F. Scott Fitzgerald

Bold lover, never, never oust thou kiss
Though winning near the goal—yet, do not grieve

—Ode on a Grecian Urn

F. Scott Fitzgerald

Under the Influence

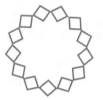

E. Ray Canterbery and Thomas D. Birch

First Edition 2006

Published in the United States by
Paragon House
1925 Oakcrest Avenue, Suite 7
St. Paul, MN 55113

Library of Congress Cataloging-in-Publication Data

Canterbery, E. Ray.
  F. Scott Fitzgerald : under the influence / E. Ray Canterbery and Thomas Birch.-- 1st ed.
      p. cm.
  Includes bibliographical references and index.
  ISBN 1-55778-848-0 (pbk. : alk. paper) 1. Fitzgerald, F. Scott (Francis Scott), 1896-1940. 2. Authors, American--20th century--Biography. I.
Birch, Thomas D. (Thomas David), 1955- II. Title.
  PS3511.I9Z576 2006
  813'.52--dc22

                                                                    2005037741

The paper used in this publication meets the minimum requirements of American National Standard for Information Sciences—Permanence of Paper for Printed Library Materials, ANSIZ39.48-1984.

Manufactured in the United States of America
10 9 8 7 6 5 4 3 2 1

    For current information about all releases from Paragon House,
        visit the web site at http://www.paragonhouse.com

Contents

Introduction

THE SECOND FITZGERALD REVIVAL UNDERWAY IS A "POPULAR" RENAISSANCE; as with all things Fitzgerald, it has layers of intricacies. Approaching three-quarters of a century after his death, F. Scott Fitzgerald continues to intrude on the consciousness of the Western world and especially America. In his lifetime, recognition came from his defining an age even as his literary reputation faded. Immediately afterward, Fitzgerald's literature was newly appreciated by a few but still disparaged in a whispering campaign by many of his most influential "friends." In the beginning of Scott's career and soon afterward, the notoriety of Scott and Zelda's behavior was pervasive. Some prominent writers did come to the defense not only of his novels but also of a lifestyle tame by twenty-first-century celebrity standards. Still, even today when it is said that Fitzgerald was "under the influence," popular notice quickly turns to Prohibition-era gin and Zelda—though, oddly enough, not to his first Golden Girl, Ginevra King of Lake Forest, or his last, Sheilah Graham in Hollywood.

As to influences on Fitzgerald, we dare not dismiss the usual suspects; rather, we begin by toning down the exaggerations. Equally, we make no attempt to separate Scott and Zelda from the American culture and history that they helped create. It is the reverse influence that seems to us relentless. American capitalism and its values, at home and abroad, continue to resonate with the same contradictions and remain vulnerable to Fitzgerald's bold social criticism. Scott's personal experiences even while confronting these contradictions in Anglo-American values go a long way toward explaining another revival. His literary and popular influence—powerful as it is—surely is based on a deeper intellect than he was given credit for in his lifetime or since. Zelda's influence is quite different and in recent times has been misappropriated. This, too, is a stain on Scott, the writer *and* the man, but he can be cleansed by the whole story.

F. Scott Fitzgerald was an artist of extraordinary literary talent who tried to synthesize the ideas and events that surrounded him and give them personal expression. Well, he was more than that. He and Zelda were personal participants who defined and helped shape much of what is American. Their lives and American life are so intertwined that they seem impervious to an unwinding. They defined the Jazz Age through self-advertisements; then, Scott gave the epoch its name. Americans generally were obsessed with clever advertising and easy money in a booming stock market. But there is more, much more.

Fitzgerald's life and novels continue to personify the great contradictions in American culture and in American capitalism. Fitzgerald's novels—especially *The Beautiful and Damned, The Great Gatsby,* and *Tender Is the Night*—can tell us about our past but just as much about the present and our future. Notably, Scott had originally set *Gatsby* in the Gilded Age, an age of excesses similar to those of the 1920s. Today the Casino Economy—beginning in the early 1980s and becoming global—has remarkable parallels to these earlier epochs.

Then, the inevitable; the crashes came. A banking panic in 1907 ended the Gilded Age though not the gild, the Crash of 1929 ended the Jazz Age though not "all that jazz," and the collapse of the technology-driven Nasdaq in 2001 brought an end to some of the most notorious players in the Casino Economy, though not its legacy. Zelda, on the precipice at an earlier age than most supposed then or since, crashed shortly after the stock market. Although the public was unaware of Zelda's plunge, only the Great Depression upstaged Scott's "crack-up." As he dispassionately acknowledged, his literary reputation had gone the way of the economy, as had his earnings from the *Saturday Evening Post* that sustained his little family.

Though Scott's novels have long been on required reading lists around the world, Scott and Zelda's cultural presence ebbs and flows. There nonetheless was, of course, a "first" Fitzgerald revival. It came during the early 1950s—being first literary, but inevitably leading to a renewal of his cultural significance. The Fitzgerald revival now under way is, if anything, even more confounding because it follows some serious academic studies, yet derives its inert velocity from the vibrant personalities of Zelda and Scott while its deeper significance once again is properly attributed to Scott.

✧　✧　✧

The second revival—as in the movies—is a sequel to the first, to which we necessarily return.

A 1945 *literary* revival doubtless contributed to the popular revival. The publication of *The Crack-Up* that year included Fitzgerald's autobiographical essays and selections from his *Notebooks* as well as letters and tributes to him from other authors. *The Crack-Up* uniquely provides insight into Fitzgerald as a writer and as a person of *at least* literary intelligence as well as immense dignity and a seriously underrated humor. Quickly thereafter came *The Portable F. Scott Fitzgerald,* a collection selected by friend and humorist Dorothy Parker and introduced by friend and novelist John O'Hara, who wrote, "All he was was our best novelist, one of our best novella-ists, and one of our finest writers of short stories," an assessment that seemed as effusive at the time as it is poorly expressed and inadequate today. The collection included *Gatsby* and *Tender Is the Night* as well as nine stories. Bantam also reprinted *Gatsby* as a paperback for the masses the same year; then, in 1949, *Gatsby* was adapted for a film starring Alan Ladd, who came up short in more than one respect.

The first cultural revival came immediately thereafter. In

death as in life, a rough cut of Scott's popular legacy always lay in Hollywood, and at the time, in the hands of screenwriter Budd Schulberg.[1] How fitting for a popular American audience. Fitzgerald's novels and stories—even he as a character—often found their way into movie scripts. Scott's closest early brush with life imitating art was when he and Zelda were asked to star in a movie based on *This Side of Paradise* at a time when the glamour and wealth of the early movie industry in New York City already was looking westward toward Southern California. This flirtation with movies, movie stars, and the westward expansion of American industry, fused with Scott and Zelda's most notorious antics, commanded only the early years of sudden fame even as it helped create the legend. Absent Schulberg, Arthur Mizener's *The Far Side of Paradise* (1951), the first book-length Fitzgerald biography, may have gone unnoticed. Instead, it rode the coattails of Schulberg's novel, *The Disenchanted* (1950), a biographical "exposé" of Scott that included his and young Budd's alcoholic escapades (on a 1939 movie studio assignment) deep in the winter snow of the Dartmouth Winter Carnival.

Over cocktails, the famous Hollywood screenwriter had regaled Mizener, a young and obscure professor, with this singular event in Fitzgerald's life. Two nights of tales became the basis for Budd's novel as well as material for Arthur's biography. Ernest Hemingway, once Fitzgerald's "best friend," gave Mizener a doubtlessly biased sample of Scott and Ernest's correspondence. This intoxicating blend of gossip, fiction, and fact landed Schulberg and Mizener on the *New York Times* best-seller list for fiction and "nonfiction," respectively and even disreputably. The Schulberg-Mizener double play brought Fitzgerald back into popular consciousness even as his reputation was further damaged at home plate.

Fitzgerald would have appreciated the delicious irony; as in the beginning, near the end and afterward, notoriety had served him well. At the time of his "crack-up," bad publicity had let Hollywood know that Scott was still alive despite premature beliefs of his death. In turn, Hollywood provided income and ideas for his final but unfinished novel—published as *The Last Tycoon;* it helped ignite the literary revival.

As with the first cultural revival, the high regard for Fitzgerald's novels plays a leading role in the second. Scott would not have had it any other way. His fascination with naming historical benchmarks, going back to epochs set by his and Zelda's personal experiences, also is well served.

At the risk of being less accurate than Scott's record-keeping would have been, let us say that the public's veneration for Fitzgerald's novels had come full circle by Thursday, April 4, 2002, at about 3:45 P.M. Oprah Winfrey, sufficiently an early twenty-first-century celebrity to be identifiable only by her first name (as in Madonna, Cher, and Britney), canceled her televised book club. Oprah's selections of fiction led reliably to sales of a million or more copies. She had a stray, inferior club pick, but she often picked serious and demanding works.

The Oprah happening epitomized a typically American aspiration of intellectual self-improvement and a hunger for the seriousness and stimulation of good literary fiction, an aspiration Fitzgerald had not only understood but had urged. Still, critics said that her program drew undue attention to the *personalities* of the authors. In truth, Oprah found it more and more difficult to find books to be really passionate about: She wanted to take time to return to the classics. She had spent the previous weekend rereading *The Great Gatsby,* a title to which the audience expressed knowing "oohs, ahhs and nods." In a brief time Oprah had run out of good books *except* for *Gatsby*.[2]

Scott Fitzgerald would not have missed the looking-glass irony in this pop cultural moment wherein the focus on authors' personalities *by a celebrity* was the subject of critical wrath. Oprah had used the "low" medium of TV to bridge the high-low cultural chasm of the American literary landscape. Much earlier, Fitzgerald had used the pages of the *Saturday Evening Post* and his short stories to achieve the same purpose—promotion of his novels and their serious social commentary while providing considerable income. Moreover, in their lives together and apart, Zelda and Scott as celebrities often overshadowed Fitzgerald's literary reputation.

Scott would have noted a second and more recent date: In midsummer 2004, the *New York Times* serialized *Gatsby*—that classic tale of an earlier New York City and Long Island summer. Just as Oprah was hoping to gain not only more attention for her authors but more viewers, the *Times* was borrowing from newspaper history to draw readers and advertising dollars. (Serializing the novels of many great and not-so-great writers in newspapers and magazines was once a common practice.) The newspaper ran the entire novel, *Gatsby*, over the course of a week in its New York metro editions. The advertising sponsor was a group of BMW dealers from the New York area, hardly the Rolls-Royce salesmen Jay Gatsby could have bragged about. Once again nonetheless, *Gatsby* was being read along the same railway route that used to take Scott and Zelda to New York City from Long Island and sometimes back.

Besides Oprah's moment and the *Times*'s new treatment of *Gatsby*, confirmation of not only a popular revival but also of a deeper appreciation of an author still remembered for his Budd-Light cleverness is found. Notably, a second edition of *Some Sort of Epic Grandeur*, the standard Fitzgerald biography first published in 1981 by Matthew J. Bruccoli, the dean of Fitzgerald scholars, appeared in 2002. It wraps up a sequence of revised editions beginning during the early 1990s, preceded by Bruccoli's more academic Fitzgerald bibliographies and critical assessments of Fitzgerald's novels.

A flurry of new books and collections from other Fitzgerald scholars has critically appraised Scott's novels and shorter stories or mused about the sources of his ideas. This mushrooming gathering evokes a commendable, if narrow, erudition while providing sundry insights into a personality much more complex than the one acknowledged during Fitzgerald's lifetime, and often afterward. All of which has culminated in the appearance of the first journal devoted entirely to Scott, the *F. Scott Fitzgerald Review*.[3] The *Fitzgerald/Hemingway Annual* filled part of the fissure between the first and second revivals, much as this new literary separation suitably reflects schisms in the friendship and literary reputations of the two leading lights of the "lost generation."

We dare not neglect the wife's abiding presence—more often in sickness than in health. Zelda, the original Jazz Age flapper who often upstaged Scott in those early giddy years in New York or on the

French Riviera, has emerged from his shadow as a "stifled genius." Zelda, the subject of revisionist biographies (the first in 1970 and the most recent in 2004) as well as an often-rumored Broadway musical, suddenly became competitive with Scott, a delusion she had earlier shared with him as mental illness enveloped her. Seemingly downplaying the severity of Zelda's mental illness, *her* biographers nonetheless have exaggerated any rational judgment of her artistic talents. Worse, they have claimed that Scott caused her terrible illness, echoing the willful misjudgment of Zelda's family and naive opinion of her childhood friend, Sara Mayfield. As we will come to note, in her times of mental clarity Zelda nonetheless would have strongly disagreed with her biographers' assessment of her talents as well as their unfair judgments of Scott.[4] Zelda cannot be erased nor the residue—the abiding irony.

✧　✧　✧

Why was the first Fitzgerald revival incomplete? Put differently, why is a reassessment of Fitzgerald indispensable? A partial answer is found in lingering verdicts from Fitzgerald's time. Scott was described as a playboy who had a natural but uncultivated gift for exploiting his *own* biography, as if on autopilot and auto-plot. What he did was effortless, it was said, but he squandered his gift for prose. With effort he could have become an important literary figure instead of the early failure that he never transcended.

Critics mourned not only Scott's failure to live up to the early promise of *This Side of Paradise*, but strongly hinted—Ernest Hemingway, most famously—that he was too much a part of the wealth and illusory culture depicted by his fiction. Worse, he idealized the rich. Worse still, he lacked intellectual depth and substance. Even *Gatsby*, a commercial failure by Scott's account and condemned as a critical failure by many who then counted, was at best "promising." Even Fitzgerald was ambivalent about the ambivalent character of Jay Gatsby. At the time, Fitzgerald personified a narrow slice of American history and culture, but in the end he could not rise above it. His fame went down in flames.

Too many writers sustain or even embellish this image of the Jazz Age legend, impugn Fitzgerald's intellectual depth with his Irish lightheartedness, confound his illness with his efforts, and confuse Zelda's influence with his authorial genius. Fitzgerald's fiction, even his short stories, *did* contain autobiographical material, but its importance has been greatly exaggerated. He is, it is said, the most self-described writer of the twentieth century, especially "under the influence." If alcohol is a truth serum, in some of his letters we know exactly what he meant. True, but his fiction *did* transcend autobiography. Besides, if he had not had long periods of sobriety, he never could have been so productive. He wrote better than he lived, and the social and cultural sweep of his stories is much broader than his personal experiences. Scott was the sophisticated thinker, artistic genius, and supportive spouse—not Zelda. Zelda was at once a vital but ultimately destructive influence.

The darkest cloud over Fitzgerald's self-expressions is his least understood tendency. He was his own cruelest critic; moreover, when Scott expressed his self-doubt or wrote of his abject failures, his insecure critics did not simply accept his judgment, they publicized it. He had, he sometimes said, squandered his deeper literary talent as an essential part of the decadence, but these were often fleeting doubts. Fitzgerald's friends and critics nevertheless took his own self-effacing word for it—that he was a failure. Once, in a reflective mood, Fitzgerald famously wrote: "I talk with the authority of failure—Ernest [Hemingway] with the authority of success." What are we to make of this, coming from a writer who carefully chose words to convey several layers of meaning? If we take such statements literally, we need at least recognize the cultural and historical reach of his self-appraisals.

Our efforts begin by rejecting notions of Fitzgerald as "a failure," especially of intellect, as being far too facile. Moreover, his insecurities come into perspective within view of his self-serving critical "friends" and the personal attacks from an unstable Zelda. In the end we gain a deeper respect not only for Scott's intellectual courage but also for his humanity as a highly professional writer *and* as a man loyal and generous even to those who betrayed him.

As the recent Oprah event and the *New York Times* serialization suggest, the magnetism of Fitzgerald's fiction for mass media as well as for the literary elite remains forceful. Contrary to romanticized legend, the lasting significance of Fitzgerald's life and fiction stems from his immersion in the intellectual trends of his time as well as from his critical depiction of American themes about wealth and aspiration. A growing and ever more respectful literature notwithstanding, there remains a failure to fully appreciate Fitzgerald's intellectual reach *and* grasp of the social and economic forces defining not just American but Western civilization. Although we do not readily associate Fitzgerald with social and economic historians of the likes of Thorstein Veblen and Karl Marx or with philosophers as diverse as Henri Bergson and Oswald Spengler, the influence of their works—some assigned in Scott's *College of One* curriculum constructed for Sheilah Graham—add considerable dimension and, in the end, respectability to Fitzgerald's life and work. An artist laboring "so desperately hard to develop a hard, colorful prose style," as he put it, to be taken seriously as well as entertainingly, is poetic justice.[5]

Beyond this clarification, we also want to explain the neglect—the turning of cheek by friend and foe, often one and the same. The neglect is partly from a hasty reading of Fitzgerald's short fiction, snubbed by critics and even Fitzgerald, the latter from a lofty height. This assessment nonetheless is far too convenient because his friends as critics had the talent and intellect to properly judge Scott's work. More subtle forces underlie the lies.

The image of an intellectually engaged Fitzgerald does not fit well with some of the distorted and contradictory characterizations that have fueled his celebrity status—a helpless drunk and slave to wealth and to Zelda (etched by Ernest Hemingway) and, most recently, a domineering and abusive drunk who stifled the creative genius of his wife (Zelda's revisionist biographers). As Fitzgerald came to understand, drinking *was* his Achilles' heel and at times did trigger his worst self-destructive and imperialistic traits. But to distort his least respectable behavior while under this particular influence to the exclusion of the "entire man" who Scott strived to be would be the wrong accompaniment to the Fitzgerald revival under way.

We thus seek to bridge the huge chasm between Fitzgerald as the youthful legend of the Jazz Age and Fitzgerald as a professional maturing far earlier than many of his biographers seem aware. Thoughtful substance and social concerns were always a part of the life Fitzgerald created, not only for himself but also for others. True, Fitzgerald was the romantic dreamer whose longings and ambitions fit well the aspirations and the idealism uniquely defining the American character. His personal obsession was his central theme. Still, his grasp exceeded his reach.

Scott Fitzgerald exposed the shallowness of American aspiration and unmasked the self-corrupting nature of the American Dream, not only in its consumerism but also in its destruction of the soul. Scott and Zelda's conceit was living the contradictions even as Fitzgerald revealed them, bringing his personal experience in line with what his intelligence and intuition perceived. In the early 1920s his living the American Dream in style, career, and earnings was theater—part of the exhibitionism in which he and Zelda conspired. Soon, however, he became a participant in Zelda's self-destructive behavior to the detriment of his own health. He came to believe that his self-described "too light" or "too commercial" writings were the sole route to affording Zelda even as he greatly underestimated these contributions to the quality of his professional life.

He fully understood the capitalist way of doing things even as he felt that he was "selling out." Not only did he and Zelda master and exploit the American advertising that came of age during the 1920s, he maximized their income by finding the most lucrative markets, nimbly adapting when those markets changed. Even when his earnings were substantial, Fitzgerald always needed more. He called himself a "Socialist," but he was continually losing, in his judgment, a competitive capitalistic rat race that had Darwinian overtones. The "failure" Scott mostly wrote about, his crack-up essays and some self-regarding letters or notes notwithstanding, was the decline of Western society at home and abroad—a perspective influenced not only by Spengler but also by Veblen, Marx, John Hobson, and others.

The global reach of Scott Fitzgerald's thinking and intuition also remains underappreciated. During his time, four great contradictory forces were at work—capitalism, socialism, communism, and imperialism. Among his literary friends, Scott alone had the deepest, even prophetic understanding of these "isms." Fitzgerald despised Social Darwinism and sided with that great iconoclast Veblen, even as he flirted with Marxism while hating Joseph Stalin and losing respect for many of the card-carrying communists in the American film colony. Though many of his Hollywood friends supposed that his lack of active political support of socialism was just another "sellout," Scott understood the differences between communism as an ideal and "communism" or "socialism" under dictatorship as practice. He had a communal sympathy for the Russian peasant whose life might be improved under true socialism, but had no sympathy for Hollywood's handsomely paid screenwriters such as Dorothy Parker and her husband striking for higher salaries under Stalin's Red banner.

Fitzgerald understood imperialism in a way comparable to Veblen and Hobson's thinking. The Great War was the outcome of the great powers, including America, acting imperially. Like the English economist John Maynard Keynes, Scott had concluded that Versailles was a Carthaginian peace that had sowed the seeds of a second Great War. He was not being contradictory when he assailed Adolf Hitler's imperialistic speeches *and* opposed American isolationism. Imperialism—American, German, or global—was disreputable. Scott's impugned patriotism led him to oppose American imperialistic policies as well as those policies that were wrong for the right reasons. Historical events since make some of his screenwriter friends look naive.

F. Scott Fitzgerald creatively put these revelations—complete only amidst their contradictions—within reach of the book-loving public. That he remained a romantic whose intuition—personal but with a global reach—bordered on the paranormal is all the more remarkable. Only his life contained more irony. Perhaps this is why no other writer has combined irony and humor to such good effect.

Toward the end a familiar judgment—"F. Scott Fitzgerald, a failure"—shadowed his Hollywood experience. His westward migration was pushed by capitalism in broad decline during the

Great Depression and pulled by capitalism's positives from its creative destruction. The push came from Scott's rising personal debt tethered to declining advertising revenues at the *Saturday Evening Post*. The pull came from Fitzgerald's understanding of a shift in American tastes and the way the movie industry would expand to meet it. His response was typically creative. Scott, believing that Hollywood films would replace his novels, engaged the enemy by writing screenplays while secretly writing a novel about Hollywood that would "restore his reputation" as a novelist. In turn, his earnings as a screenwriter kept him well situated with cigarettes, Coca-Cola and his final Golden Girl even as his other expenses mounted. Ironically, the ascent of high romance in American films and of their stars coincided with a descending economy that married culture to economics. This convergence mirrored what critics defined as Fitzgerald's final decline, another facile judgment that also happens to be wrong. In Scott's final Hollywood years we find an innovative screenwriter who aspired to be a director.

No wonder then that the disentangling of Fitzgerald's life and American life has never been completed to our satisfaction. While others have drawn indistinct parallels, the interplay of life, creation, and reality has not been properly or fairly judged. Against this broader background a biography of Fitzgerald becomes a critical social and economic history of American life and, broadly, of Western values. Even if we sometimes tip in favor of the latter, in a remarkable feat of authorial self-restraint, we will not call it a "tipping point."

Through it all, there was F. Scott Fitzgerald, the man and the professional writer. He was a legend by the age of twenty-three, heralded as a *potential* literary lion as he slid into alcoholism; still loyal to beautiful Zelda, who was quickly going mad beyond any hope; furiously writing short stories for the *Saturday Evening Post* and screenplays in Hollywood at top dollar so that he could pay the bills while buying the time to write that last great novel, whether it be *Tender Is the Night* or *The Last Tycoon*. Like his novels, Fitzgerald's life personifies many of the contradictions of modernity wherein the idea of a sovereign self is being shattered. In Hollywood, Scott was still paying Zelda's exorbitant medical bills and their daughter's tuition and living expenses at Vassar. Against these apparently insurmountable odds, his intellect and writing talents nonetheless prevailed even as he ended his life with his most mature and satisfying love affair while writing at the top of his game. Remarkably, he did do it with dignity and, finally, with sobriety.

Ironic, isn't it?

Endnotes

1. Schulberg is perhaps best remembered for his 1941 Hollywood novel and screenplay *What Makes Sammy Run?*

2. Kathy Rooney, a poet and writer living in Washington, D.C., was present at the ending. Winfrey's reference to *The Great Gatsby* was heard only by the studio audience, of which Rooney was a select member. For this and more, see Kathy Rooney, "Oprah Learns Her lesson," *The Nation,* May 20, 2002, pp. 56, 58, 60.

3. Volume 1 of the new journal was published in 2002 with a 2003 copyright. Leading up to and immediately after the publication of this new journal of essays was the mounting academic literature. From mid-1994 through mid-2004 there were 344 articles, books, dissertations, and unmentionable library items on F. Scott Fitzgerald. Among these were 95 "peer-reviewed" journal articles, those articles most seriously considered (brows-furrowed) "academic." Ironically, Fitzgerald may have not taken "seriously academic" articles seriously because he judged his most renowned professors at Princeton ignorant of the best literature. In retrospect, he appears to have been correct.

4. Our summary judgment of Zelda as well as the nature of her lifelong relationship with Scott finds further support in Jackson R. Bryer and Cathy W. Barks, editors, *Dear Scott, Dearest Zelda* (New York: St. Martins Press, 2002). Their collection includes many unpublished letters between Zelda and Scott from the Princeton University Library Collection. We otherwise would not have been able to read all of these letters, the least known being from January 1939 until Scott's death. The correspondence not only testifies to Scott and Zelda's enduring love but to their ultimate emotional maturity. Zelda's later letters clearly exonerate Scott of any responsibility for her illness while praising him for his relentless loyalty and support, not only for herself but also for their daughter, Scottie. The well-written introductions to each segment of their lives provide a kind of minibiography of the Scott-Zelda romance, one that endured to Scott's death. For these reasons the Bryer-Barks volume is an excellent supplement to our biography.

A "box" of Zelda's letters reside in the F. Scott and Zelda Fitzgerald Museum in Montgomery, Alabama. However, we were not able to examine or copy these; they may well be copies of her letters at Princeton University.

5. Quote is from a letter to Scottie, July 1937, in Andrew Turnbull's *The Letters of F. Scott Fitzgerald* (New York: Dell Publishing, 1963), p. 16.

One

●

Growing Up Amidst the American Dream

FRANCIS SCOTT KEY FITZGERALD WAS BORN IN ST. PAUL, MINNESOTA, AT 3:30 P.M. on September 24, 1896, at 481 Laurel Avenue in a building called the San Mateo Flats in the Summit Avenue neighborhood. He was named for his second cousin thrice removed and the author of "The Star Spangled Banner." Having lost two daughters the same year (ages one and three), Scott's parents' pride in their heritage and hopes for the future glowed like "bombs bursting in midair." And, although Fitzgerald's mother, Mary (Mollie) McQuillan, the daughter of an Irish immigrant, and his father, Edward, from Maryland, pled allegiance to the Old South and the Confederacy, F. Scott, like many Irish at the time and since, seemingly grew up as the quintessential American. Mary and Edward were married February 12, 1890, in what is often considered nearly the exact dividing line between the Old North and the Old South as well as many other things—Washington, D.C. About half Black Irish, Scott's consumption of alcoholic drinks was less frequent and in lesser quantities than is often the stuff of Irish legends, and watered-down gin, his favorite drink, was the drink of choice of many Americans during the astonishingly wet era of the allegedly dry Prohibition era, which usually refers to the period of "enforcement" from January 1920 to December 1933. Fitzgerald attended the dream college of his American generation, and, like many Princeton students at the time and recently, prided himself on underachieving, at which he succeeded not only admirably but with great élan.

From an early age, Scott's father instilled in him an appreciation for the aristocratic elements of the American South while his mother brought a wealthy standing to the family—at least for the granddaughter of an Irish immigrant. This upper-middle-class status combined with America's turn-of-the-century economic prosperity ensured, however, that Scott's class consciousness would be of the leisure, not laboring, type—at least initially.

Although the Fitzgeralds lived in the affluent Summit Avenue area, they moved frequently. They had moved in April 1898 to Buffalo, New York, returning to St. Paul in July 1908. Fitzgerald and his sister Annabel lived with their grandmother, Louisa Allen McQuillan, at 294 Laurel Avenue, while their parents lived nearby with a friend until April 1909, when Grandmother McQuillan went abroad and the Fitzgerald family was reunited at her apartment. In September they rented a house at 514 Holly Avenue and moved often in the Summit Avenue area, living in rental houses or apartments, including 509 Holly Avenue, 499 Holly Avenue, and 593 Summit Avenue. This pattern of rentals rather than home ownership and frequent moves would follow Fitzgerald throughout his life.

While growing up in the Summit Avenue area of St. Paul, Minnesota, Fitzgerald had a commanding view of a small Midwestern city with a highly stratified society. He was fascinated by the pairings of money and of power, of material wealth and moral failure—of beauty, glamour, and their rapid depreciation. In turn, these always were among his strongest fictional themes. He lived in nice homes in a nice neighborhood. James J. Hill, a financial ally of J. P. Morgan and owner of the Great Northern Railway, lived in the most magnificent mansion on that avenue. Scott's all-too-real family, however, lived on and moved around the edges of this wealthiest neighborhood in St. Paul, usually living at the *end* of its finest street, aptly named Summit Avenue, and never at the center of wealth and power. True, the Fitzgeralds had a comfortable life, and reminders of their social and economic respectability surrounded them. With wealth at his doorstep but just out of his reach, however, Scott grew up feeling socially insecure. So, to adolescent Scott, James Hill epitomized the American Dream and revealed to him the boundless power that resides in wealth. Hill reappears in *The Great Gatsby* as one of the models for Gatsby's wealthy patron, the fictional Dan Cody.

James J. Hill was among the robber barons, an appellation also applied to Jay Gould, John D. Rockefeller, E. H. Harriman, William Rockefeller, Jim Fisk, George F. Baer, J. P. Morgan (Hill's financier), and many other industrialists who celebrated their twenty-fifth birthdays between 1860 and 1870. Their adult attitudes and cutthroat competitive behavior emerged during the years immediately before and after the Civil War. Meanwhile, they mastered at least one problem posed by the war: mass production and the attendant necessity for large-scale production. These relatively few men controlled American industry during the final quarter of the nineteenth century, going into the twentieth.

For Scott Fitzgerald, therefore, entrance into membership in this new American aristocracy was a different matter: At the turn of the century, aristocratic attachment required being in the mainstream of the country's rapidly expanding industrial and financial wealth, a trajectory nullified by his father's many failures in the business world. Edward bounced around from being a furniture salesman for the St. Paul Furniture factory and then as a salesman for Procter & Gamble in Buffalo, but once again lost his job. It could have been a soap opera: in time, however, his death was that of a salesman.

Like P&G, the robber barons were not their own salesmen; they had publicists. With good public relations, they could justify their control of American industry. Religion had a lot to do with it. Besides their mastery of mass production, the robber barons also had something else in common: At least seven were churchgoers, and six were actively engaged in church affairs. J. P. Morgan was probably the most prominent layman in the Protestant Episcopal Church, whose communicants included about half of the seventy-five multimillionaires in 1900 in New York City. The Rockefeller brothers were prominent Baptists. None were Irish Catholic.

John D. Rockefeller said, "God gave me my money," and Baer attacked labor during the coal strike of 1902 by saying, "The rights and interests of laboring man will be protected and cared for—not by the labor agitators, but by the Christian men to whom God in his infinite wisdom has given the control of the property interest of this country."[1]

Rockefeller ruthlessly drove competitors out of business, but he sang hymns with the Sunday School children of the Euclid Avenue Baptist Church. Henry Ward Beecher, then the most renowned of American divines, and others taught the goodness of richness from their pulpits, but they were preaching to the choir of Morgan, Harriman, and Rockefeller.

Faith can stretch only so far; just as the tobacco barons ultimately needed expert medical doctors to explain the health benefits from tobacco use, the robber barons increasingly needed science's blessing. Luckily, for them, they got it.

Herbert Spencer took Darwin's ideas (which he misunderstood) and turned some physical science ideas on their heads and merged them into a "scientific sociology." It came to be known as Social Darwinism. Essentially, in Spencer's view, the fact that the rich get richer and the poor get poorer was just nature's way of improving the species and the economy at the same time. This was a tableau agreeable to the robber barons and their attendants and retainers as well as to the middle class (those who, while not rich yet, were reassured by the American Dream that it was just a matter of time).

Since the evolutionary process tends toward increasing order, writes Spencer, his scientific sociology does not conflict with the most dismal laissez-faire doctrines in economics. Because humanity's conditions were getting better and better and society was becoming more orderly through natural law, humans should not interfere with natural progress. To aid the poor, either by private or public aid, interfered irreparably with the progress of the race. The Darwinian law that the fittest, most adaptable members of a species, survive was construed to mean that the existing order of things was "best" since it was from a natural, selective process.

The incongruities were transparent only to those not committed to this "scientific" ideology. While Horatio Alger's heroes in his boys' stories could achieve in fiction the American Dream of rising to the top, the doctrines of the Social Darwinists would have preserved a social process that made sure such successes were in fact infrequent. Social programs to improve the odds for success and allow some of the "unfit" to move up would have been repugnant.[2]

Social Darwinism was the conventional wisdom and its lesson was not entirely lost on young Scott Fitzgerald. If he had devoutly believed this "scientific" truth, Scott would have thought that James Hill living in his mansion on Summit Avenue was part of the natural arrangement and that any effort to make that long climb to the top was doomed. Therefore, living contiguously to one of St. Paul's wealthier neighborhoods increasingly symbolized family pretensions and aspirations rather than *actual* status. When young Scott did go east in the fall of 1911 to attend the Newman School, it was with borrowed money from a relative (his Aunt Annabel, who had been a maid of honor at the wedding of James Hill's daughter). Early on, Scott took a view contrary to the conventional wisdom. If Hill could emerge out of St. Paul as an important figure, believed F. Scott Fitzgerald, so could *he*. Not only was Fitzgerald a dreamer from an early age, not only was he attracted to wealth, power, beauty, and glamour, but he also aspired to be an artist of repute and significance.

Mollie, Scott's mother, of eccentric dress and peculiar behavior (often blurting out embarrassingly frank remarks without understanding their effects on even insensitive acquaintances while wearing one black shoe, the other brown), spoiled her only son. Scott, quite embarrassed by his mother, truly loved his father, Edward, whose fondness for drink may have imperiled his business success. He, a small man who dressed stylishly and had fine Southern manners, also loved his delicate "pretty" son. As a boy, Scott had fine, nearly feminine features, blue eyes, and blonde hair. At an early age he realized that females adored him, a condition from which he never fully recovered. By twelve he had mastered ballroom dancing because he realized that young women loved to dance with well-dressed young men.

At that age Scott entered a private nonsectarian school in September 1908, St. Paul Academy at 25 North Dale Street with its forty boys between the ages of ten and eighteen. He failed to achieve his goal of popularity because he not only observed but also criticized the faults of other boys. As later at Princeton and even in the army, he was not a student and spent most of his time writing. He wrote juvenile adventure stories for the school newspaper and melodramatic plays for the Elizabethan Dramatic Club. Scott's first published story, "The Mystery of Raymond Mortgage," reflected the title and characters of Poe's "The Murders in the Rue Morgue." Even then, Fitzgerald began the lifelong habit of writing draft after draft. In his later fiction, Scott calls St. Paul Academy "St. Regis," and writes of his wasted school years there. He was resentful of authority and indifferent to his work; by Scott's own later account, he was considered both conceited and arrogant.

His own account appears to be right on the button. Fitzgerald played football and baseball and became a debater, but remained a poor student. His arrogance was sufficient to gain mention in a 1909 issue of the school newspaper, the *St. Paul Academy Now and Then,* which printed this note signed by Sam Kennedy: "If anybody can poison Scotty or stop his mouth in some way, the school at large and myself will be obliged." Headmaster C. N. B. Wheeler remembered Fitzgerald as:

> A sunny light-haired boy full of enthusiasm who fully foresaw his course in life even in his schoolboy days…. I helped him by encouraging his urge to write adventures. It was also his best work; he did not shine in other subjects. He was inventive in all playlets we had and marked his course by his pieces for delivery before the school. He wasn't too popular with his schoolmates. He saw through them too much and wrote about it…. I imagined he would become an actor of the variety type, but he didn't…. It was his pride in literary work that put him in his real bent.[3]

His poor performance at St. Paul Academy is what led his parents to send Scott east to the Newman School in September 1911. It was a stricter Catholic boarding school in Hackensack, New Jersey, about ten miles and forty minutes northwest of midtown Manhattan. At Newman, by any reasonable measure, Scott remained a poor student, both academically and, more important for an upwardly mobile

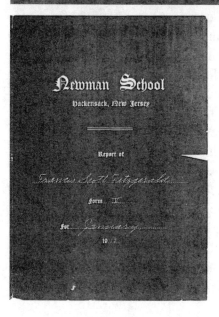

Scott's Newman School transcript. The quoted grades and remarks are in the handwriting of Headmaster Locke.

adolescent—financially and socially. He graduated with a C– average. A report card for January 1912 was typical: 60 percent in history, algebra, geometry (where below 60 percent was "unsatisfactory"); 62 percent in English; 48 percent in Latin Composition and 65 percent in Latin; 62 percent and 68 percent in English Composition and French, respectively; and, finally, a charitable 87 percent in Christian Doctrine. Except for mathematics, it is hard to imagine a more defective predictor of Scott's aptitudes. The headmaster's written remarks were much closer to the correct marks: "Naturally bright and with different application could attain a high rank."

Some of the best and most entertaining insights into young Scott come from some of his later autobiographical short stories in which he *is* Basil Duke Lee. Therein, clearly "high rank" to Scott had a different meaning than intended by his headmaster: It meant being the most popular among his classmates and a star athlete, something especially American now as it was then. These achievements would fit into his larger plan of "conquest of the successive worlds of school, college and New York," a retrospective revelation in his 1928 Basil story, "The Freshest Boy."[4] As luck would have it, Scott was about five-foot-eight, weighed only 138 to 140 pounds, and had the kind of aversion to violent physical contact that ill serves prospective football heroes. (At the time, before amateur football had turned professional, 150 pounds sans head protection easily made the team.) Arriving at prep school with what the headmaster in the Duke story called an "unusually prepossessing" attitude, Basil (Scott) acquires the nickname "Bossy," is considered a show-off, craven in football, and, perhaps without too much exaggeration, is "the most detested boy in school" his first year.[5] At Newman, Scott achieved few of his romantic or heroic goals, but eventually he gained a sense of direction.

Again, Scott naively overrated everything except his looks—athletic ability, social graces, and academic potential. He nonetheless admitted to a fundamental lack of good character—"no real courage, perseverance or self-respect."[6] Still, he was eager to be liked despite his impenetrable egotism. The frank judgment went something like this: Scott looked like a sissy and seemed to lack physical courage.

Still, in an orthodox school, his imaginative temperament, emotional sensitivity, keen observation, critical taste, and skeptical mind made him an instant misfit. These particular characteristics would plague him, as they do to all imaginative skeptics, his entire life. Despite a generous nature that would quickly evolve, even his friends would envy Scott and therefore judge him harshly.

His unhappiness the first year at Newman was transitory; Scott loved to go on school holidays to the theater in New York to see the popular musical comedies of the time such as Ina Claire in *The Quaker Girl* or Gertrude Bryan in *Little Boy Blue*. The train journeys, if nothing else, enabled him to escape the hateful judgments of his peers. To a lesser degree he also enjoyed returning to his adoring mother in an emotional attachment to the more familiar Midwest, which still left its mark in his *The Great Gatsby*. Most important, his excursions to Broadway led Fitzgerald to add the writing of a famous musical comedy to his literary ambitions.

Scott's Newman career did end on an upbeat note. His acute sense of social and economic exclusion was replaced by a gradual integration into the prep school community. Newman produced Scott's play, *The Captured Shadow,* in August 1912, which had been written on his train ride to St. Paul for summer vacation. Much later he wrote about the experience in a Basil Duke Lee story of the same title. He did win medals for elocution and track. After disgracing himself in football his first year, young Fitzgerald came back his second year to briefly star as a substitute half-back in a singular football game.

Scott at fifteen, the Newman School

In Newman's seven-to-zip victory over the Kingsley school, Scott set up a touchdown by Charles W. "Sap" Donahoe, leading to a lifelong friendship with one of Fitzgerald's first heroes. During that same school year Scott published three short stories in the *Newman News*, the school magazine edited by Donahoe, two of which foreshadow Fitzgerald's more mature treatment of young men who perform self-less acts for women who repay them with selfishness.

These athletic and writing experiences combined with the romantic possibilities of New York theater revitalized Scott's sense of personal destiny and directed him toward Princeton University and the quick train trip to Broadway. After he graduated from Newman in 1913, another Fitzgerald play, *Coward,* was produced in August, followed by his play *Assorted Spirits,* both at the St. Paul YWCA. The shows were sellouts, with Scott playing a role in the second.

Scott's interest in the theater and in theatrics would never quite abate. Characteristically, as early as *The Captured Shadow,* he wrote the best parts for himself. This quest for a mixture of community and star status was a duality that Scott would retain throughout his life and influence even his political beliefs. He retained a sense of drama to the end.

While at Newman, Scott was acutely aware, as Basil was, that "he was one of the poorest boys in a rich boys' school."[7] Money was also a near barrier preventing Scott from attending Princeton, a situation comically addressed in another Basil Lee Duke short story, "Forging Ahead."[8] Upon learning of the family's losses in the stock market, a realistic possibility in the year 1928 (though less likely in 1913), jeopardizing his attending Yale, Basil announces, "I'm going to work my way through Yale."[9] He then turns to his collection of Horatio Alger stories for inspiration—specifically *Upward Bound,* which contains a chapter championing the work ethic theme. Ironically, it is not hard work but a fortuitous stock market rally that saves Basil's dream of attending Yale and—Fitzgerald style—winning his dream girl, Minnie.[10]

At Newman, and before Princeton, Scott's isolation made him receptive in November 1912 to the attention and encouragement of one of the Catholic priests and trustees of the school, Father Cyril

Sigourney Webster Fay, age thirty-seven. Portly and so fair as to sometimes be described as an albino, Father Fay was a brilliant intellectual and fascinating talker. A great romantic, Fay made even the Church seem glamorous. Since he had a handsome private income, Father Fay could afford to combine spiritual with temporal gratifications that included good company, good food, and drink. He was a role model for Scott at age sixteen and soon his surrogate father, and may have been in love with him. The good father frequently invited Scott into his comfortable home in Washington D.C., and introduced him to men like novelist Shane Leslie and historian Henry Adams (and *possibly* French philosopher Henri Bergson). Later, at Princeton and in the army, Fay's influence became even more powerful as the older, more mature Scott began to fully appreciate one of his mentors. In turn, Fitzgerald idealized Father Fay as Monsignor Darcy in *This Side of Paradise* (1920).

The Anglo-Irish writer Shane Leslie (1885–1971), a first cousin of Winston Churchill, also became one of Scott's mentors. Shane had studied at King's College, Cambridge, had rowed for the college, and knew the great British poet Rupert Brooke. Married to an American in 1912, the year he met Fitzgerald, Leslie became acquainted with Ireland's greatest lyric poet, W. B. Yeats, and with D. H. Lawrence. Leslie would call Scott "an American Rupert Brooke" and not only recommend an early draft of Fitzgerald's first novel, but also would correct Scott's grammar and spelling before sending it to Charles Scribner on May 6, 1918. In return, in a review of Leslie's Etonian novel *The Oppidan* (1922), Scott calls Leslie "the most romantic figure I had ever known." Father Fay and Shane Leslie's friendships combined with New York theater compensated for Scott's unhappy episodes at Newman.

Next would come Princeton, in contention to be the dream university. In his scrapbook young Fitzgerald first expresses an interest in Princeton shortly after entering Newman. He had just attended the November 4, 1911, Harvard-Princeton football game (the first since 1896); on his ticket stub is "Sam White decides me for Princeton." White assured an 8–6 Princeton victory when he ran back a ninety-five-yard touchdown after a blocked kick by Harvard. Then, too, there was the proximity to Broadway and the prospects for writing his own musical comedy. He reveals in his first novel *This Side of Paradise* of still another reason for choosing Princeton over Yale or Harvard: "I think of Princeton as being lazy and good-looking and aristocratic—you know, like a spring day."[11] Later, Fitzgerald's affection for Princeton would grow with his distance from it.

✧ ✧ ✧

As Scott is making his choice of colleges, we fittingly return to Horatio Alger and the American Dream. The alternative to the Ivy League in Fitzgerald's "Forging Ahead" is the state university, portrayed in the story as a working-class institution attended by "peasants." Grandmother McQuillan made Scott's personal college choice possible by her timely death in the summer of 1913; she left his family an estate of about $125,000, or about $1,375,000 in today's dollars. Ironically, as Fitzgerald realized his dream of attending Princeton that fall, he soon learned, as he had at Newman, that his status was distinctly inferior and equivalent to belonging to the peasant class of the state university.

Scott's entrance into Princeton also confirmed another lesson he had learned at Newman, namely that the distribution of wealth in American society was unfair and seldom rooted in personal merit— in opposition to the still popular Social Darwinian view that wealth is a symbol of personal and social worth. Class divisions rooted in inequalities of wealth were evident to Scott immediately where he observed, with the stigma of an outsider, the barriers associated with Princeton's club system. Once again, Fitzgerald was a poor boy in a rich school.

Scott's exclusion initially engendered feelings of envy and regret at not belonging to the privileged class. His class consciousness nevertheless bravely retained an upward tilt. This early fascination with wealth is implanted in most of Fitzgerald's writings. Even as a child he swallowed a penny, which was never fully digested. But his belief in the magnificence that wealth *ought* to represent was so pursued by Fitzgerald that a tension would dominate his life. The

tension was between this unrealized ideal and his growing aware-
ness of the moral shortcomings of the wealthy as well as the arbi-
trary and unfair power derived from wealth.

Like Fitzgerald, the American Dream is at once elusive and
compelling; both defy precise definition yet are undeniably an
essential and enduring feature of American life and letters. The elu-
siveness of the American Dream should not deny us some characterization, no more than it could not deny Fitzgerald his central themes.
At the core of the dream is the promise of economic opportunity,
freedom, self-determination, and wealth that America has symbolized for many. Certainly by the late nineteenth century and early
twentieth century, the theme of economic mobility and advancement (in wealth) abounds in an American literature that ranges from
the popular if shallow Horatio Alger stories to a vast literature of
American immigration and internal migration, which Fitzgerald
grew up on.

In the more sophisticated of these works, an exploration into
a broader version of the American Dream can be discerned: the
hope that material, social, moral and spiritual progress can flour-
ish together in mutual reinforcement. This version of the dream has
been durable, beginning with the Puritan and New England tran-
scendental writers who were fully engaged with the problem of rec-
onciling the economic, political, moral, and spiritual dimensions of
their lives. Fitzgerald's poetic vision was to encompass both dimensions of the American Dream, just as his life was a struggle to find a
place to "settle" as he moved from place to place, from one kind of
outlet for his writing to another, and from his attempts to reconcile
his economic, moral, and spiritual dimensions. Other biographers
demur only from "political," because of Fitzgerald's "activism"
mostly through his writing. As we will discover, however, he had
keen perceptions of the real world of politics.

By the age of nine Fitzgerald understood that his father's failure
and his mother's eccentricity did not help his position within his circle
of friends in St. Paul. As he grew older he distanced himself more and
more from his failed businessman father and his socially inept mother.
Still, while his parents remained on the sidelines, Scott participated

in the social life surrounding them; he shared the lifestyle of the young Summit Avenue elite of St. Paul. Attending a premier prep school and taking very exclusive dancing classes, having access to the new University Club, going to bobsled parties at the Town and Country Club, sailing and swimming at the nearby exclusive White Bear Yacht Club, even as a young boy Fitzgerald moved gracefully among the socially successful and the comfortably rich.

✧ ✧ ✧

Already F. Scott Fitzgerald had material to write about that would include some enduring American themes. Moreover, he had the solid friendships of Father Fay and Shane Leslie. Who could have asked for better mentors than these two? Father Fay's intellect and Leslie's literary life were early beacons guiding the steep trajectory of Scott's writing career. Then, later, with the charming Basil Lee stories, Fitzgerald deftly and vividly evokes his childhood world and youthful experiences. Even then, looking back, Scott was writing of the privileged on Summit Avenue while looking out over the city of St. Paul, where the mass of ordinary people live. He writes of those of largely Scandinavian descent, living in sordid poverty just below the bluff. As he aspired to attend Princeton University, he also was aspiring to write his way out of the ordinary and create an extraordinary literary life of his own.

Endnotes

1. Frederick Lewis Allen, *The Lords of Creation* (New York and London: Harper & Brothers, 1935), p. 91.

2. For more details on the robber barons and Social Darwinism, see E. Ray Canterbery, *A Brief History of Economics* (New Jersey/London/Singapore: World Scientific, 2001), pp. 145–54, and Canterbery, *The Making of Economics,* 4th ed., vol. 1 (World Scientific, 2003), pp. 188–201.

3. Quoted in Andrew Turnbull, *Scott Fitzgerald* (New York: Scribners, 1962), p. 20.

4. F. Scott Fitzgerald, "The Freshest Boy" (1928), in Jackson R. Bryer and John Kuehl, eds., *The Basil and Josephine Stories* (New York: Simon & Schuster, 1997), p. 108.

5. Ibid., p. 93.

6. F. Scott Fitzgerald, *This Side of Paradise* (New York: Scribners, 1920) p. 25.

7. Fitzgerald, "The Freshest Boy," in Bryer and Kuehl, eds., op. cit. p. 92.

8. F. Scott Fitzgerald, "Forging Ahead" (1929), in Bryer and Kuehl, eds., *The Basil and Josephine Stories*, op. cit., pp. 182-201.

9. Ibid., p. 184.

10. Ibid., p. 190.

11. F. Scott Fitzgerald, *This Side of Paradise* (New York: Scribners, 1920), p. 27.

Two

Princeton + Ginevra

FROM SOME VINTAGE BIOGRAPHIES, WE COULD EASILY GET THE IMPRESSION that F. Scott Fitzgerald neither learned nor read anything at Princeton University. Since a myth is seldom created out of thin or even thick air, we first consider the basis for its plausibility and, second, the credibility of its sources. The initial, if less than sympathetic, plausibility is what first leaps out at us. Scott was attracted to Princeton not only by football but also by the Triangle Club, because it produced a musical comedy each fall and, during the Christmas vacation, performed it in a dozen large cities across the country. And, since his academic record at Newman was pedestrian, Fitzgerald gained admission to Princeton only by some creative cribbing and by convincing the examiners that they could not possibly reject him on September 24—*his* seventeenth birthday.

Since Scott was only conditionally admitted to the class of 1917, his admission to the university was with conditions (along with *66 percent* of the freshman class); he had to take special exams in algebra, Latin, French, and physics. When nonetheless admitted, his first thought was not of algebra, but of playing football. Differing accounts are given for his being benched the first day of practice, but the most likely story is that he was simply cut from the team. At the time football was king at Princeton, and Fitzgerald fully understood how important such nobility was for success in American society. He nonetheless had now failed twice at football. With this painful but quick ending to his athletic ambitions, Scott turned to his other early interests—the Triangle Club and writing for the *Princeton Tiger*, a humor magazine.

Fitzgerald's time at Princeton was not the happiest of his life despite his early yearning to go there. His dissatisfaction came more or less equally of two parts—from lofty ambitions unfulfilled, and from an academic curriculum ill-designed for Scott's talents.

During his freshman year, Scott roomed alone off campus at 15 University Place, as did Newman classmate Sap Donahoe. Scott's first-term courses would have intimidated even an outstanding student. They were Latin (historical literature of Rome), mathematics (plane trigonometry), English (readings in English literature—composition and rhetoric), physics (general physics), French (survey of French literature), hygiene, and physical education, as well as mathematics (algebra) to prepare to meet his entrance condition. Grading was on a scale similar to the golf handicap of a professional golfer, except more demanding: 1 (highest standing) to 7 (very unsatisfactory). Scott's first-term average of 5.17 was barely passing. Besides meeting his entrance conditions, he had to make up failed courses that would mount in number with each term. He nonetheless passed all his second-term exams except coordinate geometry.

Fitzgerald held uncommon contempt for the English Department, which he later characterized as "surprisingly pallid...top-heavy, undistinguished and with an uncanny knack of making literature distasteful to young men."[1] He spared Dr. Spaeth, who aroused his interest in the romantic poets. Much later, in 1940, Scott writes to his daughter, Scottie, about some of the professors who were teaching poetry while hating it and not understanding it: "I got in a series of endless scrapes with them so that finally I dropped English altogether."[2]

But, Fitzgerald *was* writing. He contributed to the *Tiger* throughout his freshman year while he was writing the book and lyrics of seventeen songs for *Fie! Fie! Fi-Fi!*—a musical comedy presented by Triangle and scheduled for December 19, 1914. Since

Scott began his sophomore year by failing his makeup exam in coordinate geometry, he was ineligible for extracurricular activities and not permitted to appear in the comedy he authored. That year he roomed alone at 71 Patton Hall, taking philosophy (logic), Latin (Roman comedy, Plautus, and Terence), chemistry (inorganic), English (survey of English literature), French (seventeenth-century literature), and another Latin course to meet his entrance condition. He already had established a pattern of trying to make up his failures while continuing to fail the courses that he was taking.

In his mid-sophomore year, Scott's life was disrupted in a way that would characterize much of his lifetime experience—an interlude with a woman. During his Christmas vacation, spent in St. Paul, Scott met the magnificently beautiful Ginevra King to whom he wrote many long love letters in lieu of studying.

The only males doubting Ginevra's beauty were those she never met. She was about five feet four inches in height, with a good profile and refined features. Her figure was slim, her legs and ankles pretty, her hands small and graceful. She had dark, curly

Ginevra about time of meeting Scott

hair, deep brown eyes that were lively and sparkling. Some say that Ginevra's voice was her most unique trait; it was low and expressive, with a slightly rough texture. She enjoyed singing and laughing, loved parties, adored dancing, and was unusually adept in social situations for her age, though relying on her good looks and instincts to carry the day (or evening). She was intensely competitive, desirous of winning golf, tennis, or basketball. Ginevra, an excellent golfer, could hold her own against Edith Cummings, who later won the U.S. women's Amateur title in 1923 and the Western Amateur in 1924. Like her mother and grandmother, Ginevra was named for Ginevra de Benci, the young Florentine noblewoman of Leonardo da Vinci's famous portrait (1474). In 1967 the National Gallery of Art in Washington, D.C. acquired the portrait for five million dollars.

High prices and the name, Ginevra, are companionable. Ginevra King was from upper-class Lake Forest, an exclusive suburb north of Chicago on Lake Michigan. She grew up among the great Chicago industrialists—the Swifts, the Armours, Palmers, and the McCormicks. She was the eldest of the three daughters of Charles Garfield King, a wealthy Chicago stockbroker. There was wealth on both sides of the family. Charles and his wife belonged to Onwentsia, an exclusive country club in Lake Forest, where he played golf and polo. They were the Hills of Chicago.

Scott's childhood friend and sweetheart Marie Hersey had invited Ginevra, her classmate at exclusive Westover, a Connecticut girls' school, to visit St. Paul during the 1914–15 Christmas–New Year's holidays. By then, Fitzgerald was a local boy made good at Princeton. Marie was intrigued about what—if anything—would happen when Ginevra and Scott met.

Since the holidays' social season in Chicago swept into the new year, Ginevra did not ascend from Chicago until January 4, 1915. Scott, himself only eighteen and in the midst of his sophomore year, was supposed to leave by Pullman for Princeton that night. But, truly smitten by Ginevra, Scott postponed his trip to spend an afternoon with her and to attend a dinner dance at the Town and Country Club in Ginevra's honor. The event went much as Fitzgerald describes it in *This Side of Paradise*. Ginevra was flattered and wrote in her diary that night: "Scott perfectly darling, am dipped about."[3] As early as this first book, Fitzgerald displayed the amazing ability to be very much involved emotionally in an event, but nonetheless able to stand back—observe and make notes—much like an anthropologist immersed in another culture.

He instantly fell in love with the sophisticated sixteen-year-old beauty. Ginevra had everything of any meaning—not only beauty, wealth, social status, but also pursuit by many men. Fitzgerald knew

that he had the good looks and intelligence to win "the top girl."
His autobiographical hero Amory Blaine, a much taller version of
Scott, nonetheless lacks that animal magnetism, but Isabelle (based
on Ginevra) has this admirable quality. "Flirt smiled from her large
black-brown eyes and shone through her intense physical magnetism." Ginevra was one of the "Big Four" debutantes in Chicago
at the time who included Edith Cummings, the golf champion. As
late as the 1970s, men from the area could still remember Ginevra's
beauty and grace. Such was the case, and Ginevra knew that she
possessed all of the talents required to attract men.

Ginevra King's physical beauty goes undisputed: She not only
was stunningly attractive with those big brown eyes and dark hair,
she also photographed well. Ginevra was able to impress the older
college boy with her innate superiority and sense of privilege. Her
sensual, seductive manner promised much but, as it turned out, gave
nothing. She didn't have to, and, it didn't matter. Scott nonetheless
was hopelessly in love. After writing hundreds of letters to her, he
then typed and bound them into a 275-page book.

Arthur Mizener, one of Fitzgerald's early biographers, depicts
a narcissistic Ginevra who went from man to man and never took
Scott seriously. Mizener's impression is based on a letter she wrote
to him:

> I can't remember even kissing Scott. I imagine I did. But it
> wasn't exactly a big thing in my life!… I guess I was too busy
> adding to my string to analyze my reaction to one suitor…. I
> just never singled him out as anything special…. I was [later]
> engaged to two other people. That was very easy during the
> war because you'd never get caught. It was just covering your-
> self in case of a loss.[4]

This isolated quotation gives the impression that the market for
males was much like the stock market (as brokered by her father) in
which a Ginevra simply diversified to reduce risk. If there had been
such a thing, she would have been a member of the "beta club." Still,
much of Scott's attraction for Ginevra was based on the attention

given her by many other men, a conceit she was perfectly aware of. Ginevra and Scott's romance nonetheless was much more mutually intense than Mizener and other biographers understood.

Ginevra's diary entries became more intense with each of Scott's letters.

> She received "a *sweet* one from Scott" on January 14th. Another arrived on the fifteenth: "Wonderful letter from Scott again to-day!" she notes in surprise. On January 23rd: "*Wonderful one from Scott (he is so darling).*" And on January 28th: "*Long wonderful* letter from Scott this morn." On February 6th there arrived a "marvelous wonderful heavenly letter from *Scott*—24 pages—cheered me up immensely." And on February 12th, "24 pages from Scott. *Thrills.*" Her affections, when she wrote him on February 7th, were "thriving under the stimulus of so much mail."[5]

There was nothing casual about this romance. At one time Ginevra had as many as five photos of Scott on her dresser and another on her desk. She nonetheless knew that she was a flirt and could not stop it. She had once been called "fast"—and justifiably so. She admitted to dreaming about Scott and even slept with his letters, hoping that the dreams would come in the night. There was much discussion about whether they should kiss or not, an act virtually associated with becoming engaged. When Scott visited her at Westover, her school, in February, Ginevra's diary reads: "Oh it was so wonderful to see him again. I am madly in love with him. He is so wonderful—Came up from Princeton with Joe Shanley…Marvelous time."[6]

Frequent notes of longing and frustration are found in Ginevra's letters. Her emotions spill over on March 12th: "Oh Scott, why aren't we _____ somewhere else to-night. Why aren't we at a dance in summer now with a full moon, a lovely garden and soft music in the distance. Love, Ginevra." It is the first time that she signs a letter "Love, Ginevra."[7] Whatever Ginevra *did not say* with her tantalizing long dash must have been too intimate to write for someone of her social class and personal values.

She was Scott's first Golden Girl. Her parents had just moved into a new luxurious mansion on Astor Street in Chicago. Its entry hall, however, must have been very intimidating to Fitzgerald.

The romance was especially intense during those first six months. Amazingly, their long-distance romance continued for the next two years through dances, dinners, and plays in Lake Forest and New York, at Westover and Princeton. When Mrs. King went east to pick up Ginevra for the summer, Scott was invited to meet them in Manhattan June 8. They dined on the roof garden at the Ritz Hotel; went to *Nobody Home* on Broadway, a popular play at the Princess Theater; then, on to Ziegfeld's *The Midnight Frolic,* a cabaret show in the roof garden of the New Amsterdam Theater on West 42nd Street.

Entry hall for a King's mansion on Astor Street.

Later, Scott recalled the memorable evening in his essay "My Lost City." He stopped in Chicago on his way to Montana and was able to observe Ginevra in her privileged surroundings on Astor Street. He spent much of the balance of the summer in Montana on the ranch of Sap Donahoe, his wealthy Newman-Princeton classmate and friend, getting drunk with the cowhands. This Wild West visit became the basis for his short fiction, "The Diamond as Big as the Ritz" (1922), in which Kismine Washington appears as only a narrow slice of Ginevra's superior attitude.

Scott received at least two letters from Ginevra in August. Though they had dinner together in Waterbury, Connecticut, in October 1915, he did not see her again until the following summer. Meantime, Ginevra was dismissed from Westover for flirting from the window of her room after the senior dance. In Scott's second visit to her home in August 1916, Ginevra's father, Charles King, probably uttered those now-famous words about how "poor boys shouldn't think of marrying rich girls." In any case, these were the sentiments of Mr. King's generation and class in the richer environs of the Midwest. Scott's family had much less than *any* king's ransom. The poor-boy, rich-boy polarity was brought home to Scott in this youthful relationship.

✧ ✧ ✧

We would be remiss to not return to the Princeton curriculum of Scott's sophomore year. He returned to Princeton in January 1915 to pass five of his six courses, skipping the chemistry exam. His spring curriculum included psychology, Latin (Horace and Catullus), chemistry

(qualitative analysis), English (survey of English literature, French (seventeenth-century literature), the second makeup in coordinate geometry, and a history course. In February he was elected secretary of the Triangle Club and in March was elected to the Cottage Club. He was also elected to the editorial board of the *Princeton Tiger.*

Although Fitzgerald had contributed unsigned poems, jokes and parodies to the *Tiger* early in his freshman year, in the spring of his sophomore year his work first began appearing in

Scott at Princeton

the *Nassau Literary Magazine.*

Under editors Edmund Wilson and John Peale Bishop, the *Nassau Lit* peaked in prominence both on campus and off. Fitzgerald's friendship with literary companion John Peale Bishop, who essentially tutored him in poetry while Scott simply fought with his professors, had begun in the spring of his freshman year. Bishop probably introduced Scott to Wilson, who had a great intellectual influence on Fitzgerald. Now, as a *Lit* contributor, Fitzgerald developed a closer friendship with Edmund Wilson, the *Lit*'s chair in 1915–16. They then agreed to collaborate on a Triangle Club show that would become *The Evil Eye,* the club's 1915 production. Both Bishop and Wilson remained Scott's lifelong friends; more exactly, Scott remained *their* lifelong friend. Few of his friends were as loyal as Fitzgerald and it was an endearing lifetime quality. To be fair, if we must, Bishop and Wilson *were* studious compared with Scott at the time.

In June 1915, the tense month of Ginevra and her mother's visit, Scott passed only four exams on the first try, coordinate geometry on the second, Latin on the third attempt, and failed chemistry (qualitative analysis) three times. Just as his and Ginevra's "real-world" chemistry was not working, his efforts in academic chemistry were not paying off, either. In his Ledger, Fitzgerald sums up the year as "A year of tremendous rewards that toward the end over-reached itself and ruined me. Ginevra-Triangle year." Fitzgerald nonetheless somehow survived his freshman and sophomore years.

Romances do not necessarily begin and end with academic years; as it turns out, Scott began his junior year in a failing relationship with his courses. He kicked off the fall by failing his chemistry makeup exam, which made him ineligible for campus offices, including the likely presidency of the Triangle club. He roomed alone at 32 Little Hall, taking courses that included English (the Renaissance—Spenser, Marlowe, Sidney), English (Chaucer), Italian (grammar, composition, and reading), French (the Romantic movement from Rousseau to France), philosophy (history of philosophy), and ancient art. Scott did nonetheless remain friends with Christian Gauss, the teacher for his French literature course, who was one of the few Princeton professors admired by Fitzgerald. Gauss provides some insight into young Fitzgerald.

> He was impatient of discipline…and was fascinated by the
> operatic pageantry of the pre-World War campus…. He yearned
> rather consistently to dominate the world, become president of
> Triangle Club and be a Big Man on the Campus. He possessed
> a far less solid background of reading than his friends but was
> deeply interested in the problems of art and its techniques….
> He pursued his studies only spasmodically.[8]

Though in perpetual academic difficulties, Fitzgerald still wrote for the *Tiger* and won the competition for a new football song with "A Cheer for Princeton." Then, diagnosed with malaria, which may have been a mild case of tuberculosis, he attended his last class on November 28 and went home early for Christmas. Though his transcript states "Mr. Fitzgerald was required to withdraw from the University January 3, 1916 for scholastic deficiencies," he persuaded a dean to write a letter explaining that he had withdrawn voluntarily because of ill health. The dean, conceding that he was simply going easy on Scott, given his sensitivity, was convinced otherwise. While in St. Paul in springtime, Scott continued to send his work to the *Tiger* and the *Lit,* while his script for a Triangle Club show was rejected. Scott's looming presence nonetheless remained as the Triangle Club produced his and Wilson's *The Evil Eye,* which had another seventeen song lyrics by Scott, though he was ineligible to perform. For the 1915–16 academic year, Scott writes in his Ledger: "A year of terrible disappointments + the end of all college dreams. Everything bad in it was my own fault."

Princeton was not quite finished with "Mr. Fitzgerald." He returned in fall 1916 to repeat his junior year, rooming at 185 Little Hall with Paul B. Dickey. He repeated four courses from the prior year as well as European history and qualitative analysis (which he had failed his sophomore year). Collaborating with John Biggs, Scott wrote the twenty-one song lyrics for the Triangle Club's musical comedy *Safety First,* but was academically ineligible to tour with the show. He failed three of his six courses but had good grades in English Renaissance, Chaucer, and French. Whether we should call it a footnote or, as Scott might say, a "footbawl," Ginevra King came to the Princeton-Yale game in November.

Ginevra's age probably had a lot to do with the turning point in her relationship with Scott. The tone of their letters—not only less frequent but less affectionate—began to change. If all went according to custom in her Lake Forest society, Ginevra would become a debutante at eighteen with engagement and marriage quickly following. By now a rapidly maturing Ginevra seemed to realize that she could not encourage Scott as a suitor. His social background—his being Catholic, his lower St. Paul social status, and his wealth prospects—made him unsuitable to her family and, equally important, to Lake Forest society. In January 1917, Scott notes in his Ledger, "final break with Ginevra." Scott asked Ginevra to destroy his letters; instead, she simply hid them, never revealing their contents to anyone during her lifetime. She asked him to do the same, which he did, after having that lengthy typed transcript made from them.

On July 15, 1918, Ginevra wrote Scott of her engagement announcement to William Mitchell, a naval ensign from a wealthy family, the next day. Mitchell seemed the ideal match, son of a bank president who was a friend of the King family. Scott, gathering his wits about him, replies from Camp Sheridan where he is now stationed:[9]

> Dear Ginev:
> This is to congratulate you—I don't know Billy Mitchell but from all I've heard of him he must be one of the best ever—
> Doesn't it make you sigh with relief to be settled and think of all the men you escaped marrying?
> As Ever
> Scott

Though Scott would always recall Ginevra as his first "top girl," that July was the same fateful month Scott would meet Zelda Sayre of Montgomery, Alabama.

The Mitchells prospered during the 1920s and managed to keep their wealth intact during the 1930s. Ginevra became a society matron, helping to organize and raise money for public charities. She found time to be a good golfer and a serious horse rider.

The Mitchells' second son had Down syndrome, creating a situation that put considerable strain on the marriage. Their marriage was essentially over by 1937 and they were divorced in 1939. A few years later Ginevra married an heir to the Carson, Pirie, Scott (no relation) department store in Chicago. The mature, straight-talking Ginevra wrote of her relationship with Scott: "my attitude didn't help an already supersensitive and sentimental person...Scott's and my temperaments would have clashed dreadfully and I would have undoubtedly driven him to drink a great many years earlier."[10] By default, the task fell to Zelda, the next Golden Girl of Scott's life. Ginevra died at the age of eighty-two in 1980.

Meanwhile, a young Scott was heartbroken and thought of getting even in a way only writers of fiction can: Ginevra became Isabelle Borgé in "Babes in the Woods" (1917) and *This Side of Paradise,* though her scheming and theatricality are more Fitzgerald than Ginevra; a blend of Ginevra and Zelda is found in Rosalind Connage with Rosalind's practical attitude of marriage (for the times) taken from Ginevra. While femme fatale Judy Jones in "Winter Dreams" (1922) is drawn from the young Ginevra, some of Zelda's personality is there. Most famously, Daisy Buchanan in *The Great Gatsby* (1925) is a composite. Like Ginevra she is unhappy in her marriage, has dark hair, that distinctive voice, and the security of money and social status; her recklessness and aimlessness, however, is more like Zelda's. Jordan Baker is based on Ginevra's golfing friend, Edith Cummings. The most sympathetic treatment of Ginevra is as Ermine Gilberte Labouisse "Minnie" Bibble in the Basil and Josephine stories (1928–31).

There is good reason why most of these female characters are not exactly like Ginevra. After the "loss" of Ginevra, Scott devotes his attention to Zelda Sayre, determined that his next Golden Girl would not get away. Still, Fitzgerald, in his adult fiction though less so in his life, gave women who had the ability and sufficient will to leave a wide swath of devastation, the perfect right to exact ruin among their men. Flying in the face of his sensitivity and his intensely romantic imagination, sociopathic destructiveness was a female attribute that Scott greatly admired and it attracted him. Over

time these women would be more a part of his fiction than of himself and he would find golden moments with all of them—especially
with his final Golden Girl, even as he still hungered for his first.
Dumped without "any compassion" by Ginevra for being a poor boy
in a rich man's world, Scott nonetheless would take a second chance
to woo her in his twilight years. Later, we too will revisit Ginevra
and Scott's reunion that ironically, was mutually agreed to.

At Princeton that was pretty much it for Scott's romances, but not
for his romance with the American Dream. He maintained that upward
tilt even as he was flunking out of his chosen, dream university.

✧ ✧ ✧

So, as painful as it would be for Scott, we go back for the last
time to the Princeton curriculum. In spring 1917, Fitzgerald took
Shakespeare, history of the English language, French (second term
of the Romantic movement), history of philosophy (Descartes to
Kant), and the ubiquitous chemistry (qualitative analysis). Scott's
contributions appeared thirteen times in the *Nassau Lit,* including a
short story about Princeton, "The Spire and the Gargoyle." As the
United States entered the Great War on April 6, 1917, Fitzgerald
signed up for a three-week program of intensive military training the
next month and received full credit for all his dropped courses. This
action, a paradigmatic Fitzgerald plan for recovery, probably was
the only way he could have completed the dropped courses.

Scott writes in his Ledger of this *second* junior year: "Pregnant
year of endeavor. Outwardly failure, with moments of anger but the
foundation of my literary life." Though it hardly seemed a promising start for someone aspiring to greatness as a writer, at the time
Fitzgerald may have been the only person correctly assessing his benefits from the Princeton experience. Scott would return to Princeton
in the fall as a member of the class of 1918, but would never graduate. Though not officially a member of the class of 1917 (in any
sense), Scott nonetheless was included in their yearbook, *Nassau
Herald Class of 1917*. He indicates that his future plans are to pursue
graduate work in English at Harvard and then engage in newspaper

work. In the class poll he won two votes for "Most Brilliant," two for "Handsomest," five for "Prettiest," two for "Thinks He Is Best Dressed," eight for "Thinks He Is Biggest Politician," and six as the class's "Favorite Dramatist." However harsh the assessments of Fitzgerald at Princeton, no one can ever claim that he was being ignored.

At first, but not in retrospect, it seems surprising: At Princeton John Peale Bishop and Edmund Wilson, who were publishing the works of Fitzgerald, were supremely critical not only of Scott's writing abilities, but also of his demeanor. In turn, Fitzgerald portrays Bishop as Thomas Parke D'Invilliers, in *Paradise,* as "an awful highbrow...who signed passionate love-poems in the *[Nassau] Lit.* He was perhaps nineteen, with stooped shoulders, pale blue eyes, and...without much conception of social competition."[11] Whereas Bishop and Wilson played the game of good students despite their own reservations regarding their professors, Scott did not go along. Intellectual independence would become a lifelong affliction. Somewhere between this independence and Fitzgerald's intellectual "friends," we find the genesis of an early but lasting impression of Scott as an intellectually shallow person whose aspirations greatly exceeded his true possibilities.

And, what of his intellectual competition? Though the older Bishop published his first volume of poems in 1917, the year Scott was supposed to graduate, he never achieved Scott's literary stature. As to Wilson, he never mastered the prose style required of a fine novelist and—poetically disarmed—became the penultimate critic. Wilson, or "Bunny," as Scott and others called him, was intellectual, sternly stiff, stiffly rational, and rationally self-conscious about his plain appearance. He stood in stark contrast to the dashing, handsome Fitzgerald, not to mention Scott's spontaneously intuitive and imaginative nature. Characteristically, Bishop and Wilson maintained a condescending attitude toward Fitzgerald's considerable literary achievements, even at Princeton. They looked the other way when Scott's early stories were published in H. L. Mencken's *Smart Set,* a small literary magazine greatly respected in the academic community.

In 1916 the fellow highbrows, Wilson and Bishop, published a satiric poem intended to put the popular but "shallow" Fitzgerald in his place. The contrasts are sharply drawn as they have Fitzgerald exclaim:

> I was always clever enough
> To make the clever upperclassmen notice me;
> I could make one poem by Browning,
> One play by Shaw,
> And part of a novel by Meredith
> Go further than most people
> Could do with the reading of years;
> And I could always be cynically amusing at the expense
> Of those who were cleverer than I
> And from whom I borrowed freely,
> But whose cleverness
> Was not the kind that is effective
> In the February of sophomore year....
> No doubt by senior year
> I would have been on every committee in college,
> But I made one slip:
> I flunked out in the middle of junior year.

Indeed, Edmund Wilson was the initial prime mover in creating and cultivating Scott's reputed intellectual vacuity. In an early (1922) biographical essay of Scott, Wilson strongly suggests that Fitzgerald had not read or understood anything of substance: Scott had been given only "imagination." Even Scott's dubbing Wilson as his first "intellectual conscience" had the unintended effect of implying that Scott had none of his own. While Scott was alive, Wilson at best gave Fitzgerald praise so faint as to be barely discernible. Even as late as August 23, 1953—long after Scott's death—in a letter to Lionel Trilling, Wilson writes that the trouble with Scott "is that he didn't, in the third-rate Catholic school he went to, get enough of the right kind of education to sustain his absolutely first-rate ambitions." That is, Wilson's pretentious judgment in 1953 was the same as it had been at Princeton.

John Bishop piled on by deprecating Scott's intelligence in his 1937 essay "The Missing All." He writes, "Fitzgerald partakes of that dream [of romantic self-reliance] and is too intelligent not to know it for what it is worth." So much for still more imperceptible praise, for Bishop goes on: "One can scarcely say that he [Scott] thinks; like the Rosemary in 'Tender Is the Night,' his real depths are Irish and romantic and illogical. He has an uncanny touch for probing his own or another's weakness; politically ignorant, he can see much that ails society."[12] While Wilson places Scott at not only a Catholic school but a third-rate one at that, Bishop seems to be stereotyping Fitzgerald as typically Irish. Scott is emotional and intuitive but certainly not very or naturally intelligent.

Glenway Wescott (1901–87), an American novelist whom Scott met in France in the twenties, wrote an obituary—"The Moral of Scott Fitzgerald"—no one would die for. The "moral" that

Edmund Wilson at Princeton

Wescott is alluding to essentially is "Don't waste your talent like Fitzgerald did." Wescott makes one of those needlessly invidious comparisons with Ernest Hemingway: "From the moment Hemingway began to appear in print, perhaps it did not matter what he [Fitzgerald] himself produced or failed to produce. He felt free to write just for profit, and to live for fun, if possible." Scott, lazy and fun-loving, is off the serious hook because "Hemingway could be entrusted with the graver responsibilities and higher rewards such as glory, immortality...." In stark contrast, Hemingway is the serious author taking up where Scott never really began and who "soon began to waste his energy in various hack-writing."[13] Ironically, in 1925 or 1926, when Hemingway was unknown and Fitzgerald was famous, he urged Wescott to "help [Scott] launch" Ernest's career.

Wescott deliberately went over the same ground as Wilson and Bishop—the two who knew firsthand Scott's lack of training and intellect. There was the background, from near-start to near-finish: "No doubt the ideals Fitzgerald acquired in college and in the army— and put to the test on Long Island and in the Alpes-Martitimes and in Hollywood—always were a bit second-hand, fissured, cracked, if you like."[14] Wescott also coined the most infamous of the oft-quoted nutshell phrases about Scott: "I think Fitzgerald must have been the worst educated man in the world."[15] In an obituary apparently intended to bury, not to praise, the literary Fitzgerald, Wescott did not miss anything except perhaps the charge that Zelda wrote his material, but that would have detracted from Scott's own hackmanship.

✧　✧　✧

The truth is that Fitzgerald was gifted intellectually, artistically, and, in addition, possessed an intuition bordering on the paranormal. In his first short story in the *Nassau Literary Magazine* at Princeton (April 1915), "Shadow Laurels," an estranged son returns to a tavern that his deceased father (Jean Chandelle) frequented, to learn more about him: "I want to see people who knew him, who had talked with him. I want to find out his intelligence, his life, his record.... I want to sense him—I want to know him." What follows is perhaps what Scott prophetically might have written, or what he hoped might be written, as his own eulogy: "He was educated. God knows how. He knew everything, he could tell anything—he used to tell me poetry. Oh, what poetry? And I would listen and dream...."[16] Later, we will return to some of the rest of that story.

Scott came out better with a third friend at Princeton, John Biggs. When Scott returned in the fall of 1917, not to attend classes but to write and wait for an army commission, he roomed with Biggs in Campbell Hall. Biggs wrote many issues of the college humor magazine with Scott, collaborated on *Safety First,* published two novels with Scribners, and became the youngest judge named to the Third U.S. Circuit Court of Appeals. Unlike so many others, Biggs remained a faithful friend to the end—literally—as he settled Scott's final estate and will as his literary executor.

Still, it is fair to say, a truly serious student like Edmund Wilson would easily conclude that Scott had too casual an approach to Princeton's academic life. Fitzgerald was realistic about such judgments and quite frank about his study habits. Math and physics were boring, and foreign languages were a mystery. Although Scott was most interested in English literature, his English teachers were greatly disappointing, a view shared by John Peale Bishop, who pretended otherwise. Young Fitzgerald's lack of respect for English professors was reinforced many years later when he would make a drunken, riotous visit to Dartmouth while working on the "Winter Carnival" screenplay.

The sharp, invidious contrast usually drawn between Scott's intellectual station at Princeton and that of his literary companions John Peale Bishop and Edmund Wilson is, at worst, an exaggeration.

Scott's sense of social inferiority from his Newman experience continued to be partly fed by Wilson and Bishop—at least, initially. Ironically, their own lifetime sense of inferiority had a more solid base: They eventually did realize that *they* were actually inferior in most aspects of life. Wilson had difficulty staying married, and Bishop's *earlier* crack-up otherwise resembled Scott's during the 1930s. Archibald MacLeish, who had an affair with Bishop's wife, said that her money had emasculated her husband. Bishop's career was sufficiently stagnant that he could have been (actually, in a way, *was*) a character in a Fitzgerald novel. Still, Bishop at least had sufficient loyalty to Scott to refuse Zelda Fitzgerald's invitation to bed her early in her marriage.

Besides having condescending "friends" and failing again at football, the Ivy League sport that guaranteed instant social standing, Scott had other reasons for feeling inferior in the Princeton environment. He met the privileged like Richard Cleveland (son of former president Grover Cleveland) and David Bruce (son of a United States senator, who himself later became a deservedly distinguished ambassador). Scott was a socially and financially inferior person from undistinguished Newman surrounded by rich, Eastern, Anglo-Saxon Protestants from the elite private schools. Fitzgerald himself provides an apt and concise summary of his early experiences. "That was always my experience—a poor boy in a rich town; a poor boy in a rich boy's school; a poor boy in a rich man's club at Princeton."

✧ ✧ ✧

At Princeton this lighthearted young Irishman seems to be pursuing only musical comedies, women, and gin. His intellectual friends make fun of his headlong pursuit into self-indulgence even as he outwrote and outpublished them, especially during his first five-plus years as a professional writer. He remains an intellectual lightweight; this is the way it seemed. In this conventional light or, more aptly, darkness, what comes thereafter may seem contradictory. Fitzgerald was sufficiently confident of his own mind to be supremely skeptical of Princeton's conventional wisdom as he turned his back on Princeton's literary "lights" such as Henry van Dyke, George McLean Harper, or Charles Osgood and toward his own lengthening reading lists. At Princeton a sea change already was under way as we next explore Scott's early flirtation with socialism.

We would be remiss to not at least give a hint regarding the social forces underlying Fitzgerald's transformation. James J. Hill not only made a great impression on young Scott but many others. Summit, if even in St. Paul, was not simply a street where people lived but also a higher place to which Americans aspired—not just the mansion but also other parts of the American Dream. The thoughtful person nonetheless would wonder what they might do once they reach "the top," the peak of wealth. What's more, the thoughtful *and* sensitive person might even wonder about the fate of those trampled at the bottom—the "unfit," in the key word of the Social Darwinists. As already and adequately noted, the industrialists had the Social Darwinists, God, and science right where they wanted them—on their side. Conventional wisdom is a powerful thing; it can be countered, if at all, only by a persuasive alternative. At the time there were two—socialism and, well, mild-mannered socialism, or reform of the abuses and consequences of frontier capitalism.

Endnotes

1. F. Scott Fitzgerald, "Princeton," December 1927 in Arthur Mizener, Editor, *Afternoon of an Author* (Princeton, NJ: Princeton University Library, 1957), p. 75; (New York: Scribners, 1958).

2. Matthew J. Bruccoli, ed., *F. Scott Fitzgerald: A Life in Letters* (New York: Scribners, 1994) p. 460.

3. Quoted in James L. W. West III, *The Perfect Hour: The Romance of F. Scott Fitzgerald and Ginevra King, His First Love* (New York: Random House, 2005), p. 21. West's book is based on Ginevra's diary and her letters to Scott, which were not discovered until April 2003 by one of Ginevra's granddaughters, Ginevra King Chandler. West's book appeared just in time to correct some errors in our manuscript, errors carried forward from earlier biographers. Out of loyalty to Scott, Ginevra never revealed anything from her diary or from the letters; instead, she was intentionally vague and coy in what she revealed, leading to many misinterpretations of her motives and her true relationship with Scott.

4. In a letter from Ginevra King Pirie to Arthur Mizener, December 4, 1947, Princeton University Library. This letter was written after Ginevra's second marriage.

5. West III, *op. cit.,* pp. 25–26.

6. West III, *Ibid.,* p. 35.

7. *Ibid.,* pp. 37–38.

8. Quoted in Bruccoli, *Some Sort of Epic Grandeur* (San Diego: Harcourt Brace Jovanovich, 1981), p. 68.

9. West III, *op. cit.,* p. 66.

10. Bruccoli, *op. cit.,* p. 68.

11. F. Scott Fitzgerald, *This Side of Paradise* (New York: Scribners, 1920), p. 53.

12. John Peale Bishop, "The Missing All," *Virginia Quarterly Review,* 13 (Winter 1937, pp. 115–16.)

13. Glenway Wescott, "The Moral of Scott Fitzgerald." In Edmund Wilson, ed., *The Crack-Up* (New York: New Directions, 1956), p. 325. This essay first appeared as an obituary in *The New Republic.*

14. Ibid., p. 332.

15. Ibid., p. 329.

16. The story is reprinted in John Kuehl, ed., *The Apprentice Fiction of F. Scott Fitzgerald, 1909–1917* (New Brunswick, NJ: Rutgers University Press, 1965).

Three

•

• •

Socialist Capital

SO MUCH IS HAPPENING SO QUICKLY IN F. SCOTT FITZGERALD'S STILL
young life, we pause to highlight some of the early distractions
from his studies. He enters Princeton University in September 1913
and meets Edmund Wilson and John Peale Bishop. In September
1914 his *Assorted Spirits* is produced in St. Paul. Meanwhile,
that same fall, Zelda Sayre enters Sidney Lanier High School in
Montgomery, Alabama. Shortly after Fitzgerald's first Princeton
musical comedy is produced, he meets Ginevra King in St. Paul. A
few months later his "Shadow Laurels" is published in the *Nassau
Literary Magazine.* In November Scott drops out of Princeton for
the balance of his junior year, even though his and Wilson's *The Evil
Eye* is produced. In fall 1916, Fitzgerald returns to Princeton and
soon his and John Biggs's *Safety First* is produced by the Triangle
Club. After failing to graduate, Fitzgerald is commissioned second
lieutenant in the U.S. infantry, as improbable as that may seem.
He reports to duty and begins a novel that will become *This Side
of Paradise.* In May 1918, Zelda graduates from Sidney Lanier,
and Scott reports to Camp Sheridan near Montgomery. They meet
in July (the same month that Ginevra marries her ensign); Zelda
breaks their engagement in June 1919. *This Side of Paradise* is

published March 26, 1920; Scott and Zelda are married less than two weeks later.

We set aside Scott's military duty and his courtship of Zelda for a few pages. We also put aside Ginevra King, but not as coldly as her father put aside Scott. We do so to look more deeply at Fitzgerald's self-directed learning that, oddly enough, began early on at Princeton. We observe Scott's mind at work, more or less separate from the distractions of Ginevra's coming on and off stage and Zelda's arrival in his life. After Summit Avenue and after meeting Ginevra's wealthy family, Scott's turn toward socialism is less than surprising.

✧   ✧   ✧

Fitzgerald's early and continuing flirtation with socialism was perhaps a historical inevitability given his class-conscious upbringing and the sharp contrasts among economic fortunes he observed and experienced during his and America's twenties and thirties. He personally was riding high in the twenties, knocked down in the mid-thirties, but back on top of his game in his final two years. Marxism is a recurring theme, but as Scott's complexity discloses, it is by no means the sole source of the class consciousness infusing his works. Fitzgerald carefully and widely read the writers of the left who opposed the American conservative ideology of Social Darwinism at the turn of the twentieth century. But that is not all. Through myriad experiences and self-instruction, Scott's maturation as a serious writer happened much faster than Edmund Wilson and John Peale Bishop—both *actual* graduates of Princeton—would ever admit or many of his biographers would ever recognize.

With his early, even premature view from the summit, Scott, as a writer and as a participant, always was sensitive to the pecking order. Even if it wasn't to be Princeton's class of 1917 (or any other class from which he failed to graduate), the idea of class was never far from his mind. The Princeton clubs were designed to establish one's social class; though unable to serve as a likely president of the Triangle Club, Scott *was* elected to Cottage, one of the big four Princeton eating clubs and, perhaps more important, his club of choice. It was the most architecturally elegant of the clubs and had a large Southern following. In Fitzgerald's first novel, *This Side of Paradise,* he writes of Cottage as "an impressive mélange of brilliant adventurers and well-dressed philanderers."[1] Its lavish weekend parties were intended to attract debutantes from New York, Philadelphia, and other Eastern cities. In this, it succeeded admirably. Prior to Princeton Scott had been drunk a couple of times. At Princeton he manages to drink to the point of passing out—but not that unusual for Cottageers.

Between weekends and gin, nonetheless, Scott is quietly making up his own reading list; even as his social life quickens, his reading intensifies. As Scott pursues social *and* economic capital at Princeton and well before the publication of *Paradise* (1920), he is undergoing a profound intellectual transformation. Immediately following the summer of 1917, Scott retrospectively reveals a list of readings that has at the top, author H. G. Wells and Irish playwright and critic George Bernard Shaw. Scott even half-seriously ranks himself as heir apparent to Wells and Shaw a full two years before *Paradise* is accepted by Scribners. "Did you ever notice," Scott writes his English friend Shane Leslie, "that remarkable coincidence—Bernard Shaw is 61 yrs old, H. G. Wells is 51, G. K. Chesterton 41, you're 31 and I'm 21—All the great authors of the world in arithmetical progression."[2] Then, two days after his twenty-first birthday (September 26, 1917), Scott praises Wells's *The New Machiavelli* as "the greatest English novel of the century" in a letter to Edmund Wilson. Later that fall at Princeton, bored and waiting for a military commission, Scott found some relief in writing for the *Nassau Lit* and reading "Wells and Rousseau," calling Wells's *Boon* "marvelous!"[3] Later, he refers to Wells's *Tono-Bungay* as the book "having the greatest influence on my mind" for the period 1918–20.[4] Not surprisingly, then, Scott has Amory Blaine, his taller alter ego in *This Side of Paradise,* under the influence of Wells.

Fitzgerald had been introduced to the Swiss-French philosopher, author, political theorist, and composer Jean Jacques Rousseau (1712–78) by his favorite professor, Christian Gauss (1878–1951). Rousseau was the father of Romantic sensibility, whose French prose often had a tender and musical quality. His emphasis on the free development of human potential from within (intuition), as in his *Émile,* rather than from say, Princeton professors teaching the conventional wisdom, would have been appealing to Scott. The poetic quality of Fitzgerald's own prose nonetheless emanated more from his early aspirations as a poet and musical comedy writer than as an imperfect translator of French prose. Rousseau's placement of blame for human failures on society or social arrangements often resonates in Fitzgerald's writing. Without advocating collective ownership, Rousseau's influence on Socialist thought was more along the lines of state provision of basic social needs rather than collective ownership, the kind of "socialism" embraced by Scott in the conclusion to *Paradise.*

It is no accident that *This Side of Paradise*, which Scott once sarcastically called "a Romance and a Reading List," concludes with Amory Blaine's idealistic defense of socialism. Scott's Basil and Josephine stories are frequently considered stories to illuminate his and beautiful Ginevra's romantically coming of age and to illustrate Scott's enduring romance with the American Dream. However, since even Fitzgerald's short story, "Forging Ahead," was written later—in 1928, to be exact—they also illustrate his lingering flirtation with socialism as an ideal. Thus, we begin with the end of that story.

After unsuccessfully seeking a cub reporter position with a variety of newspapers, including the *Socialist Gazette,* Basil finally lands a job building railroad cars, only to be quickly laid off. The prevailing Horatio Alger myth of self-help is further dispelled when the unemployed Basil uses a family connection to get a new job working for his wealthy great-uncle, who has recently moved to St. Paul with his second wife and stepdaughter (Basil's cousin). As it turns out, the stuck-up Basil is used as a social lever to permit his cousin to enter St. Paul society. Gradually, Basil recognizes that social capital accumulation, not individual merit, hard work, or initiative, is the path to social and economic success—so much the worse for Horatio Alger, who, in the end, is no match for Karl Marx. Reluctantly accepting his role as social networker, Basil feels "vaguely exploited" and is further disgruntled when his social obligations on behalf of his unpopular cousin get in the way of pursuing his dream girl, Minnie Bibble.

✧ ✧ ✧

To rank Karl Marx ahead of Horatio Alger is faint praise: F. Scott's youthful conversion to Marxism was never complete. Moreover, Fitzgerald's attachment to Marxism was filtered through and diluted by the ideas of H. G. Wells (1866–1946) and George Bernard Shaw (1856–1950)—progressive social reformers who were well schooled in the natural and social sciences of the day. This is so even though Fitzgerald came to know Marx the hard way—by trying to read *Das Kapital* in German and, later in life, translating some of Marx's Latin phrases for the benefit of Sheilah Graham.[5] But by the time Fitzgerald has added H. G. Wells and George Bernard Shaw to his reading list, he has toppled Marx to at least third place, perhaps much lower. Shaw acknowledges Marx's attack on capitalism, but considers his method and his economics wrong. Wells studied under T. H. Huxley, often called "Darwin's bulldog," while Shaw's discussion of Lamarckian and late-nineteenth-century neo-Darwinist theories of biological and social evolution in his lengthy preface to *Back To Methuselah* (1921) amply demonstrates the depth of *his* erudition.[6]

They also called themselves "Socialists." Shaw, along with Beatrice and Sidney Webb, founded the Fabians (1884), a mild-mannered society dedicated to transforming Britain into a Socialist state. The Fabian Society included member Wells before his leaving in a 1906 dispute with Shaw. Wells wanted the society to be in the front lines of political activism. Rather, the leaders of the Fabians envisioned the transformation of Britain by systematic progressive legislation, bolstered by persuasion and mass education, not by revolution. Even the label Fabian comes from the name of the Roman general who wore down the enemy by skirmishes and delaying tactics instead of head-on combat.

You did not have to be a Karl Marx writing in the British Museum, developing bunions while being supported by the rich industrialist Friedrich Engels, to realize that a class structure existed in England. Wells and Shaw went up against traditional Victorian values and championed social engineering as a way to break these

English class barriers and generate social progress. Gradual changes, so suited to the English temper and form of government, in the ways of better housing and better education would improve economic welfare and general well-being. As to a favored class, Wells and Shaw, in common with Marx, considered the typical working stiff the underdog; unlike Marx, they had a pragmatic plan for improving social conditions.

Fitzgerald's classmate and "friend" at Princeton, Edmund Wilson, used poorer judgment than Scott; Wilson was devoted to the original source, the fountainhead—to Karl Marx. Wilson was a devout socialist and communist not only at Princeton but later, as the 1930s ended. In a letter to Mary McCarthy on January 18, 1938, Wilson writes that he spends his evenings reading Marx and Engels ("the Owl and the Pussycat," he calls them). In a letter to Lionel Trilling on January 10, 1939, he asks Trilling where he saw a copy of Marx's Palmerston pamphlet. "I've only been able to get it in French."[7] Unlike Scott, a retail Marxist but never wholesale, Wilson later had to explain Joseph Stalin's worst behavior. Other writers such as Scott's friend Dorothy Parker also would swallow the Stalinist line. Scott was too smart or nonideological for that and avoided an embarrassment that he had, in an emergent pattern, intuitively anticipated.

✧ ✧ ✧

For us, H. G. Wells is probably best remembered for his early works of science fiction such as *The Time Machine* (1895), *The Invisible Man* (1897), and *The War of the Worlds* (1898). This first appearance as a novelist came at the end of Wells's short teaching career in biology in 1893. His books of fantasy and pseudoscientific speculations also are memorable as movies, especially for their special effects. In his first movie "appearance" in *The Invisible Man* (1933), Claude Rains's voice characterization is magnificent, though his body doesn't actually show up until the final scene. In Wells's novels of his "middle period," however, he visibly turned his back on the fantastic and tackled the realism of his world. In these, he was an imaginative social thinker, writing to wipe away the residue of

Victorian social, moral, and religious attitudes from twentieth-century life. We turn now, along with F. Scott Fitzgerald, to Wells's social thought, expressed in his mid-period realism.

As Fitzgerald read Wells's *Tono-Bungay* (1909) and *The New Machiavelli* (1911), he encountered youthful dreamers who viewed the unfettered capitalism of late-nineteenth-century England as chaotic and an obstacle to social progress. This view countered conventional Anglo-American Social Darwinism, or essentially the idea that the rich are rich because they are the fitter of the species. Richard Remington, the main character in *The New Machiavelli,* speaks for Wells when he says that laissez-faire capitalism tethered to a Victorian faith in progress has resulted in a multitude of "fresh starts, each more sweeping and destructive than the last," leaving "products, houses, humanity, or what not in its wake...." The Victorian epoch, Wells concludes, was not "the dawn of a new era," but "a gigantic experiment of the most slovenly and wasteful kind."[8] In *Tono-Bungay,* cap-

italism's waste is part of an even larger theme of social and cosmic degeneration.[9] Fitzgerald's understanding of Wells was not superficial and did not go unused.

These novels by Wells, together with *Boon*—its full title *Boon, The Mind of the Race, The Wild Asses of the Devil,* and *The Last Trump*[10] (1915)—gave young Scott a slant on society befitting his skepticism of the capitalist system and, in the case of *Boon,* his disgust at the destructiveness of the Great War.

Tono-Bungay is a devastating social commentary

H. G. Wells during his middle period when he was writing Tono-Bungay *and* Boon.

critical of both new and old wealth, which Scott would return to in his fiction—most famously in *The Great Gatsby*. In *Tono-Bungay,* George's Uncle Edward, full of energy and imaginative silliness, becomes obscenely wealthy by marketing a fraudulent medicine. The "Tono-Bungay" of the title is a placebo that Uncle Edward is marketing to an unwitting public. "The stuff was," George perceives, "a mischievous trash, slightly stimulating, aromatic and attractive, likely to become a bad habit and train people in the habitual use of stronger tonics and insidiously dangerous to people with defective kidneys."[11] In short, he is marketing an inspiring but false dream that eventually is destructive—exactly what happens later with Fitzgerald's Jay Gatsby. The English public is consumed by Tono-Bungay even as they consume it, in the same way that the American Dream consumes Gatsby.

George nonetheless is initially attracted by his uncle's vitality; it offers George a fresh alternative to the confining feudal world of his youth, the Bladesovery estate where his mother was a servant. Although Bladesovery offers a certain orderly and enduring beauty to George personified in his first love (Beatrice), its rigidities and George's inferior status within it prevent their love from coming to full fruition. However, his uncle's vulgar antidote in the world of business proves to be an inadequate tonic itself. After being recruited into his uncle's enterprise, George recognizes his uncle's "Romance of Commerce" for what it is—all facade and no substance, robbing people by engendering false hope just as the feudal system at Bladesovery robs people of even their *right* to hope. Uncle Edward becomes nothing but "a swelling, thinning bubble of assurances" drifting toward disaster.[12] While any struggle for class was futile under feudalism, it could be for win, place, but more likely show in the world of free enterprise.

Like much of Scott's own fiction in the early twenties, *Tono-Bungay* explores not only the social barriers created by wealth but their ultimately stifling effect on romance. Even the title for Scott's July 5, 1924, short story "'The Sensible Thing'" is derived from a series of episodes where George, now with his second love, Marion, is initially denied her because of his inadequate income and prospects—a rerun of his relationship with Beatrice. From Marion's initial rejection because "one has to be sensible," to the eventual engagement and marriage, George's love is commercialized, reduced to a bidding process that leaves him alienated from the original spark igniting his feelings of love. "An extraordinary bitterness possessed me at this invasion of the stupendous beautiful business of love by sordid necessity," George eloquently surmises.[13]

✧　✧　✧

The tensions among romance, endless possibilities of the imagination, and the unwelcome intrusion of necessity must have made a great impression on young Scott. The romantic vein in Fitzgerald's life and fiction is such a popular hallmark that it is easy to overlook the cold and bitter realism that underlies it. But by the time he writes "'The Sensible Thing,'" Scott will have been rejected twice—first by Ginevra and then, as we soon will see, by Zelda—on the same grounds as George and with similar effect. As we will come to notice, the lyrical luster of Fitzgerald's prose lulls the casual reader into the belief that *that* is all there is. Critics, notably his friend Edmund Wilson, even as a budding intellectual, should have been allowed less impunity when they made that kind of callous judgment. An honest and perceptive critic would have seen how the romance in Fitzgerald's novels was undone by the corruption bred by wealth.

Wells resonated with Fitzgerald not only because of the pull of socialism but also because of the push from capitalism at home and, equally important, abroad. International socialism was a source of optimism for Wells despite his view of human nature as fundamentally bestial.[14] Scott embraced Wells's view that unfettered capitalism unleashes the destructive animalistic dimension of human nature, whereas socialism humanizes these bestial tendencies of man, potentially taming what Wells calls "The wild asses of the devil" in *Boon*. It is well to remember that Scott, like Amory Blaine in *This Side of Paradise,* became absorbed with Wells in the midst of the destructiveness and disorder of the Great War, which was propelled, if not initiated, by the twin forces of capitalism and sectarian nationalism in their most destructive, imperialistic manifestations.

The new weapons of mass destruction forged in the industrial age created an important distinction between capitalistic wars and feudal wars. In the absence of giant factories, there could be no world wars. According to Amory, Scott's alter ego in *Paradise,* the Great War has "killed individualism out of our generation" and created a heroless age.[15] Giant artillery made killing impersonal. But, there is more, much more. As with the Earth's moon, nature has a dark and a light side.

Without denying the darker side of human nature, Wells provides Scott and the otherwise lost postwar generation with the *possibility* of a restorative belief in human progress. Wells's pessimism anticipated the invention of the atomic bomb while his optimism led him to support the League of Nations. Socialism would provide a measure of control and direction missing from capitalism and the powerlessness of the individual would be compensated by a higher communal ethic. Under Wells's vision in *The New Machiavelli,* which Scott had so highly praised, a new intellectual aristocracy was born not of Victorian privilege, but from an understanding that a constructive imagination could guide society toward a common aim.

✧   ✧   ✧

As to further influence, George Bernard Shaw was always just off-stage, waiting in the left wings. By commercial standards Shaw's most successful play is *Pygmalion* (1913), which satirizes the English class system through a story of poor Eliza Doolittle's transformation into a lady in the hands of Professor Henry Higgins, a phonetician. It was, after all, a motion picture, and the basis for the musical and film *My Fair Lady* (1956; 1964). And, we will be reminded of this fictional Cockney girl and her struggles to be educated when we come to the reality of Sheilah Graham, Fitzgerald's English companion-to-be in Hollywood. Although Shaw's plays brim with ideas and issues, they are vital and enthralling, made lively by his memorable characterizations, a brilliant command of the English language, and dazzling wit—all of which Scott Fitzgerald admired.

Prior to writing *The New Machiavelli,* Wells has had his falling out with Shaw and the Fabian Society, but the two literary giants remained Socialist in outlook. Edmund Wilson, by now failing as a creative writer but succeeding as the leading critic of his time, writes in 1936 that the intention of Shaw's drama is to shame people out of romantic love and interest them in social problems.[16] Shaw had this social consciousness–raising effect on Scott as well, even as Fitzgerald was falling out of love with love. Moreover, the artistry of Shaw's plays had a direct effect on the literary structure of *This Side of Paradise,* in particular the design of its subheadings such as

G. B. Shaw

His "play's the thing" for the author of This Side of Paradise: *Shaw's stimulating satire was infused with a singular poetic beauty.*

"A Kiss for Amory," "Incident of the Well-Meaning Professor," and "Temperature Normal." Indeed, there is so much going on in Shaw's plays (including gender, political, and philosophical debate) enhanced by Shaw's stature as a literary figure, that it is difficult to identify the precise influence on Scott other than that it was pervasive.

The rich leisure class of England, raw material for Wells and Shaw, illuminated the American landscape for young Scott Fitzgerald. He had witnessed the timely use but distancing of the poor from the rich under St. Paul's James J. Hill and New York's Rockefellers' tableau of capitalism. In turn, this panoramic view inspired much of Fitzgerald's best writing. Shaw's major critical plays reinforced what Scott found in Wells. *Man and Superman* (1903), which Scott was certainly familiar with by 1921 (and probably considerably sooner), would have introduced him to Shaw's brand of soft socialism. Fitzgerald also would have found satirical digs at capitalism and the leisure class in *Major Barbara* (1907), which depicts poverty, a characteristic of unbridled capitalism, as the cause of evil.

Scott's view of the Great War as derivative of Western capitalism becoming aggressive imperialism is an important, though later, theme to come under Shaw's influence. More than anything else, the outbreak of war in 1914 changed Shaw's life. For him, the war represented the bankruptcy of the capitalist system, the last desperate gasps of the nineteenth-century empires, and a tragic waste of young lives, all under the guise of patriotism. His opinions published in newspaper articles became a disaster for Shaw's public stature, and he was treated as an outcast in his adopted country, with even talk of his being tried for treason. Still, he courageously hurls his bitterness and despair about British politics and society into *Heartbreak House* (1919), a play that exposes the spiritual bankruptcy of the generation responsible for the Great War.

And, there is still more in Shaw for Fitzgerald, a man who has loved Ginevra and is already dealing with the realism that is Zelda, as he moves on to his next novels. In *Man and Superman,* there is also man and superwoman. An idealistic, cerebral man succumbs to marriage, a metaphor for a major Shavian theme—that man is the spiritual creator, whereas woman is the biological "life force" that must always triumph over him. Shaw depicts the female as a vital but destructive life force, the Zelda reality about to confront Fitzgerald but also a major theme that will breathe life into *The Beautiful and Damned* and *The Great Gatsby*.

Not surprisingly then, Friedrich Nietzsche (1844–1900) also gained prominence in Fitzgerald's mind, not only through Shaw but also through Scott's close association with H. L. Mencken (1880–1956), an editor of the *Smart Set* and later *American Mercury,* whom Scott credits as among the "chief early influences of his life."[17] Looking back from the autumn of 1922, Scott lists Mencken's *The Philosophy of Friedrich Nietzsche* (1908) among "THE TEN BOOKS I HAVE ENJOYED MOST"[18] and it probably later inspired Fitzgerald's reading of Nietzsche's *The Genealogy of Morals,* which Scott calls the most influential book he had read at age twenty-four (in 1920).[19]

The influence of Nietzsche, both directly and indirectly through Shaw and Mencken, would ultimately temper Scott's endorsement of socialism in any strict democratic or Marxist version.

Even at an early age Scott was comfortable with apparent contradictions that confounded "serious" students at Princeton. As he writes *Paradise,* Fitzgerald is attracted to two such thoughts: one is Wells's idea that society could be redirected through collective action; two is the Nietzsche notion that the individual could free himself from social constraints and become what Scott called "a personage." A belief in a "willed order"—that we are not simply dust in the wind—unites what otherwise seems a contradiction.

Shaw had doubtless lifted the "Superman" part of his play's title from the writings of Friedrich Nietzsche. As a moralist, not a systematic philosopher, Nietzsche—like Shaw and Mencken—passionately rejected Western middle-class values, depicting Christianity as decadent because of its "slave morality." He looked to the superman as the creator of a new heroic morality that would consciously affirm life and its values. This superman would represent the highest passion and creativity and would live at a level of experience beyond conventional standards of good and evil. Superman's creative "will to power" would set him off from "the herd" of inferior persons.

✧   ✧   ✧

Odd as it must have seemed to classmates Wilson and Bishop, we find Scott reading serious philosophical works even after he realizes that he won't be graduating from Princeton and before he begins his first novel. In a letter to Edmund Wilson September 26, 1917, Scott writes, "I've given up the summer [of 1917] to drinking (gin) and philosophy (James and Schopenhauer and Bergson)."[20] Too little and too much have been ascribed to Scott's lighthearted, casual statement; only the gin is remembered. It is useful, therefore, to consider what Scott might have found in philosophy.

The mention of William James (1842–1910) immediately conjures up pragmatism as a method of arriving at "the truth." The worst critique of pragmatism was when some academic said that he had tried it but it didn't work. As to the truth, once the facts are known, *everyone* is a pragmatist. James's *radical* pragmatism, however, says that values must adapt to new circumstances, a philosophy, as we shall see, underlying Thorstein Veblen's critique of capitalism—its values and institutions are too rigid to adapt to the potential benefits of new technology. Also, in a theme echoed in both Schopenhauer and Bergson, Scott would have learned from reading James that the moral energy of the individual stood as an antidote to the entropy forces and lethargy that plagued modern society, particularly within the upper classes. Another likely influence on Fitzgerald is James's rich prose, as easy to read as his pragmatism is difficult to understand.

When the Modern Library reissued *The Great Gatsby* in 1934, Fitzgerald writes in an introduction, "...I had recently been kidded half haywire by critics who felt that my material was such as to preclude all dealing with mature persons in a mature world. But, my God! It was my material, and it was all I had to deal with." It was one of those unfortunate statements showcasing Fitzgerald's tendency to be his most demanding critic, written at a low point in Fitzgerald's life and career. Critics have often used the final phrase to suggest that Scott's work was simply autobiographical. Like all fiction writers, including Ernest Hemingway, Scott *did* use his experiences in his characterizations, but that is not all.

With Scott, romance and the allure of romanticists was always in the air—hence Arthur Schopenhauer (1788–1860), a philosopher of the Romanticist generation and born the same year as poet Lord Byron. Schopenhauer surmised that desire creates images of truth, love, justice, happiness, and other alluring wants that can never be satisfied. The world is will in the sense of desire, but it is all a snare and an illusion. Art, the *one* exception to this fate, is not illusion: The desire art arouses *is* fulfilled by its object. As we will soon come to know, there is little here—be it insatiable desires, the illusions they create, or art as the sole exception—that F. Scott Fitzgerald would find disagreeable. As we will come to note, Schopenhauer also has a view of human evolution agreeable to Fitzgerald.

Henri Bergson (1859–1941), a French philosopher who went on to win the 1927 Nobel Prize in Literature, was a friend of Father

Fay's, who knew him in France. Bergson's philosophy is a kind of duel under the sun: The world contains two opposing tendencies—the life force (élan vital) and the resistance of the material world against that force. We know physical stuff through our intellect, with which we measure the world and devise the specialized canons of science. For example, the Plaza Hotel in New York City uses U.S. dollars to price 1.5-ounce cocktails at its bar. In contrast with intellect and measurement is intuition, which derives from the instinct of lower animals. Intuition gives us an intimation of élan vital, which pervades all becoming, and perceives the reality of time as duration defined by living memories not divisible or measurable.

The general idea of a life force will turn out to be important to Fitzgerald at the time of *Paradise;* a nearly infallible intuition nevertheless did not require Bergson, since Fitzgerald had sufficient intuition to realize that he had it. In one of those magnificent Fitzgerald U-turns, he later distances himself from Bergson (except to mock him) as he writes *The Beautiful and Damned* and *The Great Gatsby.*

In *Man and Superman,* Shaw anticipates Bergson's concept of "Creative Evolution" (1911)[21] and, later, in the preface to *Back To Methuselah,* endorses it. Bergson's élan vital includes a human capacity to create and direct change in the cosmos. This "willed order" allows for creative possibilities for individual and social progress, which counteracts the forces of entropy (disorder) and dissipation found in physical nature. Though many of Scott's biographers have gin winning against philosophy during that summer of Bergson and philosophy, it is a romantic exaggeration. Still, as to Bergson's more recondite ideas, a tumbler of gin would have made them go down easier.

Bergson's theory nonetheless is an important alternative to Social Darwinism—evolution governed by competitive economic forces that make humans mindless products of capitalism. Bergson's Creative Evolution, a world in which persons have minds of their own, is understandably as popular with early-twentieth-century artists as Social Darwinism is to rigid American industrialists. In *Methuselah,* Shaw calls Creative Evolution "the genuinely scientific religion for which all wise men are now anxiously looking" and invokes Schopenhauer's idea of a "will-to-live" as "the driving force behind Evolution." Shaw wants to restore human will into an evolutionary view and enthusiastically declares, "If the Western Powers had selected their allies in the Lamarckian manner intelligently, purposely, and vitally there would have been a League of Nations and no war."[22] Fitzgerald agreed about the war and soon would take up his pen to join Thorstein Veblen's attack on Social Darwinism. He also understood that life is full of novelty and creative potential, while the past is always found in the ripeness of the present moment.

Scott was attracted not only to Shaw's intellectual but also to his personal verve. As Sheilah Graham, Fitzgerald's last Golden Girl, would recall, "Scott admired Shaw for his courage in advocating unpopular causes such as socialism and atheism."[23] This admiration is confirmed by an angry February 9, 1920, letter Scott sent to a boyhood friend, Robert Clark, who apparently questions Scott for drifting under such decadent influences. Scott was writing from 38 West Fifty-ninth Street in New York City at a time in which Zelda mistakenly thought she was pregnant, more than a month before their marriage.

> Your letter riled me to such an extent that I'm answering immediately. Who are all these "real people" who "create business and politics"? and of whose approval I should be so covetous? …Just occasionally a man like Shaw who was called immoral 50 times worse than me back in the 90ties, lives on long enough so that the world grows up to him. What he believed in 1890 was heresy then—by now its almost respectable. It seems to me I've let myself be dominated by "authorities" for too long—the headmaster of Newman, S.P.A. [St. Paul Academy], Princeton, my regiment, my business boss—who knew no more than me, in fact I should say these 5 were all distinctly my mental inferiors. And that's all that counts! The Rousseau's, Marx's, Tolstoy's—men of thought, mind you, "impractical" men, 'idealist' have done more to decide the food you eat and the things you think + do than all the millions of Roosevelts and Rockefellers that strut for 20 yrs. Or so mouthing such phrases as 100% American (which means 99% village idiot),

and die with a little pleasing flattery to the silly and cruel old God they've set up in their hearts.[24]

So there! Fitzgerald did not try to conceal his real feelings.

✧ ✧ ✧

Now, something quite typical of Fitzgerald happened; Scott used part of the reactionary thought in Clark's letter to write one of his best short stories, "The Diamond as Big as the Ritz" (June 1922), a tale also based on Scott's early life. It is a recollection of Scott's 1915 visit to Sap Donahoe's (as we recall, a wealthy Newman-Princeton classmate and football hero) Montana ranch during a school vacation. In a story that draws further on Bernard Shaw, Braddock Washington, father symbol of American wealth and the omnipotent owner of a diamond mountain, attempts to cut (literally) a deal with God to save his vast wealth from destruction:

> He would give to God...the greatest diamond in the world... cut with many more thousand facets than there were leaves on a tree, and yet the whole diamond would be shaped with the perfection of a stone no bigger than a fly. He doubted only whether he had made his bribe big enough. God had His price, of course. God was made in man's image, so it had been said: He must have His price.[25]

Braddock Washington vainly tries to hide his mountainous wealth from everyone but God, a reflection of the unsuccessful attempt by the rich to prevent the estate tax legislation of 1916, or what Republicans today call "the death tax." The diamond mountain is a metaphor for the enormous coagulation of wealth from monopoly power, Fitzgerald's way of bemoaning the general trend toward industrial concentration in late-nineteenth and early-twentieth-century America. In this sophisticated story, Fitzgerald focuses as much on the destructive effects of wealth on its owners as on its aspirants.

Like Shaw, Fitzgerald's satire attacks the Social Darwinian defense for unfettered capitalism. Scott turns Social Darwinism on its head to make sense of it: Instead of man being made in God's image, God is made in man's image—by man, of course. Like man, God has H[h]is price. In truth, Braddock Washington's saying that God has His price echoes the conjectures of Washington's counterpart, Andrew Undershaft, capitalist-imperialist supreme in Shaw's play *Major Barbara,* that charity, like any other economic transaction, has *its* price. In Shaw's play, Undershaft (a munitions manufacturer), sets out to demonstrate to his daughter Barbara (a major in the Salvation Army) that the alleviation of poverty and, indeed all aspects of morality and spirituality, are derived from capitalist-generated wealth. Like the robber barons, Undershaft merges religion and capitalism so that God sides with monopoly capitalism. Mr. Undershaft is a Social Darwinist to the core.

The letter to Clark also reveals an important shift in Scott's personality—an emerging duality. Scott is the supremely self-confident individual who rejects outer in favor of inner authority (a *personage* as opposed to a personality in the language used in *Paradise;* a *Superman* in Nietzsche's and Shaw's terms). He also has a growing intellectual empathy with socialism in reaction to the sanctimonious imperialism of the Roosevelts and Rockefellers with their "little pleasing flattery" to their "silly and cruel old God." Fitzgerald's own personal experiences with the barriers erected by wealth and privilege were being vindicated by the thinkers—Rousseau, Marx, Wells, and Shaw—he most admired. As to spirituality, Scott was searching for a good God, not the God created by the Social Darwinists.

✧ ✧ ✧

Fitzgerald also was being propelled to the left by his own discovery of a new literature of American realism critical of American capitalism. Every student is a critic, but Scott was an especially astute one. Princeton's insular world had no room for the newer and darker realities of American life being revealed by writers such as Frank Norris, Upton Sinclair, and Theodore Dreiser. Scott's disdain for the Princeton "education" is reflected in his response to University president John Grier Hibben's objections to the depiction of Princeton as "the pleasantest country club in America" in *This Side of Paradise*.[26] "I had," Scott writes, "spent several years trying to fit in with a curriculum that is after all made for the average student." Still, Scott admits to Hibben that the novel overdid the gaiety and country club atmosphere of Princeton: "It is the Princeton of a Saturday night in May."[27]

In a review of Charles Norris's *Brass* in 1921, Scott writes, "No one of my English professors in college ever suggested to his class that books were being written in America. Poor souls, they were as ignorant as I—possibly more so."[28] According to Sheilah Graham, "Scott had become enthusiastic about books on social realism in 1922,"[29] but the roots of that enthusiasm originated earlier with his 1919 reading of Charles Norris's *Salt,* whose style subsequently led Scott to the writings of Charles's brother Frank as well as to Sinclair and Dreiser. After having read *Salt,* Scott was greatly disappointed with *Brass*.

By 1920, Scott had read enough of Frank Norris to write his brother Charles recommending that they bring out a memorial edition of Frank's collected works.[30] Fitzgerald tells Maxwell Perkins on February 3, 1920, that he has "fallen lately under the influence of an author who's quite changed my point of view. He's a chestnut to you, no doubt, but I've just discovered him—Frank Norris. I think *McTeague* and *Vandover* are both excellent."[31] Fitzgerald had read *McTeague* during his courtship of Zelda Sayre, who found the novel "distasteful."[32] It is likely that Scott also read Norris's *The Octopus* (1901) about railroad conspirators around this time: The novel appears later on Scott's *College of One* reading list for Sheilah Graham.[33] What's more, the novel's theme of a poet-writer dreaming of producing a romantic epic entitled "Song of the West" only to be discouraged and utterly transformed by the intrusions of powerful materialistic forces is too coincidental with the overriding theme, later, of *The Great Gatsby* to be dismissed.

By 1922, in another revelation to Maxwell Perkins, his lifetime editor at Scribners, Scott identifies himself as a Socialist while expressing his concern that power belongs to the strong, whatever the political system. Fitzgerald's concern was influenced by Mencken in conjunction with Scott's readings of Nietzsche's *Genealogy of Morals,* Sinclair's *The Brass Check,* and Dreiser's depiction of the financial superman Frank Cowperwood in *The Financier* (1912). As Scott admits, "When I read Upton Sinclair's *The Brass Check* I made my final decision about America—that freedom has produced the greatest tyranny under the sun." However, his commitment is as "a Socialist but sometimes I dread that things will grow worse and worse the more the people nominally rule."[34]

Many of Fitzgerald's critics interpreted his as an elitist position and concluded that he ignored the working class in his writings because he was too close to the rich. This too is a misjudgment based not only on a misreading of his assurance, but also of Scott's novels and his short fiction. Fitzgerald's point is quite clear: The rich manipulate the political outcomes in a democratic system, so the people only "nominally rule."

Illustration for "The Camel's Back," Saturday Evening Post

As early as 1920, in the short story "The Camel's Back," Scott is writing about the working class, however obscurely. The story is a farcical account of U.S. leadership in the postwar era symbolized by a circus party hosted by one of the "Iron Men" of the corporate world. The main character, Perry Parkhurst, obtains a camel costume to attend the party incognito, but needs someone to bring up its rear. With the mention of "money," a drunk Perry convinces a reluctant taxi driver, representative of the working class, to attend the party with him as long as he keeps out of sight in the rear of the costume. Marx's idea that workers are degraded into *things* is illustrated as Perry says " 'he isn't a fellow... He's just part of my costume.' " American capitalism requires the working class to propel it, and if the working class blindly follows the rich, then the charade of real leadership is complete.

The American rich dragging the working class behind them is not only a mockery of true leadership but also a parody of Social Darwinism.

Another story written around the same time, "A Snobbish Story," has the same theme as "The Camel's Back." Scott's undignified treatment of the working class whereby its members exhibit the pecuniary and pretentious behavior of their social and economic superiors is a systemic reflection of commercial capitalism undermining the possibility of dignified work, a personal reality Scott continued to comically communicate nearly twenty years later in his Pat Hobby stories. If most of Scott's stories concentrate on the rich capitalist class, it is because they are in the front and the working class is bringing up the rear. The truth comes through as we realize that *the capitalist* is the ass despite his apparently superior position inside the costume of capitalism.

His critics' misrepresentation of Scott's attitude toward the working class is understandable, given Fitzgerald's complexity. His sympathies were with the common man, but he was not prepared to put his entire faith in him. Scott yearned for a political leader strong enough to shelter and lift the masses out of an economic and political system ruled by powerful money interests—a "superman." In an interview given at the inception of the Great Depression,

Scott describes himself as "an autocrat in theory but a Socialist in practice."[35] As America's economic system and Scott's own little world became increasingly disordered in the catastrophic thirties, his Socialist leanings would again be revived and he would take a retrospective view of Marxism.

✧ ✧ ✧

Fitzgerald's complex motives do not end with his sympathy for a common man that he wrote of infrequently in a direct way. He and Zelda lived lives where he was unable to write effectively about the working class or perhaps was unwilling to do so in the twenties since Socialist sympathizing would not sell in the *Saturday Evening Post,* which had become his major source of income. Even if Scott had difficulty understanding the working-class situation, he certainly understood how a commercial society could be all-consuming and create mercenary attitudes within the working class (consistent with Marxist theory). Given his professional and economic aspirations, he probably preferred to address the working-class experience indirectly. As with Bernard Shaw and the Fabians, it was a soft and salable Marxism.

Although Scott recognized that he did not possess the passionate conviction of a Marxist, he nevertheless continued to accumulate Socialist capital throughout his life and was fully capable of investing it into his fiction—the very fiction that earned him a livelihood and reputation as a cash crop within American capitalism. He remained a lifelong Socialist but—through an intuition not shared with many of his fellow writers—rejected the dogmatism of communism and considered Joseph Stalin to be a ruthless dictator, *not* an authentic Marxist or Socialist.

Well before the 1930s, however, Scott was introducing a soft Marxism into his literary fiction, which was and continues to be scarcely noticed because of his conspicuous lifestyle, his presumed lack of intellectual depth, and his growing reputation as a writer for and about youth and the rich. The depth of Scott's early appreciation for the forefathers of Socialist thought extends to the aforementioned Jean

Jacques Rousseau (read by Scott, we recall, in 1917). In Rousseau's social philosophy the natural goodness of man in a peaceful state of nature was corrupted when the privatization of property introduced social inequality and unleashed unsettling emotions of envy and shame. This is the essential theme of another early Fitzgerald short story, "The Jelly-Bean" (1920), one of many thought "too light" by critics then or since to merit serious consideration.

In the story a naive Southerner, Jim Powell, confronts the barriers erected by social and economic privilege—a theme more famously treated in "May Day" (a novelette more obviously sympathetic toward socialism) and, later, in *The Great Gatsby*. Powell is treated as Rousseau's noble but shiftless savage. Jim ultimately takes solace in his own class, a kind of retreat to small-town Americana that Scott was not prepared to make in pursuit of his dreams of social and economic advancement and winning the "top girl." Since the story is among the first (if not *the* first) to engage the plot of *The Great Gatsby*, we will return to its themes in chapter 7.

✧　　✧　　✧

Like so many creative and independent thinkers, Fitzgerald was self-taught. Skeptical of the conventional wisdom being taught at Princeton, Scott decided what was important to know; he decided to read what his professors failed to assign. He aspired to be an important artist despite the considerable odds against him. In this as well as other matters, Scott's intuition was prescient. Shortly after leaving Princeton, young Fitzgerald told a bemused Edmund Wilson, "I want to be one of the greatest writers who have ever lived."[36] He was blessed with the confidence of youth; throughout his life he would struggle to remain youthful to retain that confidence. That too would be a struggle against great odds.

In his youthful apprenticeship Fitzgerald did what became for him a typical thing. While making his lifestyle a perfectly perceptible and easy target, he also became his own worst critic. Scott was almost always the first to denigrate his own short fiction, often being the rare negative voice raised. He disparaged stories such as "The

Jelly-Bean" as "commercial fiction," even though they are well crafted and are reused as themes and material for his novels. More often than not, the other critics such as Edmund Wilson were *literally* taking Scott's word for his shortcomings. They did not seem to understand how hard Fitzgerald was on himself. They certainly did not understand his strong work ethic.

At least three themes critical of Fitzgerald reemerge every few years. First, F. Scott, an academic failure in prep school *and* at Princeton, was a pseudointellectual who was clever but shallow. Second, since he wrote short stories only for money, these stories are devoid of literary value and diverted Fitzgerald from his true calling, writing novels. Third, Zelda was not only the source of his material, but she wrote much of the content of Scott's stories and novels. As we will see, the motives behind these charges are myriad. Some of the early criticisms may have been driven by envy of Fitzgerald's apparently easy, early, and amazing success with his first novel. Yet, as we next will note, in his hurry to complete *This Side of Paradise* and afford Zelda, he masks some of his talent. The numerous textual mistakes in *Paradise*—not all his—can be cited to this day as justifying his harshest critics.

Already we have disabused readers of the notion that young Fitzgerald lacked intellectual depth. At the same time his intellectual sophistication belied his gift for prophecy. Ultimately but sooner than many imagine, he sees Zelda as another mistake even as he "wins" a second Golden Girl. We turn now, as the eyes of men and women of the Jazz Age did, to Zelda.

Endnotes

1. F. Scott Fitzgerald, *This Side of Paradise* (New York: Scribners, 1920), p. 47.

2. Letter to Shane Leslie dated February 1918, Matthew Bruccoli, ed., *F. Scott Fitzgerald: A Life in Letters* (New York: Simon & Schuster, Touchstone, 1995), p. 20.

3. Letter dated fall 1917, *ibid.*, p. 12. In this letter Scott makes a reference to the ages of Shaw, Wells, Chesterton, Leslie, and himself as he did in his later letter to Shane Leslie.

4. Matthew J. Bruccoli and Jackson R. Bryer, eds., *F. Scott Fitgerald in His Own Time: A Miscellany* (New York: Popular Library, 1971), p. 271.

5. *Das Kapital* was in Fitzgerald's personal library; his copy in the Fitzgerald Collection at Princeton University Library contains as many markings in Scott's handwriting as any of his other books, most probably made from his *College of One* teachings to Sheilah. He paid particular attention to the chapter on "The Working Day." There are a great number of Socialist-Marxist books in his collection, including *Program of the Communist International*.

6. Lamarck's theory of evolution, or Lamarckism, introduced in the first decade of the nineteenth-century, claims that all life forms have evolved by a continuous process of gradual modification throughout geologic history. Lamarck's claims that new traits in an organism develop because of a need created by environment was rejected altogether as the principles of heredity were established. Still, Lamarck's theory of evolution was a forerunner of the work of Charles Darwin, who documented a modified influence of environment in evolutionary processes. In his *On the Origin of Species* (1859), Darwin envisioned a continuing struggle for survival. Those variations (differences among members of the same species) helpful to a plant or an animal in its struggle for existence better enable it to survive and reproduce, a process he called "natural selection." In turn, those characteristics favorable for survival also survive over successive generations. Darwinism did not initially distinguish between acquired characteristics, which are not transmissible by heredity, and genetic variations, which are inheritable. Still, Darwin's basic outline is now universally accepted by scientists.

7. David Castronovo and Janet Groth, eds, *Edmund Wilson: The Man in Letters* (Athens, Ohio: Ohio University Press, 2001), pp. 113, 67.

8. H. G. Wells, *The New Machiavelli* (New York: Duffield & Company, 1917), p. 42.

9. Wells once considered titling the novel *Waste, A Picture of the World: One Man's View of England*. Lengthy titles were popular in this time.

10. Speaking of long titles, Wells appears to be going for the record with this very long title of his novel, shortened hereafter to simply *Boon*.

11. H. G. Wells, *Tono-Bungay*, Everyman (Publisher): J. M. Dent (London, England) and Charles D. Tuttle (Rutland, Vermont) 1994 [1909], p. 120.

12. Ibid., pp. 68, 267, 198.

13. Ibid., pp. 108, 125, 150, 159.

14. Wells, *New Machiavelli*, pp. 61, 290.

15. Fitzgerald, *This Side of Paradise*, p. 194.

16. Edmund Wilson, "Bernard Shaw at Eighty" [1936], reprinted in his *Triple Thinkers* (New York: Oxford University Press, 1963) [1938], p. 169.

17. Bruccoli and Bryer, eds., *F. Scott Fitzgerald in His Own Time*, p. 283.

18. From an article in the *Jersey City Evening Journal*, April 24, 1923, p. 9. Reprinted in Matthew J. Bruccoli and Judith S. Baughman, eds., *F. Scott Fitzgerald on Authorship* (Columbia, South Carolina: University of South Carolina Press, 1996), p. 86.

19. Bruccoli and Bryer, eds., *F. Scott Fitzgerald in His Own Time*, p. 272.

20. Andrew Turnbull, *The Letters of F. Scott Fitzgerald* (New York: Dell Publishing, 1963), p. 318.

21. Henri Bergson, *Creative Evolution* (New York: Random House, 1944 [1911]).

22. Bernard Shaw, *Back To Methuselah* (Baltimore, Md: Penguin Books, 1961 [1921]), pp. 15, 25, and 55 respectively.

23. Sheilah Graham, *College of One* (New York: Viking Press, 1967), p. 83.

24. Bruccoli, ed., *Life in Letters*, p. 45. The references are, of course, to Jean Jacques Rousseau, Karl Marx, and Leo Tolstoy. Here, as elsewhere, except as otherwise noted, significant spelling errors are silently corrected.

25. F. Scott Fitzgerald, "The Diamond as Big as the Ritz" (1922), in *The Stories of F. Scott Fitzgerald* (New York: Macmillan, 1951), pp. 33–34.

26. Fitzgerald, *This Side of Paradise*, p. 40.

27. Written at Westport, Conn., June 3, 1920; Bruccoli, ed., *Life in Letters*, pp. 37–40.

28. The review is reprinted in Bruccoli and Bryer, eds., *F. Scott Fitzgerald in His Own Time*, p. 126.

29. Graham, *College of One*, p. 122.

30. John Kuehl, "Scott Fitzgerald's Reading," in Matthew J. Bruccoli, *Profile of F. Scott Fitzgerald* (Columbus, Ohio: Charles E. Merrill, 1971), p. 50.

31. Turnbull, *Letters of F. Scott Fitzgerald*, pp. 143–44. *"Vandover"* refers to Norris's *Vandover and the Brute* (1914), which would influence Fitzgerald's de-

piction of Anthony Patch in *The Beautiful and Damned.*

32. In February 1920; Matthew J. Bruccoli and Margaret M. Duggan, with Susan Walker, *Correspondence* (New York: Random House, 1980), p. 52.

33. Fitzgerald wrote on the flyleaf of Sheilah Graham's copy: "Frank Norris after writing three great books died in 1902 at the age of just thirty. He was our most promising man and might have gone further than Dreiser or the others. He claimed to be a disciple of Zola the naturalist, but in many ways he was better than Zola" (Princeton University Library).

34. Turnbull, *Letters of F. Scott Fitzgerald*, p. 154.

35. Bruccoli and Bryer, eds., *F. Scott Fitzgerald in His Own Time*, p. 284.

36. Fitzgerald is quoted by Wilson in Edmund Wilson, "Thoughts on Being Bibliographed," *Princeton University Library Chronicle* 5, no. 2 (1944): p. 54.

Four

Zelda

BORN VIRTUALLY WRAPPED IN THE AMERICAN FLAG AND UNLIKELY TO graduate as a member of the Princeton class of '17, Fitzgerald joined the army that year and was commissioned a second lieutenant in the infantry. He reported to Fort Leavenworth, Kansas, on November 20; soon, he expected to be at the Hun's front. Yet, as for so many of his actions, Scott went into the army for social reasons, not out of patriotism. After all, to die or even be seriously wounded in battle would suit his keen sense for drama. Despite being trained in exercises, calisthenics, and bayonet drills by the legendary (then captain) Dwight D. Eisenhower, and despite the smart uniforms Scott had ordered from style-setting Brooks Brothers, the nation—on several counts—can consider itself lucky that the war ended before Fitzgerald was sent to Europe. Even wrapped in Brooks Brothers, Scott was ill suited to be a soldier.

Though in uniform, Scott Fitzgerald had other things on his mind. At Leavenworth he was secretly and intensely working on his first novel. Few soldiers write novels while on duty, but many before and since have fallen in love while assigned to a military post. Later but coincidentally, Scott met and fell in love with the woman of his dreams—eighteen-year-old Zelda Sayre, a beautiful, celebrated

Southern belle—at an encampment near Montgomery, Alabama. The youngest daughter of a judge, Zelda was not only electrifying at Camp Sheridan but was singeing the very foundations of Old South values. From that moment on, Scott's life, in varying degrees over time, would be under Zelda's influence. And her influence on that first novel was as mixed as the praise it received.

Zelda came from the heart of the Confederate establishment; her father, Anthony, was an aloof, conservative judge of the Alabama Supreme Court, and her mother, Minnie, the artistic member of her family and a frustrated poet, was from Kentucky. Zelda, suffocating in a quiet, backward small city of forty thousand, found a larger world among the thousands of soldiers and aviators pouring into nearby Camps Sheridan and Taylor. There were, she later wrote, "men from Princeton and Yale who smelled of Russian Leather and seemed very used to being alive...."[1] Beyond those boundaries were fraternities in nearby colleges and universities that pledged their true love for Zelda.

She had no inhibitions and had no concerns regarding a "bad" reputation spreading through the region like a wildfire. Still in high school, she broke all existing rules and doubtless inspired some new ones for other young Southern women. She necked with the boys in cars at night, she smoked, and she drank gin or corn liquor cut with Coke. If she became hot at summer dances, she would begin removing underwear, slipping it into her date's pockets. Because of her beauty and her recklessness, she was wildly popular with men. Zelda compared herself to the mythical salamander that Plato said could pass through fire unscathed; she thought she could live in the fire without getting burned. Ultimately she would be fatally wrong about the fire, even as it would symbolize her all-consuming passions.

Fearless even as a child, Zelda knew how to gain attention. On one summery day in Montgomery, she called the fire department and told them that a child was on a rooftop and couldn't get down. Then she got a ladder, climbed atop the roof of her own house at 6 Pleasant Avenue, pushed the ladder aside, and waited. When the fire engine came clanging its bell, the neighbors rushed out to ask, "Where's the fire?" Zelda sat marooned on the roof and was absolutely delighted by the disturbance she had caused.

Long after Plato, Owen Johnson published the best-selling novel *The Salamander* in 1914, a book that greatly affected Zelda's as well as many other young women's attitudes. Sufficiently popular, it became a Broadway play and a film in 1916. Zelda was entering her junior year at Sidney Lanier High School, a fine example of gothic architecture, in Montgomery at the time. (Classes are still being held in the Sidney Lanier High School building at this writing.) Like Dore Baxter, the heroine in *The Salamander,* Zelda was not like any other woman; she liked the fun of dashing toward precipices, depending on others to prevent her from going over the edges—or picking up the pieces when she did. Like Dore, Zelda avoided the ordinary and expected to marry a man who would provide her with plenty of money. Dore and Zelda's romantic intrigues ran in parallel.

Later in her life, Zelda described her childhood. She was independent, courageous, and "without thought of anyone else." She also remembered herself as a "sensualist." She often walked on the open roofs of houses under construction, liked to dive and climb in the tops of trees. She said that she "did not have a single feeling of inferiority, or shyness, or doubt, and no moral principles." For the most part she would remain true to that lack of principles.[2]

The same Zelda was to be fatally attractive to F. Scott Fitzgerald. They met in July 1918, at a country club dance about a month after her graduation from Lanier. (The Montgomery Country Club was virtually an auxiliary officer's club.) As he had been at Princeton, Fitzgerald again was the poorest boy in a rich man's club. Zelda had not planned to go but relented when she was asked to do a dance, the "Dance of the Hours." Zelda's fondness of dancing later would become a compulsion foreshadowing her first mental breakdown. Scott, at the country club dance, thought her to be the most beautiful girl he'd ever seen, and he was probably right.

Zelda blotted out from Scott's mind any lingering love for Ginevra King. Zelda's vivacity and beauty rivaled Ginevra's, but she had something more and something less. Like Ginevra, Zelda had total confidence in her good looks and attractiveness to men. Even at fifteen Zelda was striking—her skin flawless and creamy and her hair golden. By the time she met Scott, she was the most spectacular belle Montgomery would ever have the pleasure of knowing. In describing the physical characteristics of Rosalind Connage in *This Side of Paradise* (1920), Fitzgerald is really describing Zelda's beauty, at which all criticism ends.

> There was that shade of glorious yellow hair, the desire to imitate which supports the dye industry. There was the eternal kissable mouth, small, slightly sensual, and utterly disturbing. There were gray eyes and unimpeachable skin with two spots of vanishing color. She was slender and athletic, without underdevelopment, and it was a delight to watch her move about a room, walk along a street, swing a golf club, or turn a "cartwheel".... She was perhaps the delicious, inexpressible, once-in-a-century blend.[3]

Zelda between meeting Scott and the publication of his Paradise

Besides, "her vivid, instant personality escaped that conscious, theatrical quality that Amory had found in Isabelle [Ginevra]."[4] Scott does not address Zelda's nose—very straight and almost hawklike in profile. Later, Ernest Hemingway would not misjudge that profile.

By all personal accounts of Zelda's early beauty, Scott's description of her physical attributes is faithful. Even then Zelda did not photograph well; she looked like a different person in every photo, partly due to personality disorders. As her mental health declined, earlier than most have surmised, she looked less and less like the "original." Her soft voice seldom betrayed her aggressiveness. When she came into a ballroom, all the other girls would want to go home because they knew that the boys would go after Zelda. She danced cheek to cheek at country club dances, then considered improper. She ignored the chaperones, the rules, and the genteel conventions of the Old South. Perhaps much of her early beauty was a projection of a very forceful personality.

Clearly, however, Zelda's social position did not equal Ginevra's world of Eastern finishing schools. Never mind. Scott could swing wide open the door to that world. But at once he knew that Zelda was not perfect. Fitzgerald again provides the most exacting description of Zelda, the complete package, in that long, memorable passage in *This Side of Paradise*. Perhaps most telling, for what was to come, parts of the passage came from one of Zelda's letters. We can see that he fell for her destructive tendencies—hook, line, and sinker. At this point the heroine, Rosalind, *is* Zelda.

> She is one of those girls who need never make the slightest effort to have men fall in love with them. Two types of men seldom do: dull men are usually afraid of her cleverness and intellectual men are usually afraid of her beauty. All others are hers by natural prerogative…. she wants what she wants when she wants it and she is prone to make every one around her pretty miserable when she doesn't get it—but in the true sense she is not spoiled. Her fresh enthusiasm, her will to grow and learn, her endless faith in the inexhaustibility of romance, her courage and fundamental honesty—these things are not spoiled…. She is quite unprincipled; her philosophy is carpe diem for herself and laissez faire for others…. She is by no means a model character…. She danced exceptionally well, drew cleverly but hastily, and had a startling facility with words, which she used only in love-letters.

But all criticism of Rosalind [Zelda] ends in her beauty.[5]

While this passage defines the "real" Zelda, it too bares young Scott. "Rosalind" was not only Fitzgerald's Golden Girl, but the "new woman" that he created in his fiction out of the whole cloth that was Zelda. Zelda, the salamander, would become Zelda, the flapper, illustrating the Jazz Age that Fitzgerald named and defined. Her beauty and other attributes described by Fitzgerald also reveal his Achilles' heel.

His woman demands that he be a hero while challenging him in such a way that he will utterly fail. Her demands will be contradictory and therefore impossible to achieve. He will have to make great amounts of income but spend all his time attending to her personal needs. His physical courage will be invidiously compared with hers, which is based not on courage but senseless recklessness. She will demand that he perform sexually on her command: when he does not, she will belittle him and draw unfair comparisons with other men she has known and even accuse him of homosexuality. Because of his sensitivities and romantic illusions, he will in turn lose sexual interest in her. Then—for sure—he won't be able to meet her physical demands; then, she will reject him. His woman is selfish, conceited, and uncontrolled; since these are his own early traits (in his youth), he is especially aware of them. The selfishness made the woman play the game even harder, her lack of control put him in awe of her, and her conceit was interrupted only by delicious moments of remorse and self-denunciation, making her dear to him.

✧　✧　✧

If Zelda was a Golden Girl, Scott was the "Golden Boy." They could have passed for brother and sister. Scott's short but erect build was kept in shape in his younger years though swimming, golfing, and boxing. He dressed fashionably and carried himself in a manner that suggested greater height. His head was comparatively large, centered with engaging emerald eyes "cold as the Irish sea," and topped with light golden brown hair, at times unruly but neatly trimmed and tapered like manicured moss in the back. His nose and ears were delicate and, he, not Zelda, had the prettier legs. His hands, though they seemed large for his body, nonetheless also were delicate. The color of his eyes changed with his moods, which explains why some acquaintances claimed his eyes were blue. When they danced at that country club dance, Zelda later remembered, "there seemed to be some heavenly support beneath his shoulder blades that lifted his feet from the ground in ecstatic suspension, as if he secretly enjoyed the ability to fly but was walking as a compromise to convention."[6] Late in his life he still looked, according to Zelda, like the man in the Arrow collar ad.

Scott cultivated the voice of a tenor. He spoke in a dramatic manner, something he acquired from acting in plays in private school and later, at Princeton. And Fitzgerald loved to talk. His voice can still be heard reciting *Ode To a Nightingale,* a second poem, and a stanza from Shakespeare in three recordings he made for radio in Los Angeles late in life. For *Ode* his voice has the sound of a hesitant and sensitive old Rolls-Royce, too dignified for the repair shop despite the need. *Ode* was one of his favorite poems, from which he derived the title of his fourth novel, *Tender Is the Night.* Of these recordings, the best is the Shakespearean recitation in which Scott uses the full range of his voice in dramatic fashion, just as if the world were his stage, as it once had been. Fitzgerald's sense of the melodramatic was magnified by his lifelong tendency to throw his arms around in an imaginative manner while relating stories, jokes, or anecdotes. Though he never said it or wrote it, Scott also fell in love with Zelda, in part because of *her* conversational stamina. Often they would talk all night, examining every side of every question.

Fitzgerald also was intelligent, charming, imaginative, and energetic. When barely eighteen years of age he theatrically rejected his formal Catholic religion by stalking the pulpit at St. John's Episcopal Church in St. Paul during a Christmas service and then exiting the opposite aisle. Still, he had a strong conscience, a profound sense of spirituality, and often was attracted by the occult. The latter attraction was common during the 1920s and even understandable, given Fitzgerald's gift for prophecy. Scott remained Catholic in his great capacity for guilt and, often, his even greater capacity for being forgiven.

Informal photo of Scott around time he met Zelda

Although (at an early age) Fitzgerald knew about James Hill, Horatio Alger, individual initiative, and Christian good fortune, his own aspirations were far more romantic. The *Dream* was more important than its American aspect. Scott's Dream was not only to be artistically successful, but also to be financially secure and have Zelda at the same time. Perhaps it was too much or too contradictory an aspiration. As the American woman of the 1970s would have put it, "He wanted to have it all."

As it turned out, the two—success and marrying Zelda, the salamander reimagined as the flapper—were hopelessly intertwined. Later, in his own lifetime, the same could be said for Scott's view of failure.

His writing talents, his means to the Dream, had begun to take shape at Princeton—this despite his flunked examinations in Latin and chemistry and thus his ineligibility for the literary prizes and offices that he had won with intense purpose. He also had developed those important friendships, most notably with Edmund Wilson, who would not only be the most important literary critic of his age and an ambivalent friend but initially Fitzgerald's chosen intellectual conscience. Some good for his later literary efforts did come from his failures, as he began to read more widely than ever. Finally, his deep longing for Zelda was to ignite his writing ambitions. Maxwell Perkins's rejection of Scott's book manuscript, *The Romantic Egotist,* came in August 1918, near the end of the summer that Scott met Zelda. Scott sent a chapter about the increasingly Zelda-like heroine to Zelda and it appealed to her sense of great importance. Zelda was not only an object of his Dream, she was considered at the time a large part of the means.

Fitzgerald's army career was not quite over. In November 1918 he reported to Camp Mills, Long Island, to await embarkation to the front, and though Scott had that romantic fantasy of dying in battle, the end of the Great War came before either passage. From Camp Mills, officers could take leave in New York City, where Fitzgerald went on drinking binges, perhaps because of his disappointment at sitting out the war. After being caught by the Hotel Astor house detective with a naked girl, Scott was confined to Camp Mills for safekeeping. When his unit was ordered to return to Montgomery that month, he was in New York, AWOL, and was left behind. Somehow he managed (as only Scott could) to meet the troop train in Washington D.C., along with a bottle of gin and two girls. Back at Camp Sheridan and Montgomery, he was made an aide-de-camp to Gen. J. A. Ryan. When Scott fell off a horse during a parade, General Ryan ordered him to take riding lessons. The army and Scott finally had a mutually agreeable separation in February 1919.

Meantime, Scott often would come to 6 Pleasant Avenue in Montgomery to visit Zelda. For Zelda, however, there were many others. An aviator with a mustache entertained her for a time, until he proposed. Astonished at being turned down, "he asked her why she had kissed him, and she replied that she'd never kissed a man with a mustache before."[7] Aviation officers performed stunts in their airplanes over the Sayre house until they were finally forbidden after two officers crashed on the nearby speedway, one of whom the astonished mustached flier. According to an entry in Scott's Ledger, he had fallen in love with Zelda on September 7. The exactness of dates was important to Fitzgerald, even when he got them wrong. Still, Zelda continued to encourage her many suitors because she fully understood that Scott considered her more desirable if other men also wanted her. Besides, she always did what she pleased without concern about how it would hurt Scott or anyone else. And, besides that, Scott had no visible means of support despite the appearance of his shoulders on the dance floor. He pressed Zelda for a commitment she refused to give.

Several biographers relate a darkly implausible account of Scott's first invitation to dinner late that summer at the Sayres': Zelda teased her father until, in a rage, he chased her around the dining table with a carving knife. Probably Zelda did tease her father, for she considered him too perfect to be human. The staid, conservative judge chasing anyone with a knife, however, is improbable. Mrs. Minnie Sayre and the Judge considered their family to be quite normal, though Minnie warned Scott that Zelda was "special," never clarifying what she meant by "special." Scott, hopelessly in love, completely missed the dark undertones. He might have had a better understanding of those underlying dark forces had he known more at the time.

Minnie's mother and sister had both committed suicide. Zelda had three older sisters—Marjorie, Rosalind, and Clothilde—with ages ranging from nine to eighteen at Zelda's birth, and a brother, Anthony, who was then six. Marjorie had a nervous breakdown and suffered from mental illness throughout her life. Anthony left Auburn University without a degree and, in 1933, after recurrent nightmares about killing his mother, committed suicide by leaping from the window of his hospital room in Mobile, Alabama. The stern Judge Sayre always rented the family's homes because he disavowed debt; financial strains may have led to his nervous breakdown. Neither the Sayres nor anyone else told Scott of this harrowing pattern of breakdowns, insanity, and suicide in Zelda's family.

To the Sayre household, *Fitzgerald* was the strange one. He was Irish, Catholic, a Princeton dropout, a Midwesterner, a writer, and "someone who drank too much." Scott's dearth of religious devotion surely made his faith a moot issue. The giving of Zelda's hand was rejected by Zelda's father mostly because he believed Fitzgerald too fond of gin and otherwise futureless; in truth, the financial prospects of a writer and college dropout (even if it was Princeton) were meager.

Zelda herself was hot and hotly pursued by many suitors, including a handsome golfer named Roger Jones whom Zelda had met at a golf tournament at the golf links of East Lake in Atlanta—then and later, the legendary *Bobby* Jones's home course.[8] Zelda remained unwilling to marry any man who did not have substantial financial prospects. The family, but especially Rosalind, eventually would not only use Scott's weaknesses against him but blame him for Zelda's mental illness.

On January 10, 1919, while still in the army, Scott learned of Monsignor Fay's death. Before he learned the news, Fitzgerald had a seizure of trembling, a supernatural experience that would find expression in his fiction. After his discharge in February 1919, Scott went to the city favored by young American men seeking a fortune—New York! New York!—so he could win the Sayres' consent, if not Zelda's love. Scott was employed as a low-salaried copy editor at Barron Collier Advertising Agency, where he tried his hand at business success by day and commercial fiction success by night. While not composing ads to be posted as trolleycar cards, he lived in a room at 200 Claremont Avenue, near Columbia University, writing short fiction at night. Mostly, his short stories, though better than his jingles, were rejected. His lone sale was his revised 1917 *Lit* story "Babes in the Woods," sold to the *Smart Set* for thirty dollars. From New York City, Scott sent Zelda his mother's ring on March 24, and they became "engaged," at Scott's insistence; to Scott the engagement was serious, to Zelda it was a mere *in*formality. In fairness to Zelda, her parents did not take the relationship seriously, either.

Zelda remained beyond Fitzgerald's grasp even as she remained in the arms of many men in her native South. Zelda would include Scott in the family's Christmas dinner and then desert him to go with boys to proms at Auburn and Georgia Tech. Fitzgerald would go into a jealous rage, get drunk, pick a quarrel, at the end of which Zelda usually said she doubted that Scott would ever make enough money to marry her. In one letter Zelda told Scott of a wild drive to Auburn "with ten boys to liven things up" and a trip down Commerce Street near the river and in the worst part of Montgomery, where she donned men's clothes and went to the movies with a gang of boys.[9] Fitzgerald was not happy about her escapades. Later, Scott, Shane Leslie, and Zelda in men's clothes would repeat the experience along London's notorious dockyards, the stalking grounds of Jack the Ripper.

On April 15, Scott took a holiday and went to Montgomery and to Zelda. He considered the trip a complete failure and wrote in his Ledger: "I used to wonder why they locked princesses in towers," a phrase Zelda would never forget.[10] Not only was romancing

Zelda a full-time pursuit, so was commercial fiction. It is difficult
to know which put the greater strain on their relationship. Was it
Fitzgerald's failures at business and professional writing? Was it
the great distance between New York and Zelda's herd of devoted
men in uniform in Montgomery? Was it Zelda's need to quench her
immediate passions? Whatever, these pressures led Zelda to break
their "engagement" in June 1919. With so many sorrows to drown,
Scott went on one of his epic drinking sprees, ending three weeks
later, and quit his advertising job. Retrospectively and confidently,
he dated the start of the Jazz Age with his drinking binge.

✧   ✧   ✧

Sometime in early July, Scott was sufficiently sober to make what
became an unconditional decision: He would stake his future and his
rewinning of Zelda on a revision of his novel. Years later he called
the novel his "ace in the hole."[11] And so, instead of writing letters to
Zelda, he went to the top floor of his parents' home at 599 Summit
Avenue in St. Paul and worked intensely on his novel for the balance
of the summer. As he relentlessly pursued success as an artist, Zelda
was seldom far from his mind or from his novel. Rather than drinking
and partying, Scott's relaxation was conversation with friends such
as Donald Ogden Stewart, a Yale graduate then working for AT&T.
Reciting poetry to Stewart, Fitzgerald repeated his favorite line from
John Masefield: "Be with me, Beauty, for the fire is dying." (Later,
with help from Scott, Stewart became a popular humorist during
the Jazz Age.) The unattainability of Zelda, the American beauty
personified, intensified Scott's aspirations. She was at least half his
Dream, half of his inspiration.
    Meanwhile, within the sphere of traditional rationality,
Edmund Wilson had urged Fitzgerald to pay more attention to form
in his drafting of what would become *Paradise*. Wilson compared
Fitzgerald's novel to a trivial current best-seller by the preadoles-
cent Daisy Ashford and made fun of Scott's intellectual pretensions:
"As an intellectual [Amory] is a fake of the first water and I read his
views on art, politics, religion and society with more riotous mirth

than I should care to have you know." But of course, Wilson had just told him. Wilson also warned him about the cheap effects of commercial stories compared with high art. He thought that Scott "might become a very popular trashy novelist without much difficulty."[12] Fitzgerald's Princeton "friend" resented Scott's creativity even before he had a reason to envy his financial successes.

Thoughts of Zelda never diminished Fitzgerald's lifelong fondness for actresses—perhaps because, well, they were so dramatic. In the same month (November) that he had received that letter of faint praise from Edmund Wilson, Scott had a fling with the English actress Rosalinde Fuller. Rosalinde had the kind of beauty that landed her in *Vanity Fair*. Judging from her diary of this affair, vanity might have had something to do with it. (Rosalinde also had an affair with the author Max Eastman, her brother-in-law.) As to Fitzgerald, he may have been retaliating for Zelda's promiscuous adventures or he might have been looking for one final fling before an eternal commitment to Zelda. Since he could not be absolutely sure about Zelda's commitment to *him,* we lean toward the spurned lover's motive.

As they rode through New York City in a closed horse-drawn carriage, Rosalinde describes how their sexual appetites were aroused: "Eager hands feeling in warm secret places under the old rug, while the bouncing of the horse's bottom was our only contact with the outside world. 'You have Egyptian ears,' she whispered to Scott" (who could resist his "Egyptian ears"?) " 'and the look of a naughty boy.' "[13]

Scott took as much of Edmund Wilson's advice as he found useful, and he was truly appreciative, a lifelong habit. Fitzgerald sent the new, revised draft of his novel—now titled *This Side of Paradise*—to Maxwell Perkins at Scribner's, who accepted it in September for publication on March 26, 1920. Scott pleaded for the earliest possible publication because "I have so many things dependent on its success—including of course a girl—...I'm in that stage where every month counts frantically and seems a cudgel in a fight for happiness against time."[14] Scott's euphoria upon his "Early Success" is described in an essay seventeen years later. "Then the postman rang," Fitzgerald writes, "and that day I quit work and ran along the streets, stopping automobiles to tell friends and acquaintances about it—my novel…was accepted for publication." He concludes the essay: "The compensation of a very early success is a conviction that life is a romantic matter."[15] In turn, it was a conviction he held virtually for life.

Before March and the publication of his first novel, Scott was still seeking financial returns as he revised earlier, rejected stories. The *Smart Set*, under the prestigious editorship of H. L. Mencken and George Jean Nathan, took several, including "The Debutante" (November 1919), "Benediction" (February 1920), and "Dalyrimple Goes Wrong" (February 1920). In "Dalyrimple," a war hero rises from a career of burglary to the state senate, an ironic treatment of the Horatio Alger success story. The more plausible story would have had a state senator turning to crime, an easier transition. The next month Fitzgerald's first novel would appear.

Described by its author as a "quest novel," *Paradise,* set mainly at Princeton, traces the aspirations and failed loves of Amory Blaine, a character greatly resembling a tall version of the young Fitzgerald. Scott, only twenty-three years of age, became famous as in one of the many versions of the American Dream. A first printing of 3,000 copies sold out in three days, and this first novel sold 47,075 copies during 1920–21. The early ads used Fitzgerald's line, "a novel about flappers written for philosophers," better than anything he had written at the advertising agency. Unlike Zelda, Fitzgerald's striking good looks photographed well; youth combined with brilliance cut a handsome, romantic figure. In turn, *Paradise* was commercially the most successful of Fitzgerald's books during his lifetime, an irony we can appreciate.

Straddling the seductive *Paradise* were two *Saturday Evening Post* stories that would define the flapper as the new American woman. Scott's short story "Head and Shoulders" (February 21, 1920) was sold to the *Saturday Evening Post* for $400 plus movie rights to MGM for $2,500. This was Fitzgerald's first foray into a mass-market magazine and his first rubbing of shoulders with agent Harold Ober. It was soon followed by a second flapper story, the first to gain national prominence, "Bernice Bobs Her Hair" (May 1, 1920), sold to the *Post* for $2,500, now effectively competing with MGM prices.[16] In these stories, Scott takes the concerns of youth seriously, distinguishing himself from other writers. *Paradise* and the *Post* stories made him famous virtually overnight, as Fitzgerald had predicted.

Scott had wisely postponed his visit with Zelda until late November 1919. Their reunion went well, and though the engagement was not renewed, Scott was confident that he would win back his "top girl." One of his best short stories, "The Ice Palace" (*Post*, May 1920), was based on this trip to Montgomery and his accurate weather forecast of a Southern women's reaction to a Minnesota winter before Zelda had ever gone that far north. Worried about the health risks of the same kind of cold Minnesota winter and his distance from Montgomery, Scott moved to New Orleans in January 1920. While living in a rooming house at 2900 Prytania Street, he corrected proofs for *This Side of Paradise,* wrote more stories, and started a novel called "Darling Heart," of which no pages survive. From New Orleans, Fitzgerald visited Zelda twice, bringing her a six-hundred-dollar platinum-and-diamond wristwatch paid for by writing "The Camel's Back," a short story later bought for a movie. Sometime during these months Zelda agreed to marriage, but the new "engagement" was not announced until March 28—two days after the publication of Scott's first novel and six days before the wedding. By now, Zelda was confident of Scott's success, a belief doubtless enhanced by Fitzgerald's own dramatic, enthusiastic reassurances.

For Scott the early money was as easy as the Big Easy and his spending soon became a studied recklessness. Earlier, in February 1920, Scott, nonetheless already bored in New Orleans, had moved to the Murray Hill Hotel and then the Allerton in lively New York City. He was able to add fuel to the fire of literary success with easily acquired bootleg gin in the city. Fitzgerald began to carelessly spend, giving huge tips out of his social insecurity and generally showing contempt for money. Since his income nicely doubled every month during early 1920, he presumed exponential income growth was a natural law. It hardly seemed a luxury, then, for Scott to move to the Cottage Club and be at Princeton when *Paradise* went dark with print.

Zelda was the other side of Scott's coin of recklessness. Isabelle Amorous (yes, apparently her real name), a sister of a Newman friend, had presciently congratulated Scott when his first engagement with Zelda ended. In a February 26 letter and reply, Fitzgerald admonished his woman-friend's judgment even as he vindicated it. "Any girl who gets stewed in public, who frankly enjoys and tells shocking stories, who smokes constantly and makes the remark that she has 'kissed thousands of men and intends to kiss thousands more,' cannot be considered beyond reproach even if above it," writes Scott of Zelda.[17]

✧ ✧ ✧

Ms. Amorous and the others were missing the point: Scott's marriage to Zelda fulfilled his second great quest—for the American beauty. Whether this achievement, one of the most enduring male versions of the American Dream, depended entirely upon Fitzgerald's financial and popular success is a matter of great debate. A couple things are clear. Despite having just spent a weekend with a football player from Georgia Tech and tending a romance with Auburn's starting quarterback, Zelda is bored in Montgomery and ready to try New York. By now her future husband has earned a considerable amount of income and stature, especially by Montgomery standards. Zelda's judgment already may have been impaired by her emotional instability. Scott, on the other hand, is not sure that he could recapture his intense romantic feelings about Zelda. Perhaps he never did.

Zelda and Scott's wedding took place in the vestry of St. Patrick's Cathedral on April 3, at noon. Zelda's sister Marjorie accompanied her to New York. Although Zelda's other two sisters Rosalind Smith and Clothilde Palmer were living there and in attendance, the bride and groom's parents did not appear. Scott's friend Ludlow Fowler was best man, and Rosalind Smith, Zelda's sister, was matron of honor. Rosalind never forgave Scott for having no party or wedding lunch. This slight did not slow Mr. and Mrs. F. Scott Fitzgerald's departure from the church for their Biltmore Hotel honeymoon at

Forty-third Street and Vanderbilt Avenue. Their marriage coincided with the early months of what Fitzgerald would name the Jazz Age. Not only would Fitzgerald be the spokesman for this new age, he would be identified with the times, and he and Zelda would come to represent all the excesses of the Roaring Twenties—not just Prohibition but the stock market bubble as well.

The Fitzgeralds were not alone as mythic figures of the twenties. It also was the age of Rudolph Valentino, Charlie Chaplin, Greta Garbo, Bix Beiderbecke, George Gershwin, Bessie Smith, Babe Ruth, Jack Dempsey, Al Capone, Man o' War, and Charles Lindbergh. All contributed to the roar and most did a lot of drinking with the exceptions of at least Man o' War and the notoriously dull Charles Lindbergh. In an age when a "reformer" was defined as someone afraid that somebody somewhere was having a good time, drinking increased in the big cities despite its "prohibition." While Lindbergh may not have been a buyer, Al Capone was a supplier to the speakeasies. And, not surprisingly, heavy drinking fueled the social activities of the Fitzgeralds.

It too was a time of accumulations of great wealth with little of it trickling down. The inequities created by disparities in wealth became further evident to Scott through his own experience. Zelda's loathing of Scott's poor economic prospects had initially blocked the Fitzgeralds' marriage. Scott soon related this bitter and hardening experience in "'The Sensible Thing'" (1924). His inner transformation during this time was recounted years later, in one of Scott's *Crack-Up* essays (1936).

> It was one of those tragic loves doomed for lack of money, and one day the girl closed it out on the basis of common sense. During a long summer of despair I wrote a novel instead of letters, so it came out all right, but it came out all right for a different person. The man with the jingle of money in his pocket who married the girl a year later would always cherish an abiding distrust, an animosity, toward the leisure class—not the conviction of a revolutionist but the smoldering hatred of a peasant.[18]

Fitzgerald's bold statements are as revealing as they are dramatic. By the time he wins "the top girl," Scott is disillusioned.

The making of money, for the moment, was without question. Like so many American celebrities, Fitzgerald then made and went on to make a considerable income. The careful record in his Ledger shows his total income from 1919 to 1936, before he went the third time to Hollywood, was $374,922.58 (after deducting literary agent Harold Ober's 10 percent commission on magazine sales) or close to $4 million in today's dollars. In contrast, members of the House and Senate were paid $10,000 yearly during the twenties, and they, by any standard, were overpaid. Scott and Zelda, however, spent *more than* $400,000, being almost always in debt.

Having once admired money and the power it brings, in his hands Scott has no interest in it and, if money has any power, he never uses it to buy favors. He continues to generously tip strangers and offer loans to friends even when he is broke. He and Zelda seldom owned anything, certainly nothing of any pecuniary value, and never experienced positive net worth. While symbolizing a golden age of American capitalism, their fascination with *capitalist accumulation* was *zero*. Zelda, irresponsible in most things, did not exclude money management from her devotion to carelessness. Scott and Zelda nonetheless are celebrated in New York and, later, in Paris; he is a legendary author and—with Zelda at his side—the first author-celebrity.

The pell-mell rush to win Zelda nonetheless had high personal and literary costs for Fitzgerald despite the commercial success of *This Side of Paradise* and some positive early reviews. In his review, the normally acerbic H. L. Mencken calls it "the best American novel that I have seen of late."[19] An unnamed reviewer in the *New York Times* writes, "As a picture of the daily existence of what we call loosely 'college men,' this book is as nearly perfect as such a work could be." Over time, however, its critics did not give Scott the artistic praise he truly sought. At the time of his composition, splicing pieces of rejected short stories with completely revised chapters of *The Romantic Egotist,* Fitzgerald is a young writer in a hurry. One reviewer dismisses the novel as "the collected works of F. Scott Fitzgerald."[20] Its production by Perkins, as dreadful as a copy-editor as he was a genius as an acquisitions editor, was shabby. Errors of spelling and of literary reference marred the book; they never were quite corrected, despite many almost comic efforts by Scott to do so.[21] Fitzgerald wanted to make a decent living, but most of all, he wanted Zelda. Moreover, Zelda had given him every reason to believe that only quick and great accomplishments could win the prize, the "top girl." She was a young woman in a hurry.

Still, *Paradise* remains, like Fitzgerald, magical. Like his other novels and stories, this first novel reveals the author's poetic imagination, dramatic vision, and his seemingly effortless craftsmanship. It, like the others, bears Fitzgerald's ineffaceable stamp of grace. The enchantment lies in the heartfelt romantic imagination that transfigures his characters and settings while creating the sound of his prose. Even this early, flawed novel infused the greenery and gothic spires of Princeton with a spirit, with campus life. The Princeton that Amory Blaine loved—"its lazy beauty, its half-grasped significance, the wild moonlight revel of the rushes," did not really exist.

Even then, still a very young man, Scott Fitzgerald did more than smoke and mirrors. Once past the magical imagery and language of *Paradise,* Fitzgerald's effect transcends the bounds of fiction to reveal a deep social reality and inexplicable irony. *Paradise* was widely regarded as the first *realistic* American college novel, but at a time when Princeton was an exclusive, glamorous school. Fitzgerald's satirical depiction of Princeton as a country club still offends university officials even as new generations of Princeton students continue to recite Fitzgerald's farewell sonnet: "The last light fades and drifts across the land—the low, long land, the sunny land of spires."

Fitzgerald soon would become aware of the shallowness of many of the variants of the American Dream even as he lives them. He and Zelda immediately begin an extravagant life as young celebrities in New York. Despite Scott's aspirations for a serious literary reputation, his and Zelda's playboy-playgirl personas get in the way of proper critical assessment of his writing. After a gin-laced summer in Westport, Connecticut, Fitzgerald would write his second novel, *The Beautiful and Damned,* a tale of the debauchery and self-indulgence of Anthony and Gloria Patch. Young Scott already was moving away from writing of the aspiration and attainment of "beauty" to writing of the corruption in its pursuit. Already, as noted, in *This Side of Paradise,* Fitzgerald advocates socialism and portrays the Socialists sympathetically in "May Day," one of his best stories. Soon he would begin to mock the American Dream as he situates himself closer to the caustic but evolutionary critic of American society, Thorstein Veblen, than to the revolutionist Marx.

But we need never forget Fitzgerald's beginnings because he didn't. *Before* his disenchantment he was a pure dreamer, an American dreamer. As a youth he was attracted to wealth and beauty and aspired to be an artist of repute and importance. He desperately wanted celebrity status, but *only* on his terms. His life evolved in a manic-depressive evocation of that Dream, a life blending financial and aesthetic success and failure that reflected not only his personal struggles to succeed but also the influence of the Dream on American society. After the great rush of early success and celebration, Fitzgerald was endlessly torn between the *need,* if not the desire, to make money *and* the aspiration to be a great, critically acclaimed novelist. He sought critical approval even as he chased dollars out of apparent necessity. Ironically, in his early attachment to Zelda and his drive to achieve her, Scott built a lifetime path dependency to earnings. He needed income not only to support his lifestyle, but to appease Zelda—later, to pay for her hospital bills, to sometimes assuage his own guilt, to provide schooling for his daughter, and, ultimately, to repay his mounting debts.

✧　✧　✧

We briefly pause, and rightly so, for anticipation is a great part of every dream. This is hardly the end of Fitzgerald and the American Dream. The parallels between his own fortunes and misfortunes and the swings in American society from the Roaring Twenties to the Great Depression to the aborted recovery prior to the destructiveness of World War II continue. His classic portrayal of the illusions does not come until the publication of *The Great Gatsby* in 1925. In his time, Fitzgerald, like the American Dream he evokes, was generally viewed as a flower that never fully bloomed and whose beautiful prose was destined to be damned with more promise than praise. These assessments were shrouded in a sense of personal disappointment with his literary career. Even afterward, Ernest Hemingway darkly intimated how Scott was too much a part of the wealth and illusory culture, which his fiction celebrated yet vilified. Worse, Fitzgerald lacked depth and substance. Fitzgerald may have personified a small slice of American history and culture, but he, like Zelda, could not rise above it. The flames of both would burn brightly but briefly, defying eternity. But, defying his critics by living with deft irony, Fitzgerald infuses his dream with a new vitality in his final unfinished novel about the land of dreams, Hollywood.

Soon we will move on to detail *The Beautiful and Damned* years; then, follow those with the years of Fitzgerald's greatest achievement, *The Great Gatsby*. But, seemingly ending Scott's *personal* American Dream was the *financial* failure of *Gatsby* by his own lofty standards and, worse, a failure contributing adversely, though temporarily, to his emotional well-being. Despite barely falling short of critical acclaim upon publication, *Gatsby* was not appreciated by critics for its intellectual depth and richness. The eternal resurrection of F. Scott Fitzgerald would not begin until the early 1950s. He died a decade too soon to enjoy the new celebration. Had he lived, probably he would have toasted us all with his favorite though ultimately destructive drink, watered-down Prohibition gin. By then, Zelda—unlike the mythical salamander—had been burned beyond recognition.

Endnotes

1. Zelda Fitzgerald, *Save Me the Waltz* (New York: Charles Scribner's Sons, 1932), pp. 34–35.

2. These remarks are found in records kept during Zelda's stay at Les Rives de Prangins, June 5, 1930, to September 15, 1931, where she was being treated by Dr. Oscar Forel, who first diagnosed Zelda a schizophrenic. These records were discovered by Nancy Milford, Zelda's sympathetic biographer. See Nancy Milford, *Zelda: A Biography* (New York, Evanston, and London: Harper & Row, 1970), p. 8.

3. F. Scott Fitzgerald, *This Side of Paradise* (New York: Charles Scribner's Sons, 1920), p. 159.

4. Ibid.

5. Ibid., pp. 158–59.

6. Zelda Fitzgerald, *Save Me the Waltz,* p. 35.

7. Milford, *Zelda: A Biography,* p. 33.

8. A newspaper article in Zelda's scrapbook mentions a golfer named Roger Jones along with Perry Adair at the "golf links of East Lake" in Atlanta deep in conversation about Zelda "whom they had met at the recent tournament over there" (Zelda's scrapbook, Fitzgerald Collection, Princeton University Library). Some biographers understandably confused Roger with Bobby Jones since East Lake was Bobby's home course.

9. Letter from Zelda to Scott, April 1919, Princeton University Library.

10. A copy of F. Scott Fitzgerald's ledger resides in the Princeton University Library.

11. F. Scott Fitzgerald, "Early Success," quoted from the critical text in "Notes on the Text of F. Scott Fitgerald's 'Early Success,'" *Resources for American Literary Study* 3 (1973): 94.

12. Edmund Wilson, *Letters on Literature and Politics, 1912–1972,* ed. Elena Wilson (New York, 1977), pp. 45–46.

13. Quoted by James Mellow, *Invented Lives: F. Scott and Zelda Fitzgerald* (Boston, 1984), p. 82.

14. Princeton University Library, correspondence with Perkins.

15. F. Scott Fitzgerald, "Early Success" (1936), in Edmund Wilson, ed., *The Crack-Up* (New York: New Directions, 1956 [1945]), p. 89.

16. Joan Micklin Silver adapted Fitzgerald's "Bernice Bobs Her Hair" for a television movie produced in 1977.

17. Matthew J. Bruccoli, Margaret M. Duggan, eds., with Susan Walker, *Correspondence of F. Scott Fitzgerald* (New York: Random House, 1980), p. 53.

18. Fitzgerald, "Pasting It Together" (1936), in Wilson, ed., *The Crack-Up*, p. 77.

19. *The Smart Set* 62 (August 1920).

20. R.V.A.S., *The New Republic* 22 (May 12, 1920).

21. For a complete or nearly complete history of the writing of *This Side of Paradise,* see James L. W. West III, *The Making of This Side of Paradise* (Philadelphia: University of Pennsylvania Press, 1983). Scott, who spelled by ear, never really learned to spell well, though he often was inventive in the use of "invented" words. Since Scribners was a famous publisher, Fitzgerald expected an editor to correct spelling, punctuation, and grammar. Nonetheless aware of his deficiencies, Scott had hired a grammarian in St. Paul to go over his manuscript and make suggestions. Some of the suggestions taken were good but others taken made some of the dialogue stilted. Then, Scott's typist introduced other errors by taking it upon herself to "correct" some things in the manuscript. Over the years Fitzgerald made lists of corrections for Perkins; however, often the editor misinterpreted the corrections or disagreed with them, compounding the errors.

Five

The Conspicuous Consumers

TO THOSE STROLLING FIFTH AVENUE OR EVEN SITTING IN THE PLAZA HOTEL bar, F. Scott Fitzgerald, the young professional writer, seemed under the influence of *only* Zelda. It was an understandable but, even then, a mistaken presumption. Before her marriage, Zelda was a celebrity, even *if* in Montgomery; Fitzgerald, in New York, now was the famous one. At the beginning, Zelda did not seem to mind because she dominated their relationship with her stronger personality—her aggressiveness. Scott, though still under Zelda's powerful influence and solicitous of her opinions, was seeking other sources of inspiration as well.

None of Fitzgerald's biographers have noted the strengthening influence of Thorstein Veblen (1857–1929). Still, Veblen's writings can explain the Fitzgeralds' behavior even as Scott is coming ever more under Veblen's influence. To complete the irony for both, Veblen died a few months before the Great Crash of 1929 that also marked the death of Scott and Zelda's Jazz Age as well as the decline in Scott's reputation. Veblen and Fitzgerald had other things in common. Both grew up near St. Paul. Both had great wit and the ability to be ironically detached from the reality they were describing. Veblen openly took an anthropological view of society, from which he was estranged; Fitzgerald used the same powers of detached observation even when it involved his own emotions and intense role in American society. Veblen, like Fitzgerald, was influenced by the English novelist Joseph Conrad's precise but difficult prose style.[1] Both were treated badly by their chosen professions during their careers. Both encountered difficulties with women, including wives suffering mental illnesses. Veblen's affairs—real or imagined—led to one expulsion after another from American universities. Zelda and Scott's wild, loud parties led to their frequent expulsion from hotels and homes. After the Biltmore asked the Fitzgeralds to leave because of their rowdiness, they moved two blocks to the Commodore Hotel and proceeded to celebrate by spinning the hotel's revolving door.

Veblen began his advanced studies at Yale in 1882, the year Social Darwinist Herbert Spencer began a grand tour of the United States, culminating in a "last supper" at Delmonico's, even then a famed watering hole of the New York rich. Later, during the 1920s that mirrored the 1890s, Zelda, Scott, and movie stars often could be found at Delmonico's. Veblen described a nation controlled by a few millionaires, those robber barons who had accumulated vast wealth not through production, but largely through financial manipulation. Passing critical judgment on the 1890s, Veblen's first and most popular book, *The Theory of the Leisure Class* (1899), introduced a number of terms, bitingly sarcastic at the time but destined to become a part of the English language, such as leisure class; pecuniary emulation (popularly known as "keeping up with the Joneses"); and, most famous of all, conspicuous consumption, a phrase he coined for ostentatious display of wealth. Later, Scott Fitzgerald would use the same terms.

For the leisure class, writes Veblen, "the incentive to diligence and thrift is not absent; it is action so greatly qualified by the secondary demands of pecuniary emulation, that any inclination in this direction is practically overborne and any incentive to diligence tends to be of no effect."[2] As Veblen could observe firsthand around the turn of the century, Commodore Vanderbilt—an entrepreneur who also robbed the public with abandon—spent $3 million to build a house, the Breakers on Long Island, providing his suitably corseted wife (for the sake of being a conspicuous "trophy") with something more than minimal shelter. James Hill of St. Paul could have done the same thing, but had settled for the heights of Summit Avenue. Vanderbilt was able to buy Vanderbilt University for only a half million, a sum that causes his conspicuous household consumption to appear wasteful.

To Veblen, conspicuous consumption *is* wasteful. As he puts it, "throughout the entire evolution of conspicuous expenditure, whether of goods or of services or human life, runs the obvious implication that in order to effectually mend the consumer's good fame it must be an expenditure of superfluities. In order to be reputable it must be wasteful." In the early months of his marriage to Zelda, Scott did not understand the close connection between his and Zelda's conspicuous consumption and waste. Before going forward to Scott's self-revelation, we find the Fitzgeralds living the lives that Veblen damned. Scott first *experienced* much of what he would next write. To compound the irony, Scott Fitzgerald soon would express his disillusionment with the lifestyles of the rich and famous even as he glamorized an era quite similar to the 1890s.

With the publication of *This Side of Paradise* and his marriage to Zelda, Fitzgerald suddenly encountered a new personal and social reality. F. Scott's first novel had filled a latent public demand for novelty, which had provided him with a considerable financial lift and, of more lasting significance, transformed him into a public figure. As to wealth, Scott's was perhaps indistinguishable from other successful novelties riding the wave of postwar consumer demand. Still, journeying prowlike through Manhattan perched atop a taxi with his "trophy" wife as the hood ornament, Fitzgerald projected an image of upward mobility symbolic of an entire class of nouveau riche. They were invited to all the parties and could be seen jumping into fountains for the joy of it. Suddenly, Scott and Zelda became celebrities engulfed in a social and economic movement not only much larger than themselves, but beyond their social abilities to control. The Fitzgeralds embodied a new social era while being engulfed by it. Thorstein Veblen had described such a cultural transformation of the 1890s with routinely ironic detachment.

At first impulsively, and then compulsively, the Fitzgeralds revel in their new fame. New York City becomes a stage for a continuous public performance by Zelda and Scott, an effortless performance because of their natural bent for the dramatic. As Scott's popularity grows with the clocklike regularity of his well-paid short stories in the staid *Saturday Evening Post,* Zelda becomes loosely identified with the class of rebellious and vivacious young women on display in "Head and Shoulders" and "Bernice Bobs Her Hair," the flappers whose behavior is rocking conventional morality. Together, Scott and Zelda's exuberant and celebratory lifestyles forge an imperial alliance that, if not exactly conquering an unconquerable city, reflects its dynamic spirit and captures the media's attention along with its insatiable audience. In her autobiographical novel *Save Me the Waltz*, Zelda provides a description of the theatrical atmosphere of the Fitzgeralds' New York City in the early twenties:

> The city fluctuated in muffled roars like the dim applause rising to an actor on the stage of a vast theater. *Two Little Girls in Blue* and *Sally* from the New Amsterdam pumped in their eardrums and unwieldly quickened rhythms invited them to be Negroes and saxophone players, to come back to Maryland and Louisiana, addressed them as mammies and millionaires.[3]

Nor are the party and pretense confined to the nouveau riche:

> The shopgirls were looking like Marilyn Miller.... They were having the breadline at the Ritz that year. Everybody was there. People met people they knew in hotel lobbies smelling of orchids and plush and detective stories, and asked each other where they'd been since last time. Charlie Chaplin wore a yellow polo coat. People were tired of the proletariat—everybody was famous.[4]

The public's identification of Zelda with the vivacious flapper and fickle society girl was not entirely undeserving since Zelda's unpredictable and audience-grabbing behavior suited her for the

Cover Art: Biography of Veblen *by John Patrick Diggins, published by Princeton University Press*

part. At heart, she was an exhibitionist. Moreover, Zelda's portrayal of the American flapper in "Eulogy on the Flapper" (1922) and, later, "What Became of the Flapper?" (1925) are not so much condescending satires as sympathetic portraits of a class of social artists, female entrepreneurs who were defining a new culture of morality congenial with her own: "I believe in the flapper as an involuntary and invaluable cupbearer to the arts. I believe in the flapper as an artist in her particular field, the art of being—being young, being lovely, being an object."[5]

Zelda—certainly a lovely object! In stark contrast to the Victorian virtue of visible restraint distinguishing conventional female morality, however, the uninhibited flapper values excess, as does Zelda, and wears not only audacity but considerable rouge. Zelda admires her freshness, her love of novelty and change, and her search for pleasure in the present moment: "I refer to the right to experiment with herself as a transient, poignant figure who will be dead tomorrow."[6] Hinting of her own economic philosophy of discounting the future, Zelda stripteases present-value business accounting: "Flapperdom…is making [youth] intelligent and teaching them to capitalize their natural resources and get their money's worth. They are merely applying business methods to being young."[7]

Perhaps. At the time neither Scott nor Zelda was particularly trustworthy in designing balance sheets or a budget. For these and other reasons, neither would have been a poster child for today's "moderate Republican."

Consider nonetheless what the newly flaming youth are challenging in Fitzgerald's *This Side of Paradise*. Some 12 percent of Fitzgerald's Princeton class regard casual kissing as morally wrong. Worse, a serious kiss meant an expected proposal to marry. Fitzgerald's potentially sensational chapter on "Petting" is actually about kissing. Despite "HE: Rosalind, I really *want* to kiss you. SHE: So do I. (*They kiss—definitely and thoroughly*)," Amory and Rosalind are not led into more daring sexual acts. This coming-of-age novel is daring only in its *recognition* of youthful sexual impulses and in its *celebration*—just after the

Scott and Zelda: studio portrait

beginning of the futile "enforcement" of Prohibition—of the freedom of drinking and sex. Alone among Fitzgerald's novels, *Paradise* often is considered naive and out-of-date today.

More than anything, the flapper was filled with the *possibilities* of a Ginevra King, teases betrayed by empty promises. Not only did Fitzgerald persuade Scribners to advertise *Paradise* as "A Novel about Flappers Written for Philosophers," but with Zelda in mind, he popularized the term "flapper" derived, appropriately enough, from a "wild Duck," though Zelda was more of a "wild and crazy Duck." In the early nineteenth century, flapper meant "a young harlot," at the turn of the twentieth an immoral girl in her early teens, in 1905 a young girl with her hair not yet put up, and finally in the 1920s an independent young woman with short hair. Freed by wealth, alcohol, and the auto, youth was behaving like Amory and his girlfriends. Not only did Scott Fitzgerald name and baptize the Jazz Age in his favorite bootlegger's gin, he made hedonism fashionable while revolting against prewar respectability and protective parents. Youth was embracing the freedom from repression.

✧   ✧   ✧

Fitzgerald expected all of his books to achieve the same financial success as his first. He spent what he expected in future income, and the lavishness of his expenditures indelibly mark him as nouveau riche. Having developed luxurious tastes, he was willing to go deep into debt to maintain his and Zelda's ostentatious living style. Scott provided his family with maids, governesses, nannies, nurses, fine dining out, expensive hotels, luxurious (though *used*) autos, private schools, the "best" bootlegger, and the finest hospitals. They initially stayed in the finest hotels near the best restaurants in New York City. Before the honeymooners at the Biltmore were thrown out for rowdiness, several of Scott's classmates showed up to help celebrate. The newlyweds served Orange Blossom cocktails and entertained Edmund Wilson, John Peale Bishop, Alex McKaig, Ludlow Fowler, and Lawton Campbell.

Being newly wed did not discourage Zelda from flirting and trying to sleep with John Peale Bishop, Scott's friend, telling him that kisses were not to be considered an end, but merely a means. Edmund Wilson, working with Bishop at *Vanity Fair,* says that Zelda would exclaim how hotel bedrooms excite her. Though it seems a quaint idea today, what Wilson does not state explicitly is the implied eroticism that excites this strange man. At the Commodore, unfortunately, Zelda's bedroom was the Fitzgerald's *only* room, and it was a bedlam of food, paper, and clothing strewn everywhere. The disorder and confusion of hotel rooms made it virtually impossible for Scott to write, even as Zelda demanded everything *at once*, if not sooner. Fitzgerald, however, was unable to work on a second novel. In New York he produced only the long story "May Day" that went into the *Smart Set* for a mere two hundred dollars.

Continuing an emerging pattern, the manager at the Commodore asked the Fitzgeralds to leave again because of their loud parties. The Fitzgeralds realized a need to leave the New York hotel life behind them and find a place where Scott could work and Zelda could continue to amuse herself and swim. On May 14, 1920 they rented the large Wakeman cottage at 244 South Compo Road in suburban Westport on Long Island Sound. Thus began a pattern of rentals that were much larger than the Fitzgeralds' needs. Once in Westport, the laundry continued to pile up in closets, Zelda continued to destroy cars by running them over fire hydrants, and the lavish parties for their weekend arrivals never quite ended.

Zelda swam daily as a member of the Longshore Beach and Country Club while Scott worked on his second novel, "The Flight of the Rocket", later titled *The Beautiful and Damned.* (The working title was under the influence of the aforementioned Henri Bergson who had used a rocket metaphor to explain how his élan vital occurred through periodic creative explosions in which physical matter is temporarily transcended, but then settles back to earth.) An Asian houseboy named Tanaka was hired to do what Zelda had never been required to do as a Southern belle—assist with housekeeping and party preparations. Scott was equally useless at chores—repairing things or mowing the lawn. Tanaka, as it turned out, could barely speak English, but had his endearing idiosyncrasies.

In July 1920 they bought a secondhand Marmon automobile that turned out to be horribly unreliable. Thus began another pattern, the purchasing of used and unreliable luxury cars. Forced frequently to borrow from his only (magazine) agent, Harold Ober, and his only book editor, Max Perkins at Scribners, Fitzgerald's payments for stories and book royalties never quite caught up with family spending.

Embarking on "The Cruise of the Rolling Junk." The Fitzgeralds' July 1920 trip from Westport to Montgomery in their used touring car later became a humorous travel article.

Sudden wealth and fame created an immediate conflict for young Fitzgerald. He wanted to be known as a serious novelist but knew that he needed to write commercial stories to pay the bills and his mounting debts. Fitzgerald's price for a *Saturday Evening Post* story steadily increased, peaking at $4,000, or about $44,000 in today's dollars, for "At Your Age" (August 17, 1929), published just before the Great Crash. Serious novels almost always earn fewer royalties than popular novels. They still do. Fitzgerald ended the year 1920 with better than $18,000 in earnings or nearly $200,000 in today's dollars, but was already in debt to two of his loyal friends, Ober and Perkins.

Still, having met H. L. Mencken and George Jean Nathan, editors of the *Smart Set: A Magazine of Cleverness*, at about the same time as he became friends with Perkins and Ober, Scott had an outlet for his stories that were too serious or too intellectual for the *Saturday Evening Post*, such as two of his masterpieces—"May Day" and "The Diamond as Big as the Ritz." (A third classic, "The Rich Boy," was published in *Redbook* in 1926.) Mencken was fiercely devoted to Fitzgerald's work, considering him one of the greatest men in the country. Mencken—like so many men—also was enchanted by Zelda as Nathan began a dangerous flirtation with her. Mencken nonetheless believed that Zelda's extravagance and carelessness fed Scott's desire for money, distancing him from serious art: "His wife [Zelda] talks too much about money. His danger lies in trying to get it too rapidly."[8]

Even as the fever of the parties rises, a sense of pessimism and looming tragedy begins to surround the Fitzgeralds' marriage. Zelda is still beautiful; moreover, what the Fitzgeralds do in New York City and in Westport is new and fun. Still, Zelda and Scott behave like small children with about the same disregard for consequences, but with no parents to restrain them. They commute to parties in Manhattan or hold weekend parties in Westport.

We would be unkind not to put this behavior into perspective. We are observing a man only twenty-four years of age and a woman of a mere twenty years, barely graduated from high school. Moreover, overnight or perhaps over a fortnight, they have become extremely well-to-do (by the economic standards of the time) *and* national celebrities. In more recent times rock, movie, and rap stars have fared much worse than Scott, the celebrity. *Playboy* magazine, a sumptuous reminder of today's young leisure class, includes an ode to actor Robert Downey Jr. among its annual "celebrity" carols. One stanza (to the tune of "Frosty the Snowman") goes:

"Robbie, the snowman,"
That's my rep in Hollywood.
Cause I'll do a line most any time,
and in any neighborhood.[9]

Cause and effect of being a celebrity is more difficult to fathom in Zelda's evolving mental illness. Just as "being easy" isn't always easy, being a member of the leisure class sometimes can be a struggle. Zelda was becoming increasingly bored, perhaps because she had *too much* leisure time on her hands. Her husband often was distracted by his work and his quest to be the best writer of his generation. Scott was not sufficiently attentive to a woman who had nothing to do—she did not keep house or cook and feared that she would become compulsive pursuing a hobby. Still, she loved to swim, and she played golf and tennis. But she did not enjoy doing any of these things alone. What was she to do if she had no one to do it with? She decided to flirt with many men, just as she had done in Montgomery. There was much idle time to fill.

Zelda invited only men to the parties. In July 1920, George Jean Nathan, Mencken's coeditor of the *Smart Set* flattered Zelda when he offered to publish her diaries, an offer that Scott was able to vigorously refuse. Dapper, urbane, and exceedingly witty, Nathan, eighteen years older than Zelda, was unlike any man she had encountered. In Westport that summer they flirted openly—exchanging suggestive notes, dancing cheek to cheek, and brazenly expressing their mutual affection. During all-night parties near the water, Zelda and Nathan often disappeared. They got along swimmingly and may have depended exclusively on the breaststroke for exercise.

Not to be completely outdone, Scott squired several attractive women around Westport; they included the actress Miriam Hopkins and Tallulah Bankhead's older sister Eugenia ("Gene"). Like her little sister, Gene drank heavily, took drugs, smoked continuously, and, though married, was openly promiscuous. Whether Scott's relationship with Miriam Hopkins was intimate or not is open to question; however, he did have a brief affair with the wilder Gene.

During this time of mutual dalliances, Zelda was taking the train into Manhattan to meet Nathan at his West Forty-fourth Street Royalton Hotel suite, directly across the street from the Algonquin Hotel and its famous literary and theatrical Round Table gathering (including George S. Kaufman, Dorothy Parker, Robert Benchley, Alexander Woollcott, Helen Hayes, Harpo Marx, Lynn Fontanne,

Tallulah Bankhead, and occasionally Ring Lardner and Scott Fitzgerald). Zelda combined the appearance of youthful purity with reckless spirit, a mix that Nathan found sexually irresistible. Though smitten, Nathan feared Scott's anger, especially after Zelda had brazenly shown Scott one of Nathan's amorous letters, apparently to heighten Scott's jealousy. Zelda was somewhat less appealing to David Bruce, Scott's Princeton friend who became a noted diplomat, suggesting that she "can drink more than any other woman he has ever seen, and is a trifle ordinary and Alabamian, but has brains."[10]

But, there was more, or less. Zelda had the habit of unexpectedly stripping off all her clothing so everyone could admire her beautiful body, locking herself into other people's bathrooms, and then taking prolonged baths. Often she asked the most available male to bathe her. One evening at Nathan's, Zelda, quite drunk, disrobed before everyone, as usual, and headed for the bath. She managed to cut her tailbone on a broken champagne bottle near his tub, requiring three stitches. Scott was not amused. Once, during one of their fights, Fitzgerald broke down a bathroom door in someone else's home. He was aware that after sexual intercourse, Zelda always bathed. Her bathing fetish might have been the source of Scott's use of "clean women" compared with "unclean" in his novel in progress that would become *The Beautiful and Damned*. If so, it has a deeply ironic meaning

There already were visible signs that the newlyweds were getting irritated with each other, but they *were* still in love, a condition H. L. Mencken had called a state of perceptual amnesia. The intimately frank diary of Scott's Princeton classmate, Alexander McKaig, confirms the newlyweds bickering without judging their "love," whether unforgettable or amnesiac. On one weekend in Westport, he notes: "Fitz and Zelda fighting like mad—say themselves marriage can't succeed." Later in the summer he saw an even more bitter fight, with Zelda, drunk, deciding to leave and walking on the railroad tracks nearby with Scott in hot pursuit.[11]

In Westport, Zelda was becoming increasingly restless, once claiming that she simply wanted to be amused, another time saying she wanted the life of an "extravagant." At times McKaig felt that Zelda was going beyond her usual harmless flirtation and making direct sexual overtures to him. Though McKaig—like most men at the time, David Bruce being a notable exception—considered Zelda to be the most beautiful and brilliant woman he had ever met, his loyalty to Fitzgerald prevented him from pursuing sex with Zelda, while her "loyalty" did not prevent her pursuit of McKaig.

The snowballing effects of Scott and Zelda's behavior were beginning to signal danger. Their widely publicized pranks at Princeton, in New York, and Montgomery are soon notorious. Earlier, when Scott took his teenage bride to an April 24 weekend at his Cottage Club at Princeton, he introduced her to everyone as his mistress. Zelda, acting the salamander, poured applejack on her pancakes at breakfast and then set them aflame. Scott also got the first of many black eyes at a wild party there. As expected, he took it badly when the Cottage Club suspended him (temporarily) for drunken behavior. Afterward, he and Zelda exuberantly jumped into the fountain in Union Square and into the fountain near the Plaza Hotel, a Fifth Avenue landmark known the world over for its palatial elegance.

Away from the city in quiet Westport for the summer of 1920 and bored, Zelda once again called the fire department. When asked where the blaze was, Zelda struck her breast and exclaimed: "Here!" Amidst this chaos, nonetheless, by August 12, Scott was able to relate the plot of his new novel to Charles Scribner II: It concerns the life of one Anthony Patch, about how he and his beautiful young wife are wrecked on the shoals of dissipation. It seemed apt. Zelda, meanwhile, would continue her exhibitionism. During a March 1921 visit to staid Montgomery, at a Hawaiian pageant, Zelda bent over, lifted her grass skirt, and wriggled her pert behind.

Excessive use of alcohol fueled some of these exhibitions, making their consumption still more conspicuous. By the time that *both* were bored with Westport, the Fitzgeralds returned to New York City and rented (October 1920 until April 1921) a flat at 38 West Fifty-ninth Street near the Plaza Hotel, from which they ordered their meals. The Plaza, which sits at the southeast corner of Central Park, was described as the greatest hotel in the world when it opened on October 1, 1907, a grandeur it had preserved. The flat, though in close proximity to one of Manhattan's legendary gathering places, did not improve the Fitzgeralds' relationship. McKaig writes in his diary: "If she's there Fitzgerald can't work—she bothers him—if she's not here he can't work—worried of what she might do." Also, according to McKaig, Scott was getting drunk every night through the winter and spring of 1921. He was well on his way to alcoholism at an early age.

As the Fitzgeralds began to drink more, some episodes became malicious rather than simply spontaneously gay. In April 1921 Scott, having challenged the authority of a bouncer in The Jungle, a New York cabaret, was asked to leave. Since Fitzgerald was not quite drunk and the bouncer was a much larger man, Scott was inclined to do so. When sober, Fitzgerald's courage was intellectual, not physical. However, Zelda, having had far too much to drink, goaded Scott to stand up like a man and take on the bouncer. This time—though well past "happy hour"—Scott got two black eyes instead of only one.

Now feeling obligated to live the public roles that they had created, Zelda and Scott began to stage their exhibitions. They were now flirting with dissipation. What had once seemed coy and delightful, such as Zelda's extravagances and flirtations, became intolerable. Their lifestyle was ruining their marriage.

✧ ✧ ✧

The prospect of parenthood often has a sobering effect on young couples. In February 1921, Zelda discovered she was pregnant. Fitzgerald hastily completed a draft of what would become *The Beautiful and Damned.* They then rocketed to Europe on May 3, 1921, while Zelda could still travel. On this, the Fitzgerald's first trip to Europe, they actually *sailed* on the *Aquitania* and docked in Southampton. Again, they stayed in the best hotels such as the Hotel Cecil on the Strand in London and dined in the best restaurants. Perkins had given Scott an introduction to John Galsworthy (whose pessimism absent irony disappointed Fitzgerald). They visited with Shane Leslie, the British writer-friend who had recommended

Paradise to Scribners. Like Gatsby later, Fitzgerald ordered quantities of English suits and shirts. They went on to France but quickly
tired of sightseeing and knew no one there. While staying at the
Hôtel de Saint-James et d'Albany, Zelda repeatedly tied up the cage-
style elevator with a smelly uncured goatskin to assure its availability when she had finished dressing for dinner. The Fitzgeralds were
asked to leave the hotel.

The whirlwind continued. In early July the Fitzgeralds cut
short what was a disappointing trip, sailed home on the *Celtic,* went
to Montgomery, possibly to settle, and to visit the future grandparents. A very pregnant Zelda found the heat unbearable. So did Scott,
and both resented living in a "dry" household as Judge Sayre swore
to uphold the law. Suddenly they fled north and rented the Mackey
J. Thompson house in Dellwood near the other future grandparents,
on White Bear Lake, just northeast of St. Paul. Minneapolis society
retreated there until fall. Though contracted to stay a year, they carelessly allowed a pipe to freeze and burst, causing severe water damage, and were asked to leave in November (as they had been asked
to leave the Biltmore, Commodore, Cottage Club, and the Hôtel
de Saint-James). The evictees moved to a different Commodore,
an apartment hotel in the Summit Avenue area, and Scott wisely
rented an office in downtown St. Paul. Then, in November 1921 the
Fitzgeralds rented a Victorian house at 626 Goodrich Avenue near
Summit Avenue.

Prior to the St. Paul visit, Scott had managed to keep Zelda
apart from his family. Fitzgerald's mother, who lacked the glamour that he had attained as a rising literary icon, continued to be a
source of embarrassment. Though he still loved his father, he probably resented his failures. Edward, the father, nonetheless reportedly
enjoyed being driven in his son's Buick touring car to the Grotto
Pharmacy for his favorite Tom Moore cigars. Zelda, bored by her
husband's family, became active along with Scott among the young
married crowd.

They were a popular couple in part because Scott now was a
famous author. In return, Scott relished all the attention. Although
very uncomfortable as a public speaker, Fitzgerald spoke to the St.

Paul Women's City Club on December 1, 1921. Joking that his topic would be "South America," he actually talked about his literary life. He became friends with Thomas A. Boyd and his wife Peggy, then literary editor of the *St. Paul Daily News*. Beginning a lifelong role as talent scout for Scribners, Fitzgerald found two novels for publication, the first by Peggy and the second, *Through the Wheat,* by twenty-three-year-old Tom Boyd.

Despite these madcap adventures and wanderings, Frances Scott Fitzgerald, always known as "Scottie," managed to be born in St. Paul on October 26, 1921.

✧   ✧   ✧

Meanwhile, Fitzgerald did manage to do some writing. At this early stage of his career he already sensed the social paradoxes in American life even as he lived them. Giving breath to these paradoxes in short fiction provided substantial material for his novels. One of Scott's best stories, "Winter Dreams," was appropriately written near the snowbanks of White Bear Lake and published in December 1922 (*Metropolitan* magazine). Scott's experience with Ginevra King animates these social paradoxes. Dexter Green (aka Scott), the central character, personifies the ambitious young man described by Horatio Alger, Jr. Green aspires to wealth and is driven by illusions. Dexter is from a middle-class background (his father owns the "second best grocery" in town), and dreams of not only associating with the wealthy, but of possessing "the glittering things themselves."

The animate object of Dexter's desires is Judy Jones (aka Ginevra King with Zelda-like behavior), a child of wealth whose selfishness, manipulations, and infidelities are overlooked by Dexter in favor of her physical beauty and "passionate energy." Having served as a golf caddie for the rich at the local country club (and later earning his fortune cleaning their dirty laundry), Dexter observes the corrupting effects of wealth on Judy, whose family belongs to the club. Although repulsed by Judy's golf etiquette and the culture surrounding her, Dexter remains powerfully attracted to her: "No disillusion as to the world in which she had grown up could cure his illusion as to her desirability."[12] That, if nothing else, has the ring of authenticity.

Fitzgerald subtly reveals some of Dexter's confusion regarding Judy in their first kiss:

> Then he saw—she communicated her excitement to him, lavishly, deeply, with kisses that were not a promise but a fulfillment. They aroused in him not hunger demanding renewal but surfeit that would demand more surfeit...kisses that were like charity, creating want by holding back nothing at all.[13]

The irony is that although Judy's kisses appear to be "holding back nothing at all," Dexter soon learns that Judy is concealing the fact that she is stringing along an array of suitors just like him with false promises of engagement. This, of course, was the treatment Scott received in the arms of Ginevra and Zelda. Also, by "creating want," the "charity" of Judy's kisses perverts its meaning since charity involves a gift designed to help alleviate needs, not create new wants.

The language of wealth and economic appetite surrounding the kiss portends Judy's arousal of an insatiable desire in Dexter, leading to insufficiency amidst abundance rather than any sort of "fulfillment." Earlier, Veblen had described how economic wants are open-ended simply because they are based on created desires, not on necessities. (And, before Veblen, we earlier noted how Schopenhauer—on Scott's summer 1917 reading list—had written of desire creating insatiable wants.) Like her alter ego Daisy Buchanan in *The Great Gatsby*, Judy Jones represents wealth in the form of an encumbrance—a perpetual "promise to pay" that never materializes. IOU displaces "I love you."

Later, John Commons (1924), a follower of Veblen, would detail the various forms of invisible and intangible forms of wealth inherent to twentieth-century capitalism while emphasizing the importance of "futurity" in defining wealth. If, as Commons succinctly observes, "all value is expectancy," then the American wealth that Fitzgerald observes as he begins his literary career in the twenties not only has its roots in monopoly and inheritance, but also is profoundly speculative, linked to an uncertain future, and potentially illusory.[14]

In "Winter Dreams" Fitzgerald writes of such speculation *prior* to John Commons and just prior to Dexter Green and Judy Jones's (Ginevra's) problematic kiss. Dexter confesses to Judy that "I'm nobody.... My career is largely a matter of futures."[15] Although intended to be a portrayal of his economic status, by story's end "the matter of futures" is transformed from a financial (Commons's futurity) to a philosophical statement about human identity and culture in a state of flux.

In this way "Winter Dreams" heralded an economic culture taking root in the United States in the early twenties that was devoted to material wealth, novelty, and change. The literature of that culture gained its highest expression in *Gatsby*. As Fitzgerald recognized, advertising had a lot to do with it. In *Advertising the American Dream,* Roland Marchand explains how advertisers in the twenties built on the public's "expectation of change" and viewed themselves as "missionaries of modernity" who "championed the new against the old, the modern against the old fashioned."[16] Rather than reinforcing brand-name recognition or providing textlike rationalization of product, advertisers increasingly appealed to the imagination and economic aspirations of middle-class Americans by creating a climate of wealth, availability, excitement, motion, and expectation in their ads and displays.

Aided by growing disposable income and installment buying plans, consumers responded by purchasing the latest product or style in an endless quest for novelty and economic status. In this context, Dexter's pursuit of Judy becomes less symbolic of an American middle-class pursuit of wealth (which Dexter quickly attains) than a cultural conversion to an ethos of novelty being advertised to the middle-class public as a luxury previously reserved only for the very rich. Advertising and other marketing strategies could manipulate and distort consumer choices.

Like *The Great Gatsby* and anticipating it, "Winter Dreams" is a morality tale warning against the notion that wealth brings lasting happiness (Dexter accumulates a fortune but the "trouble and pain" of trying to hold on to Judy leaves him discontented and unfulfilled).[17] However, and more fundamentally, the story invites an exploration into Dexter's philosophy (a prescient description of the speculative American consumer and investor attitudes that were to evolve in the twenties) that defines reality in dreams and aspirations.

Speculation is a part of the dream and the aspirations, but they defy reality. The illusion is dramatized as Dexter—lured by Judy—breaks a long-standing engagement to a wealthy and dependable girl, Irene Scheerer, to accept Judy's "promise" of marriage. By abandoning Irene and putting his faith in Judy, he rejects security and stability in favor of change and possibility. This choice, however, completes Dexter's personal corruption: By callously "playing through" Irene, he exhibits the same selfish behavior that originally repulsed him about Judy on the golf course. It was the kind of bad etiquette observed by Scott when playing golf with Edith Cummings, Ginevra King's friend and one-fourth of the "Big Four," who went on to become amateur champion and the model for Jordan Baker in *Gatsby*. What is also striking about this episode is Dexter's complete lack of remorse. Dexter's only regret comes years later when he learns that Judy has settled down and realizes that "The dream is gone."[18] Dexter, like Gatsby later, cannot avoid corrupting himself while pursuing the American Dream.

Judy Jones, too, is a more complex character than Fitzgerald's critics realize. She is also a victim of a world that strings women along as mere puppets. Fitzgerald laments not only the lost dreams of Dexter, but those of Judy as well. The story involves an impassioned attack on the habits and attitudes—the institutions—that served to limit women's role in society. There is the bright *and* the wasteful: Judy is full of the kinetic energy that the New Woman was at last allowed to unleash; however, as that energy is channeled mostly into consumerism it proved vital but wasteful.[19] Later, Daisy Buchanan can be viewed in a similar manner. They are composites of Fitzgerald's New Woman.

Again, Zelda embodied Scott's image of the New Woman even as she became her own reflection. Zelda became pregnant again in

January 1922, but decided not to have another child so soon after Scottie. In March she had an abortion. Early that month (March 4, 1922), Scott's novel *The Beautiful and Damned* was published.

✧   ✧   ✧

F. Scott Fitzgerald was to survive the battles and afflictions of the leisure class in the early twenties with both penalty and reward. His fame and fortune came overnight or, perhaps, over a fortnight. The penalty, guilt, came from knowing or at least believing that he had partly squandered his talent by commercializing his art and had come dangerously close to losing what Veblen has called his "instinct for workmanship." What was intuitive self-knowledge for Fitzgerald was social and economic theory for Veblen. Wasteful leisure and conspicuous consumption, to Veblen, along with the atavistic honoring of predatory behavior, was antithetical to nurturing this "instinct for workmanship," a basic human desire for efficiency, achievement, and purposeful work. Fitzgerald, above all, thirsted for acclaim as a serious writer, but he was struggling with the demons of his own creation.

Endnotes

1. Joseph Conrad's best-known book is *Heart of Darkness,* a novel that has been made into several movies.

2. Thorstein Veblen, *The Theory of the Leisure Class,* with an introduction by John Kenneth Galbraith (Boston: Houghton Mifflin, 1974 [1899]), p. 41.

3. Zelda Fitzgerald, *Save Me the Waltz* (1932), in Matthew J. Bruccoli, ed., *The Collected Writings of Zelda Fitzgerald* (Tuscaloosa, Ala.: University of Alabama Press, 1951), p. 48. Zelda *also* used some unique spellings, and also silently corrected here. Moreover, her use of mixed metaphors and jarring word combinations was typical. Her later writings are even more bizarre.

4. Ibid.

5. Zelda Fitzgerald, "What Became of the Flappers?" (1925), in Bruccoli, ed., *The Collected Writings of Zelda Fitzgerald*, p. 398.

6. Zelda Fitzgerald, "Eulogy on the Flapper," (1922), ibid., p. 392.

7. Ibid., p. 393.

8. From a letter to James Branch Cabell: see James Branch Cabell, *Between Friends: Letters of James Branch Cabell and Others*, ed. Padraic Colum and Margaret Freeman Cabell (New York, 1972), p. 254.

9. Robert S. Wieder, "Celebrity Christmas Carols," *Playboy*, December 2001, p. 109.

10. Quoted by Jeffrey Meyers, *Scott Fitzgerald* (New York: Cooper Square Press, 1994), p. 70. We have been unable to find the orginal source, which is most likely David Bruce himself.

11. Alexander McKaig Diary, Collection of Robert Haft, New Peterborough, New Hampshire.

12. Fitzgerald, "Winter Dreams," in *The Stories of F. Scott Fitzgerald*, edited by Malcolm Cowley (New York: Charles Scribner's Sons, 1951), pp. 130–38.

13. Ibid., p. 136.

14. John R. Commons, *Legal Foundations of Capitalism* (New York: The MacMillan Company, 1924), p. 25.

15. Fitzgerald, "Winter Dreams," p. 136.

16. Ronald Marchand, *Advertising the American Dream* (Berkeley: University of California Press, 1985), pp. 1, xxi.

17. Fitzgerald, "Winter Dreams," p. 139.

18. Ibid., pp. 142–43, 145.

19. A similar perspective is found in Quentin E. Martin, "Tamed or Idealized: Judy Jpnes's Dilemma in 'Winter Dreams'" in *F. Scott Fitzgerald: New Perspectives,* eds. Jacksopn R. Bryer, Alan Margolios, and Ruth Prigozy (Athens, GA: University of Georgia Press, 2000), pp. 159-172.

Six

The Beautiful and That Damned
Thorstein Veblen

IT WAS ALWAYS ABOUT BEAUTY AND CLASS, WASN'T IT? F. SCOTT FITZGERALD never lost his appreciation for beauty—whether it was symbolized in the responsibly wealthy or embodied in his "top girl." He nonetheless soon began to understand beauty's dark side. In this regard, Fitzgerald began to think and write along Veblenian lines. Exactly *when* Thorstein Veblen began to intrude on Scott's thoughts is difficult to pinpoint. He certainly was familiar with Veblen's devastating satire of the upper classes and their admiring underlings in *The Theory of the Leisure Class*.

Contrary to Marx's class *struggle,* Veblen depicted a struggle for *class,* exactly the kind of struggle that engaged Fitzgerald in reality and, now, in his writing. Some of Veblen's initial influence probably was filtered through author Sinclair Lewis, who made a timely visit during the Fitzgeralds' first summer (1922) at White Bear Lake. Lewis had published *Main Street* the same year as Scott's *Paradise* and was to publish *Babbitt* the same year as Fitzgerald's next novel. Underscoring Fitzgerald's early Marxian perspective as well as his appreciation for Veblen was his admiration of Upton Sinclair's *The Jungle* (1906), a dramatic portrayal of worker exploitation, employer coercion, and the fate of a reserve army of unemployed workers (even during a period of overall economic growth) for whom work was a grim necessity rather than the realization of the American Dream. In his compendium of capitalism, Sinclair captures the disintegration of the American Dream for many immigrant workers, from the initial lure of economic opportunity to its coercive and morally destructive consequences.

In Sinclair's *Jungle* it is difficult to know where satisfaction ends and waste begins. Sinclair concludes his novel with a summary of the various types of waste generated by American capitalism, which finally draws as much on Veblen as on Marx. He writes of the wastes of competition, such as the losses from industrial warfare—the ceaseless worry and friction. He complains of the idle and unproductive members of the community, the frivolous rich and the pauperized poor, the wastes of social ostentation. Money, he writes, is necessarily the test of prowess, and wastefulness the sole criterion of power.[1] His character, Schliemann (a prominent Socialist), goes on to complain about some 30 percent of the population busily producing useless things, while 1 percent is busily destroying them.

Worse. The poison penetrates the whole social body because beneath "the hundred thousand women of the elite are a million middle-class women, miserable because they are not of the elite." And, beneath them "are five million farmers' wives reading fashion papers' and trimming bonnets, and shopgirls and serving-maids selling themselves into brothels..." He knowingly bemoans the ultramodern profession of advertising as "the science of persuading people to buy what they do not want,"[2] an anticipation of John Kenneth Galbraith, who also was under Veblen's influence.

Fitzgerald was familiar with such persuasion, not only as an enthusiastic partner with Zelda in a newly emerging consumer culture but also from his brief, unhappy stint writing advertising slogans in his first employment in New York. Although Veblen had the robber barons of the Gilded Age engaged in self-advertisement, the connection between advertising and Veblen's concept of emulative spending was fused during the Jazz Age. Advertising was increasingly used to point out the inadequacies of our current consumption for attaining an adequate social stature, a persuasion contributing to a negative sum game of spending on both consumption and advertising. The embodiment of consumption was the housewife, and much Jazz Age advertising was aimed directly at her.

In a departure from Marx, who rooted capitalism's class distinctions on a strict materialistic basis involving the ownership of capital, Veblen based class distinctions on social prestige. Social prestige was originally rooted in honor as in late medieval chivalry, but under modern capitalism icons of wealth and leisure had become *proxies* for honor, proxies to be exercised by the newly rich. In practice, one could attain social stature without owning economic wealth provided one could obtain credit or otherwise create the *illusion* of wealth as with *conspicuous* displays of consumption. By also claiming that modern capitalism was divorcing human beings from an underlying need for

Zelda looking like Elizabeth Arden

creative and fulfilling work, Veblen's critique dovetails with Marx's theory of estrangement under capitalism, a condition personally experienced by Fitzgerald and mirrored in his fiction. After all, the Fitzgeralds comprised a poster family for conspicuous displays.

Veblen extended this economic and social behavior to the nation. Instead of capitalism's downfall coming from an excessive and concentrated capital accumulation, Veblen fancied economic self-destruction whereby consumption drives the economy to ever higher levels of wonderfully wasteful production. By identifying a "law of conspicuously wasteful expenditure of time and substance,"[3] Veblen provided a new critique of capitalism, critically canvassing the consumer culture culminating at the turn of the American century. In contrast to the boldfaced class conflict between the worker and the capitalist of Marx, Veblen blunts social distinctions as the middle class emulates the upper class, conspicuous consumption being more participatory than simply the ownership of capital.

✧ ✧ ✧

Fitzgerald read proofs of *The Beautiful and Damned* in St. Paul, beginning in mid-October 1921, completely rewriting various parts but especially the ending. In the novel, Fitzgerald reflected upon a Veblenesque portrayal of the leisure class as well as changes in his own social and marital status that had taken place in Westport. The novel covers the same prewar to postwar period (roughly 1910 to 1920) as *This Side of Paradise*. It also describes the personal history and genteel romanticism of a wealthy and attractive young man. Anthony Comstock Patch, a youthful representative of the leisure class, a grandson to a millionaire industrialist turned moral crusader, has nothing to do but *wait* for his expected inheritance. Since he did little while waiting, it became synonymous with leisure and, so, Anthony fraternizes with his leisure class brethren. Anthony's middle name ironically alludes to both Anthony Comstock, a contemporary crusader against vice, and to the Comstock Lode, the most valuable silver deposit in the United States.

In stark contrast to the lightheartedness of Fitzgerald's first novel, *The Beautiful and Damned* is ponderous and tragic—the title suggesting the protagonists' movement from the rich and pampered life of the beautiful to the suffering of the condemned, a damnation caused mostly by wealth and alcohol. The *absence* of "the" before "Damned" was carefully crafted by Fitzgerald. The story *is* partly autobiographical in its capturing the arc to Fitzgerald's early career following the publication of *Paradise,* but, like all of Fitzgerald's fiction, reverberates with larger social themes including the nature of class structure in early-twentieth-century America. Money plays a dominant role, but Anthony's relentless pursuit of wealth is quite different from Amory Blaine's lengthy attack on capitalism in *Paradise*.

Fitzgerald describes a middle-class cabaret crowd in which the women "poured out the impression that though they were in the crowd they were not of it.... They were forever changing class, all of them—the women often marrying above their opportunities, the men striking suddenly a magnificent opulence: a sufficiently preposterous advertising scheme...."[4] Gloria Gilbert, the youthful beauty of the novel, identifies with the cheap display and artificial striving: "I'm like these people," she says, "I'm like they are—like Japanese lanterns and crape paper, and the music of that orchestra" filling the room with sounds of "careless violins and saxophones."[5] Gloria identifies with the "bogus aristocrat," the restless social actress whose makeup will take on a variety of forms: "You will be known during your fifteen years as a ragtime kid, a flapper, a jazz-baby, and a baby vamp."[6] The public identifies Zelda as Gloria, the flapper, as well they should.

Joseph Conrad by now is Fitzgerald's most admired stylist. And—though Marx, Lewis, and Veblen sustain Fitzgerald's social themes—ironic echoes of Joseph Conrad's "Youth" frame this second novel. "Youth" is a story of a ship (the ironic *Do or Die*), which is exposed to every conceivable adversity on an ill-fated voyage to Bangkok. In the hopeless struggle to complete its mission, the effort, courage, and endurance of the crew nonetheless establish an inner sense of honor and realm of human dignity, which defies the contiguous indifference of the natural world. In contrast to this tale of honor attained through struggles, Fitzgerald's Anthony Patch creates an *imaginary* world of honor and significance for himself. Not having worked a day in his life or even exerted the least bit of effort, he views life mainly in theoretical nuts and bolts:

> As you first see him he wonders frequently whether he is not without honor and slightly mad, a shameful and obscene thinness glistening on the surface of the world like oil on a clean pond, these occasions being varied, of course, with those in which he thinks himself rather an exceptional young man, thoroughly sophisticated, well adjusted to his environment, and somewhat more significant than any one else he

knows…. In this [latter] state he considered that he would one day accomplish some quiet subtle thing that the elect would deem worthy…. Until the time came for this effort he would be Anthony Patch—not a portrait of a man but a distinct and dynamic personality, opinionated, contemptuous, functioning from within outward—a man who was aware that there could be no honor and yet had honor, who knew the sophistry of courage and yet was brave.[7]

Fitzgerald's portrayal of Anthony Patch is drenched in irony. Cutting to the truth, Anthony is leading an aimless life without personal honor *or* social function. His environmental "fitness" is having the leisure to take luxurious baths (as Scott did on his honeymoon and Zelda pursued as a fetish), engage in the "theoretical creation of essays on the popes of the Renaissance," and contemplate the meaninglessness of life while falling asleep with his bedside light on.[8] Telling his grandfather that he is *thinking* of writing a history of the Middle Ages, Anthony much prefers to talk about his "work" than to actually *do it,* as Nike would have it today. He is a well-intentioned *potential* scholar, and always will be.

Anthony's leisure class status is set against the churlish Jewish German immigrant Joseph Bloeckman, a self-made businessman who, as a member of New York City's nouveau riche, represents a vague threat to Anthony's aristocratic status. Despite possessing no advantageous inherited social or economic status, Bloeckman achieves financial success in the emerging movie industry and establishes an initial claim to the beauty of the novel, Gloria Gilbert, whom he has met through her father, a celluloid supplier to the film industry. "Celluloid" suggests that we can see through Bloeckman, as indeed we do. Just as Scott and Zelda were to be urged to do a screen test for a movie adaptation of *Paradise,* Bloeckman offers Gloria a screen test. Bloeckman's unrefined taste and manners, his commercial attitude toward art and entertainment, his plodding achievements from "peanut vendor with a traveling circus" to the vice president of "Films Par Excellence," all serve to place him as socially inferior to Anthony Patch.

Anthony and Gloria marry despite their many heated arguments. Meanwhile, they can only dream of the time when they will have more money upon the death of Anthony's grandfather. Anthony soon understands that Gloria is a woman of great nervous tension and of the most high-handed selfishness; she discovers that Anthony is an utter coward. This is not much on which to base a solid marriage; both drink heavily and live beyond their means. Their relationship only comes to terms when the attitude of not giving a damn for consequences being a mere tenet of Gloria's becomes not only the entire solace for what they do but its justification. Their marriage nonetheless leaves a wide path of ruin. Scott and Zelda do come to mind.

Whatever satirical condescension Fitzgerald levels at the unsophisticated and business-minded Bloeckman, however, the *deeper* ironies of the novel are aimed at the leisure class presumption of Anthony Patch. Although Bloeckman never fully captures nor captivates Gloria Gilbert, he is a resolute menace to Anthony and at least has the dignity of having struggled to earn *his* economic and social status. The success of his struggle makes Bloeckman tougher and *more fit* than Anthony. As the novel progresses in this evolutionary way, Anthony becomes faintly aware of the existence and strength of "harder" men seasoned by life's struggles and from whom he has been shielded. Bloeckman's appearance gradually becomes sufficiently dignified and established that "Anthony no longer felt a correct superiority in his presence."[9]

Fitzgerald is introducing Veblen's repudiation of Social Darwinism, amplifying Scott's earlier absorption of George Bernard Shaw and Henri Bergson's criticism of this contrived defense of monopoly capitalism. Veblen uses a Darwinian biological metaphor in a new way. The Darwinians had said that in evolutionary development of biological organisms, natural selection allows the fittest to survive. Veblen *counters* that institutions also evolve, but there is always a *cultural lag* between the ideas of today and today's institutions based on the ideas of yesteryear. "Institutions," says Veblen, "are products of the past process, are adapted to past circumstances, and are therefore never in full accord with the requirements of the present."[10] Veblen hangs Social Darwinism upside down, where evolution is a suffocating force. Right side up (i.e., being upside down), the surviving institutions are the *least fit* for the present. Whatever *is*, is wrong! Fitzgerald proceeds to view Anthony's leisure from a long-expected inheritance—based as it is on heritage—as outmoded and unfit for the times.

Part of Anthony's objection to Bloeckman is that he finds the movie business itself vulgar and objects to Gloria pursuing an acting career on the grounds that he hates "theatrical things."[11] Yet, as a member of the sham nobility from the distant past, Anthony's entire life has been staged, largely a performance. At last, in a futile attempt to establish superiority over Bloeckman, Anthony insults Bloeckman's heritage by calling him a "Goddam Jew," though Anthony himself has no heritage absent his grandfather's inheritance and proves to be worthless without it.[12] Anthony's shield—his membership in the *lagging* leisure class—becomes a liability in a new world where life is governed by acquired rather than inherited characteristics. Bloeckman decks him for the insult and, in a parallel theme, the movie industry subordinates Anthony's friend, Richard Caramel, a fiction writer who abandons serious work in favor of Hollywood scriptwriting, art imitating Fitzgerald's own Hollywood screenwriting experience for D. W. Griffith (1921) and anticipating Scott's future.

Anthony Patch's fate is both bitter and comical as is Conrad's portrayal of the fate of the crew in "Youth." While having sufficient income so that he does not have to work, Anthony does not have quite enough to sustain his and Gloria's expensive lifestyle. The final irony occurs in Fitzgerald's concluding pages when Anthony Patch, having finally won a legal marathon for his grandfather's wealth, sits in a wheelchair on the deck of *The Berengaria* (an ironic play on Anthony's supposed transformation) while imagining himself as a heroic and victorious general in an epic battle:

> He was thinking of the hardships, the insufferable tribulations he had gone through. They had tried to penalize him for the mistakes of his youth. He had been exposed to ruthless misery, his very craving for romance had been punished, his friends had deserted him—even Gloria had turned against him. He had been alone, alone—facing it all…

Great tears stood in his eyes, and his voice was tremulous as he whispered to himself. "I showed them," he was saying. "It was a hard fight, but I didn't give up and I came through!"[13]

Zelda and Scott somehow had survived a particularly bitter St. Paul winter. Zelda despised the St. Paul cold and writes to Ludlow Fowler that she is grateful to be spared the fate of the monkey—a reference to the expression that "it was cold enough to freeze the balls off a brass monkey."[14] They were eager to return east for the March publication of *The Beautiful and Damned*. With a $5,600 royalty advance in hand, the Fitzgeralds left Scottie with a nanny and checked into Room 644 at the Plaza Hotel in New York for a monthlong celebration. They went to nightclubs, new speakeasies, and parties at Nathan's, whom Fitzgerald had somehow forgiven for his romantic interest in Zelda. Then, there were many luncheons with John Peale Bishop, Edmund Wilson, and Donald Ogden Stewart. Once Scott had introduced Stewart to Wilson, Scott along with Edmund provided entrée into publishing for Stewart and, later, Stewart would introduce Scott to Hemingway in Paris. Zelda and Scott avoided only Alex McKaig, who had been in a fight with Scott—most likely, over Zelda. Years later, they too reconciled.

The bouncing from place to place was to continue. Scott and Zelda celebrated their second anniversary at the Biltmore and then returned to St. Paul the first week of April 1922. Fitzgerald wrote and directed a musical revue, *Midnight Flappers,* for the Junior League Frolic in which Zelda played the role of a Southern flapper. With all the travel and spectacular events, it is difficult to believe that Scott and Zelda had been married only two years.

The *Metropolitan* magazine serialized *The Beautiful and Damned,* running from September 1921 to March 1922, after cutting forty thousand words from Fitzgerald's text. The magazine paid Scott $7,000 for the privilege. Scribners' three printings totaled 50,000 copies, with $12,000 in royalties for Fitzgerald in 1922 (of a total $15,000, excluding the serial rights). These sales were sufficient to place the novel on the *Publishers Weekly* best-seller lists for March, April, and May. The best seller of 1922, A. S. M. Hutchison's

If Winter Comes, however, sold 350,000 copies. Scott was greatly disappointed in the sales of his own novel and his royalties, but today few remember Hutchison's book and nearly everyone remembers Fitzgerald's. Scott sold the movie rights to Warner Bros. for a modest $2,500. Once again, several producers expressed an interest in starring the couple in a film version of *The Beautiful and Damned.* Ultimately, Warner Bros. cast Marie Prevost in the role that Zelda apparently pined for. In a letter to Oscar Kalman, a St. Paul stock broker, sometime after December 10, 1922, Fitzgerald writes that the 1922 movie is "by far the worst" he'd ever seen.

✧ ✧ ✧

The critical praise for the novel was so faint it could barely be heard. H. L. Mencken writes in the *Smart Set* that Fitzgerald deserves praise for attempting something much more difficult than *Paradise;* even if it is a near miss, it is worthy of respect. Mencken could not be extremely critical because he knew that Scott was following Mencken's lead. John Peale Bishop writes in the *New York Herald* (March 5, 1922) that Scott's novel also is an advance over *Paradise,* but its ideas, vocabulary (e.g., "at the mercy of words with which he has only a nodding acquaintance"), aesthetics (e.g., "awkward with his own vigor"), and literary taste are extremely flawed. As usual, Edmund Wilson's commentary in *The Bookman* (March 1922) was the most damaging. In a long survey of Fitzgerald's work, Wilson concludes that Fitzgerald is a gifted writer lacking intellectual power and control without anything interesting to say. His ultimate putdown: "He [Fitzgerald] has been given a gift for expression without very many ideas to express." Bishop and Wilson's overall tone is, as ever, condescending. Fitzgerald soon admitted that the novel needed more structure (though it was not as loose as *Paradise*) and in places had a confusing point of view.

Zelda wrote a humorous review in the *New York Tribune,* "Friend Husband's Latest." She refers to Scott's attribution of fragments of her old diary and some of her letters, to Gloria: "Mr. Fitzgerald," she writes, "seems to believe that plagiarism begins at home."[15] Later, she would view such use of her material in a quite different light. Zelda sold three other articles in 1922—"The Super-flapper" (never published), "Eulogy on the Flapper" *(Metropolitan),* and "Does a Moment of Revolt Come Sometime To Every Married Man?" (a companion piece to a Fitzgerald article in *McCall's*). Zelda had no serious literary ambitions at the time.

In June 1922 the Fitzgeralds managed *somehow* to rent once again a cottage in Dellwood, at the White Bear Lake Yacht Club. A surviving scorecard from the White Bear Yacht Club golf course suggests that Zelda and Scott played several rounds of golf. Although the scorecard is signed "F. Scott Fitzgerald" as the "scorer," the scores for "Mrs. Scott Fitzgerald" and "Ringer" are recorded.

"Ringer" sounds like the kind of ironic name Scott would have used for himself. The score of 81 for Scott on a generously parred 87 course of 6,211 yards (from the ladies' tees) is most likely his average for the year. The score for Zelda is recorded only for the back

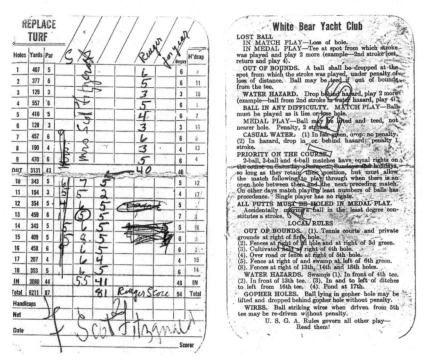

Scott and Zelda's golf scorecard, White Bear Yacht Club

nine, a 55 compared with Scott's 41. This, too, despite a report that a rich friend from St. Paul, Xandra Kalman, and Zelda played in a golf tournament and won.

Zelda and Scott also attended dinners and the Saturday night dances of the University Club in St. Paul, becoming the focus of local social life. When Zelda danced with young men at parties, she made them nervous by saying such things as, "My hips are going wild; you don't mind, do you?" In August, Scott and Zelda were again expelled from their cottage because of their loud and wild parties. This was par for their course. By now, however, they were ready to return to New York in anticipation of a work being completed by Fitzgerald.

During the summer of 1922, Fitzgerald somehow found time to become involved in another movie project. Outlook Photoplays took a three-thousand-dollar option on *This Side of Paradise*. There were serious discussions about the Fitzgeralds taking the roles of Amory and Rosalind. The planned movie project fell apart when Outlook failed to pay the option money.

Fitzgerald was not finished with the theater. Late that summer at White Bear Lake, F. Scott was crafting a play that, he believed, would make him rich and free him to write only novels. In September, Scott wrote the story "Winter Dreams" (*Metropolitan*, December), its themes, style, and tone anticipating *The Great Gatsby*. A telltale photo of Zelda that summer reveals her nervously twisting back her left hand in a strange way—a typical mannerism of schizophrenics. Fitzgerald felt that the year in St. Paul had been mostly wasted. His *Ledger* account of his twenty-fifth year: "A bad year. No work. Slow deteriorating repression. Outbreak around the corner." Zelda's behavior was beginning to annoy Scott even more. Despite the apparent good American fortune, Zelda and Scott's unhappiness was escalating. Amidst prevailing Midwestern values and declining temperatures, the Fitzgeralds were unwilling to face another season of arctic winds and ice floes; in October 1922 they again returned to the Plaza Hotel, once the center of their legendary lifestyle in New York City. They now were situated in the center of literary life where they could keep in touch with old friends and meet new writers such as John Dos Passos, Theodore Dreiser, Rebecca West, P. G. Wodehouse, Van Wyck Brooks, and Carl Van Vechten. Among these, Thorstein Veblen would inspire Dos Passos's novel *The Big Money* (1936), the third in his *U.S.A.* trilogy beginning in 1930.

In a house-hunting excursion with John Dos Passos, they searched for a place in Great Neck, Long Island, but did not find a suitable house that day. They did manage to visit Ring Lardner, who was quite drunk. Heading back to the city, Scott, Zelda, and Dos Passos stopped at a Manhattan carnival. Zelda and novelist Dos Passos rode a Ferris wheel. Zelda continued to insist on riding the old, rickety Ferris wheel long after Dos Passos wanted to stop. She frightened him with her actions and attitude; later, Dos Passos realized that he had seen the frightening fissure in Zelda's

Zelda at White Bear Lake and twisted left hand

mind. Scott and Zelda later found a place to rent for three hundred dollars a month from mid-October 1922 to April 1924 at 6 Gateway Drive in Great Neck Estates, an affluent town on the north shore of Long Island, and only a half hour by Long Island Rail Road to Broadway's theater district. They also bought a used Rolls-Royce and settled down with a live-in servant couple, a nurse for baby Scottie, and a part-time laundress.

✧ ✧ ✧

Great Neck was the home of many in show business and their wealthy families, including the noted host Herbert Bayard Swope, executive editor of the *New York World,* whose lavish parties would inspire Jay Gatsby's. In the early 1920s, American films were a New York industry. Among the Fitzgeralds' neighbors were Eddie Cantor, Ed Wynn, Leslie Howard, Groucho Marx, Basil Rathbone, Mae Murray, and Sam Goldwyn. The popular actor Ernest Truex was a Fitzgerald neighbor. Down the street also was the sportswriter Ring Lardner, who became Scott's close friend and drinking buddy. Unlike Scott, Ring was an alcoholic who generally could hold his drink. Ring was as reserved as Scott was ebullient. Scott convinced Max Perkins to publish Lardner's work, the result being a collection of Ring's short stories.

The two—Ring and Scott—often stayed up all night talking and drinking gin. Eventually Ring would stagger to his feet and announce: "Well, I guess the children have left for school by this time—I might as well go home."[16] His son later recalled how his father would often arrive home in a taxi as he was leaving for school and would have to be helped into the house. Zelda and Scott often would go to parties at the Palais Royal, the Plantation, the Rendezvous, or the Club Gallant in New York City. Paul Whiteman and his Band frequently played at the Palais Royal, one of New York's most popular nightclubs. Odyssey would better describe their outings; their Japanese "houseboy" usually found them asleep on the lawn the next morning. When not in New York, their friends from New York would spend the weekends at the Fitzgeralds in Great Neck.

These and other stories became suburban legends—not all bear repeating; especially those that cannot be verified. When, we might ask, did Scott ever find time to write? How was he able to write so much during this era and write so well? He usually wrote when he was sober and usually at night. Writing while not under this particular influence continued until about his twenty-eighth year. Until then, he had been a facile, quick writer, though one who did many revisions. In any case the Fitzgeralds lived this way in Great Neck while Scott managed to produce enough stories for the magazines to keep them going in the style to which he and Zelda now were accustomed.

In 1923, Scott finished his play in Great Neck and was about to renew his keen interest in the theater. *The Vegetable: From President To Postman* was a political satire of the already corrupt, madcap Harding administration as well as a parody of Horatio Alger Jr.'s stories for boys. As noted, Alger's stories depict the American Dream at its most shallow end (or beginning). The strange and—except perhaps for vegetarians—quite unappealing title of the play comes from Mencken's satiric essay "On Being an American," which attacks the Babbitt-like conformity of America: "Here is a country in which it is an axiom that a businessman shall be a member of the Chamber of Commerce, an admirer of [the steel magnate] Charles M. Schwab, a reader of the *Saturday Evening Post*, a golfer—in brief, a vegetable."

Fitzgerald's satirical plot reverses the log cabin to White House mythology. On the eve of Warren Harding's nomination, Jerry Frost, an unhappily married postman, gets drunk and is surprised to learn that he has become the Republican candidate for president. In a dream sequence, Frost suddenly finds himself and his small-town family in the White House. However, his tenure in office is a series of disasters. He is threatened with impeachment, a call to war from a belligerent general, bankruptcy of the Treasury by his Bible-toting father, and self-righteous lectures from the Supreme Court. Frost wakes up to find it has all been a dream (or a nightmare) in the final act. He finds his true calling as a postman.

"Friend" Edmund Wilson, who had admired Fitzgerald's fantasy and humor when they collaborated on an undergraduate musical comedy at Princeton, misjudged the play as "one of the best things you ever wrote" and "the best American comedy ever written."[17] Based on Wilson's endorsement, the play was published. Scott concluded that the play is "outrageously funny, the greatest comedy ever written." Later, Wilson was quite fuzzy about this endorsement, contending that the final play was different and he did not approve of that version. (Later, Wilson turned down an offer from Charles Scribner III to write an introduction to a published version of the play on the same grounds.)

Wilson's endorsement is doubly strange since he had made a

vicious attack on Scott the same month (April) that the play was published. Wilson wrote an imaginary dialogue between Van Wyck Brooks and "Mr." Scott Fitzgerald to contrast the two authors. Wilson gave his own ideas and the best lines to Brooks. The learned and scholarly Brooks, it seems, "knows far more about American literature than anybody else in the world."[18] Wilson's mouthpiece censures Fitzgerald for haste, superficiality, and commercialism. According to Wilson's Brooks, Fitzgerald has allowed himself to be corrupted by high-paying magazines like the *Post*. Wilson's influential and oft-reprinted essay portrayed Scott as shallow, foolish, and completely outclassed by Wilson himself. Perhaps Wilson believed that a bad parody was the best writing that Fitzgerald could do. For Wilson, Fitzgerald never outgrew his academic record at Princeton.

Ironically, Fitzgerald had begun a draft of what would become *The Great Gatsby* that summer, but had laid it aside until his play was produced. Besides, drinking and partying seemed to be the proper way to prepare for a Broadway production. Fitzgerald's Ledger entry for July 1923 reads: "Tootsie [Rosalind] arrived. Intermittent work on novel. Constant Drinking. Some golf. Baby begins to talk. Parties at Allen Swans, Gloria Swanson and the movie crowd. Our party for Tootsie. The Perkins arrive. I drive into the lake." Many of the experiences in Great Neck nonetheless would instruct Scott's new novel. The postponement of its completion may have been a financial and professional mistake. At the time Fitzgerald was so confident of the success of his play that he and Zelda had moved to Great Neck to be within an easy commute of Broadway. Its publication attracted backers, and Fitzgerald persuaded his Great Neck neighbor and popular actor, Ernest Truex, to take the role of Jerry Frost.

The Vegetable did open on November 10, 1923, in Atlantic City, New Jersey. The play not only failed at its Atlantic City tryout in November 1923, its failure was apparent even to Fitzgerald, who squirmed through the opening act. Fitzgerald uses a pun on his character's name to describe the event: "It was a colossal frost... After the second act I wanted to stop the show and say it was all a mistake but the actors struggled heroically on."[19] Scott was not finished with the theater.

In the meantime Fitzgerald had been able to use his contacts with Great Neck movie people to add to his income. Film Guild paid Scott $2,000 for his short story *Grit*: The movie starred Glen Hunter and Clara Bow. Scott also earned $500 for writing the titles for the silent film *Glimpses of the Moon*. New interest in a movie version of *This Side of Paradise* was revived about the time that *The Vegetable* was fading. Famous Players-Lasky paid Fitzgerald $10,000 for the movie rights: Scott was to help write the screenplay, but the movie was never made. Including this sale or resale, Fitzgerald earned a total of $13,700 in 1923 from the movies. A significant part of these funds were put into Liberty bonds, soon to be cashed to meet the high expenses of life in Great Neck.

Ironically, Scott had expected to make a fortune, first from the play and then from the never-produced *Paradise* movie, freeing him to write "serious novels." Instead, he will have to continue to write short stories for—of all places, the *Saturday Evening Post* that he lampoons in his play—to repay those mounting debts. Ironically, the *Post* could afford to pay him high fees because every issue had nearly 3 million readers and earned $5 million from advertising. Besides some structural faults, Scott's play failed because what he was satirizing was unfolding in the Teapot Dome and other scandals of the Harding administration. His satire was overtaken by real-world events.

✧   ✧   ✧

As to the broader social reality, both Scott and Zelda admired William Thackeray's novel *Vanity Fair,* a novel about the art of display and social ambition in early-nineteenth-century England.[20] In fact, Zelda once remarked in a magazine interview with Scott that she thought the novel's central female character—the social-climbing, wily, and manipulative Becky Sharpe—to be the most interesting figure in literary fiction. Zelda's choice is not surprising since she, too, was a daring, shrewd, and then an independent woman who knew how to play to an audience, particularly of men, to gain personal and social notoriety. Not only were the Fitzgeralds expert in utilizing the arts of display—conversation and entertainment as a source of female power—these means were appealing options to the Victorian ideal of a submissive, domestic, self-sacrificing wife. Indeed, Scott must have sometimes felt like he was playing the part of Becky's naive husband, Rawdon Cawley, who, like Scott, was constantly living on credit to subsidize his own as well as his wife's extravagant lifestyle. This is but one of several angles to Scott's brilliant satire, "How to Live on $36,000 a Year," whose title is a play on a chapter title in Thackeray's novel *Vanity Fair,* "How to Live Well on Nothing a Year."[21] As a footnote to Becky's fate, her audacity ultimately ends in scandal.

Scott's essay, written for that awful *Saturday Evening Post* (April 5, 1924), satirizes the Fitzgeralds' inability to live within their budget in Great Neck, Long Island, in 1923 and the presumptions of the class of nouveau riche to which they had quickly become members. On the expenditure side, Fitzgerald provides a precise accounting of their monthly expenditures only to discover that a thousand dollars per month is unaccounted for—a parody of the "economy" chapter in *Walden* in which Henry David Thoreau calculates to the penny his expenses for a life of simplicity. On the income side, Fitzgerald turns the dismal science on its head by applying relentless demi-Malthusian logic to his own economic circumstance: "My income had a way of doubling every month... I had made only thirty-five dollars the previous August, while here in April I was making three thousand—and it seemed as if it was going to do so forever. At the end of the year it must reach half a million...."

This exuberant extrapolation, characteristic of Scott's optimism, coupled with a twist of economic logic which holds that a rational response to an expectation of exponentially rising income is a shift in time preference toward the present, leads Fitzgerald to the ineluctable conclusion that it is much more efficient to consume than to save: "...with such a state of affairs, economy seemed a waste of time." Moreover, current expenditure—no matter how wasteful, fleeting, or unaccounted for—is really an asset: "...one satisfaction nobody could take from us. We had spent $36,000, and purchased for one year the right to be members of the newly rich class. What more can money buy?"

Fitzgerald's essay mocks not only his and Zelda's inept household management, but also the wasteful and conspicuous consumption of the entire class of nouveau riche who aspired to be members of the upper class. The larger real-world irony of the essay, however, is that by headlining their undisciplined spending, the essay itself becomes a self-promoting public display of wealth and expenditure, a grand self-advertisement specifically designed to attract the public's attention and enhance Scott's literary career. Fitzgerald credits Zelda with this masterful publicity stunt. In response to his complaint that "If we just had something to show for it [i.e., all the spending] I wouldn't feel so absurd," Zelda replies that "the only thing you can do…is write a magazine article and call it 'How to Live on $36,000 a Year.'" And, of course, that's what Scott did! Displaying wealth becomes an investment in social capital just like the parade of riches in Thackeray's *Vanity Fair*.[22]

The penurious influence of Zelda on the Fitzgeralds' household is probably even larger than conventional biographers hold. A short time later, Scott wrote a sequel, "How to Live on Practically Nothing a Year" in the *Saturday Evening Post* (September 20, 1924), now a humorous description of the Fitzgeralds' futile attempt to economize by living on the Riviera in the summer of 1924. Scott describes how they bought a car that "had the power of six horses—the age of the horses was not stated—and it was so small that we loomed out of it like giants.…" On the road, "We started for Cannes in it, and except for the warm exhaust when other cars drove over us, we found the trip comparatively cool."[23] "Paint and Powder" (1929), an article published in the *Smart Set,* which was credited to Scott but actually written by Zelda, baldly states that "almost all the superfluous wealth of America goes into display. If this is decadence, make the most of it—but I should think the sign of decadence would be surfeit, and not a lust for more and more—more of those delicate luxuries that account for twenty billion dollars a year of the wealth of the United States, more doodads, jimcracks, fads, fashions, fooleries, and fripperies, the making of which keeps thousands of workers in Fords and radios.…"[24] For Zelda, not only does wealth "trickle down" to the workers, but consumption spending is a sign of energy and progress, not waste. To Scott, it was waste.

Although Zelda's endorsement of this new consumer's ethic fueling the American economy of the twenties has economic merit in its totality up to some limit, its benefits to the Fitzgerald household ultimately are dubious. In the "How to Live on $36,000 a Year" essay, Scott chides Zelda's "Let's go to the movies" response to the discovery that they are broke, and although the uselessness of his purchase of a $1,000 Liberty bond is mocked by Fitzgerald, his heart is clearly in the work and thrift that it represents. Now playing Rawdon Cawley to Zelda's Becky Sharpe, young Fitzgerald was willingly led into this consumer culture and the related commercialization of his own art. His essay on living on $36,000 provides an early, self-aware glimpse into the troubling discrepancy that this culture had begun to create for Fitzgerald, the tension between a glamorous appearance and a growing empty inner reality, an inner reality that more and more was *his*. In truth, although Zelda's influence on Scott's literary career was in some respects supportive (her lifestyle and letters *did* provide *some* raw material for his fiction), it was often damaging and sometimes nearly fatal.

Zelda pushed Scott toward an extravagant and reckless lifestyle that, given his predilection for drink, was irresistible. The objection that this extravagant lifestyle was unsustainable was overcome by the thinking (when sober) that if money could not be saved, the experiences derived from exhausting one's income and living for the amusements of the present moment also could be husbanded and used in perpetuity for future literary production. One could live off consumption and waste indefinitely, it seemed, because wasteful living for the Fitzgeralds was in Zelda's view a social investment, a source for Scott's future literary output.

To a considerable but ultimately constrained degree, Zelda was right. Beyond the penalties that Fitzgerald incurred, his reward was that he had gained a deeper appreciation for what it took to be a great writer and, despite lapses, had retained a glimpse of that faint green light that was to be so visible in his greatest novel. By his own standards, Scott considered *The Beautiful and Damned* to be a great disappointment. Nonetheless, H. L. Mencken wrote that Fitzgerald had ceased to be a wunderkind and had begun to come into his maturity. Presaging what was to come, Zelda's review of the book, her first professional publication under her name and partly a joke, criticized the novel's intellectual pretentiousness and noted how plagiarism apparently "begins at home." By the time Scott had completed only his second novel, however, he knew that he was dangerously close to becoming a Dick Caramel or an Anthony Patch, but Fitzgerald had a new resolve to establish himself as a serious artist as he began constructing his next book, a masterpiece that would define the Great American Novel.

✧　✧　✧

The imperial alliance Scott and Zelda forged when they took to the footlights of New York City would begin to break apart as Scott pursued a more serious literary career and Zelda sought her definition of self in detachment from her husband's literary success. Their experience personified a great but tragic love story. In some ways the story of the Patches paralleled that of the Fitzgeralds, but for them the worst was yet to come. By the end of the story, the Fitzgeralds' tragedy had surpassed even Scott's fiction. There was not only a vast wasteland ahead of them, but also a great amount of still more waste.

Endnotes

1. Upton Sinclair, *The Jungle* (New York: Bantam Books, 1988 [1906]) p. 338.

2. Ibid.

3. Thorstein Veblen, *The Theory of the Leisure Class,* with an introduction by John Kenneth Galbraith (Boston: Houghton Mifflin, 1974 [1899]), p. 82.

4. F. Scott Fitzgerald, *The Beautiful and Damned* (Oxford and New York: Oxford University Press, 1998 [1922]), p. 60.

5. Ibid, p. 60.

6. Ibid, pp. 28–29.

7. Ibid., p. 9.

8. Ibid., p. 16.

9. Ibid., p. 164.

10. Veblen, *Theory of the Leisure Class*, p. 133.

11. Fitzgerald, *The Beautiful and Damned,* p. 240.

12. Ibid., p. 340.

13. Ibid., p. 349.

14. Zelda's Correspondence, Princeton University Library, December 22, 1921.

15. Zelda Fitzgerald, "Friend Husband's Latest," *New York Tribune* (April 2, 1922), magazine section, p.11.

16. Ring Lardner Jr., *The Lardners: My Family Remembered* (New York: Harper Colophon Books, 1976), p. 164.

17. Edmund Wilson, *Letters on Literature and Politics, 1912–1972*, ed. Elena Wilson (New York, 1977), p. 84.

18. Edmund Wilson, "Imaginary Conversations: Mr. Van Wyck Brooks and Mr. Scott Fitzgerald," *New Republic* 38 (April 30, 1924), p. 249.

19. F. Scott Fitzgerald, "How to Live on $36,000 a Year" (1924), reprinted in *Afternoon of an Author* (New York: Charles Scribner's Sons, 1957), pp. 93–94.

20. The fourth film version of *Vanity Fair* appeared in 2004. If anything, Thackeray's novel as movies fared even worse than most of Fitzgerald's novels as movies.

21. William Thackeray, *Vanity Fair* (Boston: Houghton Mifflin, 1963 [1848]), pp. 350–58.

22. Quotes from Fitzgerald, "How to Live on $36,000 a Year," (1924), pp. 88, 94, and 94, respectively.

23. Quotes from F. Scott Fitzgerald, "How to Live on Practically Nothing a Year," *Saturday Evening Post* 197 (September 20, 1924), pp. 17, 165–66, 169–70.

24. Zelda Fitzgerald, "Paint and Powder" (1929), in *The Collected Writings of Zelda Fitzgerald*, p. 416.

Seven

Gatsby and All That Jazz

IN JUNE 1922, SCOTT FITZGERALD WROTE TO MAX PERKINS ABOUT HIS thoughts for his next novel, which he "may" or "may not" start. Its locale, Scott wrote, would be the Midwest and New York of 1885, he thought. The next month Fitzgerald told Perkins of his intention to write something new, extraordinary, beautiful and simple yet intricately patterned. Scott's July description, in the end, was on target. Although during the subsequent months Fitzgerald would be dealing with winter in St. Paul, writing and producing *The Vegetable,* preparing *Tales of the Jazz Age* for publication, and writing a movie synopsis for David Selznick (for actress Elaine Hammerstein titled "Trans-Continental Kitty," that led nowhere), the new novel was in the back of his mind. And, as had become a pattern that Scott, friends, and critics failed to acknowledge, much of his novel would be tested in short stories.

Other matters were typical—for the Fitzgeralds. As noted, they had employed three servants full-time, with a part-time laundress, to manage their little household in Great Neck, Long Island. Life in Great Neck in 1922–23 was much like life in Westport in 1920. New York City was too close to avoid, and weekend parties on Long Island were rarely interrupted by work. Then, too, there was that close companionship of Scott and the alcoholic Ring Lardner. For Scott, being "on the wagon" meant drinking only beer or wine. Apparently from his failure in chemistry at Princeton, Fitzgerald believed that beer and wine were soft drinks. After the failure of *The Vegetable,* however, life in Great Neck was looking exceedingly expensive. Writing virtually nothing commercial save for the failed play, Fitzgerald was about $5,000 (some $55,000 in today's dollars) in debt. His 1923 income still amounted to $28,759.78, but included an advance of almost $4,000 on his *next* novel and that $10,000 for *This Side of Paradise* film rights. His expenditures, as noted, exceeded this income, including his borrowings.

When knowing what he had to do, Fitzgerald did it! First, he gave up drinking. By the summer of 1923, Fitzgerald already was beginning to work on what would become *The Great Gatsby*. Then, between the end of 1923 and March 1924, he wrote ten stories and four articles. He was writing, you might say, at "Great Neck speed." He earned $16,450 from the stories and then he wrote that story about writing them, earning another $1,000. Still, little progress, in Scott's jundgment, had been made on his new novel. The situation reminded him that mass marketing only bought time for his more serious literary efforts. Scott continued to dismiss the usefulness of his short stories in framing his novels. Moreover, he might have underestimated the life he led as a continuing source of materials for his next novel. He published "Absolution" in the *American Mercury* in June 1924. It was intended to be a picture of Jay Gatsby's early life. That he chose to cut it to preserve the sense of mystery about Gatsby does not diminish the importance of the story to the novel. Gatsby's invisible fictional background would remain part of Gatsby's mystique in the novel. Importantly, Scott began to regret his reliance on Zelda for approval on everything he wrote. He senses a new creative power *within* himself. Nonetheless, in his subconscious, he continues to remain anxious of the judgments of Wilson and Bishop.

After a winter-into-spring of moneymaking, Fitzgerald found himself in an unimaginable condition—$7,000 ahead. Zelda and he could not live reasonably well at Great Neck on this amount, but they could in Europe, where, everyone agreed, it was very cheap because of the weak European currencies. Among the weaker was the French franc at 14 francs per dollar. The Villa Marie in the south of France would rent for only $79 a month compared with their Long Island rent of $300. With all that extra income from his short fiction and these cheap francs, Fitzgerald could focus on his novel. Besides, Zelda and Scott were trying to find a new rhythm for their lives. After a typically confused trip they ended up at St. Raphaël on the French Riviera. Scott's commitment combined with his resources would carry the day.

For a while the freshness of their experiences kept them happy, and Scott grew optimistic about finishing his new novel. For once, not even Zelda could interfere: Hence, Fitzgerald initially did not even notice Zelda's new romance. It may have been the only time that Scott devoted all of his energy and talent so single-mindedly to a novel. Perhaps he lived in his novel, not in his life at that moment in time. Then suddenly, in July, trouble arrived in the form of a handsome French aviator named Edouard Jozan. By this time the Fitzgeralds' marriage was fragile. What happened next would alter forever Zelda and Scott's relationship. Later, we will return to the dramatic events of that summer. But, for now, we will focus on Scott's maturation as a serious novelist.

Great Neck had not been a total waste. The writer most in his mind when doing the initial writing on *Gatsby* in Great Neck was Joseph Conrad, whose *Nostromo* he thought to be the great novel of the past half century. Conrad greatly relieved Fitzgerald's feelings of inferiority as a writer that had been stoked by Wilson and Bishop. The power of the artist, according to Conrad, had nothing to do with brilliance or depth of thought. The appeal of the artist is not through wisdom, but through a capacity for delight and wonder, to a sense of mystery surrounding our lives. Art, in short, appeals to the senses. Fitzgerald no longer felt compelled to compete with the "intellects"—that is, those who had the better grades at Princeton. Conrad renewed Fitzgerald's artistic self-confidence.

Literature is lucky to have had Conrad's reassurance. Fitzgerald, nonetheless, still was putting himself down, through his admission of being less the intellect, less the intelligent writer, less the intuitive thinker than the likes of Wilson, Bishop, and even Mencken. Ironically, Fitzgerald's next novel would be such an artistic achievement that its deep social context would be missed by most readers, even by experienced literary critics. Fitzgerald the artist would transcend the deeper social meaning of his novel, cloaking his intellectual sources.

Great Neck had not been a total waste in other ways. Besides Lardner, Tommy Hitchcock, a patrician war hero and polo star, became his friend. Hitchcock, born wealthy (at the goal post and thinking that he had scored) in 1900, joined the legendary Lafayette Corps during the war while still in his teens. Shot down, wounded, he escaped to Switzerland by leaping off a moving train. He was to earn the Croix de Guerre with three palms, hands down. Postwar, he attended Harvard and (like the fictional Jay Gatsby) spent a term or two at Oxford. After marrying a steel heiress, he became a successful investment banker with Lehman Brothers while dominating the international polo scene as a player from 1919 to 1939. David Bruce, Scott's Princeton friend and renowned future diplomat, shared an apartment with Hitchcock during World War II and considered him to be the only "perfect man" he had ever met.

Predictably, Fitzgerald idolized Tommy, who had so many of the qualities Scott desired but was presumed not to have. Hitchcock's wealth, social class, and breeding were competitive with Gerald Murphy (not to be met until 1925), and Tommy's good looks, athletic prowess, and war record were competitive with Ernest Hemingway. More to the present point, Tommy Hitchcock was Scott's inspiration for Tom Buchanan in *The Great Gatsby* (and later Tommy Barban in *Tender Is the Night*). Why Buchanan? Despite his urbane, charming persona, Tommy had to be ruthless, even brutal, to become the greatest polo player in the world.

Great Neck had other great attributes. In the early 1920s, before films moved west to Hollywood, not only show business but also many other celebrities lived in Great Neck. Among them—*New York World* editor Herbert Swope—had those lavish parties that inspired those of Gatsby. Then, there was Scott's ever-drinking but talented friend Ring Lardner. Later, Scott portrayed Lardner as the alcoholic composer Abe North in *Tender Is the Night*. Still more years later, the Great Neck experience would provide further contacts for Fitzgerald's final assault on Hollywood and the movies.

Then again, there were the parties. Often they lasted all night. Sometimes they gravitated to downtown New York City, where jazz was gaining popularity. Although Fitzgerald's first contact with the black roots of jazz may have been during his brief stay in New Orleans in 1920, just before marrying Zelda, Scott probably followed friend Carl Van Vechten (author of *Nigger Heaven*) to Harlem nightclubs and probably received an invitation (like Van Vechten) to the Paul Whiteman jazz concert at Aeolian Hall on February 12, 1924. In turn, the Aeolian Hall concert was the prototype for "The Jazz History of the World" alluded to in *The Great Gatsby*.

Meanwhile, in Great Neck and New York City, the partying *and* the drinking were virtually nonstop. When the drinking got out of hand, Scott and Zelda sent apologetic notes to the offended. By the standards of the Roaring Twenties, these were happy times. But, there were the hangovers. With the Fitzgeralds defining the Jazz Age, the hangovers were quickly forgotten.

✧　✧　✧

What, we may ask, did jazz have to do with it? Jazz had preceded the 1920s, just as the ideal of the American Dream had been born earlier. Then, ultimately, Fitzgerald's *The Great Gatsby* would personify, even romantically define, the Jazz Age even as it tarnished the American Dream. Fitzgerald had written of the American Dream as well as of the Jazz Age before he wrote his masterpiece. Scott's romance with the Jazz Age, however, did not fade until the age itself had vanished. To him the realization that the American Dream may be empty was ultimately less tragic than the failure to idealize life, recognize life's *romantic possibilities,* and retain the capacity to wonder. Because of Jay Gatsby's longings, Nick Carraway, narrator for *The Great Gatsby,* concludes that Gatsby is "worth the whole damn bunch put together," a line that echoes an assessment of a somewhat altered Jim Powell character (from lowly "Jelly Bean") in Fitzgerald's "Dice, Brassknuckles & Guitar" (1923) wherein the dream girl of the story, Amanthis, says, "You're better than all of them put together, Jim."[1] And, she was right.

"Dice, Brassknuckles & Guitar" is the story of a now relatively well-to-do Jim Powell from a "pore family background" who travels north to New York with his black servant Hugo. Along the way he meets a young beauty (Amanthis) whom he later sends for in hopes of introducing her to the high society of New York, where he has founded an academy of modern dance and music for the wealthy youth of suburban New York City (aka Southhampton, Long Island). Jim is a cultural entrepreneur who brings jazz to the North, even titling himself Jazz Master of the academy while relying on Hugo's assistance to teach the new inflections and rhythms of the music and its dances.

The story not only reveals Scott's familiarity with the Southern sources of American jazz, including its creative roots in the black subculture, but also his recognition that jazz was taking on the function of a common currency within American culture broadly during the 1920s. It often enough is claimed that all American music originated in the South. The irony or even dark tragedy—Hugo and Jim, the producers and deliverers of the new music, are excluded from the dances held by their wealthier students, an attempt by the rich to appropriate and privatize a common culture and turn a common property resource into an individual and class prerogative. This is a theme of Rousseau, Marx, and, it must be said, of Veblen, who argued in *Vested Interests and the Common Man* that the technology of society was a communal resource co-opted by the wealthy to their private economic advantage. Fitzgerald's truly is a "dicey" story that ends with a plot twist wherein Jim turns out to be Amanthis's cousin and is invited to the last party of the season to direct Rastus Muldoon's Band, a lifelong dream. Feeling manipulated and not wishing to be beholden to the rich, however, Jim leaves Amanthis behind and returns south with Hugo.

This is not the end to our story of Fitzgerald's story. "Dice" is a focal example of Scott's intellectual subtlety. In this case the "Socialist" view of modern society is shaped by the capitalist appropriation of the commons and exploitation of the laborer-producer. This alone is remarkable, but the story also displays Fitzgerald's uncanny, intuitive ability to anticipate and capture contemporary cultural trends even as they were unfolding with himself as a participant. In that regard, jazz was rapidly migrating north in the early twenties. Fitzgerald's fictional Rastus Muldoon's Band probably had its roots in black performers in New York. The legendary Louis Armstrong, for one, traveled to Chicago in 1922 to join King Oliver's famous Creole Jazz Band and later, and separately, arrived in New York to join Fletcher Henderson's band in late 1924. Armstrong merged the language and the improvisatory essence of the blues with whatever music he encountered. Whether it was opera, symphonic or chamber music, ragtime—he was able to play the blues over it. However, as jazz became popularized among the north's wealthier (white) consumers, it often did so through *all-white* bands such as the Paul Whiteman orchestra, marginalizing some of its more authentic originators. Although we might have supposed that "Paul Whiteman" was a pseudonym for "White man," he personally wanted to integrate black musicians into his band, but social norms precluded it.

Bing Crosby, a politically neutral vocalist for the Whiteman band, now is generally recognized as the first "cool" white guy in the same way that a black male was "cool." Crosby was a jazz singer before he became a "crooner." His lesser-known brother, Bob Crosby, had a lively jazz band. Much later, idolized as a crooner and actor, Bing nonetheless sang a jazz song about how jazz was made, "Now You Has Jazz," accompanied by Louis Armstrong and *his* jazz band, in the movie *High Society* (1956). The movie, a remake of *The Philadelphia Story,* is a Veblenian musical satire of haughty class distinctions in which the newly wealthy Crosby character "wastes his time" writing and singing jazz while his ex-wife (Grace Kelly) of inherited wealth appreciates only classical music. Few, perhaps none, who have appreciated Crosby's vocal and acting talents ever made the connection.

Still, as Kathy Ogren writes, "Whiteman's popular music became so closely identified with jazz that many Americans had no knowledge of its Afro-American origins."[2] According to Breitwieser, as jazz became popularized, "the distinction between real jazz and the image of jazz became more tangled."[3] It became, so to speak, "all that jazz." As the popularization of an art form entails its commercialization and mechanical reproduction, the original work of art is in danger of losing what Walter Benjamin has called its "aura."[4] In this regard, "Dice, Brassknuckles & Guitar" also perhaps provides important insights into Scott's professional life in the early twenties and his own perception of that life.

Like Jim Powell, Scott had sprung onto the American scene and became a sort of cultural messenger and spokesman through his literary art with the publication of *This Side of Paradise*. Also like Jim Powell, Scott was beginning to feel more like a servant of his audience than an instructor as he felt the financial and cultural pressure to reproduce "as on an assembly line" short stories about wealthy young debutantes. Fitzgerald's switch to short story production mirrored the reproduction of Afro-American jazz by Whiteman and Crosby.

Now successful, Scott was no longer barred from the precincts of the wealthy. Nonetheless, being a social and economic insider did not in the least dim Fitzgerald's memories of his earlier artistic and financial struggles nor diminish his understanding of how the process of assembly-line production of short stories for magazines affected him as an artist. Although not directly beholden to the wealthy (he had no patrons), Scott was mindful of the power of money as it was channeled through both the consumption and production ends of magazines like the *Saturday Evening Post* from whom he was receiving lucrative paychecks. Although Fitzgerald ultimately became an accomplice, at least initially he was experiencing a sense of exploitation as the media, if not the wealthy themselves, co-opted his name and used it to portray a glamorous image for their commercial ends. Whatever the timing and complex of influences that led to Scott's celebrity status, in the end Scott was not prepared to retreat—stepping backward—into the South like Jim Powell and give up on his dream of literary greatness. Just as Bing Crosby gave up his dream of becoming a professional baseball player to instead sing for his supper, Fitzgerald allocated more and more time to commercial writing.

Being commercially successful without sacrificing his dream of artistic greatness or his Socialist sensibilities was going to be a difficult score to compose. Still, his "Dice, Brassknuckles & Guitar" stands as a virtuoso performance, an intuitive anticipation of the

Jazz Age. It anticipates not only Fitzgerald's defining of the Jazz Age—that temporal slice of self-indulgence sandwiched between the Great War and the Great Depression—but also his most accomplished writing in *The Great Gatsby*.

✧ ✧ ✧

Although F. Scott Fitzgerald's short novel is set in the 1920s, the original setting for *Gatsby* was the middle of the Gilded Age (1885), and its theme is widely recognized as an indictment not so much of the Roaring Twenties as of the "American Dream," which had attained its honored place in American mythology well before the opening of the twentieth century.[5] After all, James J. Hill, a robber baron living atop Summit Avenue in St. Paul, remained Fitzgerald's prototype of the American business tycoon. Moreover, much of the socioeconomic satire informing *The Great Gatsby* is not original with Fitzgerald, but again reflects the influence, both directly and indirectly, of that earlier adversary of conspicuous consumption and pecuniary emulation, Thorstein Veblen.[6] And, as we have noted, Veblen had directly focused his assault on the rich of the Gilded Age. In the end, the acceptance of this double connection gives Fitzgerald much more intellectual credit than he received at the time or since. Not only did Fitzgerald possess an undeniable artistic talent, he possessed a boldness of intellectual grasp that extends into the economic realm.

When cutthroat competition and unbridled capitalism led to the accumulation of wealth and capital in a few hands during the Gilded Age (1870–1910), Veblen understood the need to justify the excesses. The justification emerged from a belief system that condoned and encouraged the accumulation of wealth as a way of doing God's work. It was everything that the robber barons themselves could have dreamed for. Since the rich of the Gilded Age chose to display their great wealth in vulgar ways, their continued respectability required some blend of science with religion to make their wealth appear not only just, but inevitable. And so, in the view of the aforementioned Herbert Spencer (1820–1903), the fact that the rich get richer and the poor get poorer is just nature's way of improving the species and the economy at the same time. Spencer's books sold by the hundreds of thousands, and his reception in New York in 1882, two years before Gatsby *originally* was to have arrived there, would have been the envy of Paris Hilton's press agent.

Being from "the other side of the pond," Spencer was a trifle too distant to sustain Social Darwinism in America. Rising to that occasion was the most eminent of the American Social Darwinists, William Graham Sumner (1840–1910), oddly enough, one of Veblen's professors at Yale. Veblen thusly heard firsthand that "the millionaires are a product of natural selection...the naturally selected agents of society for certain work. They get high wages and live in luxury, but the bargain is a good one for society." Sumner was the salve of salvation of new millionaires who already had enjoyed Horatio Alger Jr.'s injection of the Protestant ethic element from Newtonian science, the idea of a universe that rewards.

Evoking both Calvin and science, Sumner's sociology equated the hardworking, thrifty person of the Protestant ethic with the "fittest" in the struggle for survival. Monetary success in the capitalistic society was the fulfillment of an automatically benevolent, free competitive order. In the competitive struggle, people went from natural selection to social selection of fitter persons and from "organic forms with superior adaptability to citizens with a greater store of economic virtues."[7]

Sitting at Sumner's feet was an enemy of his system, and Social Darwinism met its match in Veblen's *The Theory of the Leisure Class (TLC)*. When Veblen applied the law of natural selection to human institutions, as noted, the institutions perpetually lagged behind material change. Still, the successful individuals are those who can best adapt to changing institutions—more a Lamarckian than a Darwinian process. People being also creatures of habit, changes are made reluctantly and rarely. Because the leisure class is sheltered from pressures of subsistence, its members have no urgency to change and so retain their old habits of living. The social or cultural environment makes the survival of some characteristics more likely than others.

History can be tenacious. A state of savagery requires people to be community-centered for survival. When technology advances sufficiently to create surpluses, predation and barbarism emerge, as do classes distinguished by wealth holdings. Barbarism (as in Tommy Barban and Tom Buchanan) promotes not only selfishness and emulation, but also brutality.[8] Though such characteristics assure survival in an economy of surpluses, they are neither noble nor progressive. Aggressive behavior is rewarded; the most cunning and competitive of the leisure class have the upper hand. Fitzgerald could gather from this that the "American Dream" is to become ever more affluent and that the affluent would promote more and more exclusive institutions. Satiation becomes impossible; Scott understood this point not only from his personal experience but through his acute observations.

Veblen considered *pecuniary emulation* to be an individual's strongest motive because of the person's drive toward exclusiveness. In turn, the *standard of living* shared by a particular class determines the "accepted standard of expenditure." As Veblen put it:

> To accept and practice the standard of living which is in vogue is both agreeable and expedient, commonly to the point of being indispensable to personal comfort and to success in life. The standard of living of any class, so far as concerns the element of conspicuous waste, is commonly as high as the earning capacity of the class will permit—with a constant tendency to go higher.

In the pecuniary culture, Veblen writes, "admitted expenditure for display is more universally practiced in the matter of dress than in any other line of consumption." Sharpening the knife-edge of his sarcasm, he continues, "the woman's shoe adds the so-called French heel to the evidence of enforced leisure afforded by its polish; because this high heel obviously makes any, even the simplest and most necessary manual work extremely difficult."[9] Of course, much more complex and subtle sociology is at work in *TLC*, including the woman's service as a "chief ornament" around the house and an adequately adorned "trophy" for her husband. Women indeed comprise an abused class in *TLC*.

Taboos also play roles in Veblenian consumption. In Veblen, the taboo is a way of preventing excessive emulation of the upper classes by the lower classes. Ceremonial consumption such as buying choice articles of food and rare articles of adornment becomes taboo to women and children, and, if a servile class of men exists, the taboo holds also for them.[10] Certain intoxicating beverages and narcotics are reserved for the use of men. Such taboos separate one class from another; members of the "superior class" identify themselves not only by what they consume, but also by their power to prevent the consumption of the same items by others.[11] Over historical time, nonetheless, the upper classes remain vigilant because of the danger of emulation by lower classes.

Fitzgerald recognizes the subservience of women to the pecuniary culture and the power of drinking and smoking taboos. In Fitzgerald's world of fiction, however, women gain a new kind of social independence. Indeed, until *The Last Tycoon,* women are the energizing force in Fitzgerald's fiction. At the same time, the new woman is released from taboo bondage. Zelda especially is a glass-carrying, cigarette-toting card-holding member of the drinking-smoking sensual class. Intellectually, Scott often saw Zelda as being on the same plane as himself, frequently seeking her opinion of his work. In turn, Fitzgerald transformed Zelda and other women into his fictional new women.

✧　✧　✧

The Great Gatsby, Fitzgerald's masterpiece, is the supreme Veblenian parable of conspicuous consumption, of conspicuous emulation, of pecuniary culture, and of vicarious consumption—even of waste and of the leisure class itself. Jay Gatsby wants to live with Daisy Buchanan because she is a member of the *established* American aristocracy of wealth. She is the symbol of wealth. Gatsby lacks the maturity to realize that the symbolic Daisy cannot be obtained by money alone and—in a vulgar display of conspicuous consumption—he flaunts his nouveau wealth. Despite Daisy's infinite price ("priceless" comes to mind), Gatsby is most attracted to Daisy's voice (not the supra-price), which he describes as "full of money," a voice fostering an illusion he considers real. It is the echo of Ginevra's voice in the entry hall of her family's mansion on Astor Street in Chicago, to similar effect on Scott.

Fitzgerald here has put on display Veblen's "secondary utility," based on emulation that "seized upon the consumption of goods as a means to an invidious comparison,…as evidence of relative ability to pay."[12] The "evidence" of ability to pay, however, is not the same as the *actual* ability to pay, especially in the instance of "purchasing" Daisy at her infinite price. Daisy's price exceeds Gatsby's purchasing power and is out of every man's reach except for her current "owner."

Production surpluses, so essential to Veblenian economics, allow ostentatious display; they also promote advertising. Daisy, in her star turn, is attracted to Gatsby because he reminds her of "an advertisement," the superficial illusion *he* represents. She sobs when she sees "such beautiful shirts."[13] In one respect this scene is reminiscent of Frank Norris's McTeague burying himself in his future wife's (Trina's) apparel. The artificiality and superficiality of Daisy's emotional outburst, however, stands in ironic contrast to the genuine sensual delight and personal transformation experienced by McTeague.[14] Through Daisy, Fitzgerald is ironically commenting on female consumerism in the twenties as a new form of bondage rather than as true liberation. For Fitzgerald's central characters, as for Veblen, the cultural illusions are more important than wealth.

The first dust jacket for *Gatsby* depicted the painted eyes of an oculist's billboard advertisement, the source of imagery for a business dedicated to persuasion though fallacies and exaggerations. While Daisy represents conspicuous leisure as one facet of Veblenian waste, Myrtle Wilson, Tom Buchanan's mistress, symbolizes being laid to waste by conspicuous consumption. Both Myrtle and Gatsby are killed by Daisy, the symbol of the wealth to which they both aspire. George Wilson, after his wife Myrtle's death (from the careless driving of Daisy), mistakes the "eyes" on such a sign for the all-seeing eyes of God and cannot believe that they are "just an advertisement." These eyes give George the "right" to kill Gatsby: the advertisement has the *power of God*. Obsession in the pursuit of wealth can be deadly.

As to snobbery on the shoulders of taboo, Fitzgerald's *Gatsby* again instructs. Tom and Daisy Buchanan live in a Georgian colonial mansion representing *established* wealth. Gatsby, not unlike the robber barons at the turn of the century, has purchased a pretentious, vulgar imitation of a European mansion in East Egg. Even Gatsby's ivy is nouveau and certainly not in the same league as the Buchanans'. The establishment sees clearly that Gatsby, having no sense of tradition, simply copies the style of others, much as an American university will pattern its library on a medieval Gothic chapel. Worse, Gatsby's sartorial choice, a caramel-colored suit, is as vulgar and nouveau as his gaudy, cream-colored car, his mansion, and his lavish parties.

Daisy could never leave Tom for Gatsby because she and Tom are partners in a "secret society" of wealth, one that Gatsby cannot recognize, much less join. Daisy cannot leave the trappings of the old aristocracy. Tom, having originally "bought" Daisy with the gift of a $350,000 necklace, deploys barbaric brutality to keep her—even at the far greater cost to Gatsby of his (American) dreams and his life. Though Gatsby does not know it, no matter how great his acquisitive spirits as a bootlegger, the acquisition of Daisy is taboo.

Members of the upper middle class or even middle middle class who want to emulate the rich leisure class must do so by buying cheap imitations or by borrowing, even at the risk of bankruptcy or worse, which has been called the "Gatsby effect."[15] The Gatsby effect, of course, intimates disasters beyond bankruptcy from which recovery *is* possible. After all, Jay Gatsby died for the sins of his own emulation, a conspicuous waste.

Before Fitzgerald, only Veblen seems to have captured this cultural richness and the culture of the rich with just the proper subtle balance, mixing satire, irony, and realism to expose the false values and social waste of the upper classes. At the center of the American dream as well as Gatsby's own is the belief that sufficient wealth can recapture and fix everything, even the ephemeral, illusory qualities of youth and beauty. It was the same kind of "beauty" satirized by Veblen. The values and the waste spread downward through all the social classes.

In *Gatsby,* both new wealth (Jay Gatsby's) and old wealth (Daisy's) lead to human failings, though the failings are manifested differently. Early in the novel, Jay Gatsby is observed in the attitude of a worshiper, alone, stretching his arms toward a single, faraway green light at the end of Daisy's dock across the water—the visible symbol of his aspirations. Green is the color of promise, of hope, and renewal, and, of course, of money. For Gatsby, ideals are wrapped up with wealth, and so the means corrupt the ends. But it turns out that Daisy Buchanan is unworthy of his vision of her, and her "vulgar, meretricious beauty," her pretentiousness, is a snare. Gatsby dies disillusioned while Daisy lives on, oblivious. So much for Gatsby-like hope, and so much for the shallow end of the American Dream.

✧   ✧   ✧

The Theory of the Leisure Class was a scholarly yet satirical protest against the false values and social waste of the upper classes during the Gilded Age. *The Great Gatsby* was the exemplary novel of the Jazz Age in which Fitzgerald's sharp social sense enabled him to vividly depict the excesses and false values of the upper class at a time when gin was the national drink and sex the national obsession. The two works share not only a set of themes and a moral stance, they also exhibit many of the same writing qualities—humor, satire, teasing, exaggeration, poetic imagery, symbolism, allegory, and folklore. Nevertheless, the parallels might be dismissed as coincidental, were it not for evidence directly and indirectly linking the two writers.

Fitzgerald's description of an East Egg type of society first appeared not in *Gatsby,* but in a March 30, 1924, syndicated article originally titled "Our Irresponsible Rich." Although Fitzgerald does not refer to Veblen within the article, his Ledger notes relating to it make clear that he was consciously documenting Veblen's theme of conspicuous consumption and waste. It was in May of the same year that Fitzgerald, with three chapters of *Gatsby* in manuscript and Zelda in hand, abandoned Long Island's lavish parties and escaped to the more sedate Riviera, where he completed the draft. It is thus plausible to assume that the Veblenian sentiments explored in the article were much on Fitzgerald's mind as he wrote and rewrote the novel.

One paragraph of the syndicated article is especially revealing. In it Fitzgerald writes:

> Here we come to something that sets the American "leisure class" off from the leisure class of all other nations—and makes it probably the most shallow, most hollow, most pernicious leisure class in the world.[16]

Fitzgerald continues in high Veblenian style:

> At no period in the world's history, perhaps, has a larger proportion of the family income been spent upon display....

And the waste goes on:

> All that leisure—for nothing! All that wealth—it has begotten waste and destruction and dissipation and snobbery—nothing more.... He [the young man of inherited wealth] stocks his cellar with liquor and then votes righteously for prohibition "for the good of the masses."

Fitzgerald even appears to update Veblen's view of rich, oppressed women.

> The boy watches his mother's almost insane striving toward a social position commensurate with her money. He sees her change her accent, her clothes, her friends, her very soul, as she pushes her way up in life, pulling her busy husband with her.

Overall, Fitzgerald's theme is that the American upper class had no sense of stewardship of society so that corruption, such as the Teapot Dome scandal (then afflicting the Harding administration), was to be expected, given the premises of the American Dream associating money with success. The status of the upper class is at once gracious in its advantages and privileges but unworthy of aspiration and vision in its callous treatment of those below. The inherited rich are families in decay.

An earlier direct reference to Veblen appears in a paragraph intended for a published review of a 1921 book by H. L. Mencken. "It seems cruel," writes Fitzgerald, "that the privilege [of reviewing Mencken] could not have gone to Thorstein Veblen."[17] The paragraph, deleted by a party unknown, was apparently a typical Fitzgerald joke, since Mencken had earlier published an assault on Veblen's critique of capitalism as a "wraith of balderdash."[18] In this early instance, Fitzgerald reveals no affinity for Veblen that he might or might not have had, and was simply "needling" his friend Mencken.

While Fitzgerald often refers to Karl Marx's *Das Kapital* and other Socialist writers such as Upton Sinclair, none of his *published* writings cite or even mention Veblen. And when Fitzgerald designed "courses" for the education of Sheilah Graham, he did not list any of Veblen's books, though he included Marx.[19] Nonetheless, the class distinctions made in *The Great Gatsby* are clearly Veblenian, *not* Marxist. We can only speculate about the motives for Fitzgerald's failure to fully acknowledge his debt to Veblen at the time. It may have been simply a matter of ego. Though he was generous in attributions, Fitzgerald prided himself in his originality. The parallels between his depiction of class—especially in *The Great Gatsby*—and Veblen's sharpest satire may have been too close for comfort, providing a motive for distancing himself from Veblen. Alternatively, Veblen's influence may have been more subliminal by the time Fitzgerald wrote *Gatsby*.

Other evidence of the Veblen-Fitzgerald-Gatsby connection may be lost to history. Fitzgerald had no secretary until 1932; thereafter, he retained carbon copies of his correspondence. Out of a total of 6,000 known letters, an estimated 3,000 were written prior to 1932, Fitzgerald's precarbon age.[20] Thus, much of the missing correspondence covers the *Gatsby* period. We may never know the full extent of Fitzgerald's debt to Veblen. Undisputedly, however, he was very much under Veblen's influence. Much later, as we will relate, Fitzgerald names *The Theory of the Leisure Class* as one of his favorite books and explains why.

✧ ✧ ✧

The indirect evidence of the Veblen connection is made in Nick Carraway's living room and is equally compelling. When we think of Fitzgerald, we normally do not think of textbooks. However, Fitzgerald makes an unnoted and seemingly casual reference to an economics textbook in a climactic scene in *The Great Gatsby,* one of Scott's favorite scenes in the novel. The reference signifies not only Fitzgerald's critical view of the social effects of wealth, but the textbook's content neatly encapsulates Scott's affinity with Veblen.

Jay Gatsby is in Carraway's living room nervously waiting to meet with his lost love, Daisy Buchanan, for the first time since their romance ended five years earlier. Gatsby has grown enormously wealthy and anticipates that his newly found wealth will remove the barrier that apparently caused their separation. Gatsby "looked with vacant eyes through a copy of Clay's *Economics*" during that interval.[21]

It might be supposed that Clay's text, being a part of Nick's library, simply reflects the narrator's preparation for his job as a bond dealer in a Wall Street investment bank. Perhaps that is how the book got there, but its themes critical of the capitalist system and conventional notions of wealth run counter to instruction in financial markets, and Fitzgerald clearly understood the differences. The connection between Gatsby and Clay's text in a scene already ripe with symbolism (for example, Gatsby's attempt to reset the clock, which falls from the mantelpiece with Daisy in the room) and the fact that throughout *The Great Gatsby* Fitzgerald repeatedly provides contextual depth from assorted cultural nuances, suggests other reasons why the author wants Gatsby and Clay's *Economics* in the same room at the same time.

Henry Clay's *Economics: An Introduction To the General Reader,* first published in the United States in 1919, was a popular textbook aimed at a general audience. Edmund Wilson probably introduced Scott to Clay's text, but it is clear that Scott, unlike Gatsby, understood and appreciated the text's criticisms of conventional notions of the relationship between wealth and well-being.[22] In various reviews, Clay's text was commended for its lucid portrayal of the institutional foundations of capitalism and broad inquiry into the nature of wealth.[23] Like all good textbooks, it drew upon the ideas of influential economic thinkers, including Veblen, whose critique of the lopsided wealth evolving under capitalism instructs many parts of Clay's text.[24]

Wilson may have alerted Fitzgerald to Clay's text, but Scott expertly sculpted those ideas into art. Clay states that the real measure of wealth was not money or material product, but its capacity to "satisfy human want and desire" and elevate human welfare.[25] In his naive belief that material wealth will bring forth happiness, Gatsby is blind to the many messages to the contrary contained in Veblen and restated in Clay's *Economics*. Gatsby's "vacant stare" into Clay's text is ironic because Gatsby has made the *elementary* error of confusing money with satisfaction of wants as the real basis of wealth. The purchases and possessions allowed for by his immense fortune, however, do not yet include Daisy, his true desire. Clay, Veblen, and Fitzgerald all intimately understood that satisfaction depends on the ability of possessions to fulfill our expectations, a situation relatable to Gatsby in the "vacant stare" because his unhappiness (past, immediate, and prefigured) is related to the gap between what he has in material wealth and what he hopes for but lacks (Daisy's true love and commitment). Directly referring to Veblen's pecuniary emulation, Clay observes, "the riches of the rich intensify the poverty of the poor."[26]

Clay also criticized the conventional connection made between wealth and human welfare by noting the vulgar and dangerous uses of wealth (Gatsby's motorcar and Daisy's recklessness come to mind) as well as immoral means of acquiring or promoting it (bootlegging). Both Veblen and Clay would contend that advertising and other marketing strategies could manipulate and distort consumer choices, once again driving a wedge between wealth and welfare, image and reality:

> Advertising is only one method of inducing purchasers to buy, when on purely rational grounds they would not buy; the employment of travelers, expenditure on surface finish

and fancy wrappings, the constant introduction of novelties that have absolutely nothing but their novelty to recommend them are all examples of the great waste of productive capacity which the irrationality of purchasers invites.[27]

The most famous depiction of advertising in Fitzgerald's fiction is the aforementioned billboard in *The Great Gatsby* displaying Dr. Eckleburg's blind gaze behind huge spectacles on a featureless face. The blind gaze of Dr. Eckleburg trumps the vacant gaze of Gatsby. The authority of Dr. Eckleburg over the life of New York City commuters symbolizes a spiritually void economy at the same time it reflects Veblen's and Clay's concerns about advertising being empty, wasteful, and deceptive. Fitzgerald, in fact, had written the novel's cover into the novel. Indeed, the Dr. Eckleburg ad reminds us of various illusions and misplaced devotions in *The Great Gatsby:* middle-class people committed to an insubstantial shell of materialistic values; Gatsby's tragic devotion to Daisy; and, finally, the billboard image ineluctably gives a hollow ring to Nick's final endorsement of Gatsby who, in appealing to as many people as possible with grand displays and half truths, partly functions like an advertisement in the novel.

Those who could not afford the reality could appreciate the illusion, even as it led to waste. If the function of advertising is to create wants that would not otherwise exist, if it promotes appearance over substance, and if it raises expectations at the cost of introducing a continual sense of lacking, then the wealth of a nation is in large measure a fabrication and not truly indicative of human welfare. In addition, if goods and services are being produced for the sake of change, then a consumer addiction to novelty does not elevate human satisfaction but instead holds human identity in a perpetual state of suspension. If so, in its energy, motion, and indifference to human welfare, the economic laws of capitalism resemble the amoral laws of motion governing physical matter whose entropic tendencies mirror the wastes of capitalism depicted in Scott's fiction.

Fitzgerald's fiction (before and after *The Great Gatsby*) questions the moral foundations of wealth and laissez-faire capitalism.

Scott's theme of wealth's interference with equal opportunity even predates and anticipates Clay: It enters into Amory Blaine's idealistic defense of socialism at the conclusion of *This Side of Paradise* (1920). But, of course, Fitzgerald's critique of American capitalism began as early as "May Day" (1920), wherein Fitzgerald exposes the myth of equal opportunity in both the American economy and the polity. In "The Diamond as Big as the Ritz" (June 1922), Fitzgerald again examines the barriers and destructive effects created by wealth and privilege.

The reader is easily seduced by the fantastic aura of wealth created by Fitzgerald in the story and thus becomes part of what the "Ritz" story represents: a satire about wealth and those who worship it. Fitzgerald dispels the myth that wealth is a product of hard work, reflecting something of social, moral, and spiritual value; instead, it is portrayed as a product of Algerian luck, privileged access, inheritance, deception, brute force, and manipulation. Wealth not only lacks a moral foundation, breeding deception among its possessors and pursuers, but also is itself portrayed as an illusory artifact. In the end, the wealthy are imprisoned and destroyed by their riches as much as their middle-class devotees.

"The Diamond as Big as the Ritz" is, of course, a mountainous fantasy about wealth. Fantasies are forms of speculation. It is Dexter Green in "Winter Dreams" (December 1922) telling Judy Jones that his "career is a matter of futures": It is Judy Jones sealing Dexter's fate with a kiss promising everything except fulfillment. By the turn of the century, however, American economists had already begun investigating the fantastic character of wealth, both the power it held over people's imaginations as well as its speculative nature.

Veblen writes of how wealth as business capital depends upon credit and the "presumptive future earning capacity" of both tangible and intangible forms of capital. The energies of modern business enterprise had shifted toward trade in speculative capital and advertising of product rather than in improved products for consumers. Veblen had warned of the manipulations and deceptions of financial traders and advertisers as well as the emergence of powerful new financiers whose "trust-making" deals often generated immense profits for themselves while creating instability and economic losses for a network of producers and consumers.

Fitzgerald openly returns to the moral issues of capitalism a decade later in "Six of One"—(1932), a short story in which six disadvantaged boys outperform their six wealthy counterparts when a patron, Mr. Barnes, provides them access to the same educational opportunities. In particular, "Six of One" satirizes the Social Darwinist belief that wealth is a sign of innate "fitness" or superiority, an attitude that was increasingly difficult for the rich to sustain during the massive economic tumble that followed the 1929 stock market crash. In Fitzgerald's story, the progeny of wealth are initially portrayed as "statuesque beings" in a supposedly "Periclean age," each son proclaimed to be a "natural leader" by his father. However, the skeptical Barnes deflates that image of the boys to an "ornamental bunch" who look like "cigarette ads in the magazine" and, throughout the remainder of the story, Fitzgerald further tarnishes their heroic luster.[28]

✧　✧　✧

The roar of the twenties ended in a whimper. Beginning with the 1929 stock market crash, the promise of an ever-expanding American economy proved to be equally illusory. Explanations of the business cycle circulating during the twenties typically contained the idea that peoples' changing expectations contributed to economic fluctuations, often accentuated by procyclical credit policies of the banking system.[29] Fitzgerald was aware of how psychological factors and credit could affect the economy. Referring to the twenties as "the most expensive orgy in history," Fitzgerald explained the crash this way:

> It [the orgy] ended two years ago [1929], because the utter confidence which was its essential prop received an enormous jolt, and it didn't take long for the flimsy structure to settle earthward. It was borrowed time anyhow—the whole upper tenth living the insouciance of grand dukes and the casualness of chorus girls.[30]

We should not be surprised; the interaction between economic expectations and performance is a common theme in Fitzgerald's fiction.[31] At the same time, Fitzgerald considered the lopsided income and wealth distributions as contributors to the crash and to the Great Depression. Veblen could not have written the Jazz Age denouement so well.

In part because of his artistry, the subtlety and sophistication of Fitzgerald's economic thought is easily overlooked, perhaps the cost of his being an entertaining writer. Scott's reference to Clay's *Economics* in *The Great Gatsby,* for example, appears casual and insignificant. However, Fitzgerald literally incorporated its central messages about the moral limitations of wealth and laissez-faire capitalism into his novel for ironic effect. Beyond this, the criticisms of wealth and capitalism contained in Fitzgerald's fiction closely parallel Veblen and Clay's concerns, possibly suggesting that Clay's textbook exerted an important formative influence on Fitzgerald's economic thought, or at least reinforced Fitzgerald's skepticism of the morality of capitalism, which he derived from more famous (and radical) economic writers such as Marx and Veblen.

✧ ✧ ✧

What, then, was the immediate financial destiny of *The Great Gatsby*? Scott knew at once that there was something wonderful and extraordinary about *Gatsby*. It was, he was certain, his best work to date. Fitzgerald told Perkins that the novel would sell 75,000 or 80,000 copies. If so, the royalties would free Scott to spend his full time writing novels, and his bondage to the mass-market *Post* would end. By October 1925, however, *Gatsby* had sold only about 20,000 copies, about half as many as each of Fitzgerald's earlier novels. The royalties were barely enough to repay Scott's advances. In contrast, Fitzgerald's next short story, "The Rich Boy," was sold to *Redbook* early in 1926 for $2,500, more than half the total royalties for *Gatsby* earned that year. Thereafter, Scott returned to writing short stories.

In the meantime, there were other sources of income from *Gatsby*. Film rights to *Gatsby* were sold to Famous Players for about $50,000, out of which Fitzgerald's payment was $13,500. Playwright Owen Davis did a Broadway stage version of *Gatsby* for producer William A. Brady. The play opened at the Ambassador Theatre on Broadway on February 2, 1926. The play was well reviewed and financially successful. Before going on the road, it ran for 112 performances in New York. Scott's share of box office receipts was $7,630, enough to keep him liquid in every sense during 1926. The Fitzgeralds remained in Paris and did not see the play.

Fitzgerald now had enough income to write his next novel without resorting to magazine stories. It was an opportunity that he would never again have. By now, however, Scott's life with Zelda was conflicting sharply with his professional ambitions. As he writes to Scottie in 1938, "She wanted me to work too much for *her* and not enough for my dream."[32] During the next months Fitzgerald was back writing stories for quick bucks. This despite a record total income of $25,686.05 in 1926, or about $282,547 in today's dollars, including book royalties of $2,033.20, the $19,464.21 from the film and play, and the sale of only two short stories for $3,375. Although he would begin to construct what would become his fourth novel, *Tender Is the Night,* it not only would be a long time coming, it would be his most biographical novel, and a work that would lead to heightened tensions in his marriage.

Before that, however, in Paris, Zelda's mind was losing its thin tether to reality. At the same time that Zelda was challenging Scott's masculinity with an affair in the south of France, Ernest Hemingway's looming presence would raise new kinds of searing insecurities in Scott's mind.

Endnotes

1. F. Scott Fitzgerald, "Dice, Brassknuckles & Guitar" (1923), in *The Short Stories of F. Scott Fitzgerald*, ed. Matthew J. Bruccoli (New York and London: Scribner, 1989), p. 252.

2. See Mitchell Breitwieser, "Jazz Fractures: F. Scott Fitzgerald and Epochal Representation," *American Literary History*, fall 2000 12(3), p. 370.

3. Ibid., pp. 368–69.

4. Walter Benjamin, "The Work of Art in the Age of Mechanical Reproduction" in Meenakshi Gigi Durham and Douglas M. Kellnes, eds., *Media and Cultural Studies: Key Works* (Malden, Mass.: Blackwell Publishers, 2001), p. 51.

5. The original time and locale in "the Midwest and New York City" are characterized in a letter to Max Perkins, Fitzgerald's long-time editor. The letter is reprinted in Jackson Bryer and John Kuehl, eds., *Dear Scott/Dear Max* (New York: Scribner's, 1971), p. 61.

6. Previous work on Fitzgerald's social and economic thought has emphasized its Marxist-Socialist dimensions rather than the influence of Veblen. As examples, see Richard Greenleaf, "The Social Thinking of F. Scott Fitzgerald," *Science and Society* 16 (1953): 97–114; Malcolm Cowley, "F. Scott Fitzgerald: The Romance of Money," *Western Review,* 17 (no. 4), (1953): 245–55.

7. William Graham Sumner, *The Challenge of Facts and Other Essays*, ed. Albert Galoway Keller (New Haven, Conn.: Yale University Press, 1914), pp. 90, 57.

8. Thorstein Veblen, *The Theory of the Leisure Class* (New York and London: Penguin Books, 1994, [1899]), especially chapter 9.

9. The quotations are from Veblen, *The Theory of The Leisure Class,,* pp. 111–12, 167, and 171, respectively.

10. Ibid., p. 169.

11. For a full explication of anthropological influences on Veblen, see Anne Mayhew, "Veblen and the Anthropological Perspective," in *The Founding of Institutional Economics: The Leisure Class and Sovereignty*, ed. Warren J. Samuels (London: Routledge, 1998), 234–49. For more details on Veblen, Darwin, and biology, see Rick Tilman, *The Intellectual Legacy of Thorstein Veblen: Unresolved Issues* (Westport, Conn. and London: Greenwood Press, 1996), 47–71. For a broad yet deep intellectual survey of the Veblenian themes common to Fitzgerald and other American novelists, see John Patrick Diggins, *Thorstein Veblen: Theorist of the Leisure Class* (Princeton N.J.: Princeton University Press, 1999). For a readable but complete overview of Veblen's ideas, see E. Ray Canterbery, *A Brief History of Economics* (New Jersey, London, Singapore: World Scientific, 2001). For an intellectual treat and harmless fun, read Veblen, the orginal.

12. Veblen, *Theory and the Leisure Class*, p. 154.

13. F. Scott Fitzgerald, *The Great Gatsby* (New York: Charles Scribner's Sons, 1925), p. 93.

14. The apparel immersion scene appears in Frank Norris, *McTeague* (Greenwich, Conn.: Fawcett Publications, 1960, [1899]), pp. 60–61. We recall that Frank Norris was one of Scott's favorite naturalist writers.

15. E. Ray Canterbery, "The Theory of the Leisure Class and the Theory of Demand," in *The Founding of Institutional Economics: The Leisure Class and Sovereignty*, ed. Warren J. Samuels (London: Routledge, 1998), pp. 142–46.

16. F. Scott Fitzgerald, "What Kind of Husbands Do 'Jimmies' Make?" (also titled elsewhere, "Our Irresponsible Rich"), *Baltimore American,* March 30, 1924, p. 7.

17. Matthew J. Bruccoli and Margaret M. Duggan, *Correspondence of F. Scott Fitzgerald* (New York: Random House, 1980), p. 75.

18. H. L. Mencken, *A Mencken Chrestomathy*, ed. H. L. Mencken (New York: Knopf, 1949), p. 273.

19. Sheilah Graham, *College of One* (New York: Viking Press, 1967), p. 213.

20. Bruccoli and Duggan, *Correspondence*, p. xv.

21. Fitzgerald, *The Great Gatsby,* p. 56.

22. Economist Ray Fair plausibly concludes that Wilson was Fitzgerald's source for Clay's text. See Ray C. Fair, "The Great Gatsby: Yale, Princeton, Columbia, Harvard, Oxford," *Eastern Economic Journal* 29, no. 2 (spring 2003): p. 162.

23. Harvey Wooster, book review, *American Economic Review* 9 (1919), p. 538, reviews Clay's text. Joseph Dorfman, a renowned institutionalist and follower of Veblen, provides more background on Clay's published work and career in Joseph Dorfman, *The Economic Mind in American Civilization*, vol. 4, 1918–33 (New York: Viking Press, 1959), pp. 175, 179, 269.

24. Henry Clay had a considerable reputation as a distinguished British economist, whose career included posts at the University of Manchester, Oxford University, and the Bank of England. An indication of Clay's stature and international reputation is his presence as the keynote speaker at a twenty-fifth anniversary conference sponsored by the Wharton School on "The Conditions of Industrial Progress," which included Wesley Mitchell, John Maurice Clark, and other leading economists as presenters. Mitchell and Clark were members of the American institutionalist school, whose founder is Veblen. It is through his widely reviewed textbook, however, that Clay gained recognition with the general public and, in turn, touched Fitzgerald.

25. Henry Clay, *Economics: An Introduction To the General Reader* (New York: Macmillan, 1918), p. 215.

26. Ibid., pp. 402–3.

27. Ibid., p. 372.

28. Fitzgerald, "Six of One' " in *The Short Stories of F. Scott Fitzgerald*, ed. Mathew Bruccoli (New York: Charles Scribners Sons, 1989 [1932]), pp. 677, 668.

29. For a survey of business cycle theories during the 1920s, see W. C. Mitchell, *Business Cycles* (New York: Arno Press, 1975 [1927 edition]).

30. Fitzgerald, "Echoes of the Jazz Age," in *The Crack-Up* (New York: Charles Scribner's Sons, 1957), p. 18.

31. Another example is provided in the little-known "Bridal Party" (1930), a short story set amid the progressive weakening of the stock market, in which the relationship between psychology and economics complexly relates to the broader economic concerns of the day.

32. Andrew Turnbull, ed., *The Letters of F. Scott Fitzgerald* (London: Penguin Books, 1968), p. 47.

Eight

Slipping Out of the
City of Light

THE FITZGERALDS HAD ENTERED THE WORLD OF AMERICAN EXPATRIATES IN
Paris. They saw their friends, visited literary salons, sat in cafés, drank
in bars, and ate in the best restaurants. They frequented Left Bank
cafés such as the Dôme, the Coupole, Lipp's, the Deux Magots, and
the Closerie des Lilas as well as the cabarets of Montmartre. They
were also regulars at Bricktop's, Zelli's, and le Perroquet. Bricktop's
was a nightclub presided over by an American negro singer, who
took protective custody over Fitzgerald's money when he flashed
a large roll of it. Fitzgerald also drank at the Ritz and Crillon bars,
often patronized by wealthy Americans. He lunched at Ciro's, la
Reine Pédauque, and Foyot, and sometimes dined at the Trianon on
the Left Bank, James Joyce's favorite restaurant. Fitzgerald tipped
generously, and more than in proportion to the amounts he drank.

The Fitzgeralds not only escaped the moral and intellectual
confinement of American society, they escaped Prohibition. They
could live inexpensively by their bewildering standards and create
their own celebrated social roles. In time, nonetheless, freedom in
the city deepened their differences. Zelda became more insecure and
Scott continued to drink excessively. He spent his time at parties,

dances, and those nightclubs instead of focusing on his profession. Meanwhile, a new friendship—with Ernest Hemingway—deepened the Fitzgeralds' personal difficulties even as it helped shape Scott's art and his recognition that he was on the road to ruin.

Edmund Wilson had told Fitzgerald about Hemingway. Scott already had become an admirer when he and Ernest first met in Paris's Dingo Bar in early May 1925, only two weeks after publication of *The Great Gatsby* and six months before Hemingway's trade edition of *In Our Time*. Hemingway was little known and writing for the little magazines; Scott was writing for 3 million *Saturday Evening Post* readers for a lot of money and was three successful novels older. In contrast to both Wilson and Hemingway, the Fitzgeralds were famous.

In literature, the "City of Light" will always be remembered as the Paris where Hemingway and Fitzgerald first met. The warmth of their friendship would be sustained until springtime 1929, just before the stock market boom was to noticeably cool. Between the beginning and end of that solidarity, and during the Fitzgeralds' early friendship with the storied Sara and Gerald Murphy in Paris and on the Riviera, Zelda's slipping grasp on reality was becoming visible. All this was about to begin at a time when Fitzgerald's reputation was peaking.

✧ ✧ ✧

After publication of *The Great Gatsby* (1925), Fitzgerald was at the pinnacle of his professional career and had earned considerable respect among his peers. Edwin Clark, in his review in the *New York Times,* writes that it is a "curious book, a mystical, glamourous story of today. It takes a deeper cut at life than hitherto has been enjoyed by Mr. Fitzgerald. He writes well—he always has—for he writes naturally, and his sense of form is becoming perfected." Although there was no consensus that *The Great Gatsby* was "the best American novel ever written" as Fitzgerald boasted to his editor Maxwell Perkins in a letter on August 27, 1924, no less of an authority than T. S. Eliot writes, "It seems to me to be the first step that

American fiction has taken since Henry James...."[1] John Dos Passos, who also was influenced by Veblen, writes more broadly of Scott's talent: "When he talked about writing his mind... became clear and hard as a diamond...he was a born professional. Everything he said was worth listening to."[2]

Ernest Hemingway had not considered Fitzgerald a serious artist and described Fitzgerald's pattern of revising his short stories for commercial sales as "whoring," a phrase first and often used by Fitzgerald himself, but *The Great Gatsby* earned Hemingway's initial respect and eventual envy. Hemingway's remembrance: "To hear him [Fitzgerald] talk of it, you would never know how very good it was, except that he had the shyness about it that all non-conceited writers have when they have done something very fine...."[3] Fitzgerald's self-effacement contrasted with Hemingway's macho swagger.

Fitzgerald was in many ways Hemingway's most important mentor. A ten-page letter from Scott to Ernest written in May 1926 recommending substantial revisions in style and organization of *The Sun Also Rises* (1926) had a significant effect on the reworking of the beginning of the novel. Fitzgerald also made numerous suggestions for revisions to *A Farewell To Arms* (1929), which were taken seriously by Hemingway. During this time in the mid to late twenties, Fitzgerald also gave Hemingway substantive literary and professional guidance on at least one of his short stories, "Fifty Grand," eventually published in 1927 in a revision along the lines originally suggested by Fitzgerald in late 1925.

Prior to leaving for Europe in mid-April 1924, Fitzgerald had been an influential adviser to Maxwell Perkins, alerting him to promising young writers in the United States, most notably Ring Lardner and Thomas Boyd. Upon arriving for the second time in Europe with the intent (amusing as it may seem) of leading a slower-paced life, Fitzgerald could not resist taking on the unofficial role of colonialist for Scribners, initially encouraging Perkins to sign up the redoubtable Gertrude Stein, among others. For some authors this is a natural instinct. Fitzgerald, exposed to Hemingway's work in early 1924 by the looming presence of Edmund Wilson, sent a letter of endorsement to Perkins in October, enthusiastically promoting Hemingway six months before ever meeting him, making the endorsement even more objective.

After initiating the contact with Scribners, Fitzgerald then deftly guided Hemingway's novel toward publication with Perkins. In the "campaign" to get Hemingway published with Scribners (and released from his contract with his original publisher, Liveright), Fitzgerald has been described as being "commissioned" by Hemingway "to serve as his lieutenant in making the change."[4] Such an assessment, however, obscures Fitzgerald's central guiding role in the whole affair. It was Scott who first "discovered" Hemingway and recommended him to Perkins, thereby setting the stage for Hemingway's beneficial shift to Scribners. Then, throughout 1925, Fitzgerald continued to privately correspond with Perkins and tout Hemingway's work while, separately, advising Hemingway on literary and professional matters.

Fitzgerald was commander in charge and not subservient to Hemingway during this period. After all, the correspondence with Perkins was confidential—there was *no* reporting back to Hemingway. Thereafter, in January 1926, Perkins sent a cable to Fitzgerald (*not* to Hemingway) committing Scribners to publish both *The Torrents of Spring* (a novel rejected by Liveright, which released Hemingway from his contract with them) and *The Sun Also Rises,* relying almost exclusively on Scott's judgment of Hemingway's potential since at this point Perkins had seen neither novel. Hemingway subsequently signed with Scribners following a personal meeting with Perkins in New York City in February 1926. The often-mentioned claim that Scott's underlying motive for undertaking to launch Hemingway's career was a desire to be loved by his superiors (that old black magic, hero-worship) is not credible since Perkins and he always treated each other as equals and Hemingway was still a novice. Perkins ultimately became Hemingway's editor in much the same sense that he was Fitzgerald's editor.

Besides Fitzgerald's influence as a professional boaster of Hemingway's work, by all accounts (except later alternations by Hemingway), their early friendship was deep, meaningful, and mutual. Mutual friends Gerald and Sara Murphy have told much of that story.

During the several days that they spent in Paris in May 1924, Scott and Zelda met the Murphys. Fair, tall, slender, and elegant, the still handsome Gerald had been Skull and Bones at Yale; graduated, he hated the idea of going into his father's prosperous New York leather goods store. Sara, older, was a beautiful heiress from Ohio. Both lived in Paris on private incomes from their families. By the time that he had met the Fitzgeralds, Gerald had decided that he wanted to become a painter. More exactly, taking as their motto the old Spanish adage "Living well is the best revenge," the Murphys sought, cultivated, collected, and entertained artists living in Paris and soon came to know not only Picasso, Miró, and Juan Gris, but also other kinds of artists such as Stravinsky, Léon Bakst, and Braque. Gerald and Sara were already close friends of John Dos Passos, Archibald MacLeish, and a then unknown young writer, Ernest Hemingway. Paris was at its artistic peak and everyone, including the artists, seemed very young.

The Murphys had discovered the off-season Riviera through American composer and lyricist Cole Porter (1893–1964), a friend from Yale (who—like Scott at Princeton—never graduated). The Murphys liked the Riviera's gardens and proximity to the sea and began to build a villa at Antibes. After they told Scott and Zelda of the attractions there, the Fitzgeralds went to the south of France at the end of May. By June they came to St. Raphaël: Scott famously wrote about the gay red-roofed houses and the air of carnival. Thereafter, forgetting their pledge to economize, they rented the spacious Villa Marie—high above the sea, surrounded by lemon, palm, pine, and silver olive trees, with a winding gravel drive up to its entrance and its Moorish balconies of white-and-blue tiles. It was an exotic fortress facing the Mediterranean.

The Murphys especially liked the highly individualistic and beautiful Zelda. Otherwise, at times it is unlikely that the sophisticated expatriates would have put up with Scott alone. But, even for Scott, the summer began well. He was writing every day. They had household help and a nanny for Scottie. Zelda at age twenty-three, almost twenty-four, had little to do but swim and sun on the beach. They soon met some French aviators stationed nearby with whom they drank and danced at night in the casino behind the *plage*. With

Scott intensely preoccupied with *The Great Gatsby* manuscript, Zelda decided to fly solo.

✧ ✧ ✧

The solo "flight" was with at least one of the young aviators, Edouard Jozan (b. 1899). They began to meet in the afternoons to swim together, lie on canvas beach mats in the sun, and invent new cocktails. Jozan, like Scott, was handsome. Unlike Scott, he was tall, deeply tanned, and had dark, curly hair. Unlike Scott, he also enjoyed taking physical risks—more like Zelda. He looked like the leader he would become as a vice admiral in the French navy (1952), having an air of assurance lacking in Scott. He greatly resembled the dashing young aviators from Montgomery who earlier had wooed

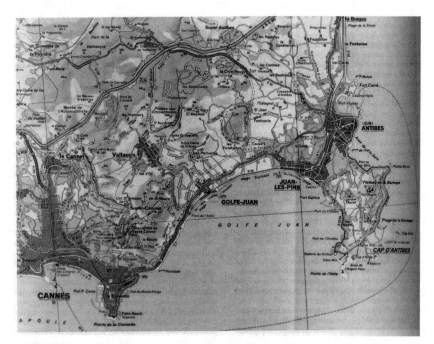

The Riviera. The Fitzgeralds migrated among the coastal towns and cities highlighted on this map.

Zelda. Edouard, too, did stunts with his airplane above Villa Marie, dropping his plane's wings dangerously close to the Villa's red-tiled roof. We are inclined to believe that he performed the stunts at Zelda's urging. Scott, too, admired these characteristics in the young pilot.

Zelda fell hard for Jozan: The young aviator was not romantically serious, looking mostly for a summer fling before being transferred elsewhere. To Zelda the relationship was more than physical; it was deeply emotional. Her attraction with this aviator was much greater than with those who had stunted over her house in Montgomery. Scott, quite accustomed to men falling in love with his wife, had not expected such heated reciprocity. Once Scott understood what was going on, he put an end to it in typical Fitzgerald fashion. He insisted that Zelda not leave the Villa Marie. Zelda and Jozan were no longer on the beach together, and Scott wrote in his Ledger: "The Big Crisis Over—13th of July.... Zelda swimming everyday." Despite Scott's optimism about the pair, the romance between Scott and Zelda would never again regain its former intensity. Parts of the marriage had been irreparably broken.

In early August, Gilbert Seldes and his bride arrived at Villa Marie to spend a few days of their honeymoon. Seldes noted no obvious disharmony in the couple. He did, however, remember the trips he and his wife made down to the beach with the Fitzgeralds, on a road that had been built originally for carriages. On each trip down they came to one particular point that was dangerously narrow and curved. Every time, precisely at that curve, Zelda would turn to Scott, the driver, and say, "Give me a cigarette, Goofo."[5] During the moments of fearful silence, Scott did manage to give Zelda her cigarette and negotiate the narrow turn with the barely reliable Renault. For the Seldes it

Admiral Edouard Jozan in 1957

was harrowing, and they both thought it strange that Zelda made the same request every time at the same turn of the narrow road.

Soon there would be another crisis. Early in September, Zelda attempted suicide by taking an overdose of sleeping pills. Sara said that Scott came to the Murphys early one morning. "He was green-faced, holding a candle, trembling—Zelda had taken an overdose of sleeping pills. We went with him, and Sara walked her up and down, up and down, to keep her from going to sleep. We tried to make her drink olive oil, but Zelda said, 'Sara,...don't make me take that, please. If you drink too much oil you turn into a Jew.' "[6] No explanation for her act was given to the Murphys, but they presumed that it was related to Jozan. This, despite Scott's Ledger notes in August—"Trouble clearing away," and then, "Last sight of Josan."[7] Years later Scott admitted to a relative that Zelda had told him that she loved Jozan and had asked Scott for a divorce. Scott might have thought that to be a truly "crazy" idea, and he was probably right.

✧   ✧   ✧

With *Gatsby* safely in the mail to Scribners by the end of October, the Fitzgeralds decided to go to Rome. For many reasons, it was a bad decision. Both were ill during the dreary winter months. Scott took an instant dislike to the Italians and began to drink heavily. Despite this, he soberly revised the *Gatsby* proofs. By the first of the year they went to Capri for warmth and, hopefully, recovery. Zelda became ill with colitis and both were anxious about her health during the year. This illness, too, probably was related to her failed love affair with Jozan. Zelda began to paint while Scott assured John Peale Bishop: "Zelda and I sometimes indulge in terrible four-day rows that always start with a drinking party but we're still enormously in love and about the only truly happily married people I know."[8] He meant it, and it appears retrospectively, he was correct about the enduring love.

In April, Scott and Zelda drove their rapidly depreciating Renault back to southern France. The top of the car had been damaged and Zelda insisted it be removed. The car broke down in Lyon, where they abandoned it for a train to Paris. Though, as Scott put it, that spring was made up of "1000 parties and no work," they did finally meet Ernest Hemingway, the writer that Fitzgerald had heavily promoted sight unseen. Soon they were best of friends.

Scott and Ernest's trip to and from Lyon is now legendary. Scott took Hemingway along to pick up the abandoned Renault. At the time both writers had wonderful things to say about each other; they apparently had a great time drinking and talking on the two-day trip. *Gatsby*, published in April 1925, was a critical if not unqualified success, and Hemingway was curious about its author. Although *Gatsby* sold much less than Scott's expected 75,000 or 80,000 copies, Gilbert Seldes and Gertrude Stein, combined with T. S. Eliot's high praise, convinced Fitzgerald that the book was a great achievement. He and they were right.

The Zelda-Ernest relationship was quite different: They took a quick and intense dislike for each other. Ernest reportedly told Scott, "You know, Scott, she's crazy." Hemingway believed that Scott would never write another great novel if he stayed married to Zelda. As Ernest saw it, Zelda was jealous of Scott's work and was doing everything she could to keep him from writing. For her part, Zelda saw through Ernest's macho demeanor as being largely bogus. She simply did not believe that any man was as "male" as Ernest claimed to be. But Zelda was going to prove Ernest right long before his deep insecurities and dark side would be discovered.

The Fitzgeralds left Paris for Cap d'Antibes in August and joined the Murphys for dinner at a scenic inn at St.-Paul-de-Vence in the mountains above Nice. The inn's dining terrace hovered about two hundred feet above the val-

The Murphys in the 1920s

ley with a sheer drop from its outer walls. When Scott realized that Isadora Duncan, the fabled dancer, was seated at a nearby table, he immediately went to her and sat at her feet in his most excellent worshiping mode. Although she was quite heavy and past her prime, according to Gerald Murphy, "She ran her fingers through his hair and she called him her centurion."[9]

Zelda was quietly watching until she suddenly leaped atop her chair and then across both Gerald and the table into the dark stairwell behind him and just in front of the wall. Although the Murphys were certain that she was dead, Zelda reappeared within seconds and stood quite still at the top of the stone stairs. Sara wiped the blood from Zelda's knees and dress. The Murphys were greatly unnerved by such self-destructive and gratuitous violence. Besides, as Gerald was to note, the Fitzgeralds didn't want ordinary pleasures such as fine food and wine, but were straining to create some kind of action that they did not even understand or were able to control.

Despite these difficulties, the affection between the Murphys and Fitzgeralds was genuine and deep. In September, Gerald wrote to the Fitzgeralds after they had left the Riviera:

> There *really* was a great sound of tearing heard in the land as your train pulled out that day. Sara and I rode back together saying things about you both to each other which only partly expressed what we felt separately. Ultimately, I suppose, one must judge the degree of one's love for a person by the hush and the emptiness that descends upon the day,—after the departure. We heard the tearing because it was there,—and because we weren't able to talk much about how much we do love you two. We agreed that it made us very sad, and sort of hurt a little—for a "summer holiday"…you two belong so irrevocably to that rare race of people who are *valuable*. As yet in this world we have found four. One only *really* loves what is rare and valuable to one, in spite of the fact that one loves first.[10]

That same month Scott notes to himself: "Futile, shameful use-less but [for] the $30,000 rewards of 1924 work. Self disgust. Health gone."[11] That winter in Paris was little better for the Fitzgeralds. Their apartment, near the Etoile, long neglected, damp, and in ill repair, lent them little cheer. Zelda continued to take no interest in decorat-ing, preparing meals, or cleaning. Meanwhile, *Gatsby* had opened on Broadway. In early March 1926, they returned to the warmer Riviera, renting the Villa Paquita in Juan-les-Pins. A reporter for *The New Yorker* visited that year and wrote "That the Fitzgeralds are the best looking couple in modern literary society doesn't do them justice.... Scott really looks more as the undergraduate would like to look, than the way he generally does."[12] He also noted that the Riviera was quiet until the beautiful Fitzgeralds arrived. Their lifestyle and illnesses had yet to alter their enthusiasm or features.

And, they were still embraced by the literati. The Hemingways, Murphys, and the MacLeishes joined the Fitzgeralds in May. Scott generously offered the use of their villa to the Hemingways (with six months of free rent to go). Scott and Zelda took a larger place in Juan-les-Pins, the Villa St. Louis, and remained there until the end of 1926. Conveniently, a beach and a casino were only one hundred yards distant.

Suddenly that summer, Zelda's behavior became even more bizarre. Very late one evening in the casino at Juan-les-Pins with the Murphys, Zelda stood, raised her skirt above her waist, and began to dance. It was virtually a repeat performance of her Montgomery Country Club exhibition. Zelda was focused entirely on the dance: She looked neither left nor right. She looked at no one, not even Scott. She remained aloof and remote, sometimes with a strange little smile suddenly, inexplicably, crossing her face. The dances were merely exhibitions and she seemed to be having no fun. It was the same summer that Zelda was asked about Hemingway's novel *The Sun Also Rises*. It was, Zelda said, "Bullfighting, bullslinging, and bullshit."[13] Zelda was more and more jealous of Hemingway's relationship with Scott as her own ties to Scott were deteriorating.

They continued to see the Murphys, often. But there were inter-ruptions. Scott began to sense that the Murphys had greater respect for Ernest than for him. At one social event, Fitzgerald began to throw Sara Murphy's delicately blown Venetian glasses over the edge of their garden. After two (free) throws, Gerald stopped him and suggested that Scott not come back for a while.

The Murphys remained fond of Zelda but did not fully realize that her "complexity" was a part of her worsening mental illness. Her mind seemed to make different connections than most persons'. She would say whatever happened to occur to her without any intended effect. Once she asked Gerald, for no apparent reason, "Don't you think that Al Jolson is just like Christ?"[14] And, no matter how rude Scott's drunken behavior became, Zelda always remained loyal to him. As to Sara, she thought that Zelda was becoming really spooky. And, she was right.

Zelda's behavior continued to be destructive. On the rocks high above the sea there were notches cut at five feet, ten, up to thirty. It was a high dive, a dangerous dive, especially at night. One mistake in timing and the diver would be smashed on the rocks below. Zelda, stripped to her slip, would very quietly ask Scott to go for a swim. One night Scott was visibly trembling as he followed Zelda who had challenged him to a high dive. The last dive was at thirty feet: Scott made the dive after Zelda had surfaced. One slip, and they would have been killed.[15]

Another time (in 1926), after considerable drinking at the Villa St. Louis, Zelda became hysterical. A doctor arrived and gave her a shot of morphine to calm her. The episode scared both Scott and Zelda. They had good reason to be frightened: now, we know that hysteria associated with drinking alcohol is a symptom of schizophrenia. At a farewell party hosted by the Murphys for Alexander Woollcott and "Chato" Elizaga, Zelda tired of the verbal and liquid toasts, rose, and said something about "What are words?" Then she took off her black lace panties and threw them at Woollcott and Elizaga as "gifts."

✧　✧　✧

At the end of the year the Fitzgeralds returned to the United States. Although Zelda had been ill much of the past year, Scott had completed *Gatsby,* learned a great deal, and was deeply absorbed writing a new novel.

Scott had written for the movies and knew that a fortune could be made writing screenplays. Upon their return to America, Scott was offered a job by United Artists to write a screenplay for actress Constance Talmadge. Scott and Zelda had run out of money and the offer was too tempting at $16,000 (about $176,000 in today's dollars) if UA took the script and a $3,500 advance (some $38,500 in today's dollars) if it didn't. Anyone with any understanding of capitalism could see it as a win-win situation even if one loses the opportunity. The screenplay, *Lipstick,* was to be an original flapper comedy set in Princeton.

The Fitzgeralds headed to Hollywood for the first time. They stayed at the fashionable Ambassador Hotel in Los Angeles; Scott and Zelda shared a four-apartment bungalow with hard-drinking John Barrymore, author Carl Van Vechten, and an actress friend, Carmel Myers. Actor Pola Negri was a neighbor.

Scott's screenwriting on this particular visit was not as memorable as his infatuation with a young actress, Lois Moran. She was only seventeen but already a worldly movie star. Not only was Zelda bored and restless, she greatly resented Scott's intense interest in the young and beautiful actress. Lois and Scott's feelings apparently were mutual; she wanted Fitzgerald to be her leading man in a film and arranged a screen test for him just as Rosemary Hoyt would later arrange one for Dick Diver in *Tender Is the Night.* Zelda resented even more Scott's insinuation that Ms. Moran not only had done something with herself, but something requiring both talent and effort. Offended by the invidious comparison, Zelda burned (in the bathtub) all of the clothes that she had designed for herself while Scott was off dining with the young star. It was another of those odd things that Zelda had been doing.

As usual, Fitzgerald's attitude toward Lois Moran informed a *Post* story he wrote that spring called "Jacob's Ladder." Another of his *Post* stories, "Magnetism," of March 3, 1928, is about an actor much like Scott who plays opposite a young actress much like Ms. Moran. In this story about Hollywood, George Hanaford discovers that to possess a magnetic personality is to be confronted with special, ironic responsibilities. In a now familiar pattern, this same magnetism and much of the prose in this short story would reappear in *Tender Is the Night*, as Dick Diver's charm drew many into his circle. What Fitzgerald failed to achieve in reality he could always attain in his imagination.

Scott and Zelda later appeared uninvited at a costume party given for the Talmadge sisters by producer Samuel Goldwyn. The Fitzgeralds were at the front door on all fours, barking, and asked if they could come to the party. After Zelda came indoors, she went upstairs to the bathroom, slipped out of her clothes, and took a bath. The Fitzgeralds often made themselves conspicuous by their presence. Despite these distractions, Scott finished the script in eight weeks.

The *Lipstick* script is about an unjustly imprisoned girl who is given a magic lipstick that makes her so magnetic that men want to kiss her. United Artists, however, decided not to use the screenplay, and Scott and Zelda went back east. The producer, John Considine, was notorious among writers and actors for having little sense—for example, rejecting Fred Astaire as the most awful thing he had ever seen. Three years later Busby Berkeley came to Hollywood and made *Whoopee* with an idea much like Fitzgerald's. Scott luckily was able to keep the $3,500 advance, for he had already spent it.

Though not making the big money on this trip, Scott did have a memorable meeting with producer Irving Thalberg, who was then dating the flapper-in-waiting, Constance Talmadge. As a parting gesture to Tinseltown, the Fitzgeralds stacked all the furniture in the center of their Ambassador apartment with all their unpaid bills perched on top. On the trip back east, Zelda and Scott continued to quarrel about Lois Moran, who Scott had invited to visit them when they had a place.

In March 1927 they leased a mansion called Ellerslie near Wilmington, Delaware. John Biggs had discovered it for them. Friend Biggs and editor Max Perkins thought that Wilmington would be less distracting to Scott's efforts on his new novel than would the area around New York City.

As luck would have it, the Fitzgeralds soon had Lois Moran as a weekend guest, a weekend that included the day Charles Lindbergh landed at Le Bourget. Soon, too, Scott and Zelda were again throwing their wild parties and quarreling. John Dos Passos was a frequent guest. Both Scott and Zelda were drunk much of the time and were smoking heavily. Once again—this time after still another quarrel about Lois Moran—a doctor had to be called to give Zelda a morphine injection. It was another indication of deepening mental illness. The tranquility they sought remained elusive. By midsummer Zelda impulsively decided to take ballet lessons.

On one of his trips to New York that fall—most likely for a tryst with Miss Moran—Scott met with H. L. Mencken and Mencken's young assistant on the *American Mercury*. Scott got up, pacing the room, and quickly outlined his ideas for his new novel.

Lois Moran, the movie actress, at the time of meeting Scott

It's about a woman who wants to destroy a man, because she loves him too much and is afraid she'll lose him, but not to another woman—but because she'll stop loving him so much. Well, she decides to destroy him by marrying him. She marries him, and gets to love him even more than she did before. Then she gets jealous of him, because of his achievements in some line that she thinks she's also good in. Then, I guess, she commits suicide—first she does it step by step, the way all people, all women, commit suicide, by drinking, by sleeping around, by being impolite to friends, and that way. I haven't got the rest of it clear in my head, but that's the heart of it. What do you think Henry?

"Well, it's your wife, Zelda, all over again," Mencken replied. Fitzgerald reacted with a great emotional outburst, which turned into tears. Afterward, Mencken told his assistant that Scott would never amount to anything as long as Zelda was around.[16] Mencken seldom (never) minced words.

Though he had been working on his new novel since the summer of 1925, Fitzgerald had done little writing in 1927. An ill-timed visit by Zelda's sister Rosalind and her husband, Newman Smith, in February 1928 provided a further interruption. Scott had been invited to Princeton to speak at the Cottage Club on the honor system, of all things. He was too drunk to give the speech and returned home late that night, weeping. During an ensuing argument with Zelda, who also was drunk and possibly under the influence of morphine, Scott threw a favorite vase of Zelda's into the fireplace. After Zelda sarcastically called his father an Irish policeman, Scott allegedly slapped her, causing a nosebleed and outrage from Rosalind. As Scott remembered it, the fight happened when Zelda, "a raging maniac" when drunk, resisted his trying to put her to bed and he inadvertently hit her nose when she rushed at him. Zelda ignored her sister's plea to leave Scott, once and for all. Zelda told her that they remained deeply in love. Around this time Scott was drinking in order to be able to work, something he had never done before.

Now thoroughly fed up with their own behavior, it was time to go back abroad in April 1928, their third trip to Europe. The Fitzgeralds rented an apartment opposite the Luxembourg Gardens at 58 rue Vaugirard, so that Scottie could play outdoors. In the same month, Scott's first of the eight-story Basil Duke Lee series, "The Scandal Detectives," was published in the *Saturday Evening Post*. They soon visited with the Murphys, and Gerald introduced Zelda to the head of their daughter Honoria's ballet school, Madame Lubov Egorova. Though Zelda had returned to dancing apparently in defiance of Scott's praise of Lois Moran, dancing now became Zelda's sole compulsion. Yet, as Gerald Murphy described her dancing, her intensity was grotesque. Her legs looked muscular and ugly. He wanted to hold his breath until it was over.

Scott was doing little better, though he had better-looking legs. In July he notes in his Ledger: "Drinking and general unpleasantness." In August: "General aimlessness and boredom." After returning to the U.S. on October 7, 1928, to Ellerslie: "back again in [a] blaze of work and liquor." On his thirty-second birthday: "Ominous [underlined three times]; No Real Progress in any way and wrecked myself with dozens of people." All were insightful and honest evaluations. Fitzgerald made no progress on his novel that winter, either.

Back at Ellerslie, Zelda began dancing lessons in Philadelphia, with new determination. At home she was brooding and silent, practicing her ballet endless hours. She also began writing a series of short stories for *College Humor,* the first published being "The Original Follies Girl" (July 1929). Generally, she ignored both Scott and Scottie. Scott, for his part, had brought from Paris a taxi driver and ex-boxer, Philippe, to be his chauffeur and drinking companion. To Zelda's disgust, Scott and Philippe boxed together and separately, getting into bar fights at three or four in the morning, only to be rescued by an increasingly reluctant John Biggs. Zelda also disliked Mademoiselle, Scottie's French governess. Ellerslie brought Scott and Zelda no more satisfaction than before.

✧ ✧ ✧

When the Ellerslie lease expired, Scott's novel had yet to be completed. In March 1929, as the Jazz Age was nearing an end, the Fitzgeralds boarded the *Conte Biancamano* and sailed for Genoa. It would be their fourth trip to Europe. Scott promised Max Perkins that he would send the chapters from there. As they said their good-byes, John Biggs was shocked by Zelda's agitation and nervous distraction. He knew that Zelda did not like him; indeed, as he noted, Zelda never got along with anybody who liked Fitzgerald. He, like Hemingway, attributed her behavior to jealousy. From Genoa, Scott and Zelda went to Nice, stopping briefly, then on to Paris in April, where Zelda resumed her dancing lessons with Egorova. By now Zelda was infatuated with her teacher. Again, her world was consumed by compulsive dancing. Scott drank, though he had given up any objections to Zelda's compulsive behavior.

After spending the summer at the Villa Fleur des Bois in Cannes, Scott, Zelda, and Scottie settled at Juan-les-Pins. Tallulah Bankhead, the actress, saw Zelda that summer and noted her strange behavior. "She had gone into a flower shop and suddenly for her all the flowers had faces."[17] Zelda began to laugh with a mixture of wild delight and terror; her speech patterns began to change. One evening the Fitzgeralds and the Murphys were watching a documentary about underwater life at a cinema near Antibes. When an octopus appeared on the screen, Zelda became hysterical and screamed "What is it? What is it?"[18] These were portents of worse things to come.

As the stock market crashed in the United States in October 1929, the Fitzgeralds returned to Paris by car through Aix, Arles, Pont du Gard, Vichy, and the château country, arguing much of the way. Scott was driving their car through the mountainous Grande Corniche when Zelda suddenly seized the steering wheel, shouting "God's will," and tried to hurtle the car over a cliff. Fitzgerald managed to regain control of the car, stopping it at the lip of a precipitous cliff. Zelda could not explain why she had done it. Most likely, however, she had heard voices telling her to do it. Scott had prophetically written a similar scene with Eleanor's character in *This Side of Paradise*. The scene was based on a wild streak in Zelda that caused her to do crazy things, even in her teens. In the novel, Eleanor raced her horse toward a cliff, throwing herself off the horse just before it plunged off the cliff.[19] Now life was imitating art, imitating life. The Grande Corniche incident marked the beginning of a darkening period for Zelda.

In Paris they rented another musty apartment at 10 rue Pergolèse. Zelda returned to Egorova's dance studio, resuming her ballet with manic intensity. Fitzgerald, thinking that a vacation might improve Zelda's condition, booked a tour of Algeria in North Africa for February 7, 1930, with stops scheduled for Biskra, Constantine, and Algiers. Zelda, however, was ill with a fever and could not put ballet or Egorova out of her mind. In Algiers she begged to return to Paris. Scrapbook photographs show that she was on the verge of collapse. Her only comfort, or so she thought, was to be near Egorova.

Out of Algeria and back in Paris, events turned from the bazaar to bizarre. From her early sexual adventures, it is difficult to imagine Zelda as a lesbian. Nonetheless, Fitzgerald told Zelda's doctors that her "first indications of lesbianism 'were' directed towards Egorova...and her utterly uncharacteristic tendencies toward lesbianism 'manifested' usually with liquor."[20] Zelda began to befriend several members of Paris's lesbian community. She met other lesbians at Sapphic bars such as the Monocle on boulevard Edgar-Quinet, Bal de la Montagne Saint-Genevieve (opposite the Ecole Polytechnique on a hill behind the Pantheon). Zelda developed a close relationship with bisexuals Dolly Wilde and Emily Vanderbilt. Hemingway wrote of Scott's new source of pain:

> At this time Zelda could drink more than Scott could and Scott was afraid for her to pass out in the company they kept that spring and the places they went to. Scott did not like the places nor the people and he had to drink more than he could drink and be in any control of himself, to stand the people and the places.[21]

As ever, Zelda felt no guilt or remorse. Her emotional and sexual relationships with women brought her fulfillment that she was to rationalize as God's plan. Gertrude Stein had a similar attitude, but absent any help from God.

Sexual ambiguity is now known to be a symptom of schizophrenia. When the schizoid split happened to John Nash, the 1994 economics Nobel Prize winner, he began a long period of homosexual experiences. This ambiguity seems to go along with all the other confusions of persons suffering this mental illness. For example, neither Zelda nor John Nash could distinguish the voices of actual persons from the voices inside their brains. On her part, Zelda leaped higher at dance class to quiet the voices inside her head. The new sexual fulfillment eventually would come to an end as Zelda continued her downward spiral into madness.

✧　✧　✧

The legend of Scott and Ernest in Paris and on the Riviera would grow. The dangerous escapades of Scott and Zelda would never be forgotten. As Scott was to relate it much later, he and Zelda had much more fun than the disturbed characters in what would be his next novel. In some ways it was the best of times for the Fitzgeralds—in other ways, the worst. A storm was gathering over the City of Light, and a special kind of darkness was closing in on Scott and Zelda. Ernest Hemingway was to play a major role in the drama.

Endnotes

1. Edmund Wilson, ed., *The Crack-Up* (New York: New Directions, 1945), p. 310. Letter from T. S. Eliot to Fitzgerald, December 31, 1925.

2. Ibid., p. 129.

3. Ernest Hemingway, *A Moveable Feast* (New York: Charles Scribner's Sons, 1964), p. 155.

4. Scott Donaldson, *Hemingway v. Fitzgerald: The Rise and Fall of a Literary Friendship* (Woodstock & New York: Overlook Press, 1999), p. 73.

5. The quote is from an interview with Gilbert Seldes by Nancy Milford and appears in Nancy Milford, *Zelda* (New York: Harper & Row, 1970), p. 111.

6. This account is given by Calvin Tomkins in an interview with Nancy Milford, January 4, 1966. The quote is from Milford, *ibid.*

7. F. Scott Fitzgerald, Ledger, July and August, 1928 entries, Princeton University Library. Spelling as usual, by ear, the entry reads "Josanne" instead of "Josan."

8. Andrew Turnbull, ed., *The Letters of F. Scott Fitzgerald* (New York: Scribners, 1963), p. 357.

9. From an interview of the Murphys by Nancy Milford, quoted by Milford, *Zelda*, p. 117.

10. Fitzgerald correspondence, Gerald Murphy to Scott, September 19, 1925, Princeton University Library.

11. Fitzgerald, Ledger, p. 180.

12. John Chapin Mosher, "That Sad Young Man," *New Yorker*, April 17, 1926, pp. 20–21.

13. This is the way that Zelda's friend from Montgomery remembers it. Sara Mayfield, "The Fitzgeralds: Exiles from Paradise," Comment, *University of Alabama Review 4*, (winter 1965), p. 45. Mayfield, not always a reliable source, would have had no reason to exaggerate Zelda's comments.

14. From an interview with Gerald Murphy by Nancy Milford in Milford, *Zelda*, p. 123.

15. From an interview with Sara Murphy by Nancy Milford (See Milford, *ibid.*, pp. 124-125).

16. Charles Angoff, *H. L. Mencken: A Portrait from Memory* (New York: Thomas Yoseloff, 1956), pp. 98-99. Angoff had been Mencken's young assistant.

17. Tallulah Bankhead, quoted in Brendon Gill, *Tallulah* (New York: Holt, Rinehart and Winston, 1972), p. 122.

18. As quoted by Gerald Murphy in Milford, *Zelda*, p. 155.

19. F. Scott Fitzgerald, *This Side of Paradise* (New York: Charles Scribner's Sons, 1920), p. 217.

20. F. Scott Fitzgerald, medical history of Zelda's condition, F. Scott Fitzgerald Papers, Craig House Files, Princeton University Library.

21. Hemingway, *A Moveable Feast*, p. 179. What Hemingway wrote in this book is not always reliable. This comment, nonetheless, seemed to summarize Scott and Zelda's experiences at the time in Paris.

Nine

○

Hemingway, the Count of Darkness

THE JAZZ AGE WAS ABOUT TO END WHILE SCOTT AND ZELDA'S PERSONAL crash was ongoing. Of the two, Zelda was the first to completely collapse. Pathologically dependent on Egorova, her ballet teacher, and mentally and physically exhausted, Zelda had her first breakdown. She was admitted to the ominous-sounding Malmaison Clinic outside Paris on April 23, 1930, almost exactly a decade after she and Scott's marriage. The clinic's report states that upon admission, she was continually repeating a prophetic litany: "This is dreadful, this is horrible, what is going to become of me, I have to work, and I will no longer be able to, I must die, and yet I have to work. I will never be cured, let me leave."[1] Thereafter, though Zelda would voluntarily go in and out of various clinics and mental institutions to which she had been committed, she would never again resume a normal life.

Zelda discharged herself from Malmaison after less than a month and returned to Paris to resume her ballet lessons. There, she experienced hallucinations and attempted suicide. On June 5, 1930, she was admitted to Val-Mont Clinic in Glion, Switzerland, and was examined by Dr. Oscar Forel. Dr. Forel had her transferred to his own clinic, Les Rives de Prangins at Nyon, a kind of country club for the mentally ill, on lovely Lake Geneva. Shortly thereafter, the Fitzgeralds wrote two very long letters reminiscing about their lives together. However, the letter written by Scott probably was never sent.

Fitzgerald writes of their earlier time in France with their friends Gerald and Sara Murphy and of Ernest Hemingway as his equal and his kind of an idealist. "I got drunk with him on the Left Bank in careless cafés and drank with Sara and Gerald in their garden in St. Cloud but you were endlessly sick and at home everything was unhappy."[2] But as Scott turned to their most recent experience in France, he notes how Gerald and Sara did not see them, and when Hemingway and he met, Ernest was "apprehensively telling me his whereabouts lest I come in on them tight and endanger his lease." It did not help Scott's self-esteem. Back on the beautiful Riviera, Fitzgerald had developed an ugly inferiority complex and could not face anyone unless he was drunk. Writing of the trip to Africa, he tells Zelda, "You were going crazy and calling it genius—I was going to ruin and calling it anything that came to hand." Scott ends the letter with little self-recrimination. "We ruined ourselves—I have never honestly thought that we ruined each other." If indeed Fitzgerald never sent the letter, he was demonstrating a growing maturity and understanding of Zelda's mental problems.

✧ ✧ ✧

Scott had made many bad personal choices. Not only did he often make bad choices in his women, Fitzgerald also did not always choose his heroes wisely. As Scott had noted, Ernest Hemingway also was in Paris that spring of 1929. By now, however, a chill had invaded his and Scott's friendship. Ernest had recently remarried, was irritable, and avoided his old drinking companions. Besides, Ernest's new wife, Pauline, did not approve of the Fitzgeralds. Besides that, Hemingway was working hard to complete his new novel, *A Farewell To Arms*. He nonetheless had reluctantly given Scott the manuscript to read. Fitzgerald drafted a nine-page memo of suggested changes on which Ernest wrote, "Kiss my ass."[3] In turn,

Scott read portions of it to Morley Callaghan, a young Canadian writer he had met in Toronto who was now visiting Paris.

The Hemingway manuscript gave Callaghan an opportunity to take a close look at Hemingway and the Fitzgeralds. He noticed the changes in Hemingway and thought him overly competitive in wanting to engage in boxing and drinking bouts with him. Meanwhile, Morley *and* his wife were as impressed with the Fitzgeralds' handsomeness as they were surprised by Zelda's silence. The strain of the ballet lessons was taking its toll.

During 1929, the age that Scott Fitzgerald had named crashed with the stock market. At the time the Fitzgeralds and the Hemingways were living in the same neighborhood of Paris. However, they saw little of each other, and that was the way Ernest wanted it. Scott felt the chill of Hemingway's way. Scott and Zelda hoped that their return to Europe in March might alter the uneven rhythm of their lives. Hemingway sailed for France on April 5. Meanwhile, their editor Max Perkins was increasingly worried about Scott's health and his unfinished novel.

Summer did not take away the chill; June 1929 marked a watershed in Scott and Ernest's personal relationship. One June afternoon in Paris, Ernest and Morley Callaghan invited Scott to serve as timekeeper for a few practice rounds at a local gym during which Callaghan, an adept boxer, decked Ernest. Callaghan's recollection is that Scott appeared "mystified" by Callaghan's superiority in the ring, wore a "shocked expression" when Callaghan cut Hemingway's lip with a right jab, and then, after Callaghan knocked Ernest down, suddenly cried out "'Oh, my God!'" and confessed that he had mistakenly let the round go too long. Callaghan recalls that Hemingway responded to Scott's admission with "fierce words." "'All right, Scott,' Ernest said savagely, 'if you want to see me getting the shit knocked out of me, just say so. Only don't say you made a mistake.'" Callaghan's impression was that by lashing out with those bitter, angry words, Ernest had practically shouted that he was aware that Scott had some deep hidden animosity toward him. "Shaken as I was, it flashed through my mind, is the animosity in Scott, or is it really in Ernest?... What is it? Not just that Scott's a drunk. I knew there was something else."[4]

That "something else" that Callaghan had detected beneath the affable exterior of "Papa" was Ernest's resentful, aggressive, and sometimes malicious nature, particularly when his heroic manly stature was threatened (always associated with craftsmanship by Hemingway in his life and art). When the *New York Herald Tribune* later that year (November) inaccurately reported that Hemingway had been knocked "out cold" by Callaghan, Ernest pressured Scott—who Ernest still held responsible—to send a cable to Callaghan demanding a retraction. Unknown to Scott and Ernest, Callaghan had already sent a letter of correction to the *Tribune* in which he made light of the event, playfully concluding that "I do wish you'd correct that story or I'll never be able to go to New York again for fear of getting knocked about"—that is, by Hemingway, who Callaghan understood might take the misrepresentation more seriously.[5]

Indeed, Ernest was not amused when he learned that Callaghan also had recently repeated a rumor then circulating that Ernest was a homosexual. He angrily lashed out in a letter to Maxwell Perkins: "There should be a limit to what lies people are allowed to tell under jealousies.... There will be a certain satisfaction in beating up Callaghan because of his boasting and because he is a good enough boxer."[6]

As it would turn out, Ernest's personal code of honor would not preclude jealous boasting and self-promotion, nor hitting below the belt, either, particularly when it came to circulating damaging and misleading associations about Scott. In another letter to Maxwell Perkins in August 1929, Hemingway exaggerates his boxing prowess (by implying he was drunk at the time of the Callaghan bout) and blames Scott for the knockdown, claiming that instead of a one-minute round, "He had let the round go three minutes and 45 seconds—so interested to see if I was going to hit the floor!"[7] Later, in 1951, over a decade after Scott's death, Hemingway told Scott's biographer Arthur Mizener that Scott had let the round go for thirteen minutes. Scott's lapse seemed to increase exponentially with time itself. Unfortunately for Scott, the most damaging of Ernest's exaggerations and misleading associations were yet to come.

In a letter to Scott later that year (December 1929), Ernest did apologize for his outburst, admitting that he had overreacted out of "damn old animal suspecion" (Ernest's spelling) and said he believed "implicitly" all along that Scott's timekeeping error had been an honest one.[8] But the damage was done: Both had belittled the other. Ernest was not simply shadowboxing. Meanwhile, Scott had become a literary lightweight among those who mattered.

Fitzgerald's professional decline had begun earlier; it was a leading indicator of the market crash to come. With the collapse of the stock market, Scott later notes, "the most expensive orgy in history was over."[9] Agriculture had sunk long before the Great Crash, and Fitzgerald's stature had begun to go with the outgoing sales tide of *The Great Gatsby*. Hemingway was among the first to take notice. The ebb tide became an undertow as Fitzgerald failed to publish another novel until *Tender Is the Night* (1934), and as he faced the lingering charge, first by Edmund Wilson and John Bishop, then by Hemingway, and later (posthumously) by Glen Wescott, that he lacked intellectual substance. This indictment diminished his ranking among the leading men of American letters.

Worse, Scott's petulant "hero," Ernest Hemingway, was the archvillain of the caviling bunch. Not only did Hemingway energetically promote his view of Fitzgerald, he also engaged in a smear campaign against Scott. One of Hemingway's motives was to obscure his literary debts to Fitzgerald. Even if the artistic debt owed by Hemingway to Fitzgerald is judged trifling (which it was not), Scott's promotion of Hemingway's professional literary career surely was not—indeed, Fitzgerald's professional advice had a lasting influence.

✧　✧　✧

Aside from initiating a fissure in their friendship, the boxing episode also opened up a new dimension to their relationship: the importance of public image as portrayed by the media. By the late twenties and early thirties, both writers were public celebrities, and both recognized that image was important to their "author" status. In truth, Hemingway's macho image as courageous war hero, rugged outdoorsman, and skilled athlete was nearly as carefully marketed and overstated as Scott's early image as spokesperson for the young and wealthy. Aside from his bruised ego, this helps explain Ernest's subsequent distortion to Perkins of the Callaghan bout. While Hemingway instinctively sensed the importance of cultivating a public image to be a heavyweight contender in the literary marketplace, Scott was attempting to shed the lightweight image he had acquired in the twenties.

From the start, Scott was suspicious of his early fame, though it befitted his romantic view of the author as a cultural producer and leader, a vision he had begun to project upon Ernest. In "Early Success" (1937), Scott recalls how following "Bernice Bobs Her Hair" he came by the label of "'the Author'" but realized that "one wasn't really an author any more than one had been an army officer, but nobody seemed to guess behind the false face."[10] Unfortunately, the "false face"—the public image of youth, vitality, and wealth that he along with Zelda and the media had helped cultivate—had created a separate reality.

In the long hiatus between *The Great Gatsby* and *Tender Is the Night*—the years during which Ernest distanced himself from Scott— there had surfaced in Scott's professional life a tension between two conflicting ideas of an "author." On the one hand, Scott aspired to be a cultural leader who created and guided his audience by creating works of art of social significance and literary distinction. In opposition to this romantic conception of an elite autonomous "author" was the idea of an author as a socially constructed figure shaped by public taste and the media, a "brand name" product marketed by commercial concerns circulating independent of the writer's intentions and control. The former type of author was manly, independent, and strong—just like Ernest; the latter effeminate, dependent, and weak. Scott would later refer to Ernest as his "artistic conscience"[11] and shared the creed contained in Hemingway's remark that "All art is only done by the individual,"[12] but it was also increasingly and disturbingly clear to Scott that the profession of literary author was much more than a romantic vision of autonomy, a premonition of later postmodern conceptions of authorship.

Fitzgerald had hoped that *The Great Gatsby* would be the bridge between these two perceptions, permanently establishing him as a serious "author" while still preserving his public popularity, but Scott overestimated his ability to mediate his media image. Although Fitzgerald had received significant critical praise for the novel from highly respected literary peers like T. S. Eliot, Edith Wharton, and Gertrude Stein as well as from prominent literary critics such as Gilbert Seldes, other reviewers lumped *Gatsby* with his earlier work, and Scott became "depressed" when sales fell well short of his heightened aspirations. Scott believed that the main reason for the disappointing sales was that "the book contains no important woman character and women control the fiction market at present," but it is also true that the novel's brilliance, including its intellectual undercurrents, was overlooked by many reviewers who dismissed it as just another Fitzgerald story about the wealthy and confirming one of Scott's fears expressed in a letter to Perkins just before the novel came out in April 1925.[13]

A related issue was Hemingway's depiction of Scott's short story writing, which first Scott and then Ernest called "whoring." Perhaps to impress Ernest with his ability to command both the commercial and artistic realms of his professional life, Scott claimed that he deliberately altered his short stories by inserting "twists that made them into saleable magazine stories" to earn money in support of his novel writing. Hemingway recalls Scott asserting: "Since he wrote the real story first…the destruction and changing of it that he did at the end did him no harm." However, Hemingway was skeptical of Scott's prowess. He believed that Scott's short story writing was wasting his talent, a waste promoted by Zelda who, out of jealousy, encouraged her husband to drink so as to distract Scott from his "real" work on his novel, itself not immune to harsh attack.[14] Hemingway believed that the laudatory reviews of *The Great Gatsby,* particularly the one by Gilbert Seldes, who proclaimed that "Fitzgerald has certainly the best chance at present of becoming our finest artist in fiction," had "constipated" Scott, who, Hemingway thought, was too intent on creating a masterpiece in his next novel (although, in retrospect, Scott had accomplished exactly that in *The Great Gatsby*).[15]

Despite an increasingly invidious bent to Ernest's remarks, there was nevertheless a scent of truth to Hemingway's criticisms, and Scott was increasingly sensitive to them as his literary stature, public image, Zelda, and, most important, the work on his next novel began to fade. In truth, Scott was enchanted by favorable reviews such as Seldes's, which located him among the literary elite and cultural leaders, but the reality was that Scott was struggling with his next novel and in 1929 earned a total of only $31.71 from the sale of his previous novels, thereby compelling him to perform new tricks with his short fiction writing to stay financially afloat but leaving him artistically and spiritually "undernourished." In this regard, by April 1930, Scott had published "First Blood" in the *Saturday Evening Post,* the first of a five-story Josephine Perry series. Scott also was drinking too much, a fault Ernest also would prominently display in his memoir *A Moveable Feast* and which Scott himself acknowledged, recalling visits to "the Ritz Bar where I got back my self esteem for half an hour."[16]

Hemingway's attacks were first personal but, later, professional. When Scott dedicated *All the Sad Young Men* (1936), "To Ring and Ellis Lardner," a jealous Ernest admonished Scott: "Your friend Ring is hampered by lack of intelligence, lack of any aesthetic appreciation, terrible repressions and bitterness."[17] While faulting Zelda, Hemingway ultimately held Scott responsible for his shortcomings, referring to them a month before the Great Crash of 1929 as "self-made," an assessment that Scott accepted even as Ernest began a campaign to discredit him.[18] As the thirties progressed, Hemingway's criticisms would turn from being brutally honest to brutal and dishonest, variously suggesting that Scott was effeminate, cowardly, captivated by wealth, and lacking the discipline and intelligence needed to be a great artist, all of which caused lasting damage to Scott's fragile self-image while alive and his public image then and thereafter.

Evidently determined to insure that Scott's literary reputation would not be entirely self-determined, Ernest first went public with his criticisms in 1933 with a short story in *Scribner's* magazine titled

"Homage to Switzeraland" which took a jab at Scott's *This Side of Paradise*. This was harmless enough, but it was followed by a much more damaging reference to Scott in Hemingway's deservedly famous long story "The Snows of Kilamanjaro" in *Esquire* in August 1936. There, the fisherman rubbed salt into Fitzgerald's many wounds as Ernest derogatorily depicted Scott as a minor character:

> He remembered poor Scott Fitzgerald and his romantic awe of them [the rich] and how he had started a story once that began, "The very rich are different from you and me." And how some one had said to Scott, Yes, they have more money. But that was not humorous to Scott. He thought they were a special glamorous race and when he found they weren't it wrecked him just as much as any other thing wrecked him.[19]

By quoting from "The Rich Boy" (1926), Hemingway is reaching back to a short story post-dating and extending *The Great Gatsby*. Ernest must know that he is mocking Fitzgerald's grand theme.

It is a depiction etched into literary memory and not soon forgotten. And, of course, it happens to be wrong. On the narrower issue of Fitzgerald's alleged shallowness regarding the rich, Hemingway reveals his own lack of depth by missing the point. "The Rich Boy" is very sophisticated: It is much more a subtle portrayal of the psychology underlying imperialism than a tale regaling the glamour of wealth and class. More broadly, too, Hemingway's criticism of Fitzgerald is misdirected: It was not admiration for the rich that was laying Fitzgerald to waste, but a complex of factors, some internally and some externally imposed, which Fitzgerald courageously and openly explored in "The Crack-Up" (beginning just six months earlier in *Esquire*).

"The Rich Boy" also has many of the themes and character types more fully developed in *The Great Gatsby*. Scott wrote the story in Capri while awaiting publication of *Gatsby* and revised it in Paris. A greatly revised version of the story was printed in *All the Sad Young Men*. In the latter version, an unnamed narrator begins the story with an analysis of the "very rich" that differs substantially from Hemingway's fictional version of Fitzgerald's fiction:

They are different from you and me. They possess and enjoy early, and it does something to them, makes them soft where we are hard, and cynical where we are trustful, in a way that, unless you were rich, it is very difficult to understand. They think, deep in their hearts, that they are better than we are because we had to discover the compensations and refuges of life for ourselves.[20]

Fitzgerald was "deeply hurt" by Hemingway's passage, later complaining to Sheilah Graham that "it was as though I was already dead."[21] In a curt letter to Hemingway, he angrily instructed him to "Please lay off me in print. If I choose to write de profundis sometimes [i.e., in "The Crack Up"] it doesn't mean I want friends praying aloud over my corpse…when you incorporate it (the story) in a book would you mind cutting my name?"[22]

Scott's anger was understandable. Hemingway now had Scott on the ropes, once "The Crack Up" and other "confessional" essays were in the ring. We reserve the knock out punch for a later chapter.

✧ ✧ ✧

There is still another marker for the dramatic shift in the comparative literary status of Hemingway and Fitzgerald. The two essentially equal literary giants met in Paris—also in the chill of that June 1929—and ended up discussing alternative ways of ending a novel. At this gathering, as Scott recalls in a letter to H. L. Mencken on April 23, 1934, he and Hemingway together "worked out" the literary device inherited from Conrad of concluding a novel with a "dying fall" rather than with an "emotionally heightened staccato."[23] Fitzgerald revisited the discussion in a letter to Hemingway on June 1, 1934, after his harsh criticism of what turned out to be Scott's "new" novel, *Tender Is the Night*. Although Fitzgerald was the more knowledgeable regarding Conrad's theories of literature (having long ago been under the literary influence of Conrad's preface to *The Nigger of the Narcissus*), in his letter, Scott tactfully inverts their teacher-pupil relationship to express his debt to Ernest for showing him how to end his novel *(Tender)* on a gradual fade to produce a lingering emotional effect. However, it already had been the device used by Scott to end *The Great Gatsby*. Fitzgerald's suggestion to Hemingway for altering the conclusion to *A Farewell To Arms* was dismissed.

The tide of literary authority had begun to turn as early as 1926 with the publication of Hemingway's *The Sun Also Rises*. A second successful Hemingway novel, *A Farewell to Arms,* appeared in 1929. During these times and afterward, Fitzgerald was publishing some of his weaker short stories (principally the Basil and Josephine series) to keep his household financially afloat while trying to rescue *Tender* in the outgoing tide. Certainly by the time Mencken had read Fitzgerald's letter in 1934, it was widely recognized that Hemingway had emerged as "the shining hero of American letters"[24] while Fitzgerald had fallen into relative obscurity.

Ironically, Fitzgerald's steadfast loyalty to Hemingway—against all odds—probably detracted from *Tender.* In a dubious act of "authorship," Scott would create a new character, Philippe, based on Ernest Hemingway, for stories on the way to a new novel. It is a project widely ignored by biographers who do not understand its importance to Scott, and, as it turns out, to Hemingway.

The conceived Philippe novel is set in France during the Middle Ages.

In a *Notebooks* entry, Scott notes: "Just as Stendal's portrait of a Byronic man made *Le Rouge et Noir* so couldn't *my* portrait of Ernest as Philippe make the real modern man."[25] In his depiction of Philippe, Scott was returning to Schopenhauer and Nietzsche's idea of a "will-to-power" as the evolutionary force behind modern Western culture, an idea Scott had more recently encountered in volume 2 of Oswald Spengler's *Decline of the West*. A March 1929 letter to Hemingway reveals Scott's enthrallment with Spengler and Hemingway, which would congeal to inspire his projected novel: "Spengler's second volume is marvelous. Nothing else is any good—when will you save me from the risk of memorizing your works from over-reading them by finishing another?"[26]

Scott would never complete the Philippe novel (although he continued to hold out hopes for its completion until his death), but parts of it were published as short stories in *Redbook,* beginning with "In the Darkest Hour" in October 1934—a story that begins in A.D. 872, the approximate birth date of Western culture designated by Spengler, who locates it in the tenth century A.D. According to Spengler, Western culture began and evolved from a cosmic force that adhered to exceptional individuals whose actions personified the modern quest for power and propelled its historical destiny. "In the Darkest Hour" is set at a "time when Europe was so overrun by Northmen, Moors and Huns that it had fallen into a state of helpless and sub-bestial degradation. Leaderless, the wretched farmers had no protection from the fiercest hordes...." Into this political, economic, and cultural void (reminiscent of H. G. Wells's Wild Asses description of World War I) rides Philippe whose forceful personality and innate sense of command begins to create order out of disorder.

In a historically accurate depiction of the shifting power and

Hemingway in bigger-than-life "macho" mode

property relations that established the feudal order of Europe, Philippe (the nascent nobility) offers the peasant class protection in exchange for their military service, creates a strategic alliance with the Church to keep foreign invaders (and, in a later story, the king) at bay, and taxes the merchant class to secure his fief. It is notable that Philippe is at once productive and destructive in establishing his authority. His "seizing power by force and cunning" creates a new cultural order that prevents Europe from continuing in its present "state of helpless and sub-bestial degradation," but it is an achievement tainted by an egotistical sense of destiny that ruthlessly sacrifices the weak and whose methods include spreading false stories as part of a divide and conquer strategy.

Hemingway's forceful personality, macho lifestyle, and desire to rule are all reflected in Philippe, but the cunning manipulations of Philippe suggest that Scott's "hero-worship" of Ernest's *person* was not as naive as often presumed. Despite these reservations regarding Hemingway's personal traits, Scott unequivocally admired Ernest's talents as a literary artist including the fact that his fiction grew directly out of World War I and brilliantly captured the mood of a "lost generation." Hemingway's simple declarative sentences, his terse dialogue, and his repeated use of nouns (things) provided guideposts in a disorderly world while plumbing a deep emotional space. By capturing the spiritual desolation during and following World War I, and creating a new art form to describe the psychological undercurrents associated with the individual's confrontation with nada, Hemingway represented the type of cultural and artistic leader Scott aspired to be as he struggled to complete *Tender Is the Night*.

Ironically, while Scott paid tribute to Hemingway's increasingly suspect bravado and admired his art for providing a foothold in a spiritual wasteland, Scott was rapidly losing his grip both professionally and personally, a crash Hemingway did nothing to slow and indeed promoted. Zelda's hospitalization was creating a financial drain that forced Scott into writing still more short stories that, he felt, detracted from work on his novel. Meanwhile, the increasingly callous and distant Hemingway hammered away at Scott's lack of work ethic, discipline, and inability to pull himself up by his bootstraps.

After *Tender Is the Night* was finally completed, the publication of the first two Philippe stories—"In the Darkest Hour" in October 1934 and "The Count of Darkness" in June 1935, six years after the Callaghan-Hemingway bout in which Ernest's dark side was revealed to Scott, only served to expose and accentuate the increasingly bizarre disparities within Scott's professional life as "author." Although the style and content of the Philippe stories were incompatible with Scott's previous fiction, *Redbook* marketed the stories as modern romances set in the Dark Ages. In a ridiculous blurb for

"The Count of Darkness," the reader is told: "The brilliant thought quality and style of the creator of 'The Great Gatsby' are very much in evidence in this majestic story of 879 A.D." This is followed by a quote from one of several bad lines from the story:

"Hello, you baggage!" he [Philippe] said to Letgarde [his soon-to-be wife].

"May I speak sire?"

"If you don't say too much," he replied.

Critics agree; the Philippe stories comprised Scott's worst fiction. By quick dismissal, however, biographers also fail to unravel the Ernest-Scott enigma.

How could the author of *The Great Gatsby* and *Tender Is the Night* fail so massively? First, Scott's lifelong literary agent, Harold Ober, understandably had trouble marketing the stories because they stood in contrast to the public's expectation that Scott would write about "contemporary" society, with "new woman" characters exercising independence rather than being treated as chattel. It was like dropping a dark curtain upon the stage of a grand and gay party where readers and editors alike expected Scott to continue his Jazz Age performance. Like Jay Gatsby, Scott was the advertisement for the American Dream of youth, wealth, and romantic possibilities, and the American media and public would continue to project its hopes onto that mythical image. The prospect of Scott's conceiving "contemporary" society in broader historical terms was not entertaining, nor was it to be entertained. Fitzgerald remained a prisoner of his Jazz Age reputation.

A second reason might be related to the stylistic difficulty of moving from irony to satire. In an awkward way, the Philippe stories were a return to the kind of overly broad satire displayed in Scott's play, *The Vegetable,* and they partly failed for similar reasons. He was at his best with irony that sweetens bitterness and at his worst with outright parody—this, before Hemingway became a recognizable parody of himself. Paradoxically, Fitzgerald simply could not be taken seriously when he was overtly farcical.

A third reason may be related to Fitzgerald's original motivation for writing the stories. Scott wanted to write the story of Ernest as Philippe wherein Philippe embodies many characteristics of Hemingway and his work—the pride (before the fall), the bravado (before it was exposed), the reckless courage (before it became boorish), and Hemingway's skills (*still* admired by Fitzgerald). Philippe, like Ernest, is a tough guy and a romantic idealist. Moreover, Philippe is a Catholic knight while Hemingway often was called a medieval Catholic in the exercise of his faith. Only someone who knew Hemingway and his work, warts and all, as Scott did, could write about him so accurately.

The tales of darkness but dawn, sleepless nights but sunrises, and other Lost Generation halftones betray Hemingway's work. The places of action are France and Spain. "In the Darkest Hour," Philippe refuses to sleep or admit to tiredness because that is what he does—keeping watch in the darkness. In the story's last line, Philippe is described in heroic symbolism: "Embodying in himself alone the future of his race, he walked to and fro in the starry darkness" The second story, "The Count of Darkness," begins at dawn. After some conversation with the oddly named Letgarde, during which Philippe uses freshmanic Hemingwayisms, the sun also rises as the story goes on. "What do you want, little chicken?" asks Philippe-Ernest. Grabbing Letgarde and pulling her up on his horse, Philippe tells her, "Don't let go, baby, and nothing can happen to you." "Nothing" is Fitzgerald's version of Hemingway's nada.

When Philippe leaves, Letgarde is fascinated by a song being sung by a tramp about "Silver trout for streams / Whiter than the whitest pebble in the stream bottom...." Of course, there is something fishy about the trout: The tramp's little song echoes the famous opening sentences of *A Farewell To Arms* (white pebbles in the riverbed). The sentimental Philippe-Letgarde romance and the tragedy of her drowning in the Loire bring to mind Hemingway's story of the love and loss of Catherine and Frederic in Hemingway's novel. It is also in the Loire that Philippe fishes in the dark, inventing a way to get fish out of the stream despite the improbability of success.[27]

"Fishing in the dark" may be an apt metaphor for "The Count of Darkness," according to H. R. Stoneback.[28] The drowned body of Letgarde drifts downstream as the fishing scene ends. Philippe-

Ernest holds her in his arms, but eventually her body slides from him. Kneeling, he says one Ave Maria, and then, in the moonlight, he can "say nothing." He tries again. " 'Ave Maria'—he began—and it seemed as if the trees told him nothing." Philippe-Ernest, in the presence of nada, says his farewell to arms. "Choked with emotion," Philippe, controlling his emotions before his men, commands them to dig her grave. "I guess I must be pretty much of a tough," he thinks as the story mercifully ends.

Although Fitzgerald was not a practicing Catholic, he had Catholic sensibilities and spiritual yearnings. Hemingway was a devout convert and a practicing Catholic for much of his adult life, inclusive of his years of friendship with Scott.[29] Ernest once said that the "only way he could run his life decently was to accept the discipline of the Church," and he once thought that perhaps the Church could help Scott.[30] In Fitzgerald's final, unfinished Philippe story, "Gods of Darkness," Philippe strikes a deal with the devil. When Philippe is seen crossing himself and knocking on wood (the double sign that Hemingway often made), the abbot of the monastery suggests that he is acting like one of the superstitious peasant-cult members. Philippe nonetheless is initiated into the dark cult because he realizes that the "power from below" is a potent force. His final initiation takes place in a "dim cathedral," or "deep locker-room of the earth," a reference to Hemingway's athleticism and a muscular Christianity always playing to win.

Emerging from the "deep locker-room," riding home (with the sun about to rise, of course), Philippe descends into an outright parody of Hemingway. Philippe thinks of Becquette (the local "priestess" of the cult) and how he would "like to take a punch" at that "baby": "The sorer she got, the more I liked her!" The Philippe stories end with Philippe's troubled Catholic conscience struggling in his use of a new vision of darkness "Half a god—half a devil" while "playing to win." Therein remains the enigma of Fitzgerald's fascination with Hemingway, but his complete failure—according to critics—to convert it to art. Initially at least, under Scott's dire circumstances and dark state of mind, he might have been writing a parody of Hemingway for therapeutic reasons.

The reverence for Hemingway's artistry at the time precluded an appreciation of the humor in the parody. In any case, it would have been lost on *Redbook*'s readership. Besides, the magazine was advertising Fitzgerald's stories as modern, light romance set in the Dark Ages. As a failing billboard copywriter during his first job in New York, Fitzgerald would have been a better publicist.

✦ ✦ ✦

A great amount of ink has been spilt over Scott's lifelong "hero-worship." It is a great part of the legend of Fitzgerald and Hemingway. The image of Fitzgerald as subordinate is reinforced even though Fitzgerald never lost his desire to dominate. This contradictory tendency can be found in relationships with both his friends and his literary peers as well as—later, and less obviously—in his selection of readings from the biographies of Julius Caesar and Abraham Lincoln as preparation for writing *The Last Tycoon*. This last novel revolves around the life of Hollywood mogul Irving Thalberg, another of Scott's heroes. He had a tendency to develop "literary crushes," as writer John Dos Passos put it, which often led to embarrassing encounters, with Scott literally groveling at the feet of writers he respected (not to mention dancers). This propensity has led Scott Donaldson, in his *Hemingway vs. Fitzgerald,* to conclude, wrongly: "What Scott loved about Ernest was the idealized version of the sort of man—courageous, stoic, masterful—he could never be."[31] In the end Hemingway could not live up to that self-promoted image.

So, at last, did Hemingway know of Philippe? If so, what was his reaction? Carlos Baker, a Hemingway biographer, has Ernest down in "the valley of the Loire" in 1953. "Ernest amused himself by imagining that he was a medieval knight riding his horse along the riverbank. The notion stayed with him all the way south [to Spain]."[32] As related in an interview with Stoneback, Mary Hemingway recalled the incident: "We'd been up at Chartres, admiring the medieval knights in the stained glass and the sculpture. Then we drove through the Loire Valley. Maybe it was that awful Fitzgerald stuff about Ernest as a medieval knight that he was thinking about."[33] Perhaps Scott understood Ernest better than did Mary; Hemingway's Philip of Madrid, a counterespionage agent in his play *The Fifth Column*, appears to be Philippe's twin. They are both strong, tough men, imperious in command. Philippe is one with the people; Philip is with the people now and is through with the idle rich and the Riviera. Philippe comes north from luxurious Moorish Spain to France; Philip comes south from France, where he has spent much of his life in luxury, to fight for the peasants. Philippe fights the Northmen; Philip fights the Germans. Philippe will play the games of darkness to win; Philip will use counterespionage.

When Perkins gave Fitzgerald a summary of the play's action, then titled simply *Philip,* Scott replies that he is fascinated by what Perkins had said about the play and fascinated by Hemingway's Byronic intensity. On December 24, 1938, just after *The Fifth Column* is published, Fitzgerald writes to Perkins that he has decided to complete the Philippe stories as a thirty-thousand-word novelette. Did Fitzgerald recognize Philip as Philippe? Hemingway seemed to be using Fitzgerald's fictionalized version of himself as Philip. Not surprisingly, Hemingway's Philip comes across as a bad parody of Ernest because it is a parody of another bad parody, Philippe. Most critics again agree; just as the Philippe stories comprise Fitzgerald's worst fiction, *The Fifth Column* is Hemingway's worst published fiction. Though he never got around to it, Scott was intending to complete the Philippe stories, perhaps with some additional insight provided by Ernest's Philip. It would have been Fitzgerald's worst novel.

While the first five years of the Fitzgerald-Hemingway friendship greatly benefited Ernest, in the end Scott's fascination with Hemingway and Ernest's fascination with Fitzgerald's fascination with him led to artistic failures by both. A twin irony was at work: Philippe and Philip deserved each other, but *both* were Hemingway.

Endnotes

1. From the Malmaison Clinic report on Zelda, Princeton University Library.

2. The letter is an undated draft written sometime during the summer 1930, titled by Scott as *Written with Zelda Gone To the Clinique*, Princeton University Library.

3. The memo with Hemingway's handwritten comment is in his *Correspondence*, John F. Kennedy Library.

4. Morley Callaghan, *That Summer in Paris* (New York: Coward-McCann, 1963), pp. 212–14.

5. As quoted by Matthew J. Bruccoli, *Fitzgerald and Hemingway: A Dangerous Friendship* (New York: Carroll & Graf, 1994), p. 143.

6. As quoted from ibid., p. 145.

7. Ibid., p. 126.

8. Both quotes from ibid., p. 150.

9. Quote is from "Echoes of the Jazz Age," in Edmund Wilson, ed., *The Crack-Up* (New York: New Directions Paperbook, 1956), p. 21.

10. Quotes are from "Early Success" (1937), reprinted in Wilson, ed., *The Crack-Up*, pp. 85–90.

11. F. Scott Fitzgerald, "Pasting It Together," March 1936, in Wilson, ed., *The Crack-Up*, p. 79.

12. Ernest Hemingway, *Death in the Afternoon* (New York: Charles Scribner's Sons, 1932), p. 99.

13. Matthew J. Bruccoli, ed., *F. Scott Fitzgerald: A Life in Letters* (New York: Charles Scribner's Sons, 1994), pp. 105–06.

14. Ernest Hemingway, *A Moveable Feast* (New York: Scribners 1964) pp. 155–56.

15. Quotes from Bruccoli, ed., *A Life in Letters,* p. 124.

16. Ibid., pp. 187–88.

17. Ernest Hemingway, *Selected Letters, 1917–1962*, ed. Carlos Baker (New York: Scribner Classic, 2003, [1981]), p. 200.

18. See Bruccoli, *Fitzgerald and Hemingway,* p. 132.

19. Ernest Hemingway, "The Snows of Kilimanjaro," *Esquire* 6 (August 1936), p. 27.

20. F. Scott Fitzgerald, "The Rich Boy" (1926), revised and printed in *All the Sad Young Men,* (New York: Scribners, 1926) pp. 1–2.

21. Sheilah Graham, *College of One* (New York: Viking Press, 1966), p. 88.

22. Andrew Turnbull, ed., *The Letters of F. Scott Fitzgerald* (New York: Dell, 1965), p. 311.

23. Bruccoli, ed., *A Life in Letters*, p. 256

24. Graham, *College of One*, p. 88.

25. Matthew J. Bruccoli, ed., *The Notebooks of F. Scott Fitzgerald* (New York: Harcourt Brace Jovanovich, 1972), p. 159.

26. Quoted from Bruccoli, *Fitzgerald and Hemingway,* p. 105.

27. The quotations from these stories are from F. Scott Fitzgerald, "In the Darkest Hour," *Redbook,* October 1934, pp. 15–19, 94–98 and F. Scott Fitzgerald, "The Count of Darkness," *Redbook,* June 1935, pp. 20–23, 68, 70, 72 (with the blurb from p. 20).

28. See H. R. Stoneback, "A Dark Ill-Lighted Place: Fitzgerald and Hemingway, Philippe Count of Darkness and Philip Counter-Espionage Agent," in Jackson R. Bryer, Alan Margolies, and Ruth Prigozy, *F. Scott Fitzgerald: New Perspectives* (Athens and London: University of Georgia Press, 2000), pp. 231–49. A Catholic theme similar to that developed here but in a much more elaborate fashion can be found in Stoneback's essay.

29. This has been established by H. R. Stoneback, "In the Nominal Country of the Bogus: Hemingway's Catholicism and the Biographies," in Frank Scafella, ed., *Hemingway: Essays of Reassessment* (New York: Oxford University Press, 1991), pp. 105–40.

30. The Hemingway quote appears in Carlos Baker, *Ernest Hemingway: A Life Story* (New York: Scribners, 1969), p. 333.

31. Scott Donaldson, *Hemingway vs. Fitzgerald* (Woodstock, N.Y.: Overlook Press), p. 322.

32. Baker, *Ernest Hemingway*, p. 511.

33. Stoneback, "A Dark Ill-Lighted Place," p. 242.

Ten

All That Waste

"WASTE" OR SIMPLY "WASTED"? IN A LITERARY CAREER FRAMED BY TWO world wars and hollowed out by personal, family, and economic depression, it is not surprising that Fitzgerald dealt extensively with the topic of waste. Approaching the idea of waste—whether it is in his life or his writing, the two often blurred, literally—F. Scott Fitzgerald cannot be assessed without coming to terms with his alcoholism. Any obsession with the issue is blunted by its cavalier treatment in the biographies of other writers who had the common denominator of alcohol and being Irish. Many wrote under the influence.

Certainly by 1928 in Paris the Fitzgeralds' drinking pattern had changed. During most of the 1920s people seemed to drink to have a good time. "Happy hour" was an apt metaphor. As Scott remembered it, "There was a kindliness about intoxication—there was that indescribable gloss and glamour it gave, like the memories of ephemeral and faded evenings."[1] Now, the drinking was more from habit, from boredom, or because of an increasing dependency on alcohol. In a *Saturday Evening Post* story, "A New Leaf" (July 1931), Fitzgerald seems to be explaining his own addiction through the eyes of his character, Dick Ragland. "About the time I came into money I found that with a few drinks I got expansive and somehow had the ability to please people, and the idea turned my head. Then I began to take a whole lot of drinks to keep going and have everybody think I was wonderful."[2]

But now, Zelda told her friend Sara Mayfield, "two drinks puts him in a manic state, absolutely manic, he wants to fight everybody, including me. He's drinking himself to death."[3] Scott was going down the path already taken by his friend Ring Lardner in Great Neck. Fitzgerald's daily consumption was as high as a quart of gin and thirty beers. His character Dick Ragland again describes Scott's situation. "Just when somebody's taken him up and is making a big fuss over him, he pours the soup down his hostess's back, kisses the serving maid, and passes out in the dog kennel. But he's done it too often. He's run through about everybody."[4]

As the 1920s continued, Zelda was doing little better, but sensed her increased loss of control as she watched Scott. In her (downward) spiral notebook, Zelda designed a plan of moderation for both her alcohol and cigarette use. She writes: "10 cigarettes a day, 1 aperitif before breakfast, white wine, champagne, an aperitif before lunch, two water glasses of red wine [she had crossed out one and substituted two] and a cocktail before supper and white wine."[5] This could have been considered only a moderate regimen in her time. Zelda described a typical night of drinking to Mayfield:

> We've been on a party. Nobody knows where it started, when it'll end, or whose party it is. All of the people were white, I think. But one of the women had slept with a Negro, a six-day bicycle racer, and a prizefighter that sniffs cocaine. Mere pec- cadilloes, ma cherie. Another one says she sleeps with men for money and women for fun. And she looked like such a nice, simple home-loving type. Just some of the swell friends Scott's picked up at the Dingo Bar. All they talk about is sex plain, striped, mixed and fancy.[6]

✧ ✧ ✧

The disappointing sales of *The Great Gatsby* doubtless contributed to Scott's problem. He told his friend John Biggs that "I drink because I'm the top of the second rates."[7] Scott ignored others' advice to moderate his drinking. In particular, when Zelda complained, he drank still more. Scott was dependent on alcohol, but Zelda's obsession with ballet was also very disturbing and abnormal. Back at Ellerslie, both of these health problems worsened. There had been one too many "happy hours": The idea that there was less to be happy about seemed to enter the collective conscience in Paris and in the New York area. That others were similarly afflicted did not diminish the mounting difficulties for Scott and Zelda.

Did Fitzgerald's Irish heritage have anything to do with it? Despite his accurate portrayal of alcoholism in *Tender Is the Night*, "The Crack-Up" essays, and "The Lost Decade," he never really explained his personal compulsion, only to rationalize and therefore to confirm it. Zelda probably contributed to and enabled his drinking before her first visible mental breakdown in 1930, and Scott's alcoholism intensified thereafter. In the 1920s, Zelda had encouraged him to drink as a kind of spectator sport. Anytime that Fitzgerald tried to write instead of paying attention to Zelda, she called him a "killjoy" or "spoilsport." Hemingway, as noted, believed that Zelda was insanely jealous of Scott's work.

The cultural and social attitudes of the time are important to note: If a man drank heavily, he was not presumed ill; rather, he was judged by his ability to function under the influence. To function well under the influence made him "manly" in the way Ernest Hemingway was admired. As to mental illness, we recall that Zelda was "charming" to the Murphys because of her "honesty" and her unusual use of language. What later would be understood as symptoms of mental illness made Zelda more attractive to the Murphys on the Riviera than Scott. By the same token, Hemingway's charm under the influence of alcohol was unmistakable, but Scott was rude and childish. What, we might ask, does this say for the mental acuity of the Murphys? Or, for that, the cultural prejudices of the time?

Besides Scott Fitzgerald, those writers of the Irish drinking class have produced some of the best in American literature. They include

Eugene O'Neill, John O'Hara, William Faulkner (half Ulster stock), and John Steinbeck. Unlike his contemporary O'Neill, Fitzgerald did not entirely despise his Irish background or himself for being part Irish, but he did set most of his stories in the Jazz Age, on the Riviera, among the nouveau riche, not in the lace-curtain Irish St. Paul where he grew to manhood, a term Zelda quickly disabused when speaking of Scott. St. Paul, too, is identified with the iconoclastic Scandinavian liberal Thorstein Veblen.

More to the point, whether heavy drinkers are writers, Irish, other types of celebrities, or construction workers, they usually drink on at least two occasions—when they are happy and when they are sad. Well, too, they drink on special occasions and at the end of the day. They drink to dull pain and to make the good things in life seem better. They drink to loosen the tongue and to stifle words of love and affection. They all have more drinks than reasons for them, though many are the reasons. Drink for heavy drinkers is a singular form of escape, whether it be for O'Neill, O'Hara, Faulkner, Steinbeck, Hemingway, or Fitzgerald. Of them all, Scott Fitzgerald seemed to have more pain to dull. Still, Fitzgerald had more control over his alcoholism than is commonly claimed. He was a functioning alcoholic; moreover, the binge nature of his drinking left periods of sobriety and intense productivity.

Nor are the Irish unique among the drinking class. Other ethnic drinkers drink *as much:* among regular drinkers—WASPs, Slavics, and Native Americans. In truth, the Irish are somewhat *less likely* than people of Slavic or English heritage to suffer serious alcohol problems. Some 88 percent of Irish Catholics in the United States drink wine, beer, or spirits compared with two-thirds of the overall population. This does not mean that Irish Catholics drink more per capita. While some of the reasons for drinking appear to be genetic, others are cultural: For example, the American Irish drink more with more problems than do their Eire cousins. Being *American and* grasping for the American Dream may have something to do with it.

Since the late nineteenth century in Irish America, these facts have not prevented literature from stereotyping drinking as an ethnic Irish compulsion. The most celebrated thing on American St. Patrick's Day is conviviality by the glass. "Danny Boy" is sung in Irish bars to mourn a weakness for drink and drunkenness. In truth, however, a family history of alcoholism or growing up in a culture that promotes adult drinking remain the most important traits influencing alcohol addiction.[8] Such cultures include the French for wine, the Germans and Austrians for beer, the English for ale, and the Americans for martinis. F. Scott Fitzgerald drank straight gin, a *very* dry American martini. Scott's family history was not dominated by alcoholism, but his father, born in America, was a heavy drinker, and his drinking probably hampered his work as a salesman. In the fictional biographical portrait of his father in the early short story "Shadow Laurels," Scott describes his "small, heavy-bearded black eyed" father as a would-be poet, "always sleepy" from drink, and an inveterate slacker.[9] Scott prophetically knew that he had inherited from his father both a love of storytelling and of drink. When Scott went off to college, the student culture at Princeton University promoted it. Its reputation as "the pleasantest country club in America" preceded Scott. Perhaps most important, no culture promotes the drinking of alcohol as much as the USA.

Today, experts generally agree, early onset alcoholism, as in Fitzgerald's case, is the most difficult to cure. Scott may have been on the edge of alcoholism by his twentieth year. Already he was taking the train from Princeton into New York City and disappearing into bars for several days and nights. Invited by Sap Donahoe, a St. Paul and Princeton friend, to his family ranch near Bozeman, Montana, in the summer of 1915, Fitzgerald had a good time drinking with the cowboys and winning fifty dollars in a poker game. Once elected to Cottage, one of the "big four" clubs at Princeton, Fitzgerald drank himself through those lavish weekend parties. Scott returned to Princeton only to await his commission in the army at age twenty-one rather than to get his degree. Princeton's most famous alumnus (Brooke Shields aside) never graduated. From the beginning, gin may have had something to do with his failure as a serious student, but it was more complicated than that—*much* more complicated.

After all, there was that beautiful, selfish, and irresponsible Southern belle, Zelda. Scott was twenty-two and Zelda eighteen when they met; already both were drinking heavily. No one has a complete record of the rounds, but Zelda probably was a heavier drinker than Scott at the time. Zelda was not only American, she was from Alabama, where drinking alcohol *still* is widely considered a sin. In his efforts to "afford" Zelda—as it turned out, a lifelong and elusive quest—Scott took that unappealing job with the Barron Collier Advertising Agency at thirty-five dollars a week. His ads were for signs on streetcars. When not so "writing," Fitzgerald got drunk with his college friends and indulged in all kinds of sophomoric pranks. Zelda gave him still more reason to drink.

In April 1919, Scott and Zelda became informally engaged and slept together for the first time. Zelda already had dispensed with her virginity at fifteen (in an age when "purity" was greatly prized, especially in Montgomery, Alabama) and openly flaunted a "loss" that she considered a benefit. And, despite her "enthusiastic" sex with Scott, she told him that marriage was out of the question until he had achieved financial success. Having earlier been rejected by the beautiful but rich Ginevra King for his relative poverty, Fitzgerald surely was more disappointed than surprised.

But, there was more, or less. There was the Sayre family's opposition to their marriage. Zelda needed (and the family intimately knew it) a reliable, strong husband who would *want* to and *could* control her inherently wild behavior. Scott charged into Montgomery, invading the post–Civil War South—an unreliable Irish Catholic who had failed at college, had no visible career, and drank heavily with visible effects. "Post–Civil War South" was a provisional term then and perhaps even today; Montgomery had yet to admit that the war had ended. Though Zelda defended her Scott as the sweetest person in the South *or* North when sober, her daddy, Judge Sayre, sternly responded, "He's never sober."

Impatient with Scott, only two months later Zelda broke off their engagement and ended their sexual relations. Fearful of losing her to a prosperous Southern rival and the aforementioned golfer Roger Jones, Fitzgerald decided (his golf being second rate) that he would win Zelda by writing a best-selling novel. He quit the job he hated and got drunk (again). "I was a failure—mediocre at advertising work and unable to get started as a writer. Hating the city, I got roaring, weeping drunk on my last penny and went home."[10] Of course, as his contemporary author-friend Thomas Wolfe (1900–1938) would put it, in a sense Scott could never really "go home again." His style of drinking—"binge drinking" by its most respectable name—would continue intermittently until nearly the end of his life.

Doubtless the early onset of Fitzgerald's alcoholism was telling. But, there is much more to his story and his ailment. In his time excessive drinking was considered in polite company either a weakness *or* strength, not an illness. Those who saw Scott's friend Ernest Hemingway drink considered his indulgence to be not only masculine but also admirable. Hemingway, as they said of William Faulkner, could "hold his liquor." Scott, who often passed out cold after only a few drinks, could not. Hemingway often maligned Fitzgerald not for his intemperance but for his weak constitution. Therefore, Scott lacked not only verticalness, but also "discipline and masculinity." For writers, many of whom were Scott's friends, drinking was their day job; it was an accepted way of living, not a medical problem. And, for the most part, Scott himself considered his drinking a "weakness," though often a necessary one.

Few, however, have had more reasons to drink than Fitzgerald. Sometimes it kept him from writing; other times drink kept him going. His fame assured that his most notorious binges would become known—at least among those who otherwise would want to employ his great talent. Besides, when drunk, Scott's demeanor, unlike many others under the influence, was insulting, mean, and usually self-destructive. It was the kind of behavior that gave the "dark" side of the Irish their maudlin reputation. Literary peers such as Dos Passos and Hemingway as well as close personal friends like the Murphys all comment on Scott's belligerence and self-centeredness when drunk.

Eventually, drinking would virtually destroy Fitzgerald's reputation. The contrast drunk was made all the more stark by his wit and natural charm when sober. Fitzgerald was naturally blessed with the special gifts of Irish inheritance—humor, wonderful storytelling, and irony. Often sloppy and surly when drunk, his voice was exquisitely resonant when his words were not slurred. Still, it is a mistake to dwell unduly on the liquid part of Scott's personality; he remained a professional writer to the end. If those binges had never had endings, Fitzgerald could not have written so much or so brilliantly. Moreover, some of what he wrote came from his experiences while under that particular influence.

Perspective is vital. Drinking was not Fitzgerald's life, but its damages were visible at critical times in his career. Somewhere between his great artistic achievements and this damage lies the net social waste, if any. The effects of gin were mixed, even as he drank it straight. In Scott's creative process it is difficult to know how many afflictions were needed to spur his writing. He had so many; we might suppose that any one of them would do. He nonetheless was most productive during times of dire financial need. Then, too, much of the material he most often worked with came out of the way he and Zelda lived and fought. While a drinking binge was his first reaction to a new emotional crisis, his recoveries led to sobriety and intense writing activity, his professional aspiration.

There is a great deal of waste in any nation, in any era. Fitzgerald's own wastage—painful as it was to him and to Zelda—nonetheless contributed greatly to American literature. In his artistry, adversity was often Scott's only friend. How much of Scott's internal wasting was imposed on him by Zelda or by his intense professional aspirations is difficult to know because they were so intertwined. This, despite Scott's view, that neither destroyed the other.

✧ ✧ ✧

There too was a sexual dimension. Zelda's reckless affair with Lieutenant Jozan during the mid-1920s brought to the surface Scott and Zelda's sexual problems. Zelda was sensual and aggressively sexual whereas Scott was reserved; he knew at an early age that he lacked a strong sexual drive. His sexual inhibitions nonetheless—like his social inhibitions—were greatly diminished by heavy drinking.

Sexual liberation became one more reason for his alcoholism. The Fitzgeralds, desiring to have a son, tried to conceive another child during the winter of 1926. Although their failure probably was the result of Zelda's earlier abortion and miscarriages, Zelda increasingly blamed Scott. She complained that his penis was too small to give her sexual satisfaction and compared Scott unfavorably with Jozan. This invidious comparison, of course, did not help matters with the ever-romantic Scott.

Later, as Zelda became obsessed with ballet dancing, their sexual relations came to an end and she began to accuse Scott of homosexuality. Worse, she claimed that he and Ernest Hemingway were lovers, one of the least plausible sexual couplings in literary history. When Scott and Ernest were sufficiently drunk one evening, Scott asked Ernest for his opinion regarding the size of the questionable member. Ernest reassured Scott that his was quite normal. This casual male bonding had nothing to do with homosexuality; otherwise, Hemingway *never* would have related the story. Though Scott never made the connection at the time, paranoid suspicions about people's sexual orientation is one of the symptoms of schizophrenia.

Now, Zelda was unmistakably mad. She had entered La Sanitarium de la Malmaison on April 23, 1930, in an agitated, intoxicated state. She paced the floor, flirted with the doctors, told them she was in love with her dance teacher, previously had loved a friend in the Paris Opera, and insisted again that Scott was a homosexual in love with a man named Hemingway. Scott, concerned that the medical staff would believe her, explained how Zelda's hallucinations were related to a family history of mental instability on both sides of her family. The diagnosis at Malmaison was greatly understated as "anxiety" brought on by Zelda's overwork as a dancer. When, she discharged herself on May 11 it was against her doctor's advice.

Soon Zelda began again to experience hallucinations and attempted suicide with an overdose of barbiturates. It was on May 22 that Fitzgerald drove Zelda to the Val-Mont Clinic in nearby Glion, Switzerland, where she became infatuated with several nurses. Zelda claimed that she had been brought there by force, that she was a homosexual, and suspected her husband of the same behavior. Dr. Oscar Forel was retained by Scott to aid in diagnosing Zelda's condition since Val-Mont was known primarily for treating gastrointestinal problems, not mental illness. Forel, not knowing what to do, consulted with a Swiss psychiatrist, Eugen Bleuler, director of a Zurich hospital and professor of psychiatry at the University of Zurich. Bleuler had introduced the term *schizophrenia* as a substitute for "dementia praecox" in 1911 and was a leading authority on psychoses. He suspected the worst—acute schizophrenia—and moved Zelda to Les Rives de Prangins near Nyon on Lake Geneva on June 5, 1930.

Prangins looked like a resort. The Prangins building had once been the chateau of Joseph Bonaparte and occupied a one-hundred-acre park between Geneva and Lausanne. The acreage offered golf, skiing, tennis, riding, a bathing beach, and billiard and music rooms. During 1930–31, Scott paid about $13,000 (roughly $143,000 in today's dollars) for Zelda's treatment. Still, after becoming violent and attempting to escape, Zelda was forcibly restrained. She was given chloral hydrate whenever she hallucinated and placed in solitary confinement to prevent harm to herself. Her condition did not improve.

Scott commuted between Paris and Nyon and stayed in Lausanne or Geneva. Scottie was turned over to an Alsatian governess in Paris and told nothing of her mother's condition, except that she was ill. Rosalind, Zelda's sister, who was living in Brussels, did not help. She blamed Scott for Zelda's problems and demanded that she and her husband be allowed to adopt Scottie. It was a demand that Scott found easy to refuse. All of this put Fitzgerald under enormous financial and emotional strain.

Meanwhile, Zelda slipped into a deep depression. As she writes to Scott, "The panic seems to have settled into a persistent gloom punctuated by movements of bombastic hysteria."[11] Fitzgerald deposited money into Zelda's hospital account and told the doctors to give her every luxury in the line of Paris clothes and so forth that she wanted. Zelda expressed her appreciation for this and for other gestures in loving letters that she composed whenever lucid. In one, she describes her feeling while hiking in the mountains near the hospital:

Dear Sweetheart—Walking along up so high there were white stones with black moss spots like the backs of ponies grazing, and there were stones that menaced and pierced the earth like broken bones, and there were stones that the earth caught on like a garment in the wind, and there were meadows spread out to dry and the clouds moved so fast as if they could crush you and the sky was like a rippling beach and we stood on the horizon. There we were in the highest place—with the whole world rolling away like a lot of sculptors clay about our feet and we the memorial to some forgotten lyric poet. There were yards and yards of fraises du bois like an old-fashioned print, red dots hanging on a preponderance of grace and there were calves depressed like bad boys who've just had their faces washed and there was love everyplace for you. Darling, Wednesday usually comes in the middle of the week, so I won't see you for another half of a whole. It's unbearable. Dear, I love you so much that loving is like being one of those cheeses that drip through a cloth, which is you, of course—and darling and love and dear—good night.[12]

In this hospital Zelda gave up her dream of becoming a prima ballerina. (From the beginning Dr. Forel believed that Zelda's recovery depended on her giving up her ballet aspirations and Scott giving up drink.) Instead, she wanted to go home to Montgomery. To keep her in the hospital, the nurses often gave her bromides and morphine. These "sleeping cures" were widely used in Europe during the 1920s and 1930s. After one of these treatments, Zelda was calmer but covered with eczema and in excruciating pain. She told Scott that God was torturing her. Toward the end of summer Zelda was back in schizophrenia. On November 22, 1930, Forel and Bleuler agreed on a diagnosis of "schizophrenie," an organic brain disease impairing various functions and causing bizarre and dangerous behavior. They knew of no cure for a disease that tended to run in families. Today we would say that the cause was primarily genetic.

Such letters and such events must have been heartbreaking for Scott. Late that September, Scott commented on how Zelda, "in spite of tenderness toward him still makes irrational erotic remarks," and that she had become so infatuated with a red-haired girl at the clinic that Prangins had to change her living quarters. Her days at Prangins had to be carefully structured. Keeping Zelda within any limits, however, had always been very difficult. Sometimes she wanted to paint and write into the night.

Earlier in September, Scott had moved to the Beau Rivage Hotel and later the Grand Hotel de la Paiz in Lausanne. He spent some time with Thomas Wolfe, who was summering nearby. Since the doctors would not allow Scott to see Zelda, he communicated only through telephone calls and letters. Again lonely, he began an affair with a titled Englishwoman with the unlikely name of Bijou O'Connor, whom he met at his hotel. She had once worked for British military intelligence, and her wit and charm was great comfort to Fitzgerald at a time of great need. (Most likely, Ms. O'Connor is the nurse-savior figure in Scott's [much later] movie script for "Babylon Revisited.")

By December 1930, Zelda's condition had improved sufficiently that Scott and Scottie could visit during Christmas week and help trim her tree. However, the excitement was too much for Zelda, and she began to break ornaments. Scott fled with Scottie to ski at Gstaad and did not see Zelda again until after his father's funeral in Rockville, Maryland, in January 1931. Upon his return, Fitzgerald found Zelda substantially improved. He took her and Scottie to the lakeside resort of Annecy in Haute-Savoie for two weeks of sailing, swimming, playing tennis, and picnicking. Not only did everyone enjoy being together, Zelda would remember every moment of the experience. "The Crash! Zelda + America" is the way Fitzgerald summed up his thirty-third year in his Ledger.

✧ ✧ ✧

Zelda was released from Prangins on September 15, 1931. She had been there for fifteen months. The Fitzgeralds spent a few days on Lake Geneva, then checked into Paris's Majestic Hotel before taking the *Aquitania* to New York. Zelda's new passport reveals the physical toll of her illness. Softness has been replaced by coarseness, lively eyes replaced by a blank stare, a nose more pronounced on her thinner face. Determined to once again put their past behind them, the Fitzgeralds fled Europe: It would be for the final time.

In Manhattan, they checked into the New Yorker Hotel for a week or so and looked up old friends such as Alex McKaig and John Bishop. Scott met alone with Harold Ober and Maxwell Perkins, and lunched with Hemingway. By now the American economy was in a freefall and New York City had not been spared. Even New Yorkers felt a sense of defeat; it was not the New York of the Roaring Twenties, but it nonetheless was too busy and stressful for Zelda. The family went south to Montgomery, staying downtown at the Jefferson Davis Hotel; three rooms and four baths cost only nine dollars a day. Although the South had not been spared the Great Depression, most Southerners did not notice it since the Deep South had been economically depressed for so long. Zelda wanted to buy a house (they had never owned any property), but they settled on a six-month lease on a large house at 819 Felder Avenue in one of

Zelda: Before and after Prangins

Montgomery's nicest neighborhoods. (Although the house has since been divided into apartments, it still stands as a historical site with a few of the rooms devoted to a Fitzgerald Museum.) While there, Scott began to rethink his novel.

In Montgomery, Zelda swam, played tennis, visited friends, and did some painting and sculpting. She and Scott went to the country club where they first met and she sometimes joined Scott for a round of golf. They had their usual entourage: a French governess who had returned from Europe with them privately tutored Scottie, while a hired black couple cooked and cleaned.

The close proximity of Zelda's parents forced Fitzgerald to alter his drinking habits. This, as it always had, made him edgy. In late October, Scott was offered $750 a week by Metro-Goldwyn-Mayer (MGM) to revise a screenplay of Katherine Brush's 1931 best-selling novel *Red-Headed Woman,* to star Jean Harlow. He initially rejected the offer because he was working on a series of short stories as well as a novel and did not want to leave Zelda. When MGM raised the offer to $1,200 at the urging of the legendary Irving Thalberg, who wanted Fitzgerald for the job of making Harlow a star, Scott accepted. The proximity of Zelda's parents may have made his decision easier. Besides, these were handsome wages, especially during the Great Depression. Ultimately Irving Thalberg would become Monroe Stahr in Fitzgerald's *The Last Tycoon.* Since Zelda's mental condition precluded her from going, she was far less excited about the prospects than was Scott. Among other concerns, Zelda worried that there would begin another Lois Moran–type affair. Scott and Zelda, of course, quarreled at the train station.

Scott left Montgomery in early November 1931. He got off to a bad start, getting drunk at Thalberg's home and reciting "Dog," a bad Princeton party song even by sophomoric standards. He was accompanied at the piano by Ramon Navarro, but was booed by John Gilbert and Lupe Velez. Worse, Thalberg could not tolerate drunks and asked (heavy drinker and playwright) Charles MacArthur to take Scott home. Meanwhile, back in Montgomery, Zelda found the small city oppressive and unsettling without Scott. Her father, ill for the past year, was dying. Despite his deteriorating condition, he had the strength to discuss the prospects for her divorcing Scott. The Judge died on November 17. Now, Zelda had nothing to look forward to except Scott's return for Christmas. She did, however, begin to write a novel, a thinly veiled autobiographical account of the Fitzgeralds' recent life that would become *Save Me the Waltz* (1932).

Zelda had read the drafts of Fitzgerald's ongoing novel that would become *Tender Is the Night*. Meanwhile, the *Red-Headed Woman* film project was shelved, and a Harlow screenplay was written by Anita Loos. Scott's Hollywood failure combined with his knowledge that Zelda was writing a psychological novel with much of "his" material put him in a terrible mood. They argued continuously about her ceasing the writing project. Zelda began drinking again, had an outbreak of eczema, and began to hear voices in her head once again. She drank the contents of Scott's whiskey flask and was seized by hallucinations of people doing awful things to her. She had to be hospitalized.

Dr. Forel wanted Zelda to return to Prangins. Such a long trip was impractical and instead he recommended that she enter Craig House, a private sanitarium in Beacon, New York, on the Hudson River above West Point. By the time Forel's letter had arrived, Zelda had already been admitted on February 12 to Henry Phipps Psychiatric Clinic of Johns Hopkins University in Baltimore, where she remained until June 26, 1932. She was placed under the care of Dr. Adolf Meyer and Dr. Mildred Squires. By now, Zelda's mouth was twisted in an uncontrollable smile of amusement. This relapse so frightened Zelda that—perhaps for the first time—she realized the seriousness of her illness. Still, she returned to work on the novel, with the encouragement of Dr. Squires, and secretly submitted the manuscript to Maxwell Perkins at Scribners.

When Scott discovered what had happened, he was furious. He was especially angry that the novel had been written on time paid for by money he had earned writing magazine stories and Hollywood screenplays rather than his own novel that covered similar material. Scott insisted on major revisions, which he supervised during late spring and summer of 1932. The middle section of the manuscript, which was a portrayal of Scott as an alcoholic, was deleted. That section included provocative, vindictive attacks on Scott as a writer and husband as well as scandalous revelations of their private life. Scott was correct in his belief that the novel would ruin him and any prospects for his own novel.

Save Me the Waltz confirms Scott's assessment of Zelda as an amateur writer and of the consequences of her actions. It appeared in bookstores on October 7, 1932, and sold only 1,392 copies from a printing of 3,010, earning Zelda a net $120.73. The bulk of royalties earned went toward corrections in the page proofs plus repayment of Fitzgerald's long-standing debts to Scribners. It was, we must emphasize, published in the midst of the Great Depression, when most families could not afford even necessities. Nothing good came from it. Scott still viewed the novel as a personal attack on him. The financial failure was damaging to Zelda's delicate psyche, something that Scott had anticipated.

✧ ✧ ✧

Still, Zelda had sufficiently recovered to attempt a return to "normal life." In May, a month before Zelda's discharge from Phipps, Scott found a rambling, fifteen-room Victorian house on the Bayard Turnbull estate near Towson, Maryland, called La Paix. The name came from its peaceful setting, situated as it was on twenty acres with a small lake and a tennis court. The name belied the warfare between Zelda and Scott. They lived there until the end of 1933. There, Fitzgerald hired a secretary, Mrs. Isabel Owens, to type manuscripts and supervise Scottie (and become her substitute mother). She and Scott made frequent trips to Phipps, which was nearby.

The Turnbull family lived next to La Paix in a new house. Fitzgerald treated young Andrew Turnbull like the son he never had. Ultimately, Turnbull became one of Fitzgeralds' biographers. As Turnbull remembers him, "There was always something of the magician in Fitzgerald. He was the inventor, the creator, the timeless impresario who brightened our days and made other adult company seem dull and profitless. It wasn't so much any particular skill of his, as a quality of caring, of believing, of pouring his whole soul and imagination into whatever he did with us." As to Zelda, when there, she kept to herself and talked to no one.[13]

Amazingly, Scott, the embodiment of American optimism, still had hope for Zelda's complete recovery. On June 16, Zelda was able to spend the morning at La Paix and the rest of the day at Phipps. Her doctors warned that any strenuous work would lead to a relapse. In particular she was cautioned not to compete with Scott. Competition of any kind appears to be especially stressful for anyone with schizophrenia or even a lesser mental illness. Besides, writing requires great concentration, an effort very difficult for the schizophrenic. No doubt with some encouragement from Scott, her doctors recommended that she give up writing fiction. Meanwhile, Dr. Thomas A. C. Rennie was assigned to Zelda's case.

Rennie asked the Fitzgeralds to share their personal perceptions of their marriage. This request led to a remarkable dialogue. Zelda wrote, linking her recent breakdown to Scottie's constant ill humor in her presence and to her relations with her husband. Scott, for his part, linked her recent breakdown to his novel-in-progress. He saw a clash of egos in which Zelda considered herself to be as fine a professional writer as he. Again, competition, even when imaginary, can trigger a breakdown for a schizophrenic. Scott's letter to Dr. Rennie also reveals something intellectually deeper, his renewal of interest in Karl Marx, or at least Marxism.

We can put Scott's letter into context by first relating his latest flirtation with Marx. Scott began rereading Marx during the summer of 1932 shortly after moving to La Paix. The general sense of doom with which Scott (and the nation) were viewing the economy is indicated in a letter to art exhibitor Cary Ross when Scott half-jokingly referred to an eclipse on August 26, 1932, as "prefiguring, paralleling and indirectly precipitating the fall of capitalism and here one must read *Das Kapital* at last."[14] Scott had lengthy discussions with members of the Communist Party in Baltimore and was even recruited to do some public speaking on behalf of the cause. Perhaps as prep material, Scott was given a copy of a communist pamphlet entitled *Program of the Communist International.* An underlined passage (which may or may not have been Scott's marking) near the beginning gives its general tenor: "Imperialism subjects large masses of the proletariat of all countries to the dictatorship of the finance-capitalist plutocracy."[15]

As Scott immersed himself in Marx's ideas on class conflict, worker alienation, and the instability of the capitalist system, he was simultaneously experiencing a profound marital conflict with an unstable Zelda while suffering from every conceivable form of Marxist alienation—dispossessed of his

Scott and Zelda while attending a theater performance of Dinner at Eight, *Baltimore, but also looking anxious, June 1932*

work, self-worth, friends, wife, and artistic creativity. In his letter to Dr. Rennie (October 1932) at the Phipps Clinic, Scott positions himself as an exploited worker and Zelda as the capitalist-imperialist appropriating for her private gratification the "materials of our common life."[16] In particular, Scott assessed their marital difficulties as "a rather clear-cut struggle of egos between Zelda and myself" wherein "for the last five years—the two and a half of ballet and the two and a half of sickness, she has come to regard me as the workhorse and herself as the artist—the producer of the finer things such as painting, uncommercial literature, ballet, etc., such as I have not been able to mix with the damn Post story writing."[17]

Scott (the laborer) is the true producer of value: "Consciously she knows that her Literary work is founded upon mine and that she is still a long way from turning out work as the best of mine" whereas Zelda (the capitalist) appropriates (not creates) value even to the point of endangering the life of the worker who supports the capitalist:

It is significant that last February her breakdown was associated with my outlining to her a frame for what was then a new approach to my work which was a story of our eight years in Europe. I read her a chapter. What did she do immediately on her arrival in the clinic but sit down and try to write it herself, including what she must have known was some of the best material in my notebook, stuff I had often discussed with her and that she knew I hadn't touched for short stories because it belonged in a more important medium.

The letter continues in a Marxian vein connecting Scott's immiserization with Zelda's appropriation:

But the fundamental struggle continued, shown indirectly by her unwillingness to let me help her with her stories coupled with a study of my books so profound that she is saturated with them, whole fragments of my scenes and cadences come out in her work, which she admits. One is flattered—it is only when she aims to use the material of our common life, the only fact material that I have (heaven knows there's no possible harm in her using her own youth, her dancing, etc.) that she becomes a danger to my life and to us.

In principle, Scott agrees that Zelda has a "right" to what "we both observed," but asserts "that under the present circumstances I have all rights to [that store of common material]" and her continued appropriation will end up "leaving me literally nothing," like the propertyless worker.[18]

It's not known exactly *who* renewed Scott's interest in Marx and company in the early thirties, but the reason is clear: With the advent of the Great Depression and Americans on the verge of political revolt, it was impossible to repudiate Marxist thought and the Soviet alternative. Yet, symptomatic of Scott's life, which straddled capitalism and socialism, he saw fit to invest $100 in AT&T and $100 in Northern Pacific Railway (one of James Hill's companies) stocks in June 1930, just a year before he read M. Ilin's *New Russia's Primer: The Story of the Five-Year Plan* (1931) and recommended it to his ten-year-old daughter Scottie, the beginning of an ongoing education in Marxism and Soviet history for her that lasted until Scott's death in 1940. In a letter written on February 26, 1940, Scott admonished Scottie: "Some time when you feel very brave and defiant and haven't been invited to one particular college function read the terrible chapter in *Das Kapital* on The Working Day, and see if you are ever quite the same."[19] But Scott could never fully shed his aristocratic heritage, noting with regard to Scottie's "coming out" in 1939 that even Marx "made every attempt to marry his daughters into the British nobility."[20] Although under the influence of Marxist ideas in the thirties, Scott reserved the right to be in a class of his own.

Also later in the thirties, when instructing Sheilah Graham in her *College of One* course, he referred to Ilin's book as "A beautiful, pathetic trusting book—old and young, rather haunting, and inspiring like the things read and believed in youth."[21] However, Fitzgerald retained the Marxist principle of the right of laborers to own what they produced throughout his life. In another book assigned to Sheilah (James Froude's biography of Caesar), Scott wrote an extensive note to her articulating the Marxist view that workers are in effect slaves robbed of their production under the capitalist system:

> Chattel slavery, it is true, has in English speaking lands, virtually disappeared; but that was only the crude old form of slavery. Is slavery dead where men and women make wealth for others to enjoy it? The man who, goaded on by his misery or the misery of those who are dependent on him, plots & even murders to obtain a miserable wage—*he* is a slave, call him what modern name you will. The condition of things when men willing to get work cannot get work, and when other men needing what these could make cannot afford to buy—this is not *freedom*.[22]

The final sentence is a strong, eloquent argument for full employment made seven years before the passage of the Employment Act of 1946 in the United States. Yet Fitzgerald was wary of transplanting the Soviet brand of communism to the United States, a view that was way ahead of the thinking of most progressives at the time. This is Scott's position in a *Baltimore Evening Sun* article (May 1932): "In ideals I am somewhat of a communist. That is, as much as other persons who belong to what we call 'the arts group,' but communism as I see it has no place in the United States."[23]

✧ ✧ ✧

The Marxist subtext in Scott's letter to Dr. Rennie in 1932 attests to his renewed interest in Marx, perhaps because the wastes being described so closely paralleled his own. Dr. Meyer also read the Zelda-Scott letters. He acknowledged that Scott understood Zelda's case well, but until Scott gave up drinking and participated in the therapy, he did not expect Zelda to recover. We need recall that Dr. Meyer himself had an expert's understanding of Zelda's illness. Although Scott did begin treatment for his alcoholism in December 1932 with one of Dr. Meyer's colleagues, he did not continue and instead resumed his denial of any such problem. Meanwhile, Fitzgerald suggested that Zelda focus on painting, while she was secretly making notes for a second novel. Zelda's new intense focus on writing would bring still more ruin to the Fitzgeralds' marriage and still more wasting of Scott and his talents. The Great Depression would continue to mirror Scott Fitzgerald's emotions during the thirties.

Endnotes

1. F. Scott Fitzgerald, *The Beautiful and Damned* (New York: Charles Scribner's Sons, 1950), p. 417.

2. F. Scott Fitzgerald, "A New Leaf," quoted in Matthew J. Bruccoli, *Some Sort of Epic Grandeur: The Life of F. Scott Fitzgerald* (New York: Harcourt Brace Jovanovich, 1981), p. 135.

3. Zelda Fitzgerald, quoted in Sara Mayfield, *Exiles from Paradise: Zelda and Scott Fitzgerald* (New York: Delacorte Press, 1971), p. 138.

4. Fitzgerald, "A New Leaf," p. 136.

5. Zelda Fitzgerald, spiral loose-leaf notebook, Zelda Fitzgerald Collection, Princeton University Library.

6. Zelda Fitzgerald, quoted in Mayfield, *Exiles from Paradise*, p. 138.

7. John Biggs, quoted by Rex Polier in "Fitzgerald in Wilmington, The 'Great Gatsby' at Bay," *Philadelphia Sunday Bulletin*, January 1974, Sec. 4.

8. For a brilliant exploration of the romance between the American Irish and alcohol, see Maureen Dezell, *Irish America Coming into Clover: The Evolution of a People and a Culture* (New York: Doubleday, 2000), pp. 117–39.

9. John Kuehl, ed., *The Apprentice Fiction of F. Scott Fitzgerald, 1909–1917* (New Brunswick, N.J.: Rutgers University Press, 1965), p. 76.

10. F. Scott Fitzgerald, "My Lost City," in *Crack-Up*, ed. Edmund Wilson (New York: New Directions, 1945), p. 26.

11. Letter from Zelda Fitzgerald to F. Scott Fitzgerald, fall 1930, F. Scott Fitzgerald Papers, Princeton University Library.

12. Letter from Zelda to Scott, undated, Princeton University Library.

13. Andrew Turnbull, "Scott Fitzgerald at La Paix," *Publications in the Humanities* (Cambridge, Mass.: M.I.T., 1956), p. 7.

14. Matthew J. Bruccoli and Margaret M. Duggan, eds., *Correspondence of F. Scott Fitzgerald* (New York: Random House, 1980), p. 297.

15. *Program of the Communist International,* pamphlet, F. Scott Fitzgerald Collection, Princeton University Library.

16. Matthew J. Bruccoli, ed., *F. Scott Fitzgerald: A Life in Letters* (New York: Charles Scribner's Sons, 1994), p. 220.

17. Ibid., p. 220.

18. Ibid., pp. 220–21.

19. Scott's investments, unknown until now, were found in notes in the Fitzgerald Collection, Princeton University Library The quote is from ibid., p. 436.

20. Ibid., p. 388.

21. Sheilah Graham, *College of One* (New York: Viking Press, 1967), p. 123.

22. Scott's handwritten note to Sheilah appears on page 8 of Fitzgerald's copy of Froude's *Caesar*, Fitzgerald Collection, Princeton University Library.

23. "Scott Fitzgerald Seeking Home Here," *Baltimore Evening Sun*, p. 12, reprinted in Matthew J. Bruccoli and Jackson R. Bryer, eds., *F. Scott Fitzgerald in His Own Time: A Miscellany* (New York: Popular Library, 1971), p. 285.

Eleven

Not So Tender Is the Night

NOW, THE FITZGERALDS ARE IN A WRITING COMPETITION, OR SO IT SEEMS. Once again, Zelda is using material for her second novel similar to what Fitzgerald is using for his *Tender Is the Night*. For financial and professional and personal reasons Scott is anxious, even desperate, to complete his new novel. Beyond the use of similar material, Fitzgerald correctly worries that Zelda's undertaking of a long work, especially one focused on her illness and one in competition with him, will menace her health. There is a great deal at stake—Scott's future as a novelist, the caring for Zelda, the support of Scottie, and the Fitzgeralds' precarious marriage. The denouement swirls around Zelda as the femme fatale and Scott as a personage.

Zelda's moods were fluctuating daily and Fitzgerald was near the end of his rope. Zelda and her appearance dismayed a dinner guest, Malcolm Cowley. After she was served dinner alone in her room, Cowley and Scott visited with her. Cowley reports:

> Her face was emaciated and twitched as she talked. Her mouth, with deep lines above it, fell into unhappy shapes. Her skin in the lamplight looked brown and weatherbeaten, except that on

the left cheek there were four parallel red streaks where she
had raked it with her fingernails, so that she made me think of
a starved Indian in war paint.[1]

On April 10, 1933, Scott wrote Dr. Meyer asking permission to
return Zelda to Phipps. Some of it was filled with self-pity:

> (1) Is Zelda more worth "saving" than I am? (2) Zelda is strug-
> gling to learn how to write and to paint—while I make myself
> more ill with drink as I try to finish up the work, [my novel]
> of four years. (3) I began to compromise my own case—by
> loss of self-control and outbreaks of temper. (4) I will prob-
> ably be carried off eventually by four strong guards shrieking
> manically that after all I was right and she was wrong, while
> Zelda is followed home by an adoring crowd in an automobile
> flanked with flowers and offered a vaudeville contract.

Some of it went over ground now familiar to us:

> …this idea of "mutual duty" was, from Zelda's youth, the thing
> most lacking in her personality, much more lacking than in the
> average spoiled American girl.…Zelda played the baby with
> me always except when an important thing came up, when she
> was like a fire-hose in her determination.

Some related to Zelda's observed work patterns:

> She cannot work in moderation.… Her "illusion" is—that her
> work's success will give her some sort of divine irresponsibil-
> ity backed by unlimited gold.… She is working under a green-
> house which is my money and my name and my love.[2]

The debate about whether Zelda should avoid continuing a
novel using psychological material until Scott completed *Tender Is
the Night* continued, unabated. Ultimately the debate came down to
one of money, money to pay Zelda's medical bills. Fitzgerald was

the sole financial provider. Dr. Rennie stepped in to facilitate a three-way dialogue between the Fitzgeralds and himself. The session took place in the living room of La Paix on May 28, 1933, at 3:30 P.M. in the midst of the worst part of the Great Depression. The exchanges were recorded by Isabel Owens on a Dictaphone, and later transcribed. The "Rennie Transcript," as it is known at the Princeton University Library, is a remarkable discussion running 114 pages.

As Dr. Meyer knew, Zelda was not the only ill person in the Fitzgerald family. By now Scott was a deeply divided and, in many respects, broken man—some elements of which would be later revealed publicly in *The Crack-Up*. Ironically, as Scott became increasingly engaged with Marxist thought in the early thirties, he was also becoming increasingly dependent on a capitalist system (itself in decline) because his commercial short story writing had

Unemployment during the Great Depression. The photo shows the beginning of unemployment benefits, state employment service office, San Francisco, 1938.

become the sole source of family income. At the time, however, Scott's literary standing was rapidly deteriorating. Even his reputation with the *Saturday Evening Post*—his financial bread and butter—had begun to wane in tandem with the American economy: The prices paid to Scott by the *Post* peaked in 1932 at $4,000 and declined thereafter.

Stories of the indulgent Jazz Age had become irrelevant at the same time that magazine advertising revenue was falling. Persons barely able to afford necessities such as food and basic shelter do not have to be persuaded as to their wants. The medical expenses associated with Zelda's illness were mounting relative to family income that, at $15,823 in 1932, was less than half of 1931. Instead of commercial short story writing serving as a platform for Scott attaining a higher level of artistic endeavor (Fitzgerald and Marx's utilitarian compromise with capitalism), Scott was feeling emotionally and financially drained and increasingly estranged from his most creative work, the novel that would become *Tender Is the Night*.

Scott knew that successfully completing the novel was crucial if he were to maintain his professional stature among both the literary elite as well as the public audience that he engendered in the twenties—a dual allegiance that Scott equated with great authorship. All of these conflicting forces—Scott's imperialist aspirations, his Socialist leanings, and the bourgeois-capitalist realities of his life—culminate and collide in this remarkable May meeting at La Paix between Scott, Zelda, and Dr. Rennie (recorded at Scott's request). The transcript reveals Scott's apparent contradictions—his domineering, caring, and self-regarding personality traits—all of which just adds to its historic and biographical significance.

The immediate impetus for the meeting is Scott's discovery that Zelda is secretly writing a second novel whose psychiatric content might jeopardize the success of his own, the same fear he had with the initial draft of *Save Me the Waltz* before it was revised to his satisfaction. The broader motive for the meeting, however, is Scott's contemplation of a divorce and perhaps a desire for an official record in support of his belief that he is under personal and professional attack from Zelda. He is in his judgment the victim of Zelda's deceit, disobedience, and deliberate destructiveness. Scott's opening remark of his "gradually being destroyed by the present situation" is transparent. Scott proceeds to aggressively criticize Zelda's artistic ability ("third rate") and personal character ("egotism, self-love…no communal responsibility").[3]

Although these accusations are sometimes harsh and even abusive in their repetition, they are meant to establish that he is the superior writer and the only one to be trusted to think of the greater good of the family: "I say that I am a different sort of person than Zelda, that my equipment for being a writer, for being an artist, is different equipment from hers. Her theory is that anything is possible, and that a girl has just got to get along and so she has the right, therefore, to destroy me completely in order to satisfy herself."[4] The "illusion" of invincibility combined with an insensitivity to personal destruction are twin symptoms of paranoid schizophrenia.

As virtually a condition for the continuation of their marriage, Scott demands that Zelda refrain from writing unless it is approved by him and carefully supervised by medical authorities. Scott's position is crystal clear: Zelda is incapable of approaching anything close to economic self-sufficiency, and anything damaging to his career at this stage amounts to financial suicide for the family. Aside from balancing the household economy, however, is Scott's concern for Zelda's mental stability. In response to Zelda's claim that Dr. Rennie advised her to "write long things" because it was therapeutic, Dr. Rennie replies, "But didn't I also say very emphatically and haven't I said all along that for you to dabble in psychiatric material is playing with fire and you ought not to do it, and didn't you promise me really once that you would put the psychiatric novel away for five years and would not touch it for that period?"—a question to which Zelda does not respond.[5]

If Dr. Rennie indeed advised Zelda to write "long things," this activity too had risks. In a diagnosis confirmed by Dr. Slocumb in a letter to Scott nearly a year later (April 11, 1934), Scott writes that Zelda suffers from an inferiority complex that, in her artistic pursuits, translates into a competitive urge contributing to her mental instability. This first manifested itself with Zelda's manic obsession with ballet—triggered, in Scott's view, by his affair with Lois Moran, a young, successful Hollywood professional "artist"—which culminated in Zelda's first hospitalization in 1930. Scott recounts Zelda's destructive emulation again when she wrote the initial draft of *Save Me the Waltz* as a "scandalous expose of me a dirty back-sided attack on me to destroy my life by making me out a S.O.B...." In the 1933 instance, Zelda's "competition" was directed more personally at Scott and, more important, it now endangered the family's finances. With household income declining precipitously, Scott had become even more "hypersensitive" about his literary standing.[6] Under pressure from Dr. Rennie, who frames the issue as reducing "itself to the question in your own mind of your fundamental worth in comparison with your husband's," Zelda reluctantly agrees to Scott's demands by the end of the meeting.[7]

This "settlement" is far from amicable, however, and there are numerous attacks and counterattacks recorded in the transcript that reveal the tempestuousness of the Fitzgeralds' marriage. Zelda states her case. She resents Scott claiming exclusive right to their shared experiences on the basis that he is the superior professional writer; views his immediate demands as "bullying"; implies that he is a megalomaniac and mentally abusive. "Your whole attitude," Zelda says, "is that you have the right to everything, that you can sit up and reproach me from morning until night, about my not having money, about not working, and not having anything, and trying to raise hell when I do anything."[8] She even accuses Scott of physical abuse, claiming that in 1928, while living at Ellerslie, Scott returned home drunk from a talk at Princeton's Cottage Club, became violent, and bloodied her nose.

Scott is no less unsympathetic. He tells Dr. Rennie that "the first time I met her I saw she was a drunkard" and estimates fifty occasions in which Zelda needed bromide or injections of morphine to calm her down after becoming "a raging maniac" while drunk.[9] As regards the bloody nose incident, Scott says that it happened following the night of his Cottage Club scheduled talk at Princeton, but that the physical contact occurred when Zelda rushed *at him* when he tried to put her to bed at 6:00 A.M. because she had been up all night on a drinking binge of her own. In response to the charge that he "raise[s] hell" whenever Zelda acts on her own, Scott replies that "that is because you do terrible things" and adds: "Sometimes I am inclined to think you do these things because you are psychotic, and other times I think because you are just wicked."[10] So there! Indeed, it is difficult to separate psychotic acts from intentionally evil ones.

Scott's anger is as apparent as its practicality. The anger causes him to treat Zelda in a harsh and domineering manner, which does not enhance his plea to Zelda that this is the time "to be kinder" at this trying time in his literary life.[11] Scott establishing Zelda's untrustworthy character and inferior talent, however, is salient to his argument that he should have present authority over Zelda's writing because it represents a threat to his professional career and therefore to the financial lifeblood of their small family. Scott is being practical in his suggestion that Zelda is economically dependent upon him, and for Zelda to pursue her psychiatric novel at this time is the height of selfishness since it seriously threatens their small family's survival. Furthermore, Scott considers it only fair that Zelda now finally make sacrifices in light of his previous sacrifices—especially the interrupted work on his novel to earn income from his short story writing to keep the family afloat. He bluntly tells Zelda: "You have one power: You can ruin us. To make us or help us, you have not got that power. I am the only person in the world that can make us. And I can share with you the honor and the glory that I make, and the money...."[12]

Now, we may well wonder. Is Scott being more egotistical than magnanimous here, and is he indeed overreacting (or overacting)? Scott reflects upon these charges in the course of the meeting. What exactly is under attack from Scott's perspective? In particular, how could a sophisticated novel like *Tender Is the Night* possibly be harmed by Zelda whipping out a "third rate" novel (a point Zelda herself makes), even if it focuses on psychiatric material that, objectively speaking, belongs at least as much to Zelda as to Scott?

We have already given one explanation—the economic realities of the family's situation. Although *Tender Is the Night* is a sophisticated novel not principally aimed at a mass public audience, it had to be *sufficiently* aimed there if it were to be enough of a financial success to allow Scott to continue his serious work as a novelist. A psychiatric novel by Zelda threatened to compromise the commercial reach of *Tender*. Another explanation touches upon artistic purity—that Zelda's work would invariably taint *any* reading of Scott's novel and therefore compromise its literary as well as commercial value. A third explanation embraces both these perspectives. Scott's vision of literary greatness was of an author leading the masses as well as lifting the eyebrows of highbrows—a characteristic that Scott detected and admired in Irving Thalberg, a producer-director who raised standards of art in the film industry even while catering to a mass commercial audience.

A final explanation is found in the invidious comparison of Scott's artistry compared with Zelda's. That Scott was the superior artist was beyond doubt. One could only speculate about Zelda's artistic abilities even when she was, if ever, well. Part of Scott's superiority came from his ability to create historical and philosophical as well as emotional atmosphere in his fiction. An early outline draft of *Tender Is the Night* has Dick Diver as a communist who sends his son to Russia to be educated. However, in its final version, the Marxist slant in the novel is more a subtle extension of a device employed by Scott in his previous novels: the metaphorical relationship between "capital" and what Kuehl has called "the most vital character he ever created," the femme fatale.[13]

The femme fatale animates men with her beauty but ultimately destroys them, and is possessed with considerable financial and physical capital. Scott's original exposure to the femme fatale was Ginevra King. As the femme fatale takes shape in Scott's other fiction, now mostly inspired by Zelda, there is a frequent connection between her character and the destructive power of capital with Marxian undertones. Marx viewed capital as a vital but destructive force in the capitalist stage of social evolution. It is specifically described in the chapter "The Working-Day" in *Das Kapital*. The leading fictional female characters in each of Scott's *completed* novels (Rosalind in *Paradise*, Gloria in *Damned*, Daisy in *Gatsby*, and Nicole in *Tender*) are indeed possessed by Marx's description of capital as "dead labour, that, vampire-like, only lives by sucking living labour, and lives the more, the more labour it sucks."[14] It is the sorry truth.

Scott was aware of the parallel between his femme fatale who attracts then consumes men and Marx's view of the capitalist as a parasitic monster who accumulates and expands by exploiting the labor of others. The description of Rosalind in *This Side of Paradise* is filled with economic metaphor and parasitic undertones: "She treats men terribly. She abuses them and cuts them and breaks dates with them and yawns in their faces—and they come back for more. She's a—she's a sort of vampire, I think"; men "are hers by natural prerogative" and "she is one of those girls who need never make the slightest effort to have men fall in love with them."[15] Her beauty, like unearned capital, is an inalienable property right capable of yielding perpetual interest. Amory, in fact, views her as a corporation to be invested in, to which Rosalind responds: "Oh, it's not a corporation, it's just, Rosalind, Unlimited. Fifty-one shares, name, good-will, and everything goes at $25,000 a year."[16] Fitzgerald gets away with his attack on capitalism through the use of humor.

✧ ✧ ✧

In *The Beautiful and Damned,* Gloria Gilbert (Patch) is twice referred to as "la belle dame sans merci" ("the beautiful but merciless lady," from the title of a Keats poem) who at one point literally draws blood from Anthony Patch. In the novel, Fitzgerald also defines a vamp as "a picker up and thrower away of men, an unscrupulous and fundamentally unmoved toyer with affections."[17] The vamp absorbs and drains men just as the modern capitalist accumulates wealth only to expend it. In this regard, Fitzgerald's femme fatale detours from the original Marxian image of the capitalist as someone driven only by the desire to save in order to accumulate capital with secondary attention to satisfying consumer desires. The detour is toward Veblen.

Scott's femmes fatales embody capital accumulation but also exhibit the traits of modern consumerism as well. They are therefore wastrels in two ways—sucking up the labor power of a nation, and laying its produce to waste by consuming rather than investing. Capitalism does not therefore lay the foundation for a higher stage of society (as in Marx's theory where capitalism provides the physical capital accumulation necessary for socialism and the abundance required for communism) since Veblenian consumerism devours much of this foundation. Through Zelda, Scott had personal experience not only with the destructive effects of consumerism but the destructive force of her own personality.

In contrast to Gloria, who is mostly a disgusted observer of Anthony Patch's largely self-imposed ruin, Daisy Buchanan is more directly an engine of destruction since she is the driver of Gatsby's luxury car in a hit-and-run accident that kills Myrtle Wilson and seals Jay Gatsby's fate. Daisy's connection to wealth and capital is communicated through the sound of her voice, which is "full of money"[18] (from Ginevra's mouth) and her marriage to Tom Buchanan. Tom, from "old money," has accumulated enough capital (old wealth) to erect an insurmountable barrier for the would-be competitor, Jay Gatsby—an echo of the Marxian theme that accumulations of capital lead to destructive monopoly power.

In *Tender Is the Night*, the Warren sisters' store of capital (derived from their father, who was "a self-made American capitalist") proves destructive as well. As Dick Diver's labor becomes commodified when his professional work becomes dependent on Nicole's inheritance and Baby Warren's lending of capital, he is disenfranchised and robbed of his dignity. Not only is the working-class Dick dependent on the rich (his new job depends on the investment of Warren money and his catering to wealthy patients), the capitalist Nicole is also dependent as she sucks in the hardworking efforts of virtually the entire laboring class to support her consumer lifestyle. Soon we will return to this theme in *Tender*.

Although Scott was immensely gratified by the critical response to *The Great Gatsby* from those who mattered, the fact that sales fell significantly short of his expectations always shadowed him, but, one suspects, not just for financial reasons. True, part of Scott's concern was that lack of commercial success meant less financial breathing space to create further serious works of fiction.

But there were also remnants in Scott of that alter romantic egotist in *This Side of Paradise,* Amory Blaine. Like Amory, Scott had an urge to guide and protect other people that extended into his view of authorship. It is a trait embodied in the romantic egotism of Amory's "immense desire to give people a sense of security" and "to be necessary to people, to be indispensable,"[19] a quality that Jay Gatsby more successfully manages to sustain than will Dick Diver. Dick Diver's inability to protect Nicole and guide Rosemary Hoyt reflects Scott's inability to protect Zelda and is a premonition of his inability to guide a new generation of youth growing up on Hollywood. Scott's dream to be an artistic leader with the ability to entertain, uplift, and be popular among the masses, as well as impress the literary elite, was fading.

Finally, what about the apparent contradiction between Scott's magnanimous promise to Zelda and his domineering and autocratic manner on that ugly Sunday afternoon? Scott's magnanimous claims are seemingly overshadowed by the corrupt means employed—his domineering style, at times harsh and even vicious. Perhaps Scott's ultimate justification lay buried in the epigraph to the Conrad novel he admired most—*Nostromo*, named after another swashbuckling "man of the people" who had a secret mission.[20] The epigraph Conrad used to introduce his novel about imperialism, revolution, stolen treasure, and betrayal—themes that Scott was particularly well-positioned to appreciate—came from Shakespeare: "So foul a sky clears not without a storm."

For Scott at least, the storm *did* temporarily pass. Consistent with medical advice and Scott's demands, Zelda ceased writing her psychiatric novel. Scott was then able to focus on finishing his novel, which he completed and sent to Maxwell Perkins in October 1933. Also during that same summer, Scott would help Zelda rewrite her play *Scandalabra* after a disastrous dress rehearsal performance lasting nearly five hours. But Scott and Zelda's relationship would remain a mixture of dark and light—tempestuous storm and brilliant sun.

Scott nonetheless remained more sympathetic to Zelda than did others. John Peale Bishop, a frequent visitor with the Fitzgeralds during the 1920s, blamed Zelda for Scott's problems. Bishop later shared Edmund Wilson's view of Zelda: "In those years in Paris, I came to detest her. She was really a very evil creature and like all evil people, deficient in the common emotions."[21] Scott did blame Zelda for failing to take responsibility for her actions—such as trying to kill others by driving a car over a cliff. "Never in her whole life did she have a sense of guilt," writes Scott. He eventually told Scottie that Zelda had rejected universally accepted moral laws and tried "to solve all ethical and moral problems on her own."[22] Zelda had no moral compass and today would be considered a sociopath.

Scott and Scottie's passions about Zelda's destructiveness were amplified over time while being more bluntly expressed. While suffering from a bout of tuberculosis in October 1939, Scott told Dr. Carroll: "She has cost me everything a woman can cost a man—his health, his work, his money." In an important letter to Arthur Mizener, one of Fitzgerald's biographers, Scottie writes, "She was extravagant, yes, but that was part of her disease, and God knows she was an overwhelming egotist and probably a terrible tough person to live with on a day-to-day basis—and she probably ruined Daddy." Finally, even Zelda writes in 1939: "Nothing could have survived our life."[23]

✧ ✧ ✧

Unfortunately, despite Scott's bitter fight for his literary life, his premonition that *Tender Is the Night*, like Dick Diver, would suffer a dying fall and not generate sufficient sales to keep household finances intact, turned out to be all too true. Ultimately it was to send Scott back to Hollywood, but not without bringing with him the idea of a different type of conquest. It would be an entrepreneurial undertaking that would make an Irving Thalberg proud—first, in film, and then, in literature, the creation of a new novel about Hollywood.

Not surprisingly, then, more than any of Fitzgerald's novels, *Tender Is the Night* deals with darkness, destruction, and waste as well as seemingly futile attempts by Scott to emerge from beneath the forces of decay that surround him. Although completed in the

America of the 1930s and published on April 12, 1934, it is a story that takes place in Europe in the "broken universe" following World War I. Those forces of decay are evident to Fitzgerald at the time he is writing the novel, both at a personal and a cosmic level. The waste is everywhere—inside and out.

In *Tender Is the Night*, Fitzgerald makes the destructive consequences of imperious behavior evident by scattering the wreckage of the Great War throughout the novel. Although the wasteland left by contending imperialistic nation-states deepens the reach of the novel, Fitzgerald's literary focus is on personal deterioration, partly reflecting his own midcareer "crack-up," Zelda's struggle with self-definition and mental illness, and complex tensions within their marriage. The autobiographical nature of the book is particularly poignant when Fitzgerald goes into the interior of Nicole Diver's mind, her internal struggles undoubtedly mirroring Zelda's illness and sense of helpless dependence.[24] Of course, the novel is also about Dick Diver's own retrogression toward an inner wasteland where human will, the only salvation in an entropic world, is undermined and seemingly ruined beyond repair. As Fitzgerald works on Dick Diver's life in *Tender Is the Night*, he is self-consciously and painfully confronting his own transition from an ecstatic state of "becoming" in the early to mid twenties to a state of "having become" in the late twenties and early thirties.

Although Dick Diver is modeled to a modest degree after Fitzgerald's friend and patron of the artists, Gerald Murphy, the similarities between Gerald and Scott's life and art confirm rather than deny the autobiographical tilt of the novel. Murphy, like Fitzgerald, was part of an emigration of American artists to Europe in the twenties. Like Fitzgerald, in his art Murphy concentrated on depicting aspects of American culture (with Europe as backdrop), creating a collection of paintings in the twenties that reflected both modern American consumerism and its mechanized culture. His "smoothly painted" billboard like depictions of popular American products selling in Europe reflect the influence of Fernand Léger and foreshadow the work of Andy Warhol, who was also engrossed in the relationship between commerce and art.[25]

Like Fitzgerald, Murphy's work is not necessarily or always a glamorization of wealth (*The Razor,* for example, has a Yale-like skull and crossbones composition of three potentially destructive objects: a razor, a box of matches, and a fountain pen), but there is an undeniably comforting aesthetic found in paintings such as *Cocktail* and *Watch,* which seek to harmonize modern consumerism, mechanization, and wealth with art. Sheilah Graham observed that "it wasn't the actual money of the rich that appealed to Scott, although he was always in need of it [ironically, Fitzgerald received timely financial assistance from the Murphys when in Hollywood in 1939], but the way people like the Gerald Murphy's used it, to give grace to their surroundings."[26]

If Murphy attempts to give grace to the objects of wealth in his paintings, Fitzgerald makes a similar attempt in Book 1 of *Tender Is the Night*, but *only* as a deception to expose its illusory and eroding moral effects. Fitzgerald vividly captures the landscape and life on the Riviera. Fitzgerald's thrust is that, ideally, beauty should incorporate the outward forms of wealth, but such magnificence is lacking in American culture because there is much that is destructive in both the making and consuming of products. This, of course, is the central economic theme of Thorstein Veblen, and it also will become an implicit theme in Fitzgerald's *The Last Tycoon*. In Fitzgerald's world, only love offers redemption, but it too is transitory, fragile, and liable to be torn apart. At its best, art, like love, can unite us with something truthful and real, which momentarily suspends us above the entropic forces drifting toward waste.

Despite the Riviera and glamour that dots the opening chapters of the novel, marital dissolution and family disintegration are central themes in *Tender Is the Night*. These themes are reflected in both the Warren and the Diver households. The Warren family is infected by the hidden incestuous relationship between Nicole and her father (a self-made millionaire by corrupt means) born out of his perverse protectiveness and domineering nature, which has left Nicole helpless, schizophrenic, and dependent on Dick's counseling. The disintegration of the Diver household culminates near the end of the novel with the marital breakup of Nicole and Dick wherein Nicole, far from achieving independence, turns toward another domineering and overly protective father figure, Tommy Barban. All of this stands in contrast to the opening of the novel where, as seen mainly through the youthful eyes of actress Rosemary Hoyt, the Divers appear to be the ideal household economy of European antiquity, which possesses wealth, values leisure, and embodies the Aristotelian virtue of magnificence. So much the worse for Aristotle.

To Rosemary's youthful and untrained eye, the Divers are wealthy but not wasteful: "The Divers' day was spaced like the day of the older civilizations to yield the utmost from the materials at hand, and to give all the transitions their full value...."[27] The materials at hand are considerable: living off the interest of Nicole's enormous inheritance allows for an extravagance that seems costless. However, this workless world of apparent self-sufficiency and grace (the Greek ideal) does have its cost. Something is missing, a reality obscured early in the novel because much is seen through the worshiping eyes of Rosemary Hoyt. In fact, it is primarily Rosemary's work ethic (*not* her work, which is too artificial for Dick) separating her from Nicole. Rosemary's work ethic is symptomatic of the youthful energy, that attracts Dick, a reminder of vitality and intensity that he is just beginning to sense is gone. It is the kind of contrast that Scott was making between the young actress Lois Moran and Zelda.

Dick's deterioration, like Fitzgerald's, is complex. Partly it is his coping with Nicole's mental illness that drains Dick. But, after all, it is his profession to deal with such problems, so work and family are potentially compatible, although delicately balanced. Also, Nicole's illness is somewhat under control until Dick himself strays toward Rosemary (strongly suggesting an already existing personal lack within Dick, a blunting of his own work ethic and success), and the oblivious alcoholic behavior of Abe North triggers a sequence of ugly events that culminate in Nicole's relapse. Dick's personal alienation is also promoted, if not caused, by the culture of wealth surrounding him. Belatedly, he recognizes the "waste and extravagance involved" in being host to "carnivals of affection" and eventually recognizes "a discrepancy between the growing luxury in which the Divers lived, and the need for display which apparently went along with it."[28] The strains of artificial displays of comfort mandated by Veblenian social status simultaneously extend to Dick's relationship to Nicole after he falls in love with the energy and promise of Rosemary.

In addition to increasingly false and burdensome responsibilities of Veblenian display, Dick's attempts at "qualified financial independence" and maintenance of a work ethic are undermined by Nicole's wealth and possessiveness. "Naturally Nicole, wanting to own him, wanting him to stand still forever, encouraged any slackness on his part, and in multiplying ways he was constantly inundated by a trickling of goods and money." (Fitzgerald could have been writing about Zelda's dependence and the trickling of money from his short stories during the late 1920s.) We are reminded that Dick owns "his work house and the ground on which it stood" at Tarmes on the French Riviera, but instead of the independence of a self-sufficient yeoman farmer, the reality that emerges is that of a subservient laborer who has been given living quarters convenient to the owners of the surrounding estate.[29]

Dick's economic dependence is both an ironic commentary on the household economy of the ancients (a hierarchic system ruled by men with women and slaves subservient) and on the capitalist system from which springs the Warrens' wealth. In either case, Fitzgerald's Marxist perspective remains alive even as capitalism remains unwell: The economy is hierarchically structured, and economic independence is a snare and a delusion. Not only is the working-class Dick dependent on the rich (his new job depends on the investment of Warrens' money) and his catering to wealthy patients, but the capitalist Nicole is also dependent on the hard work of others to support her idle and extravagant consumer lifestyle.[30]

The economic system is unhealthy (in conflict with itself) and its disease leads to waste. Nicole's control over labor power coupled with her instability and fragility make her a pretty but an accurate symbol of the Marxian view of the American postwar economy going from boom to bust. In *Tender Is the Night*, Scott incorporates his own version of the "proletariat" novel but with a historical sweep and sophistication that almost makes it unrecognizable as such. At least his critics and the public did not recognize the novel's historic reach. *Tender* was Scott's favorite novel, perhaps because he fully appreciated the breadth of its vision.

During Fitzgerald's lifetime, especially during the Great Depression of the thirties, the idea of inherently wasteful forces operating within a free market capitalist economy was gaining prominence. In Marx and Veblen the destructive forces within capitalism included the economic waste of unemployment—rising to a 25.2 percent rate in the USA in 1933—as well as other dangers to human and social development, all of which gained new relevance during the Great Depression. Like Marx, Veblen viewed economic depression and episodes of high unemployment as inherent to capitalism. As production outstripped demand, according to Veblen, business owners responded by attempting to combine operations in order to mitigate competition, reduce output, and prop up prices. This reason for "monopoly capitalism" is somewhat different from Marx's. Unlike Marx, Veblen's producers also promoted the "unproductive consumption of goods" through advertising, development of new foreign markets, and the like.[31]

✧ ✧ ✧

And, so, the waste in the American economy was mirrored in the Fitzgerald and Diver households. *Tender Is the Night* was serialized in *Scribner's* magazine in four installments, beginning in January 1934. The final book, published on April 12, 1934, was substantially different and, in Scott's judgment, vastly superior. John Peale Bishop praised even the first installment. Archibald MacLeish wrote: "Great God Scott you can write. You can write better than ever. Believe it. Believe it—not me."[32] Novelist Louis Bromfield wired his congratulations. The novel was widely and mostly well reviewed. John Chamberlain writes in the *New York Times:* "Compared to the motivation in Faulkner, it is logic personified." Gilbert Seldes writes that Fitzgerald "has stepped again to his natural place at the head of the American writers of our time."[33] Scott received glowing letters from Carl Van Vechten, John O'Hara, John Dos Passos, Thomas Wolfe, Bennett Cerf, Christian Gauss, James Branch Cabell, and Robert

Benchley, whose opinions greatly mattered. Hemingway's disapproval had to do with the connection of the Divers to the Murphys, even though the Divers were in most respects quite unlike the Murphys. Other critics such as Clifton Fadiman, J. Donald Adams, Edith Wharton, William Troy, and Henry Seidal Canby had reservations, especially regarding the treatment of Dick Diver. As with *Gatsby,* Fitzgerald believed that even his admirers failed to appreciate what he had been trying to achieve. On both counts, he was correct.

The first printing of *Tender Is the Night* of 7,600 copies sold quickly, followed by two more printings of 5,075 and 2,520 copies. In April and May the novel achieved tenth place in the *Publishers Weekly* best-sellers lists. Scott had received $10,000 for the serialization. The book's sales, while respectable, fell far short of what Fitzgerald had achieved in the early 1920s with *This Side of Paradise* and *The Beautiful and Damned.* His royalties were only about $5,000, not enough to pay off his mounting debts. Scott had high hopes, too, concerning stage and film rights; his buddy Clark Gable had recently expressed interest in a talkie version of *Gatsby.* Another plan, which did materialize, was a reissue of *Gatsby* in Bennett Cerf's Modern Library series. Fitzgerald's faith in the enduring worth of *Tender* has been proven correct. *Tender Is the Night* has a greater scope than *Gatsby* as it illuminates the conflicting values and changing mores of post–World War I America in a manner not achieved elsewhere in literature.

Equally important, Fitzgerald was at war with himself because he was at war with Zelda. Just as Dick Diver realizes how his detachment as a medical scientist is incompatible with his commitment as a husband and lover, Fitzgerald was going through the same experience as an author. Scott was deeply conflicted. Zelda and her mental illness stood in the way of Fitzgerald's aspirations as an artist. More and more, it was clear that she would never recover. As her medical bills and the cost of Scottie's education mounted, Fitzgerald's own health was deteriorating, making it still more difficult to continue his success with the *Saturday Evening Post.* Between the publication of *Tender* and his third try in Hollywood would be his most difficult years. Often, if not alone, he would be lonely.

Endnotes

1. Malcolm Cowley, *The Dream of the Golden Mountains: Remembering the 1930's* (New York: Viking Press, 1964), p. 188.

2. Letter from F. Scott Fitzgerald to Dr. Adolf Meyer, April 10, 1933, F. Scott Fitzgerald Papers, Princeton University Library.

3. The quotes are from the "Rennie Transcript," the "Craig House" file for Zelda Fitzgerald, Department of Rare Books and Special Collections, Princeton University Library, pp. 1, 22, and 10, respectively.

4. "Rennie Transcript," p. 5.

5. See Matthew J. Bruccoli, *Some Sort of Epic Grandeur* (New York: Harcourt Brace Jovanovich, 1981), p. 350.

6. "Rennie Transcript," pp. 20 and 53, respectively.

7. Ibid., pp. 92–93.

8. Ibid., p. 68.

9. Ibid., pp. 8 and 15, respectively.

10. Ibid., pp. 68, 70.

11. Ibid., p. 71.

12. Ibid., p. 26.

13. John Kuehl, *The Apprentice Fiction of F. Scott Fitzgerald, 1909–1917* (New Brunswick, N.J.: Rutgers University Press, 1965), p. 9.

14. Karl Marx, *Capital,* vol. 1 (New York: International Publishers, 1967 [1867]), p. 233.

15. F. Scott Fitzgerald, *This Side of Paradise* (New York: Charles Scribner's Sons, 1920), pp. 157–58.

16. *Ibid.*, p. 161.

17. F. Scott Fitzgerald, *The Beautiful and Damned* (New York: Oxford University Press, 1988 [1922]), p. 147.

18. F. Scott Fitzgerald, *The Great Gatsby* (New York: Charles Scribner's Sons, 1925), p. 80.

19. Fitzgerald, *This Side of Paradise,* p. 241.

20. "Author's Note" to Joseph Conrad's *Nostromo* (New York: Doubleday & Company, 1960, [1904]), p. xv.

21. Quoted in Elizabeth Spindler, *John Peale Bishop: A Biography* (Morgantown, W. Va.: West Virginia University Press, 1980), p. 223.

22. F. Scott Fitzgerald, *Letters of F. Scott Fitzgerald*, ed. Andrew Turnbull (New York: Scribners, 1963), pp. 46, 117, 95, respectively.

23. F. Scott Fitzgerald, *Dear Scott/Dear Max: The Fitzgerald-Perkins Correspondence*, ed. John Kuehl and Jackson Bryer (New York: Scribners, 1971), p. 554; Letter from Scottie Fitzgerald Lanaham to Arthur Mizener, March 10, 1950, Fitzgerald Collection, Princeton University Press; *The Romantic Egoists: Scott and Zelda Fitzgerald*, ed. Scottie Fitzgerald Smith, Matthew Bruccoli, and Joan P. Kerr (New York: Scribners, 1974), p. 225.

Despite these seemingly harsh judgments, Scott and Zelda's love affair ended only in death. Even after Zelda's third breakdown on February 12, 1934, their correspondence was filled with mutual love, compassion, advice, and hope. See Jackson C. Bryer and Cathy W. Barks, *Dear Scott, Dearest Zelda* (New York: St. Martins Press, 2002), pp. 270–383.

24. F. Scott Fitzgerald, *Tender Is the Night* (New York: Charles Scribner's Sons, 1962 [1934]) pp. 160–62.

25. The descriptive phrase appears in Barbara Haskell, *The American Century: Art and Culture, 1900–50* (New York: W. W. Norton and Whitney Museum of American Art), p. 167.

26. Sheilah Graham, *College of One* (New York: Viking, 1967), p. 110.

27. Fitzgerald, *Tender Is the Night*, p. 21.

28. Ibid. pp. 27, 265.

29. Ibid. p. 170.

30. Ibid. pp. 176–77.

31. Thorstein Veblen, *The Theory of Business Enterprise* (New York: Augustus Kelley eds, 1965 [1904]), p. 255.

32. Matthew J. Bruccoli, ed., *F. Scott Fitzgerald: A Life in Letters* (New York: Simon & Schuster, 1995), p. 323.

33. Quoted by Bruccoli, *Some Sort of Epic Grandeur*, p. 370.

Twelve

Entering the City of Ashes

MISHAPS AND TRAGEDY CONTINUED TO DOG THE FITZGERALDS. JUST AS Scott was completing the final draft of *Tender Is the Night* at La Paix, Zelda set fire to papers and perhaps some of her paintings in a fireplace not meant for use. Once again the fire department was called. Scott insisted that repairs to La Paix be postponed until he completed his novel. Then, at the end of 1933, the Fitzgeralds moved from the still fire-damaged La Paix to a smaller, cheaper house in downtown Baltimore at 1307 Park Avenue. In August, Zelda's brother Anthony suffered a mental breakdown. At the time he had the fear that he would kill his mother. After entering a hospital in Mobile, Alabama, he committed suicide by jumping out of the window of his room. Perhaps more understandably, Fitzgerald's brother-in-law Newman Smith, husband of the irritating Rosalind, also killed himself (after Scott's death). Fitzgerald sums up the year in which he completed *Tender* in his Ledger as "A strange year of Work + Drink. Increasingly unhappy.—Zelda up + down. 1st draft of novel complete. Ominous!"

Scott's drunken quarrel in late 1933 following a lunch with Hemingway and Edmund Wilson at the Plaza Hotel in New York City is symptomatic of Scott's growing sense of personal inadequacy during the late twenties and early thirties and symbolic of his grow-ing alienation from the artistic and intellectual aspects of his work over which he most aspired to reign supreme.[1] Afterward, the ever "rational" Wilson upbraided Scott: "What I object to is precisely the 'scholar and vulgarian,' 'you helped me more than I helped you' busi-ness."[2] Fitzgerald, as usual, wrote a letter of apology for his drunken behavior to Wilson.[3] To underscore the shortcomings in Fitzgerald's life by contrasting them to Hemingway's also was becoming com-monplace. Ernest's virile athleticism in boxing, fishing, and hunting is all too effortlessly put next to Scott's "country club" athleticism and frail 135-pound body being cut from the Princeton football squad his freshman year. Even Fitzgerald's later enthusiasm for diagramming plays and sending them to Princeton's head football coaches, however humorous in intent, ineluctably takes on a pathetic shade when held up against the backdrop of his earlier failure.

As bad as conditions are for Scott, they are even more ominous for Zelda. After Anthony's death, Zelda became suicidal. She had her third breakdown at Park Avenue and reentered the Phipps Clinic on February 12, 1934. There, she began smiling to herself, was unre-sponsive, and would suddenly begin laughing for no known reason. Less than a month later, Zelda was moved to Craig House Hospital in upstate New York and was cared for by Dr. Forel's friend, Dr. Clarence Slocum. His diagnosis that she was simply suffering from fatigue was not especially perceptive. After about two and a half months at Craig House, Zelda went into a catatonic state.

For his part, Scott predictably began to drink more heavily. Between September 1933 and January 1937 he was admitted to Johns Hopkins Hospital eight times to recover from alcoholic binges or for relatively mild problems with tuberculosis. His alcohol use was rationed and he was given sedatives. Unlike Zelda's projected blame on him, he did not blame her for his illnesses. He blamed only him-self. Partly to compensate for his antagonism toward Zelda's writ-ing efforts and the failure of her play, *Scandalabra,* Scott arranged for an exhibition of Zelda's paintings during April 1934 in the Cary Ross Gallery in New York along with a smaller exhibit at the Hotel Algonquin. Zelda was allowed to leave Craig House for the opening of the exhibits. The motto on the gallery's brochure summed it up best: *Parfois La Folie est la Sagesse* (Sometimes Madness Is Wisdom). Most of the time, of course, madness falls well short of wisdom and, ironically, the psychopathic aspects of Zelda's paintings were obvious. Gross proceeds were only $328.75 and the reception was disappointing. *Time* magazine called the exhibit Zelda's "latest bid for fame." Some of the paintings can be viewed in the Fitzgerald Museum in Montgomery.

On May 19, 1934, Zelda, in a catatonic state, was moved to Sheppard-Pratt Hospital in Towson, Maryland, adjacent, ironically, to La Paix. This particular breakdown devastated Scott because now he had little hope for her recovery. When Zelda emerged from her catatonic state at Sheppard-Pratt, she made frequent attempts on her life. Once, while Scott was walking with Zelda, he caught her just before she tried to throw herself beneath a passing train. Gradually she adjusted to institutional confinement. This, though Scott knew that despite all his work to find the best hospitals, doctors, and treatments, the efforts probably were hopeless. In his *Notebooks,* he writes, "I left my capacity for hoping on the little roads that led to Zelda's sanitarium." Their great love had become a great tragedy.

Despite all of these problems involving Zelda, she and Scott had such a powerful bond, it would never be completely broken. She had read the serialized installments of *Tender Is the Night* at Craig House. In April she congratulated Scott on the work and wrote:

> The book is grand. The emotional lift sustained by the force of a fine poetic prose and the characters *subserviated* to forces stronger than their interpretations of life is very moving. It is tear-evoking to witness individual belief in individual volition succumbing to the purpose of a changing world. That is the purpose of a good book and you have written it—Those people are helpless before themselves and the prose is beautiful and there is manifest an integrity in the belief of both those expressions. It is a reverential and very fine book and the first literary contribution to what writers will be concerning themselves with some years from now.[4]

Zelda had not lost faith in Scott's ability to write, even as he entered his years of deepest self-doubt. Still, even when Fitzgerald appeared to be beaten down by forces both outside and within his control, he was never powerless. While struggling with alcoholism and living the twenties in apparent disorder, he also authored the decade, as in the pithy essay "Echoes of the Jazz Age" (1931), with a staggeringly sober objectivity that captured its restless spirit. Even while Fitzgerald witnessed the "disintegration of one's own personality" in the late twenties and early thirties, he masterfully described the seemingly incommunicable horror of a hollowed out person in a series of articles published in *Esquire* in 1936, and in fact only a person of Fitzgerald's notoriety could have ensured an interested enough audience for *Esquire* to publish them.

✧　✧　✧

It is important to revisit the mounting desolation facing F. Scott Fitzgerald and leading up to the *Esquire* "Crack-Up" essays. Scott's deteriorating condition sheds light on their contents.

After *Tender* was finally published on April 12, 1934, Fitzgerald was quite uncertain as to what to try next. Earlier, in September 1933, Scott's friend Ring Lardner had died from tuberculosis and alcoholism. As Scott wrote a moving tribute to him for the *New Republic,* he no doubt sensed the problematic parallel between their careers and shared fate. Meanwhile, promising to stay sober, Fitzgerald suggested to Christian Gauss that he be invited to Princeton to give a series of lectures on writing fiction; as we might expect, Princeton expressed absolutely no interest. Also in 1934 he tried to persuade Clark Gable to make a new movie version of *Gatsby*. Scott also had written a film script for George Burns and Gracie Allen, "Gracie at Sea," that was never used. He presented the idea originally to George Burns, who encouraged Scott "to go on." It is surprising that Scott was able to write a comical farce in his condition.[5]

On May 16, 1934, 10:00 to 10:30 P.M., CBS broadcast "The Diamond as Big as the Ritz," based on Scott's short story with a script by Stephen Fox. Scott also wrote a series of fifteen-minute playlets for CBS, each to be broadcast twice a week, but CBS turned them down.[6] He managed somehow to write three more *Post* stories during May–August 1934; although the *Post* paid Scott $3,000 for each, the magazine warned Ober that the stories were of poor quality. Scott's 1934 income was $20,032.22, of which all his books (including *Tender*) added only $58.34. Around mid-1934, Fitzgerald also began a novel based on the ill-fated Philippe stories with a hero based on Hemingway. It was, as noted earlier, Scott's greatest failure in literary judgment. He was continuing to struggle with his conflict between being a man and being a writer.

After Zelda had been moved to the Sheppard-Pratt Hospital just outside Baltimore, Scott was having his own health issues, including a lung problem and fever diagnosed as tuberculosis. His doctor and others suggested that the mountain air of North Carolina might be beneficial. After spending a couple weeks in February 1935 at the Oak Hall Hotel in the resort town of Tryon (where his friends Nora and Lefty Flynn took care of Scottie), Fitzgerald returned to Baltimore in March and April to be close to Zelda, still confined at Sheppard-Pratt. On March 20, 1935, he published his fourth collection of stories, *Taps at Reveille,* the final book to appear while he was living.

A month later X-rays revealed that Scott's lungs had deteriorated further. There was a tubercular cavity in his left lung and large infiltrations in the right one. Scott describes his condition to Harold Ober: "I am half crazy with illness and worry, and in a state where each aggravation only adds to the accumulation of anxiety, strain, self pity, or what have you."[7] It was a prevailing condition for roughly the next two years. His Baltimore physician sent him to a specialist in Asheville at a pulmonary treatment center near the boyhood home of Thomas Wolfe. Instead of entering a sanatorium, Fitzgerald stayed at the grand Grove Park Inn near Asheville. It had opened in 1913 and advertised itself as "The Finest Resort Hotel in the World." Scott must have been amused that E. W. Grove made his initial fortune with Grove's Tasteless Chill Tonic. Fitzgerald resided in two adjoining rooms at 441, a room with a view of incoming guests. The innkeepers speculated that Scott was looking for beautiful, available women; the more likely explanation, besides the lower cost of the room (since it did not provide a view of the Smoky Mountains), was Fitzgerald's search for his next story. As it turns out, Scott found at least one lovely woman on the dance floor of the inn.

For the most part Scott was ill and drinking, and probably could not enjoy the scenery or the adjacent Donald Ross golf course. (The inn is still there, and the Donald Ross golf course was restored to Ross's original 1924 specifications during 1998–2002 renovations.) The hotel desk reported that Scott was drinking 31 to 37 bottles of beer daily. In a paradigmatic example of poor judgment, Scott agreed to an interview on his fortieth birthday by a popular New York newspaper in room 441. The story portrayed Fitzgerald as a despairing drunk.[8] After reading the story, Fitzgerald, devastated, claimed to have swallowed enough morphine to kill him. Luckily, as he related it, he vomited before the potion could affect him. Quickly, however, he dismissed the act as quite foolish: Except during long drinking bouts, Scott generally was upbeat and full of life.

At the end of two years at Sheppard-Pratt, however, Zelda had made no progress. On April 8, 1936, Scott moved her to Highland Hospital in Asheville to be near him. She remained there for four years, until April 13, 1940, when she had apparently recovered sufficiently to live with her mother in Montgomery. She was in and out of that hospital three more times—back in August 1943 to February 1944 (six months), back in early 1946 to late summer 1946 (eight months), only to return for the final time on November 2, 1947.

Still, Fitzgerald continued to write. While living either in Baltimore or North Carolina in 1935, he published seven stories and essays, two in the *Saturday Evening Post,* two in *McCall's*—the others in *Liberty, American Magazine,* and *Esquire.* He received $700 for a short antiwar radio script called "Let's Go Out and Play," but other scripts based on his "Gwen" stories in the *Post* about a father-daughter single parent situation were never produced despite interest by CBS. He also wrote the first of his three "Crack-Up" autobiographical essays for *Esquire.* Even though he claimed to have no energy left to write, Fitzgerald earned $16,845.16 in 1935 at a time when college professors at Princeton were earning less than

$10,000. Still, Fitzgerald, nearing forty, was a sick, tired, depressed man often doing his worst writing.

Zelda's hospital bills were now $18,000 a year (roughly $198,000 in today's dollars). Scott's mother had died in August 1936 and left Scott just under $23,000, or about $253,000 in today's dollars, virtually all of which went to pay Scott's debts. He remains "completely on the spot" for the balance of 1936. His earnings for 1936 were $10,180.97: His nine *Esquire* pieces brought in only $2,250, while book royalties were a mere $81.18. His income continued this downward slide in the early months of 1937 and was only $3,500 in the first half of that year. By that time, Fitzgerald owed Ober over $12,000, or about $132,000 today. Until then, his main financial problem had been on the expense side of the ledger, not the income side.

✧　✧　✧

We have a couple of firsthand sources regarding Scott and his activities in Asheville. The literal first firsthand source is Fitzgerald's part-time secretary in the summer of 1935, Mrs. Laura Guthrie Hearne, a palmist who kept a diary. Scott also befriended Tony Buttitta, who ran the Intimate Bookshop in the George Vanderbilt Hotel in Asheville. Tony also wrote newspaper articles and was a publicity man for the North Carolina Symphony Orchestra while working on a couple novels, often after his shop was closed for the day. Mrs. Hearne's account does not always agree with what Scott told Tony. Fitzgerald spoke of "Rosemary," not Hearne's actual name, who, he told Tony, resembled the young actress Rosemary in *Tender Is the Night*. As he often did, Fitzgerald used his poetic imagination and his sense of the dramatic to embroider the details—to make the story, as he felt, more true than life. For his part, Buttitta wrote a book about that summer.[9]

Buttitta provides a detailed depiction of Fitzgerald's appearance at the time. Scott has a well-shaped head, a high brow, straight nose, full mouth, and slightly jutting chin. His silhouette formed a romantic profile—sensitive, handsome, and youthful, like that of a juvenile star.[10] He was a slight, blondish, collegiate-looking chap, blending into the Asheville summer social crowd, hatless and casual in gray flannels and light tweed jacket. When they first met, Scott was smoking and wavering a bit, more from absorption in himself, Tony thought, than from the effect of booze. His face was drawn, pale, and gloomy, the overhead light making it look like a detachable mask.[11] Still, Buttitta marveled at Fitzgerald's vital personality, his bold and spirited voice, his words and sweeping gestures, along with the memories, thoughts, and emotions they evoked. Buttitta noted Scott's pale, ashen complexion on several occasions.

F. Scott Fitzgerald gave to Tony Buttitta his own summary of the intellectual influences on his work up to the summer of 1935. He does so with characteristic Fitzgerald detachment and generosity, undiminished by the passage of time or the wounds of misfortune. Three of his contemporaries figured prominently in his life and work. John Peale Bishop introduced him to the Elizabethans and the English Romantic poets, Keats among them. The French Symbolists stimulated the poetic imagery of his work. Edmund Wilson, whom he described as an intellect "packed with cerebral energy," could not write novels—he being too analytic and critical. Wilson later turned to economics and political history; in *The American Jitters,* he wrote of the collapse of capitalism.[12] Ironically, Wilson's one crack at producing a great novel was his editing of Fitzgerald's *The Last Tycoon.* And, there is, of course, Ernest Hemingway. Fitzgerald said that he did all he could to help Hemingway because he had unqualified respect for Hemingway's talent as a dedicated writer. Hemingway was his "artistic conscience" who had replaced him with the success of *The Sun Also Rises* and *A Farewell To Arms.* Fitzgerald mused, "You have to be careful whom you do favors for" as he went for another glass of beer.[13]

Of literary figures, he still admired Flaubert, Anatole France, Dickens, Thackeray, Shaw, and Conrad—all masters of their craft, and the Americans—they included Frank Norris, Mark Twain, Henry James, Dreiser, Upton Sinclair, and Mencken. Some helped shape his iconoclastic thinking, others his skeptical and pessimistic outlook. *The Theory of the Leisure Class,* Fitzgerald said, was one of his favorite books. Veblen foresaw the course of American culture after our period of expansion and prosperity. Wilder's novels have what Veblen says the leisure class needs to gratify its desire for good breeding—smartness, mobility, and its love for the artistic and archaic.[14] In his ill-fated interview Fitzgerald had held forth on Nietzsche, Henri Bergson, Veblen, and Henry George, with a reference here and there to Marx and Spengler.

Mrs. Hearne, the palmist, naturally is fascinated with Fitzgerald's hands. His hand was large for a man his size, white and a bit shaky. (Buttitta writes that when lighting cigarettes, Chesterfield's, Scott's hands shook.) Not only were Fitzgerald's hands large, they were covered with soft, refined skin, almost like a young woman's. His fingers were short compared with the long palm, which was covered with many fine, flamelike lines, grilles, and forks. The top phalanges were firm and the mounds robust and full.

Mrs. Hearne, who at first did not know Scott's name and fame, judged his hands to be those of a highly creative temperament and personality. She saw contradictory traits that at times kept him from producing his best work or maintaining emotional balance. Imagination, energy, and stubborn determination were gifts from his mother rather than from his father, who endowed him with his weakness, a kind of gentility, and a sense of failure. He was a feeling rather than a thinking man, with deep stores of emotional energy and a self at war with a highly developed unconscious.

Warm, generous, deep affection—he was more aesthetic than physical, responding to sexuality through momentary passion and lust, but more satisfactorily through his imagination. Romantic, idealist, fond of beauty—he was more fanciful than realistic, more poet than novelist. He was brilliant with a strong intuition. In her diary she writes, "How exceedingly right he is when he speaks. He understands causes and what is behind all actions more than anyone I ever saw. He can even explain you to yourself which is rare indeed!"[15] This is quite a compliment coming from a professional seer. Later, she notes of Scott and Zelda, "He had foreseen all the things that were going to happen to them. They knew their marriage and money and all were too wonderful to last and that in them were the seeds of tragedy."[16] His curiosity and humanity led him to seek out people—to charm, amuse, and stimulate. His socializing took its toll when he did senseless and outrageous acts.

This much of Fitzgerald visibly remained even though everything had crashed about him that summer. He otherwise was physically, emotionally, and financially bankrupt. He smoked and drank steadily, but ate very little; he took pills to sleep a few hours, and he could scarcely write what he thought was a decent line. He was a stranger in Asheville and suffered from loneliness despite his saying that a writer must have solitude to practice his craft. His visits to Buttitta's bookshop kept him from feeling completely out of touch with the world of books and writers. He was kept alive to the end, Buttitta suggests, by the conscience and values of his youth.[17]

✧ ✧ ✧

Fitzgerald's migration had been minimal. He had migrated from the metaphorical "valley of ashes" to the reality of the "city of ash," himself going from ashes to ashen. He did get into his usual difficulty with women. Laura Guthrie managed to fend off Fitzgerald's seduction attempts; she did not want to become involved with an alcoholic. Scott was consoled when she agreed to be his secretary and companion. She found him to be "a very commanding man— say, 'Do this. Sit down. Come here' or anything that appeals to him at the moment."[18] Later, Laura quotes Scott: "I can't imagine anybody defying me in the really big things. I *must* rule." "I said, 'Napoleon was like that wasn't he?' A bright sudden smile of agreement, 'He was indeed.' Scott likes to think of the similarity between them."[19]

Fitzgerald's charm was more successful with Beatrice Stribling Dance, from a wealthy family in Memphis, and six years younger than Scott. She was married to Du Pre Rainey "Hop" Dance (apparently his real name), a rich San Antonio businessman and sportsman. Beatrice, on a holiday with her mentally ill sister at Grove Park Inn, pursued Scott and got his attention by reading *The Great Gatsby* in the hotel lobby. After dinners, dancing with Dance on the Inn's vast terrace, and, of course, drinks with Beatrice and her sister, Scott became Beatrice's lover by mid-June. Laura became a go-between for the two lovers. Beatrice, a rich woman, wanted to run away with Scott and offered to pay for everything. Scott, for his part, found Beatrice to be arrogant, spoiled, selfish, and not terribly bright (though Scott's standard for intelligence was set at a lofty bar).

The affair, despite its farcical aspects, ended badly. Hop Dance, seemingly oxymoronic, became suspicious of Beatrice and Scott. When he phoned his wife late at night, he discovered she was not in her room. Then, in early August, Hop returned unannounced to Asheville with his family physician, Dr. Cade. Scott, armed only with a beer can opener, went to the Dances' hotel room with Laura. As it turned out, they all had a nice chat and Scott instinctively liked Hop. Upon leaving, but not well enough alone, Scott boldly asked Beatrice if he could kiss her goodnight, to which she eagerly agreed, despite her husband's presence. Hop became Hopping mad (with a capital "H"), pushing Scott out of the room and slamming the door.

The next day Dr. Cade warned Scott of the possible tragic consequences of the affair; Fitzgerald agreed to stop seeing Beatrice. She took the breakup very hard, though Scott tried to console her with many letters over the years. Much later, in an October 11, 1938, letter to Beatrice from Hollywood, Scott recalls the good doctor: "You must have passed through many mutations since that August evening in 1935 when we sat downstairs in the Battery Park Hotel, and that funny doctor was going to solve us as briskly and easily as if we had been a minor operation. I am still amazed at his lack of perspicacity." Beatrice had sent him subscriptions to *Life* and *Fortune:* "I got word that *Fortune* was to smile on me again for a year."[20]

They were still corresponding as late as November 1940 after Scott had admitted to Sheilah Graham that he had been in love with Beatrice. In his *Notebooks,* Fitzgerald writes of a connection among the personalities of Ginevra, Zelda, and Beatrice. They were all from prominent families, spoiled, and behaved in a reckless, selfish fashion. He considered himself relatively balanced and conservative compared to them. "Except for the sexual recklessness, Zelda was cagey about throwing in her lot with me before I was a money-maker, and I think by temperament she was the most reckless [and most unbalanced] of all." Scott told Laura Guthrie "how Zelda made a hit on men wherever they went. Winston Churchill in England was her slave (in conversation) for several hours at a party."[21] But, in the Dance affair, Fitzgerald, usually trying to be responsible about Zelda, had become reckless himself.

The strongest of the Fitzgeralds finally would crack, but it would not be the end of his story. Fitzgerald fled his mixed emotions in Asheville for Baltimore in September 1935, but he was not finished with North Carolina or North Carolina with him. He moved into the Cambridge Arms Apartments across from the Johns Hopkins campus. He spent two despairing months feeling guilty about betraying Zelda and about the suffering Beatrice had endured. Upon impulse, he fled the cold of November and traveled south to Hendersonville, a little resort town eighteen miles south of Asheville. Perhaps as self-punishment but also to save money, he moved into a dollar-a-day room in the modest Skylands Hotel at the corner of sixth and Main Street in the town's center. According to his *Notebook* entry for November 1935, his was an ascetic existence, especially compared with the luxury of the Grove Park Inn. He was still deeply in debt (not only to Ober but to Scribners and Perkins), no longer able to eat much solid food, and on the edge of destitution.

At the Grove Park Inn, avoiding hard liquor, Scott had apparently been drinking only beer, but in massive amounts. Now he was drinking as heavily as ever, and it was gin. Doctors had told him to limit his drinking to one shot a day; following doctors' orders, he carefully measured out one shot at a time until the entire bottle was empty. He did claim to enjoy washing his own clothes and eating two eighteen-cent meals a day. After returning to Baltimore for Christmas, however, he realized that he had "tried life on subsistence level and it doesn't work."[22] He realized that he needed a decent place to generate his stories. By this time his drinking habit had taken a terrible toll. His skin was now a pale blue and ashen. He had hit bottom.

✧　✧　✧

Amazingly, while barely existing in the Skylands Hotel, Scott began to write his three "Crack-Up" essays. Arnold Gingrich (1903–1976), a long-time admirer, published them in his *Esquire:* The aforementioned "The Crack-Up" (February 1936) was quickly followed by "Pasting It Together" (March) and "Handle with Care" (April). In them Fitzgerald explores his worst characteristics. The essays comprise some of the most important documents in modern American literature. They are a mixture of self-punishment, confession, and apologia. He achieves the same kind of objectivity that he had achieved in *Tender* about his own suffering, evoking an intensity of feeling similar to Dostoyevsky. The series produces the irony of a writer writing brilliantly about why he cannot write. It is Fitzgerald's best nonfiction.

He sets his themes with two abstract premises. The first: During his years of success and fame, he had believed that "life was something you dominated if you were any good." This premise he now rejected. The second: "The test of a first-rate intelligence is the ability to hold two opposed ideas in the mind at the same time, and still retain the ability to function." He affirms this premise with brutal objectivity. The antithetical ideas in his own mind are that Zelda is permanently insane but will recover, and that he is a hopeless failure but will eventually succeed. He described his present condition in words later mocked by Hemingway. "In a real dark night of the soul," writes the insomniac Scott, "it is always three o'clock in the morning, day after day."

Hemingway, regarded the essays as cowardly and shameful. Fitzgerald's military service during World War I had always an aura of timidity when contrasted to Hemingway's—at least, to Hemingway's exaggerated claims. Stationed first in Fort Leavenworth, Kansas, then in Fort Sheraton near Montgomery, Fitzgerald was far removed from military action and had sufficient leisure time to write fragments of a novel and court Zelda, whereas Hemingway's job as war correspondent for the *Toronto Sun* and, later, his work as an ambulance driver earned him wounds and war decorations, which adds dimension to Fitzgerald's retrospective observation about himself in one of his *Crack-Up* essays that "There were to be no badges of pride, no medals, after all."[23] What to Fitzgerald was an expression of his disappointment, to others was self-pity.

Fitzgerald publicly discloses for the first time his more profound failure at Princeton, which overshadowed his "not being big enough (or good enough) to play football in college, and at not getting overseas during the war."[24] There were Fitzgerald's academic difficulties, making him ineligible for membership in the Triangle Club for whose presidency he was being groomed. This loss of social status was devastating to Fitzgerald's visions of grandeur and self-confidence: "It was a harsh and bitter business to know that my career as a leader of men was over…. Some old desire for personal dominance was broken and gone."[25]

Then, in August, Gingrich published "Afternoon of an Author," an article that took up all of two pages in the same *Esquire* issue as Hemingway's "The Snows of Kilimanjaro," justifiably a classic. It is in this lead story that Ernest writes condescendingly of "poor Scott Fitzgerald" in awe of the rich. In an article that Scott could neither define as fiction or nonfiction, he refers to his own timid steps toward "reforestation." In this surprising pairing of the two authors, Scott, for his part, reveals the fissure between his exhausted self and struggles as a writer, and the public image of him as "indefatigable." In an ironic detachment from his title as "author" and no mention of *Gatsby,* Scott sorts through his mail and discovers that "Paramount wanted a release on a poem that had appeared in one of the author's books, as they didn't know whether it was an original or quoted. Maybe they were going to get a title from it. Anyhow he had no more equity in that property—he had sold the silent rights many years ago and the sound rights last year."[26]

Hemingway was by no means the only critic who viewed Fitzgerald's "Crack-Up" essays as self-indulgent and self-pitying. At the time John Dos Passos attacked Fitzgerald for his self-involvement at a time of general conflagration in the world. The essays embarrassed Scott's editor, Max Perkins, who wished Scott had never written them. "Friend" Edmund Wilson was appalled by what he considered to be the endless self-pity. Much later, Dos Passos did more than recant. Wilson would go on to edit *The Last Tycoon,* Scott's final, but unfinished novel.

Those closest to him at the time viewed Scott as courageous. Sara Murphy, who recognized the enormous emotional and financial strain on Fitzgerald of coping with Zelda's mental breakdown (faithfully and carefully hidden from view in "The Crack-Up"), soon wrote: "your spirit & courage are an example to us all" while at the same time taking him to task for his youthful philosophy of controlling life.[27] More apt perhaps is Dos Passos' account of his second thoughts in *The Best Times*. He recalls when Scott was living in Baltimore and Adolf Meyer was then treating Zelda: "How easy it is to give your friends bad advice; it [The Crack-Up] turned out to be one of his best books." Dos Passos reserves his memoir's greatest praise for Scott, while testifying to his fortitude; Scott was "meeting adversity with a consistency of purpose that I found admirable," while "trying to raise Scottie, to do the best thing possible for Zelda, to handle his drinking and to keep a flow of stories into the magazines to raise the enormous sums Zelda's illness cost." And, as to Scott's revered "author's" role, "At the same time he was determined to continue to write first rate novels." Dos Passos concludes, "I never admired a man more."[28]

These and other defenders of Scott and the essays might as well have remained mute for they are seldom mentioned. Mark Schorer, in contrast to Hemingway, called the essays "a beautiful and moving confession; without a hint of self-pity, it is one of the most extraordinary self-revelations in literature."[29] Another defender was his editor and publisher, Arnold Gingrich at *Esquire*. Fitzgerald had hit rock bottom, said Gingrich, and any publicity—good or bad—was helpful, and the "Crack-Up" essays had a beneficial effect on Fitzgerald's career. As Gingrich suggested, at this point, sixteen years after his first fame, many people thought Scott was dead. The essays did remind Hollywood that Fitzgerald was still around. They also had an important effect on literature. "The Crack-Up" had a liberating effect on confessional poets such as Robert Lowell, John Berryman, Ann Sexton, and Sylvia Plath, who wrote of their personal anguish and mental breakdowns as well as accounts of alcoholism, drugs, and depression in works like William Styron's *Darkness Visible*

(1990). Moreover, Fitzgerald opened the door to the deliberate use of bad publicity by writers Truman Capote, Tennessee Williams, and Norman Mailer to gain attention while revealing the adversities of their alcoholism. Fitzgerald's influence—in this as well as in other matters—extended well beyond his life.

✧ ✧ ✧

One of Fitzgerald's best and wittiest *Esquire* stories was "Financing Finnegan (1938)." It is partly a private joke about Scott's financial dependence on Ober and Perkins and their tireless efforts to rescue a disaster-prone author named Finnegan [Fitzgerald]. Finnegan's career "had started brilliantly and if it had not kept up to its first exalted level, at least it started brilliantly all over again every few years." In what was part self-representation and part comedy, Fitzgerald calls him "the perennial man of promise in American letters—what he could do with words was astounding, they glowed and corruscated—he wrote sentences, paragraphs, chapters that were masterpieces of fine weaving and spinning." The ending of "Financing Finnegan" is not entirely speculation. Harold Ober had been trying to get Fitzgerald on salary in a Hollywood studio since 1935. Scott had resisted because he detested the collaborative writing system that he had experienced with Irving Thalberg. Fitzgerald concludes the Finnegan story with "the movies are interested in him—if they can get a good look at him first and I have every reason to think that he will come through. He'd better." Fitzgerald had run out of writing sources of income; he [Finnegan] knew that he'd better go to Hollywood.

Endnotes

1. For this account, see Matthrew J. Bruccoli, *Scott and Ernest: The Authority of Failure and the Authority of Success* (New York: Random House, 1978), p. 113.

2. Letter from Edmund Wilson to Scott, December 4, 1933, Princeton University Library.

3. See F. Scott Fitzgerald letter to Edmund Wilson, February 1933, in Matthew J. Bruccoli, ed., *F. Scott Fitzgerald: A Life in Letters* (New York: Simon and Schuster, 1994), pp. 226–27.

4. Zelda's Correspondence, Princeton University Library.

5. F. Scott Fitzgerald (and Robert Spafford), "Gracie at Sea," Princeton University Press. The original draft does not have Robert Spafford as coauthor.

6. The script for "The Diamond as Big as the Ritz," and at least two of the playlets are in the Fitzgerald Collection, Princeton University Library.

7. Matthew J. Bruccoli, ed., *As Ever: Scott Fitzgerald, Letters between F. Scott Fitzgerald and His Literary Agent Harold Ober, 1919–1940* (London: Woburn Library, 1973), p. 218.

8. The interview was published as Michel Mok, "The Other Side of Paradise, Scott Fitzgerald, 40, Engulfed in Despair," *New York Post,* September 25, 1936, pp. 1, 15. The story was reprinted in *Time* magazine.

9. Tony Buttitta, *After the Good Gay Times: Asheville-Summer of '35, A Season with F. Scott Fitzgerald* (New York: Viking Press, 1974).

10. Ibid., p. vii.

11. Ibid., p. 4.

12. Ibid., p. 89.

13. Ibid., pp. 90–91.

14. Ibid., p. 145.

15. Laura Guthrie Hearne's Diary, c. 1935, p. 19, Princeton University Library. Laura is quite literate and commits few spelling errors. Those few errors are silently corrected for readability in quotes from her diary.

16. *Ibid.,* p. 50.

17. Buttitta, *After the Good Gay Times*, p. ix.

18. Hearne's Diary, p. 12.

19. Ibid., p. 107. Hearne reveals how Scott was still able to write despite distractions from Zelda. When Zelda went to sleep, he "wrote half the night, wrote his 3,000 words in pencil" (p. 24).

20. Letter from Scott to Beatrice, October 11, 1938, Princeton University Library.

21. Hearne's Diary, p. 47.

22. Bruccoli, ed., *As Ever,* p. 239.

23. F. Scott Fitzgerald, "Pasting It Together (March 1936) reprinted in Edmund Wilson, ed., *The Crack-Up* (New York: New Directions, 1945), p. 76.

24. Ibid., p. 70.

25. Ibid., p. 76.

26. F. Scott Fitzgerald, "Afternoon of an Author," *Esquire,* August 1936, reprinted in Fitzgerald, *Afternoon of an Author,* Arthur Mizener, ed., (New York: Charles Scribner's Sons, 1957), pp. 181–82 and 178, respectively.

27. Matthew J. Bruccoli and Margaret Duggan, eds., *Correspondence of F. Scott Fitzgerald* (New York: Random House, 1980), p. 430.

28. John Dos Passos, *The Best Times: An Informal Memoir* (New York: The American Library, 1966), p. 209–10.

29. Mark Schorer, *The World We Imagine* (New York: Farrar, Straus & Giroux, 1968), p. 364.

Thirteen

Scott, Zelda, and the Caesar Thing

SCOTT'S DECISION TO RETURN TO HOLLYWOOD INVOLVED A REASSESSMENT of himself and his ambitions. He knew that he had once mastered the writing crafts of the commercial short story and of the novel. He also had harbored other desires to master other things, not the least of which were unconquerable women. He had tried screenplays. His main problem with screenplay writing was his lack of complete control of the project, complete control of the content. He not only enjoyed writing and directing the actions of others, he liked to command in a dramatic fashion and with flair. Fitzgerald always was part entertainer, someone who could barely resist being onstage. Moreover, Scott's desire to control—to be in charge—surfaced from a lifetime of imperialistic impulses. It is fitting irony: Fitzgerald acted out his personal imperialism mostly when drunk. He could be a strict authoritarian, but it was a mantel that he wore poorly. Beyond the personal, Fitzgerald was a literary imperialist who understood warfare emanating from grand global imperialism.

We return therefore to the sometimes contradictory but nonetheless imperialistic impulses of F. Scott Fitzgerald. In this aspect of his personality, Scott often compared himself with Napoleon rather than with Julius Caesar, but only because his knowledge of Caesar came relatively late in his life. For Sheilah Graham's *College of One* course, Scott assigned James Froude's *Julius Caesar* (1899) and sections from H. G. Wells's *Outline of History* dealing with the Roman conquest. Both copies in the Fitzgerald Collection at Princeton University Library include Scott's markings and annotations, with Wells's *Outline of History*, along with Oswald Spengler's *Decline of the West*, providing the framework for Sheilah's history lessons. Fitzgerald is reading Froude in preparation for writing *The Last Tycoon*.

As noted by Wells, the growing importance and influence of money capital in the Roman Republic made Rome, its financial center, a new sort of city that foreshadowed modern urban centers such as Fitzgerald's New York City. Wells blames money and wealth as the source of Rome's corruption and eventual decline. The Roman Senate became the political arm of this wealth and power and, by ordering the seizure of foreign lands to fuel the lavish lifestyle of Roman high society, Rome eventually ransacked Europe and embarked on "the most wasteful and disastrous series of wars that has ever darkened the history of mankind."[1] In like fashion, with the quick success of *This Side of Paradise*, money floated the Fitzgeralds off of firm ground in modern New York City and Scott would begin his lifelong running into debt while being at war with Zelda.

The parallels between Fitzgerald and Caesar are as dramatic as they are revealing. If Caesar was allied with wealth during his rise to power, in Froude's account it was not out of admiration but from expediency and with an eye toward the nobler end of reforming Rome. Fitzgerald, in his writings, made wealth a large target so that his attack would be justified. The murder of Caesar by powerful opponents constituted a betrayal by the forces that had gained enormously from his empire-building. The attacks on Fitzgerald, especially by Wilson and by Hemingway, also were defined by the size of *their* target. Out of respect and admiration for Caesar's epic greatness, Froude in his biography writes: "Human nature is equal to much, but not to everything. It can rise to altitudes where it is alike unable to sustain itself or to retire from them to a safer elevation."[2]

It is a fitting epitaph not only for Julius Caesar but also for F. Scott Fitzgerald, who found himself betrayed (Zelda, Wilson, and Ober, who eventually refused to lend any more money to Scott) and slain (Hemingway, Wescott) by those he had selflessly aided. Fitzgerald, like Caesar, also was at an altitude from which it was difficult to descend gracefully.

Ernest Hemingway's construing Fitzgerald's failures as being due to an admiration for wealth is doubly ironic. It was initially from personal experience regarding the unfairness of wealth and later, out of a regard for wealth as an important historical force, that Scott's fiction dwelled upon it. In fact, Fitzgerald could not have missed the irony that he shared with his most famous fictional character, Jay Gatsby, and one of history's most famous individuals, Julius Caesar: the fate of being perceived as incapable of rising above the corrupt influence of wealth *and* women.

In his young adult years, as noted, Fitzgerald adopted an attitude summed up as "Life was something you dominated if you were any good," a belief that was shaped by his early success when he saw "the improbable, the implausible, often the impossible, come true."[3] Scott's youthful imperialist philosophy stands in contrast to the isolationism described by Fitzgerald in the last of the published "Crack-Up" articles after revealing his emotional bankruptcy in the first installment. However, it has been far too easy for biographers to take the tone of withdrawal, retreat, and seeming surrender in "The Crack-Up" and rework Fitzgerald's life in reverse to uncover an entire trail of failure and obsequiousness in Fitzgerald's life, a perspective partly supported by Fitzgerald's own admissions.

Perhaps the most famous of these admissions is the oft-quoted *Notebooks* entry in which Fitzgerald makes his most self-damning statement to favor Hemingway: "I talk with the authority of failure—Ernest with the authority of success. We could never sit across the table again,"[4] a remark so dramatic that it serves as the subtitle to Matthew Bruccoli's contrast of the two literary giants in *Scott and Ernest* (1978). Fitzgerald was true to his word. After Scott went to a filming of *Spanish Earth*, made by Hemingway, Lillian Hellman, Joris Ivens, and Archibald MacLeish, Scott was invited to Dorothy

Parker's, where Hemingway and others were gathering. After driving Hellman to the party, Scott was reluctant to go in because he was scared of seeing Ernest, at least scared as long as he was sober.

In fact, there were contradictory assessments of Julius Caesar with which Fitzgerald would have been familiar, but as creator of Jay Gatsby and a public icon himself, Fitzgerald was used to the fictional construction of ambiguous but mythic personalities. In contrast to the stoic Caesar portrayed by Froude, Wells depicts "a dissolute and extravagant young man" around whom "scandals cluster thick." Later, as ruler, he continued in this prodigal vein by catering to the masses, spending "great sums" to covet the public. In contrast to Froude's description of the Caesar-Cleopatra relationship as distant and purely formal, Wells depicts Caesar as being virtually Cleopatra's servant. From an undisciplined Caesar absorbed by wealth and dominated by women, there emerges a man who succumbed to temptation, corrupted by the same forces he supposedly opposed or mastered. Such amorous pleasantries with a woman "mark the elderly sensualist or sentimentalist…rather than the master ruler of men."[5]

Hemingway's indelible portrait of Fitzgerald as a failure due to his enchantment with wealth, luxury, and Zelda [Cleopatra] is strikingly similar. If not for Nick Carraway, Jay Gatsby would have suffered a similar fate because the public perception would have been shaped by Tom Buchanan exposing Gatsby's sordid business dealings—so like Fitzgerald's "overly commercial" writing and Daisy's verifying false charges of manslaughter against Gatsby. At the time he was writing *The Great Gatsby,* and increasingly afterward, Fitzgerald believed that he was in similar danger of being misunderstood. In the public mind as well as among his literary peers, he was increasingly viewed as an intellectual weakling who failed to transcend the wealth and illusory culture of which he wrote.

✧　✧　✧

Parallels between Fitzgerald the personality and Fitzgerald the professional author abound. To be a literary imperialist requires a liberal education, and this we know Scott possessed from his wide-ranging interests, his carefully chosen books (now in the Princeton Library), and his reading list for Sheilah Graham's *College of One* course. About the time of his writing of *Gatsby,* Fitzgerald also became familiar with the themes in Oswald Spengler's *The Decline of the West* (1918, 1922).[6] At the time of its first publication in 1918, the debacle and aftermath of the Great World War seemed to bear out Spengler's view that Western civilization, with its faith in unbounded expansion, was in the process of going to waste. For Spengler, as for Wells, the national symbol of deterioration was the sprawling large city where money ruled, a theme echoed in the urban economic wasteland depicted in *The Great Gatsby*. People like Nick Carraway were migrating to financial centers like New York City, where "the whole life of broad regions is collecting while the rest dries up."[7] Like the mechanistic commuter traffic passing beneath the visage of Dr. Eckleburg, Spengler perceives a spiritless materialism flowing through the urban landscape.

Imperialism also was Spengler's political and international symbol of the deterioration of Western civilization, while in Fitzgerald's mind imperialism and the Great War blended. Spengler's sweeping historical perspective undoubtedly influenced Fitzgerald's perception of imperialism and his understanding of the forces underlying World War I. Spengler viewed imperialism as a manifestation of a new Faustian worldview, citing Cecil Rhodes and his phrase "expansion is everything" as being the "first precursor of a Western type of Caesers, whose day is to come though yet distant." Prophetically, Spengler proclaimed that imperialism's expansive tendency is "daemonic and immense, which grips, forces into service, and uses up the late mankind of the world-city stage...."[8] As noted, the remnants of World War I scattered throughout *Tender Is the Night* are used by Fitzgerald as atmospheric backdrop to deepen the general theme of destruction in the novel and provide ironic commentary on the new empire that Dick Diver, a medical doctor, and Hollywood are striving to create in Europe.

Besides Spengler, prominent economists such as John Hobson and Thorstein Veblen were developing theories of imperialism during Fitzgerald's lifetime, and almost certainly helped shape his perspective. For example, Hobson identifies J. P. Morgan and John Rockefeller as supporters of American imperialism. "They," he writes, "desired to use the public resources of their country to find profitable employment for their capital which otherwise would be superfluous."[9] Fitzgerald's cynicism about this influence of business on international politics echoes Hobson: "Maybe we had gone to war for J. P. Morgan's loans after all."[10] Whether J. P. Morgan and other business interests were the cause of world war, Fitzgerald does not say, but his inference is clear.

In *Imperialism: A Study* (1902) and *The Economics of Unemployment* (1923), Hobson sees imperialism as an outgrowth of the fundamental inefficiencies of the capitalist system. There are several layers of waste inherent to capitalism, all of which are traceable to the highly unequal distribution of income created in a free market economy. Within capitalist economies, the excess savings of the upper class leads to a level of consumer demand that is insufficient to ensure full employment. In the search for profitable investment outlets for the surplus savings of the wealthy and to rid themselves of surplus product, business attempts to capture foreign markets, which became the engine driving the imperialistic quests of the major powers of Europe and the United States. The thirst for hegemony leads to costly government expenditures to secure protection for business interests abroad, actions that heighten tensions between competing national powers engaged in the same imperialist enterprise.

The extreme manifestation of these moves is war—eventually two world wars. In sum, Hobson highlights some of the tremendous costs that may evolve out of the unequal distribution of income generated within the capitalist system. Although Hobson's focus is mainly on Europe, he recognizes that the United States is not immune to these imperialist forces. In fact, its technological leadership means that the U.S. is particularly susceptible to overproduction, and Hobson mentions U.S. hegemony in Cuba, Hawaii, and the Philippines as examples of U.S. imperialism, as well as adventures in South America near the turn of the century.

Thorstein Veblen, a great constant in Fitzgerald's thinking, like Hobson, views capitalism as generating considerable waste, but, unlike Hobson, does not attribute the far-reaching destructiveness of imperialism to the inability of the capitalist system to achieve full employment. Rather, Veblen argues that threats, displays of force, and political influence being exerted by big business abroad are normal strategies within the pecuniary culture of business (the revelations of the Microsoft case during the 1990s or the Enron and Tyco scandals during the early 2000s would not have surprised Veblen, nor would have the absence of effective retribution). As early as 1904, when he wrote *The Theory of Business Enterprise,* Veblen observes how international businesses had enlisted the military powers of their respective states to promote their interests abroad. The result, Veblen argues, is a growing tension between nations in the international quest for riches. Instead of business competition triggering the "wealth of nations," the mantra of classical economics, Veblen has international commerce standing out as a prophetic "inquiry into the nature and causes of the wars of nations."

Veblen also anticipates the essence of the psychological dimension of competitive warfare. To him, predatory and warlike behavior is an honorific badge in an earlier barbarian stage of society that has not entirely disappeared in modern society despite the emergence of leisure and consumption as objects of emulation. Within the business community, for example, the love of "sport" and conquest remains to the point that "warlike demonstrations have come to be a part of the regular apparatus of business."[11] In the international realm, force and fraud are routine business strategies. Fitzgerald's characters such as Jay Gatsby and "old sport" Tom Buchanan as well as the gangster Wolfsheim epitomize these human traits. The power and predation of the hereditary leisure class is a central theme in *Gatsby* and in *Tender Is the Night*. Indeed, Fitzgerald's words and themes still resonate early in the twenty-first American century as the officers of businesses use fictional accounting to manipulate stock prices to benefit their own stock options.

And, this is not the end of it. Veblen notes how "the experience of Continental Europe in the matter of armaments during the last half-century, and of all the greater nations during the last two decades, argues that when warlike emulation between states of somewhat comparable force has once got under way it assumes a cumulative character; so that a scale of expenditure for armaments which would at the outset have seemed absurdly impossible comes presently to be accepted as a matter of course."[12] Wasteful "Cold War" expenditures existed long before the Soviet-American Cold War. Even Veblen, however, did not anticipate the human cost of trench warfare during World War I, which Dick Diver in *Tender Is the Night* estimates as "twenty lives a foot."[13]

The influence of Veblen's psychology and sociology of imperialism also resonate in Fitzgerald's "The Rich Boy" (1926), the novelette so underestimated and misunderstood by Hemingway. Its themes fall, appropriately, about midway between *Gatsby* and *Tender*. "Rich Boy" is an account of imperialism writ small in the urban culture of New York City. In the story Anson Hunter ("son of a hunter") is a model of the wealthy heir who is endowed with an archaic temperament of the predatory type described by Veblen. The eldest child of an aristocratic New York City family of old wealth and elite social standing, Anson inherits not only wealth and social status but also a sense of innate superiority. These privileges, however, stunt his moral development: He lacks self-control, which contributes to an unruly hedonistic streak of excessive drinking and womanizing and, being accustomed to receiving and possessing, he is unable to make crucial self-sacrifices required for moral and spiritual growth. To sacrifice is to abandon control, an alien concept for inheritors of wealth who have predatory instincts.

Anson's personal life of reckless hedonism reflects the energetic dissipation of New York City in the mid to late twenties also described by Fitzgerald in "My Lost City." One face of Fitzgerald's also resembles Anson's—Scott's rude, combative, and domineering side when he is under the influence of alcohol. However, Anson's imperialistic disposition manifests itself most observably in his treatment of women. After his drinking contributes greatly to the dissolution of his engagement to Paula Legendre, his first (and only) serious relationship, Anson learns of her new interest in another wealthy suitor, Lowell Thayer, and is "uneasy to think that he might lose her." He returns to Palm Beach and, over a game of cards with Paula and Lowell, seizes her back. Yet once back in his possession, he fails to commit: "Why should he, when he might hold her so, biding his own time...."[14] Unable to capitulate to the golden moment with an act of self-sacrifice that love requires, he misses the opportunity of his life, the profoundest form of waste in a Heraclitan and Entropic world where life is a series of irrecoverable moments. When he meets a married and pregnant Paula years later, Anson is still unattached and notably sterile. His depression eases and confidence returns only after Paula dies in childbirth. As the story ends, Anson returns to the "hunt" and stalks a nameless woman in a "red tam" on a ship traveling to Europe.

Throughout, Anson exhibits an instinctive urge to dominate and what Veblen satirically called "prowess." Even as a Wall Street financial investment adviser, Anson is essentially an overseer "taking pleasure in helping people and arranging their affairs."[15] As with Paula, women are treated as colonies to be seized and protected, not out of charity, love, or even for what they may provide as sustenance or repute, but because the spirit of conquest is an end in itself (Paula is worth a million bucks, but the satisfaction Anson derives is from the victory of seizing her from a competitor, not from what possessing her might yield, materially or otherwise). The conquest is more important than the possession—a trait we have observed in Fitzgerald in its more benign manifestation.

Anson's behavior reflects the notorious imperialist propensity for controlling others' affairs while possessing no *self*-control, expanding into new territory without properly husbanding what is seized along the way. Ironically, women and their parents are attracted to Anson because of his appearance of sturdiness and "protective strength" but, like an empire's rhetorical assurances to its colonies, Anson's protection is more pose than reality. Seizure and control of a country is often justified as paternalistic protection against that country's own domestic turmoil or to counteract the threat of another empire's nefarious invasion. This rationalization is typically thinly disguised self-interest of imperialism's promoters who seize territory to monopolize a new market for self-gain. This is precisely how Anson behaves toward women whom he captures with his magnetic and forceful nature, subsequently neglects, and reclaims only if they seek another alliance.

To be sure, Anson's ability to exude confidence and protective strength—traits that endear him to women—are valuable business assets that seem to lend support to the idea that capitalism, by directing people's energies toward business and industry, can override imperialism's destructive tendencies. That is, it is better to tyrannize over financial assets than over nations. Anson's paternalistic care for his clients' financial affairs (often extended to their personal affairs) may be taken as evidence of a genuine priestly attribute and a confirmation of the mollifying effect that work in a capitalist system can have on latent predatory behavior. Fitzgerald's story parallels Hobson's thesis; Capitalism is as effective in channeling combative urges abroad as it is with its pacifying effects at home. What is conclusive is Fitzgerald's sophisticated recognition of the underlying psychological forces of imperialism as well as its destructive tendencies.

✧   ✧   ✧

As in so much of the life of the Fitzgeralds, the global social forces so well understood by Scott were being repeated at a personal level. Scott and Zelda's relationship often took on this character of two imperialistic nations at war. Both wanted to control, to dominate in some sense. Zelda was a manipulative woman with many controlling weapons—her beauty, her natural self-centeredness, and her skill in the social art of putting people on the defensive. As we have seen, Scott confessed an urge to dominate women, but Zelda, the dominatrix, could not be tamed. Captivated first by her physical beauty and sharp intelligence, then drawn to her unpredictable nature and taste for extravagance, Scott, even when sober, was easily kept off balance and under her direction. Alexander McKaig, the friend who kept a journal of conversations he had with the Fitzgeralds during their first year of marriage (1920), provides ample evidence that Zelda was the one promoting a reckless lifestyle that would lead to ruin:

Evening at Fitz. Fitz and I argued with Zelda about notoriety they are getting through being so publicly and spectacularly drunk. Zelda wants to live life of an "extravagant"—No thought of what world will think or future. I told them they were headed for catastrophe if they kept up at present rate.[16]

As noted, Hemingway and H. L. Mencken took an instant dislike of Zelda, consistently claiming that she manipulated Scott out of jealousy and with malicious intent to keep him from his work as a serious writer. Hemingway even said that she intended "to put him [Scott] out of business" sexually. Later, when her mental illness made domination and independence impossible, Zelda naturally reacted angrily, lashing out at Scott as overbearing and dictatorial, a technique that succeeded in putting Scott on the defensive. By 1931, Zelda was friendless and entirely dependent upon Scott. In a letter written to Scott in early March 1932 after she had suffered a significant relapse, Zelda perversely conceals her aggressive and manipulative side and admits, however obliquely, that she is now incapable of hunting her own prey (except Scott) and is dependent upon his sheltering love and understanding:

I have often told you that I am that little fish, who swims about under a shark, and, I believe, lives indelicately on its offal. Anyway, that is the way I am. Life moves over me in a vast black shadow and I swallow whatever it drops with relish, having learned in a very hard school that one cannot be both a parasite and enjoy self-nourishment without moving in worlds too fantastic for even my disordered imagination to people with meaning. So: it is easy to make yourself loved when one lives off love. Goofo—I adore you and worship you and I am very miserable that you be made even temporarily unhappy by those divergencies of direction in myself which I cannot satisfactorily explain and which leave me eternally alone except for you and baffled. You are absolutely all in the world that I have ever been able to think of as having any vital bearing on my relations with the evolution of the species.[17]

Scott nonetheless is not the prototypical predator-imperialist. His natural generosity, sense of marital duty, and residual love for Zelda that led him to be protective of Zelda during her mental fissure (which began to noticeably surface by 1926 if not earlier) is understandable and entirely consistent with doctors' orders after she was institutionalized in 1930. Scott's alleged overprotectiveness both before and after Zelda's institutionalization did not stem from a desire to dominate Zelda or stifle her creativity as often claimed by Zelda and sometimes implied by her biographers—Nancy Milford, Kendall Taylor, and the near-hysterical Sally Cline.

When Zelda tried to establish some creative outlet, discipline, and self-sufficiency to her life by pursuing a career in ballet in the late twenties, Scott was supportive of and may have actually initiated the idea, contrary to the imperialist's natural predilection to seize and control. Zelda nevertheless resented her continued (colonial) economic dependence, writing retrospectively in February 1932 that "I hated taking his money for my lessons: I wanted my dancing to belong to me, so I wrote to pay for them," now evidently viewing the professional arts (dancing and writing) as her natural vocation. Zelda perceived Scott, but not herself, as an imperialist.

In a flurry of creativity between 1928 and 1929, Zelda did indeed write five short stories (with Scott's editorial assistance and deriving characters from what Scott called their "common store of material"), which were published in *College Humor* under both their names, and one short story in the *Saturday Evening Post* for which Scott was given sole authorial credit although Scott admitted that he had nothing to do with it except for suggesting a theme and proofing the completed manuscript. His authorship was required to gain top dollar. Scott further promoted Zelda's literary work in 1930 when he had his agent, Harold Ober, send three of her short stories to Scribners. When Perkins rejected them, Scott nevertheless wrote back that he intended to press forward on Zelda's behalf and to encourage her to write some additional stories with an eye toward publishing a collection of her short stories:

> I was sorry of course about Zelda's stories—possibly they
> mean more to me than implicit to the reader who doesn't know
> from what depths of misery and effort they sprang…. She has
> those series of eight portraits that attracted so much attention
> in College Humor and… I think a book might be got together
> for next spring if Zelda can add a few more during winter.[18]

Scott did not initially promote Zelda's autobiographical novel,
Save Me the Waltz, after Zelda sent it to Scribners in March 1932
without his prior approval. Nevertheless, after demanding revisions
that would not jeopardize the status of his own novel, Scott shep-
herded Zelda's novel toward publication with Scribners in 1932 by
corresponding confidentially with Max Perkins just as he had earlier
launched Hemingway's career. At the same time, Scott counseled
Perkins to tone down any praise he might have for Zelda and her
book for fear that she would associate such praise with immediate fame and money. But as Zelda's mental condition worsened and
her angry but groundless accusations of abuse and neglect by Scott
continued, the marriage likewise continued to deteriorate. Scott's
perspective on the situation was that he was being manipulated. In
1932, Scott told Dr. Rennie that:

> In the last analysis, she is a stronger person than I am. I have
> creative fire, but I am a weak individual. She knows this and
> really looks upon me as a woman. All our lives, since the days
> of our engagement, we have spent time hunting for some man
> Zelda considers strong enough to lean upon. I am not. How-
> ever, I am now so near the breaking point myself that she real-
> izes she has me against the wall and that she can drive me no
> further. She is a little afraid of me at the present time.[19]

In Scott and Zelda's remarkable conversation with Dr. Rennie
in 1933, Scott does reveal an imperialist desire to dominate, but it
is quite different from the allegation that he wished to lord over his
wife. Rather, what surfaces is Scott's deeply felt and lifelong desire
to lead his profession:

It is all unfair. It is all unfair…I am paid those enormous prices, and not for nothing. I am paid for a continual fight and struggle that I can carry on…the whole equipment of my life is to be a novelist. And that is attained with tremendous struggle; that is attained with a tremendous nervous struggle; that is attained with a tremendous sacrifice which you make to lead any profession. It was done because I was equipped for it as a little boy. I began at ten, when I wrote my first story. My whole life is a professional move towards that.[20]

At issue in the lopsided battle between Zelda and Scott's professional literary lives is the question of what authors can legitimately claim as their own. Scott was a literary imperialist in that his writings were broadly intertextual. He borrowed from Zelda and (often credited) her ideas and materials (including private letters and entries from her personal diaries) that supported his own writings, and freely incorporated their personal experiences into his writings. But this behavior was part of a larger pattern of literary debts and intellectual and social influences that permeate Fitzgerald's literary work and vision. The same can be said of other literary figures, especially Hemingway, who used characters (including his wives) and material from real life.

Scott's use of Zelda's private letters, particularly those reflecting Zelda's private thoughts during her illness is, nevertheless, controversial in its reach, as is the public credit given Scott for some of Zelda's writings. As noted earlier, Scott himself provided two plausible reasons for his actions—he and Zelda's common economic interest and Scott's assessment that Zelda was a third-rate writer whereas he was a professional writer of the first order and spokesman for his generation. As Scott explains to Dr. Rennie, the difference between the professional and the amateur is something that is awfully hard to analyze. In a different context, he writes to Sara Murphy and refers to "the little immeasurable portion of a millimeter, the thing at the absolute top that makes the difference between a World's champion and an also-ran…."[21] Again, Fitzgerald's intuition is remarkable; only in recent years have economists estimated the fineness of this line between the champion and the also-ran.

Much of Fitzgerald's lifetime controlling behavior seemed aimed at success as an author. In that process he sometimes took great risks with friendships. On occasion, especially at the beginning of his career, Scott would feign drunkenness as a way of disarming people. Even when sober, his practice of bombarding and badgering people with personal quizlike questions (sometimes with the help of Zelda) was considered either silly or offensive. Scott's interrogations were partly a device for getting insight into people's personalities to help him construct characters for his stories, but attacking and disarming people by probing their hidden feelings was also a way for Scott to feel *in control.* This desire to dominate or absorb other people into himself as a core element of Scott's personality is revealed in his *Notebooks:*

> When I like men I want to be like them—I want to lose the outer qualities that give me my individuality and be like them. I don't want the man; I want to absorb into myself all the qualities that make him attractive and leave him out. I cling to my own innards. When I like women I want to own them, to dominate them, to have them admire me.[22]

Although Scott's concern for his family seemed controlling, it was motivated by his experience with Zelda and his rational fear that Scottie would follow in her footsteps. His imperialism generally was confined to politically understanding it and incorporating cultural and nation-state dominance into his fiction plus his own strong determination to dominate his profession. However, when Zelda revises manuscript for the novel, that she began in Spring 1933, into "Caesar's Things," she is attacking her perception of Scott's imperialism, but is unwittingly attacking his professional author's persona. Having regressed into a religious hysteria, Zelda is contemplating what is to be given to God and what is to be given to Caesar (sometimes meaning Scott). She misunderstands Scott's devotion to his art as detracting from his indulgence for her.

Despite this confusion, Zelda consistently berates Scott for his attempt to control her, despite *her* lack of control being a lifelong affliction. Sometimes she thinks of Scott (i.e., Jacob in her novel) as possessing Caesar's worst traits, as she attacks Scott in the same way she did in *Save Me the Waltz*. After writing of marriage in chapter 4, she continues: "It is a conviction that 2 egos make better tune with cosmic harmonies together than apart; it is many things besides the impetus of possession...." In chapter 5, Zelda writes that "Jacob [Scott] literally could not stand a woman's prerogative: to him women were agents...." She writes in chapter 7: "He [Jacob, aka Scott] kept nagging and asking and third-degreeing his acquaintances till it all made acceptable continuity with what he thought it ought to be dramatically...."

Scott's objection to Zelda's writing, however, is directly connected to his dual role as author and as chief bill-payer. The material being used by Zelda prior to the publication of *Tender* presents a huge problem for Scott's psychological novel. As her theme, Zelda is using the life of Vasily Nijinsky, a male dancer with the Ballets Russes and lover of its director Sergei Diaghilev. Nijinsky had gone quite mad and was diagnosed as schizophrenic. Later, in "Caesar's Things,"Zelda strains her own credibility when she writes of her meeting the French lieutenant (Jozan), "Life suddenly offered possibilities to a reckless extravagance which she didn't like...."[23] Here we need only consider the source, as well as the quite different description of her affair in *Save Me the Waltz*.

✧ ✧ ✧

Meanwhile, back in the Fitzgeralds' real world, Scott was faced with debts to repay, Zelda's latest hospital bills, and Scotties' schooling costs. Once again his eyes turned reluctantly westward. Scott's reluctance to go to Hollywood in 1937, however, was not complete. Once he finally committed to go, he went with two new imperialistic quests in mind. First, he had the idea of becoming a film director or becoming influential enough to control more than one aspect of a film—not be just a cog in the wheel like the usual scriptwriter. Second, in a lengthy letter written on September 29, 1939, to Kenneth Littauer (who, as editor at *Collier's*, was considering serializing *The Last Tycoon*), Scott indicated that he had chosen Irving Thalberg as a hero for a novel three years earlier (1936) "because he is one of the half-dozen men I have known who were built on the grand scale."[24]

In the past, "going west" generally was recommended for young men. Scott, now, as in so many other ways in the past, was breaking the mold. Now, however, he had run out of options; this was his only path to financial survival. The return to Hollywood took a lot of courage; it also required the past of a celebrity and a great amount of talent.

Endnotes

1. H. G. Wells, *The Outline of History* (Garden City, NY: Garden City Publishing, 1920), p. 401.

2. James Anthony Froude, *Julius Caesar* (New York: D. Appleton and Company, 1904), pp. 1–2.

3. F. Scott Fitzgerald, "The Crack-Up" (February 1936), reprinted in Edmund Wilson, ed., *The Crack-Up* (New York: New Directions, 1956, [1945]), p. 69.

4. F. Scott Fitzgerald, "The Note-Books," in Ibid., p. 181. The entire "Note-Books" chapter runs pp. 91–242.

5. Wells, *Outline of History,* p. 441.

6. It is possible but improbable that Fitzgerald read the original German edition of Spengler, and the first complete English translation of vol. 1 did not appear until 1926 and of vol. 2 until 1928, after *Gatsby*. Scott may have read a review of *Decline of the West* in *Century* (summer 1924), the *Yale Review* (vol. 13, 1924), or a translation of portions of it by Kenneth Burke in *The Dial*, November 1924. The conclusion remains: Fitzgerald was greatly influenced by Spengler.

7. Oswald Spengler, *The Decline of the West, vol. 1* (New York: Alfred A. Knopf, 1926), p. 32.

8. Ibid., pp. 37–38.

9. J. A. Hobson, *The Economics of Unemployment* (New York: Macmillan, 1923), pp. 76–77.

10. F. Scott Fitzgerald, "Echoes of the Jazz Age" (1931), in Wilson, ed., *Crack-Up,* p. 13.

11. Thorstein Veblen, *The Theory of Business Enterprise* (New York: Augustus M. Kelley, 1965, [1904]), pp. 297, 296.

12. Ibid., pp. 297–98.

13. F. Scott Fitzgerald, *Tender Is the Night* (New York: Charles Scribner's Sons, 1962, [1934]), p. 56.

14. F. Scott Fitzgerald, "The Rich Boy" (1926), in *The Stories of F. Scott Fitzgerald* (New York: Macmillan, 1951), pp. 185–86. This story was first published in *Redbook* 46 (January & February 1926), pp. 27–32, 144, 146; and 75–79, 122, 124–26.

15. Ibid., 185.

16. Alexander McKaig Diary, 1919–21.

17. Jackson R. Bryer and Cathy W. Barks, *Dear Scott, Dearest Zelda: The Love Letters of F. Scott and Zelda Fitzgerald* (New York: St. Martin's Press, 2002), p. 154. This is the first paragraph of a four-page handwritten letter; for the rest, see Bryer and Barks.

18. Letter from F. Scott Fitzgerald to Maxwell Perkins, c. September 1, 1930, in Matthew J. Broccoli, ed., *A Life in Letters: F. Scott Fitzgerald* (New York: Simon & Schuster, 1994), p. 200.

19. Quoted by Nancy Milford, *Zelda: A Biography* (New York: Harper & Row, 1970), pp. 261–62. We have been unable to locate the original source.

20. Rennie Transcript, Fitzgerald Collection, Princeton University Library. We cannot identify the page number from our Library notes.

21. Linda Patterson Miller, ed., *Letters from the Lost Generation* (New Brunswick, N.J.: Rutgers University Press, 1991), p. 139.

22 F. Scott Fitzgerald, "Notebooks K," in Wilson, ed., *The Crack-Up,* p. 169.

23. The quotes are from Zelda's draft of "Caesar's Things," Fitzgerald Collection, Princeton University Library.

24. Quote and entire letter is found in Bruccoli's preface to his take on *The Love of the Last Tycoon*. See F. Scott Fitzgerald, *The Love of the Last Tycoon*, ed. Matthew Bruccoli (New York: Simon & Schuster, 1993), p. xiii.

Fourteen

"Old Scott" Goes West

NOW, HAVING MOVED BACK TO THE OAK HALL HOTEL IN TRYON, NORTH Carolina, in January 1937, where he had lived in February 1935, Scott Fitzgerald awaited with mixed feelings a third call from Hollywood. As they say in the barroom, it would be the "last call." He was, however, in dire straits. His anxiety focused on the $40,000 he owed and the fact that he had published, by his standards, no *important* fiction since *Tender Is the Night* in 1934. By May 1937, Ober had been unable to place a Fitzgerald story in any magazine for nearly a year. Fitzgerald's 1936 royalty payments from his books, all of which were still in print, were $81.18. Often he was forced to wire Ober for money for daily living expenses, with occasional advances from Maxwell Perkins. And, he still had Zelda's ongoing private hospital bills and Scottie's private schooling costs to pay. Characteristically, Scott refused to place Zelda in a public insane asylum or Scottie in a public school.

As his friends had warned, the publication of "The Crack-Up" essays had hurt his writing reputation. The essays, however, did let people know that Scott Fitzgerald still lived. At the nadir of his career, notoriety was better than no publicity at all. In any case a lucrative short story market no longer existed; magazines now had competition from the movies. Intuitively, Scott had long known—since about 1930—that movies would become his competition. It was only fitting: movies, as a form of entertainment, had been born the same year as Scott. They were the same age, but the movies were doing better, much better. By this time Scott had suffered greatly, but he was not cynical. Not only did he keep faith with himself and with his profession, he had arrived at a difficult maturity and a great dignity. And, he did look older. Back east, they would begin to call him "old Scott."

Despite Scott's mixed feelings about Hollywood, he had been trying to return. In August 1936, a picture possibility with RKO Radio was delayed because, according to Ober, "A friend of one of the men said he had seen you in New York when you had been drinking. I have assured them you have not been drinking this year and I think and hope things can be straightened out in a few days...."[1] In the meantime, Edwin H. Knopf—working for Metro-Goldwyn-Mayer (MGM) as a director, producer, writer, and story editor—persuaded his colleagues at the studio that Fitzgerald would be a valuable writer. Knopf's task was not easy: Fitzgerald's reputation was waning and he had publicized his "crack-up." Knopf and Fitzgerald had known each other in France at the end of the twenties, with Knopf very much an admirer of Scott. Knopf refused to believe Fitzgerald to be a hopeless case, either as a man or as a writer.

Knopf, a frustrated novelist, had written a screenplay that combined his own experiences with Scott's. Although the characters originally were called "Scott" and "Zelda," Samuel Goldwyn fictionalized the names and released the film as *The Wedding Night,* starring lanky Gary Cooper as the shortish Scott and a new sex goddess, Anna Sten, as a lookalike Zelda. Knopf apparently had fantasized himself as a taller Scott Fitzgerald and made some money from the illusion. Perhaps he wanted to give some of it back to Scott, the original legend. Perhaps he had come to understand the illusion of money as power.

As for Scott, his aspirations to dominate his profession now further extended—into Hollywood. Although periodically driven to fantasyland for financial reasons, Fitzgerald did have high creative aspirations, hoping to blend his literary talent with a new artistic medium. To some degree, as we will see, he succeeded beyond contemporary biographical judgments. Ultimately, as we also will see, Scott was unable to shape events in Hollywood or "retire to a safer elevation." Instead, he became enormously frustrated by his failure to extend his artistic reach and realize his imperialistic vision. Spengler observes in *The Decline of the West* how "like everything else that is no longer becoming but become, it has put a mechanism in place of an organism."[2]

The mechanistic character of the Hollywood factory initially overwhelmed Scott, even though he found some consolation and a little essential money in his Pat Hobby stories, which parodied the standardization of human parts, including himself, as a cog in the wheel. Dying broke while writing a novel about a creative industry leader in demise, Scott was finally defeated by the destructive forces of wealth and economic power. But his "epic grandeur" rested on a higher plane as he reflected upon the Western world, as well as his own life, in decline. As we next find, however, even Fitzgerald's decline was not sustained during his final days in Hollywood. Western civilization itself may simply have reached a plateau—the jury on the outcome of which is still out.

✧ ✧ ✧

A train carried Scott Fitzgerald westward to California. He was forty years old and it was his last chance, he believed, to recollect his life. His current opinion of Hollywood matched Dorothy Parker's, who said, "Deep down, Hollywood is shallow." Parker, a screenwriter for MGM, also had discovered "a great truth" about screenwriting, "and that is that no writer, whether he writes from love or from money, can condescend to what he writes. What makes it hard in screenwriting…is the money he gets."[3] Novelist William Faulkner was another MGM screenwriter and alcoholic who disliked the work but liked the money. Deep down, too, Fitzgerald already knew of these authorial concerns. Despite his "sincere hatred" for the place, however, Hollywood was the last hope for the money he so desperately needed. It was the kind of jam in which Fitzgerald's talents nonetheless had carried many the day. He was determined to make the most of it.

It was early July 1937 and Americans were entering the final phase of the Great Depression, a time when the official unemployment rate was hovering around a cool 14.3 percent. Although Scott was traveling through the hot, brown dust bowl of Oklahoma and Texas, he was wearing an impeccable Brooks Brothers suit and carrying a wrinkled raincoat, a battered hat, and a wool scarf. He was not drinking alcohol; rather, he was drinking one Coca-Cola after another while continuing his habit of chain-smoking Chesterfields. From the train, Scott wrote a friend, "These Texas lands are like crossing a sea—spiritually, I mean, with a fat contract at the end."[4] At least, *that* was his fervent hope.

And, though Fitzgerald had written that "there are no second acts in American lives," MGM offered him a six-month contract at the extraordinary salary of $1,000 a week, about $11,000 a week in today's dollars. *His* second act would be, of all places, in Hollywood, wherein Scott was to define three acts as making a movie. Then, with a renewed contract he received $1,250 per week for all of 1938: In eighteen months during 1937–38, he earned a total of $88,500, the equivalent of nearly a million in today's dollars. In the earning hierarchy of Hollywood screenwriters of this era, Fitzgerald's weekly earnings at MGM fell somewhere between the eighty-third and the ninety-first percentiles at the top of the scale. Of 228 writers surveyed by Leo C. Rosten for 1938, not more than a maximum of 18 were paid more than Fitzgerald—not bad for a "failure," a washed-up and forgotten novelist.[5] Scott was able to revive his career, pay off his debts, support his family, and save enough money to buy time for his next novel, which was based partly on his experiences in Hollywood during his three visits there. Equally important, Scott would have his final and most fulfilling love affair.

The match made by Scott Fitzgerald and Hollywood certainly could not have been made in heaven. Fitzgerald had written of the huge failures of those who pursued wealth without integrity and the American Dream without understanding it. In Hollywood,

Scott was, as ever, his own most severe critic. In his previous trips there in 1927 and 1931, he had drawn an enormous salary; yet he considered himself a bitter failure as a screenwriter. By the 1930s, Hollywood had *become* the premier manufacturer of dreams—the ultimate "DreamWorks." During the Great Depression, when most Americans' dreams lay in shambles, everyone looked to Hollywood to tell them, even *show* them, *what* to dream about. Although the 1930s was Hollywood's Golden Age, Fitzgerald judged these Hollywood screenplays to be the shabbiest writing anywhere, anytime. By Scott's standards, what he and other authors did in Hollywood was "whoring."

Other incongruities come to mind. When writing, Scott was aggressively independent. He worked alone with his own ideas and personal experiences. Moreover, he wrote "at home," never having an employer to order him to "come to the office from nine to five." In Hollywood, screenplays were written by a kind of floating committee. A writer would write an early part of a screenplay, then be replaced by a second, only to be replaced by a third, and so on until as many as fifteen writers completed the "collaboration." The system actually was less structured than even a floating committee, and "collaboration" lost its meaning since generally the writers came in relays, one not knowing what the previous writer had done nor what the next one might do or undo. It was a marathon relay of strangers with no clearly defined starting or finishing line, a production system invented by Irving Grant Thalberg, the "boy wonder" of Hollywood.

Fitzgerald, like many other professional writers, believed that these serial authors and revisions completely destroyed whatever integrity the original work might have had. As ever, Fitzgerald was more sensitive about others revising his work than were most authors. To Hemingway's credit, Scott believed, his hero Ernest was able to stay away from Hollywood screenwriting altogether. William Faulkner wrote the screenplay of *To Have and Have Not* (starring Humphrey Bogart and Lauren Bacall), one of two truly successful Faulkner screenplays, the other being *The Big Sleep* (Bogart, once again). Faulkner, Scott knew, was lucky to have the cerebral Bogart making up dialogue as he performed.

Scott prepared for his new profession much as he had when he studied the short story form while beginning to write short stories for the *Saturday Evening Post*. MGM's studio library screened dozens of movies for him every week during his early months in Hollywood; he carefully researched their form and content. Still, no one would ever confuse Scott Fitzgerald with a "nine-to-five" model employee. Hollywood was a notorious employer of screenwriters who were forced to come to the studio every day and work like drudges—thanks to the Thalberg model. Fitzgerald's friend Nathanael West, writing from his personal experience in Hollywood, satirized the process in his great novel *The Day of the Locust* (1939). He wrote: "There's no fooling here. All the writers sit in cells in a row and the minute a typewriter stops someone pokes his head in the door to see if you are thinking."

It may have been William Faulkner's habits during the early 1930s that spoiled "working at home" for all screenwriters. At some point flacks at MGM discovered that Faulkner was "working at home" in *Oxford, Mississippi*. Being closely supervised certainly was not Fitzgerald's style, either; besides, he did not know whether his victory over alcohol was fleeting or permanent. If a writer was drinking on the job, the omnipotent studio bosses would know about it. Besides, Scott's ultimate goal, fed by his Caesarlike side—perhaps outrageously ambitious—was to become a writer-director. The director-author duality then would preserve the quality of Scott's screenplays.

Despite the odds, Fitzgerald nonetheless was extremely conscientious. When he did infrequently fall off the wagon, it was in his usual dramatic and widely celebrated manner. There was little chance that the studio bosses would miss such episodes. In contrast, William Faulkner's alcoholism was sedate and private; like Hemingway, Faulkner could "hold his liquor." For this, public and critical opinion seemed grateful, if not sanctimonious.

At forty, Scott *had* prematurely aged. His features had widened, and he was self-conscious of the growing bulge of his stomach. His wrinkles were neither deep nor wide, but had the fineness and frequency associated with illness. Still, he was a handsome man, though looking more like an aging matinee idol than a young leading man. He carefully combed his fading yellow hair to hide its thinning on top. He was a magnificent ruin. Even as early as 1927, when the seventeen-year-old Lois Moran wanted Scott to star in a movie with her, he failed the screen test because he looked "too old" for the part, though he was cavorting in nonreel life with the young, beautiful movie star. Just as Scott and Zelda had valued youth above all else, so did Hollywood. It still does. Were he young, Scott would have been instantly in his element.

✧   ✧   ✧

Scott moved into the Garden of Allah Hotel at 8152 Sunset Boulevard across the road from the Players Club, a popular hangout. The Mocambo and the Trocadero on Sunset were two other hot spots within walking distance. Schwab's drugstore, where "sweater-girl" Lana Turner was to be discovered, also was nearby. The Garden of Allah—built by Alla Nazimova, an eccentric silent-movie star,

was a popular place to stay for a hard-drinking crowd of East Coast writers and actors. Scott moved into an upstairs bungalow apartment at the top of a flight of red-tiled steps. He entered the apartment through an arched Spanish doorway and past a large ceramic Moorish pot. Sometime thereafter, Fitzgerald wrote a post card to himself: "Dear Scott— How are you? Have been meaning to come in and see you. I have been living at the Garden of Allah. Yours Scott Fitzgerald." This reference to his literary isolation exhibited the kind of

Scott in the summer of 1937, photographed by Carl Van Vechten

irony that kept Fitzgerald sane. Meanwhile, the Garden of Allah had seen better days and resembled more a heavily used movie set than a hotel.[6] Surviving until 1959, the Hollywood branch of the Great Western Bank has since replaced it. Otherwise, the demographics of Hollywood are little changed.

Straightaway, Scott remet old friends such as Dorothy Parker, Robert Benchley, John O'Hara, and Anita Loos. All were known for their humor, with Parker being heralded as "the wittiest woman in America." She was thrown out of Catholic school, she said, for insisting "the Immaculate Conception was spontaneous combustion." Alan Campbell, her long-suffering husband, was an actor and writer-collaborator. "Dottie" was small and pretty with a soft voice and impeccable diction. Still, for Scott, a gulf had to be closed; these writers now were the important people while he was not. Anita Loos, author of *Gentlemen Prefer Blonds*, complained: "Scott had that unhealthy humility of the reformed alcoholic."[7] Still, on one occasion, Scott wrote a humorous nonsense poem about his friend.

This book tells that Anita Loos
Is a friend of Caesar, a friend of Zeus
Of Samuel Goldwyn, and Mother Goose
Of Balanchine of the Ballet Russe
Of Tillie, the Viennese Papoose
Of Charlie MacArthur on the loose
Of shanks, chiropodist—what's the use?
Of actors who have escaped the noose
Lots of Hollywood beach refuse
Comics covered with Charlotte Russe
Wretched victims of self-abuse
Big producers all obtuse
This is my birthday, but what the deuce
Is that sad fact to Anita Loos.

Anita Loos would not have to always despair about Scott's new sobriety. The pressure of old friends and the proximity of the Garden of Allah to Hollywood's most popular nightlife were destined to test Scott's resolve not to drink.

Monday, July 12, was Scott's first full nine-to-five day at the studio—in an office on the third floor of the Writers and Producers' Building, renamed the Thalberg Building, after producer Irving Thalberg's untimely death in 1936. An ugly building, the writers called it "the Iron Lung." Scott's name was written on a small square of paper on his office door. This was not Scott's first encounter with Thalberg. Fitzgerald woke Thalberg with a late-night alcoholic phone call in 1934 to try to sell him on a movie version of *Tender Is the Night*. Later, Scott thought that Thalberg not only killed the idea of using someone like Fredric March in the film, but suspected Fitzgerald of having an affair with Thalberg's wife, the beautiful and exotic movie star Norma Shearer. This was not as improbable as Scott made it sound, for Norma was attracted to Fitzgerald. Now, however, Scott was in Thalberg's building; he remembered—despite everything—that he actually *did* like Thalberg. He began his daily

Irving Thalberg and Norma Shearer. Fitzgerald greatly admired both the production head at MGM, who became "Monroe Stahr" in The Last Tycoon, *and the acclaimed actress.*

habit of bringing a briefcase of Coca-Cola. He set sharpened pencils and yellow legal pads upon his desk.

At lunch in the MGM commissary, Scott eventually joined the other writers (and several actors) at "the Left Table," left for its physical location and left for its politics. The gathering included at various times such writers as Anita Loos, Aldous Huxley, S. J. Perelman, and Ogden Nash. Comedian Groucho Marx would sometimes be an unwanted guest, who would dominate the conversation and insist that everything be a joke. Scott had known Groucho as a neighbor in Great Neck in the twenties, but in Hollywood, Scott considered Marx a sick, unfunny, old man. In contrast to Marx, Nash poetically described Fitzgerald as "very quiet but extremely attractive with a sweet nature that came through."[8]

Other days Fitzgerald would join a table with a group of writers and actors who thought of themselves as "the clique." Anita Loos and Aldous Huxley would be there. Among the actors would be legends such as Spencer Tracy, Clark Gable, and sometimes Carole Lombard. This group, rather snobbish, accepted only brainy people like Scott and was distinguished by its irreverent humor. Almost all the truly fabled actresses on the lot were excluded not on simply one but both counts.[9]

✧ ✧ ✧

That was the workaday world of Hollywood. Within hours, however, Fitzgerald's love life would brighten in an unlikely way with an improbable English woman. Only two days later Scott would meet the sexy, beautiful Hollywood gossip columnist Sheilah Graham. Scott's luck was about to improve. Sheilah—by her own account—had remained in a state of heat since her early teens. She was now aged thirty-three years and had yet to cool down.

Endnotes

1. Matthew J. Bruccoli, ed. *As Ever, Scott Fitz* (Philadelphia: J. B. Lippincott, 1972), p. 279.

2. Oswald Spengler, *Decline of the West,* vol. 1 (New York: Alford A. Knopf, 1926), p. 302.

3. Quoted by Ian Hamilton in *Writers in Hollywood* (New York: Heinemann, 1990), p. 98.

4. From a letter by Scott to Corey Ford in early July 1937, Andrew Turnbull, ed. *The Letters of F. Scott Fitzgerald* (New York: Charles Scribner's Sons, 1963), p. 550.

5. Leo C. Rosten, *Hollywood: The Movie Colony, the Movie Makers* (New York: Harcourt, Brace & Co., 1941), p. 384.

6. There are two firsthand sources on Fitzgerald's final Hollywood years and two secondhand accounts. The first is Sheilah Graham (and Gerold Frank), *Beloved Infidel* (New York: Quality Paperback Book Club, 1989), originally published by Henry Holt and Company in 1958. Because of the era of its publication, *Beloved Infidel* left out sex because it was taboo in the 1950s and left-wing ideology because of the powerful presence of the House Un-American Activities Committee. Since much of the 1930s was about sex and left-wing politics, the book became a sanitized sentimental love story. Sheilah quickly grew to dislike this version of her story and followed with *The Rest of the Story* (1964), *College of One* (1966), *The Garden of Allah* (1970, *A State of Heat* (1972), *The Real F. Scott Fitzgerald* (1976), *The Late Lily Shiel* (1978), and *My Hollywood* (1984). The latter books were complicated footnotes to correct the original autobiography.

The second firsthand source is a short book by Fitzgerald's secretary during his final eighteen months: It is Frances Kroll Ring, *Against the Current: As I Remember F. Scott Fitzgerald* (Berkeley, Calif.: Creative Arts Book Company, 1985). Ring's book reveals some things missed and sometimes unknown to Sheilah. Frances Kroll saw Fitzgerald virtually every day during this important time of his life, a time when he was writing the Pat Hobby stories and *The Last Tycoon.*

A secondhand account is by Sheilah's son, a writer: Robert Westbrook, *Intimate Lies: F. Scott Fitzgerald and Sheilah Graham* (New York: HarperCollins, 1995). Before her death in 1988, Graham bequeathed papers, diaries, notes, and correspondence to her son, the novelist Robert Westbrook, with explicit instructions to write the full story of her life with Fitzgerald, which she herself could not fully tell. As it turns out, most of what Westbrook corrects are the errors or lies that Sheilah first wrote about herself. As to Fitzgerald, except for some new details, Sheilah had most of the facts correct. In this and the next chapter, therefore, we trust the biography of Sheilah in her son's account. He is our primary source regarding her life. We quote *Beloved Infidel* or other books by Graham only if Westbrook has used the same quotes. We presume to be close to the truth wherever the son and mother are in agreement. Perhaps the most original contribution of Westbrook is his account of his mother's behavior shortly after Scott's death. As told by Westbrook, the Sheilah-Scott relationship still remains a remarkable love story.

Another secondhand account of Fitzgerald's years in Hollywood is found in Tom Dardis, *Some Time in the Sun: The Hollywood Years of F. Scott Fitzgerald, William Faulkner, Nathanael West, Aldous Huxley, and James Agee* (New York: Charles Scribner's Sons, 1976). Dardis's account is based partly on studio sources who were in Hollywood during the 1930s. Dardis's chapters on Fitzgerald probably are the best sources of published information about what Scott actually contributed to various screenplays and movies.

7. Aaron Latham, *Crazy Sundays: F. Scott Fitzgerald in Hollywood* (New York: The Viking Press, 1971), p. 5.

8. Ibid., p. 8.

9. For the most accurate, descriptive, and detailed account of Scott's day at the studio in 1938, see Latham, *Crazy Sundays,* pp . 3–25. Latham was able to interview Fitzgerald's Hollywood agent, H. M. Swanson, and producer Edwin Knopf.

Fifteen

Sheilah

ALTHOUGH SHEILAH BEGAN LIFE ON LONDON'S SEEDY EAST END AND lived many of her early years in an orphanage, she had manufactured a life at the edges of nobility. She was a Cockney girl, born Lily Shiel, who had escaped to the West End at age seventeen. As a modest salesgirl, she met Maj. John Graham Gillam, a handsome, decorated army officer of the Great War and twenty-five years her senior. Lily thought him romantic. The major quickly hired her at the John Graham Company. Soon Lily would be calling the major "Johnny." He was certain that he would become a millionaire because of his marketing skills, which turned out to be dubious. Lily was soon dating not only Johnny but also Monty Collins, a millionaire slightly younger than Johnny.

Though initially engaged to Monty, she eventually settled on Johnny, who was the better dancer and more romantic. Monty Collins, unable to bear the loss of Lily's youth and innocence from his life, committed suicide soon after her marriage. Shortly after Lily's marriage in the spring of 1923, Sheilah—a supremely physical and sensuous young woman—discovered that the major was impotent. Quickly, other misfortunes followed. Soon Johnny had no money.

Always filled with entrepreneurial spirit if not ability, Johnny borrowed funds and pushed his pretty young wife onto the London stage. Lily enrolled at the Royal Academy of Dramatic Arts, where she performed Shakespeare with a Cockney accent—to everyone's amusement. Gradually, however, her Cockney manners and speech nearly disappeared. Johnny then decided on musical comedy: Lily enrolled in private singing and dancing lessons. By now she had the classic lines of beautiful women; her legs seemed longer, her skin more perfectly smooth, her eyes more green and catlike than ever. She also had developed a more sophisticated way of moving. Johnny realized that "Lily Shiel" no longer suited her, and he renamed her "Sheilah Graham"—an astute marketing move, at last.

Johnny arranged an audition before impresario Charles B. Cochran, who immediately hired Lily to be a chorus girl in the revue *One Damn Thing after Another*. Sheilah became a "Cochran Young Lady"—famous in England for their sex appeal and beauty. Looking very much the part, Sheilah was voted "The Most Beautiful Chorus Girl in London." Many attractive bachelors and married men were in hot pursuit. Her "Stage Door Johnny" encouraged her to date the wealthy ones, requiring Sheilah to pretend that she was single, which was easier than convincing them that she could sing and dance. Meantime, Johnny became "Uncle Johnny." Thereafter came a pattern of slipping into the paternal bed of her "uncle" at one to three in the morning after romancing a sir, lord, or other handsome rich man around London.

As one example, Sheilah had been on a yacht off the south of France alone with, literally, a *Member* of Parliament. His personage suddenly pulled off his bathing suit and begged for her to whip him. When she refused, he masturbated in front of her. Beyond this possible exception, Sheilah was happy at last to have the sex but sensed that she was in a bad marriage. At heart, she, like Fitzgerald, was a romantic.

As a theatrical dancer, Sheilah was—to put it politely—clumsy. Worse, she knew she was a fraud. Still, Cochran thought her so pretty that he gave her a lead part in Noel Coward's *This Year of Grace*. Ultimately Sheilah fell or stumbled, from *Grace*. Between the stress onstage and her quadruple life off, Sheilah had a nervous breakdown. Sir Richard North, an aging millionaire who wanted to adopt Sheilah so that his incestuous fantasies would be more realistic, paid for her expensive nursing home stay and then funded a vacation for both she and Johnny in the south of France. Johnny had a wonderful time while Sheilah remained quite unsettled.

Not long after the nervous breakdown, Sheilah began to write. Her first article was a natural—"'The Stage-Door Johnny,' by a Chorus Girl." She sold it to the *Daily Express*. After a few successes, Sheilah began to move among old families of country wealth, which meant that she had to invent parents and a life growing up in Chelsea, a bohemian part of London. Along the way she met movie star Charlie Chaplin, whose stories of the Hollywood film colony intrigued her. Sheilah began to think of Hollywood as her place in the sun.

In England she could be herself only while playing squash at a club with society friends in Grosvenor Square. There, in the winter of 1932, Sheilah met an attractive young man she knew as the Marquess of Donegal; captain of the men's International Sportsman's Club's squash team. He also was the Earl of Donegal, the Earl of Belfast, Viscount Chichester of Ireland, Baron Fisherwick of Fisherwick, and Hereditary Lord High Admiral of Lough Neagh, among other titled names. He was among those in England who had more names than Sheilah! He was part of the multititled leisured rich. An aspiring courtesan could scarcely do better, and Sheilah decided that the attractive young lord would fall in love with her.

A few months later, Lord Donegal gazed into Sheilah's eyes and said, "I'm in love with you, Sheilah. I want to marry you."[1] She really was not in love with him; besides, she had the small matter of an inadequate husband to deal with.

Sheilah envisioned America as a bigger stage on which to play. Like other probable immigrants, she was enticed by her version of the American Dream. In her first visit in 1931 she explored the idea of writing a syndicated article, something that did not exist in England. In June 1933, at the age of a very young-looking twenty-nine, she sailed into New York Harbor to promote her new mystery novel. John Wheeler got her a job as a reporter on the *New York*

Mirror. Sheilah succeeded in New York with daring and brazenness, climbing through bedroom windows to get exclusive photographs, interviewing murderers, and going up in an open two-seat airplane to report on Lindbergh's return from Europe. Using wild exaggeration, Sheilah wrote in one column that in summertime New York *every* husband had an affair while his wife was out of town in the country. She believed that she did not have the talent to be a real writer and *had* to rely on sensationalism, bluffing, and showing a lot of her lovely legs to succeed.

With such self-doubts, her decision to write in California seemed unavoidable since it was thought in London that even tycoons like Samuel Goldwyn and Louis B. Mayer could barely speak English. Generally, they were right; in Hollywood, no one at the top would notice her lack of erudition. And so she left New York and arrived in Hollywood on Christmas Day 1935 in the midst of the Great Depression of the global economy and that of F. Scott Fitzgerald. She moved into a small apartment on a side street off legendary Sunset Boulevard.

Sheilah continued to stay in contact with Johnny *and* with Lord Donegal. In New York she fell in and out of love several times. She had an affair with her boss, King Vidor, the movie director, in 1936. Then, early in 1937 in Hollywood, Jock Whitney had asked Sheilah to be his mistress. Jock, as it were, made the mistake of using the term *mistress*. Her romantic side said that she wanted something more conventional—a divorce from Johnny and marriage to Lord Donegal and his many titles. She would be Her Grace, the Marchioness of Donegal; that would open a lot of doors in Hollywood. Soon she had her engagement ring. Her children would be of noble birth, quite a few steps above orphans. That was her plan.

That *was* her plan; but suddenly, Sheilah met another great romantic. When Donegal had visited her in Hollywood, Sheilah introduced him to her friends, including the redoubtable writer and comic Robert Benchley. Donegal was especially impressed with Benchley, "the most civilized American I have ever met."[2] Benchley considered the remark condescending, but nonetheless sufficient excuse to stage a party, for which he seldom needed a pretense.

Benchley (1889–1945) once said, "A great many people have come up to me and asked how I managed to get so much done and still look so dissipated." He decided to have a party with Sheilah's friends the day his lordship was to return to Hollywood and to Sheilah. It was Bastille Day—July 14, 1937—giving Benchley not one but two excuses to celebrate.

✧ ✧ ✧

A few weeks before, Sheilah had rented a house at 1430 North Kings Road in Hollywood Hills, high above Sunset Boulevard. It was on a precariously steep hill and dangerous road. Gradually, the party gravitated safely down the hill toward Benchley's bungalow below at the Garden of Allah. From there Benchley commandeered a new group of guests, including Dorothy Parker and her husband. Comic actor Frank Morgan, among others, was there.

Then, Sheilah saw *him*. The man was looking at her: He was very pale and alone in an armchair beneath the glow of a lamp. He had a Coca-Cola in one hand and a cigarette in the other. Later, she would say that he "appeared to be all shades of the palest, most delicate blue: his hair was pale, his face was pale, like a Marie Laurencin pastel, his suit was blue, his eyes, his lips were blue, behind the veil of blue smoke he seemed an apparition that might vanish at any moment."[3] Sadness seemed to envelop him, but the sadness and suffering in his face lent him an air of quiet dignity. Besides her, he was the only person at the party who was not drinking alcohol. Then, he *did* vanish. When Sheilah asked Benchley who *that* man was, he told her that he was F. Scott Fitzgerald—the writer. She, like many others in Hollywood, had thought that Fitzgerald had died a long time ago.

It was left-wing politics, never far from Fitzgerald, that brought Scott and Sheilah together the second time. Scott had always been on the lists of the left. Back on March 21, 1935, the secretary of an organization committee for the American Writers Congress had written to Scott, inviting him to a public meeting at Mecca Temple and at the New School for Social Research in New York City.[4] The

Congress was to be devoted to "the struggle against war, the preservation of civil liberties, and the destruction of fascist tendencies everywhere." There was a reference to "literary applications of Marxist philosophy" on the League of American Writers program, including defense "of the Soviet Union against capitalist aggression." Among those who had signed "the call to the Congress" were some of Scott's friends such as John Dos Passos, Thomas Boyd, and Nathanael West. The list also contained others whom Scott admired such as Theodore Dreiser, Malcolm Cowley, and Matthew Josephson.[5] This, of course, was not a good time to invite Fitzgerald to anything. We have no evidence that Scott even replied to the letter; it is doubtful that he would have been interested since Fitzgerald simply did not join associations. Besides, he would have judged the aims of the Congress as being quite naive.

It was with some reluctance, then, that Scott returned to left-wing politics. Scott reflects in "Pasting It Together" (1936), the second in the series of "Crack-Up" articles in *Esquire*, "that my political conscience had scarcely existed for ten years save as an element of irony in my stuff. When I became again concerned with the system I should function under, it was a man much younger than myself who brought it to me, with a mixture of passion and fresh air."[6] During his imperial reign in the twenties, Scott had distanced himself from leftist causes and, as the thirties progressed, remained scornful of what he called "shoddy" proletariat literature that, at its worst, bordered on propaganda. It was the attitude expressed by Scott in 1927 to his friend John Dos Passos.

Dos Passos was being kidded by his fashionable New York acquaintances for his "radical frenzies" and recalled that

> Scott Fitzgerald, with whom I had a long session during some short visit of his to New York at about this time, was particularly funny about it, kidding and serious too. He was on firm ground when he begged me to keep novel writing and propaganda separate. Even a touch of propaganda would ruin my work if it hadn't ruined it already. I can still remember the scornful look on his pale face...."[7]

Later, in 1935, in a conversation with Tony Buttitta in Asheville, Scott provided the following assessment:

> Even if I weren't used up, I don't have to tell you that the trend has changed. This rash of bogus novels about peasants, Holy Roller preachers, mill hands, union organizers, strikes—that's the thing. It's due to the Depression. We have lost confidence in our senseless *laissez-faire* economic system. Though I've read Marx, Engels, and company, the workers' world is outside my experience. I was stuck with my own crashes and tried to salvage what I could for my writing. But those bonehead critics have jumped on the proletarian bandwagon. They pile praise on the barnyard boys and dismissed my last two books as trivial and passé.[8]

Dorothy (Dottie) Parker contrariwise never met a left-wing cause that she didn't like and had little patience with anyone who didn't understand that extreme left was the only direction up. She and her husband Alan Campbell were earning more than five thousand dollars a week writing screenplays for Samuel Goldwyn. The screenwriters, mostly of the left and rabidly pro-union, were attempting to organize a labor union, the Screenwriters Guild. The producers were right-wing and believed that they might as well move to Russia if the screenwriters became unionized. Even the cerebral Irving Thalberg at MGM, who believed that *laborers* should be allowed to unionize, opposed the unionization of "artists." He attacked the leaders of the Screenwriters Guild as "sons of bitches, bastards, and Goddamn reds."[9] Otherwise, Thalberg liked writers. Dottie, applying equally abusive words to producers, was elected to the board of the struggling guild and held many recruitment meetings at her elegant home in Beverly Hills. Naturally, when her old leftist friend Scott came back to Hollywood, he became a target for her campaign.

Dottie had invited Scott to a private screening of Hemingway's film *The Spanish Earth* at actor Fredric March's house. Ernest had come to Hollywood to raise money for the Spanish Republic in still another war that Hemingway would see but Scott would not.

Fitzgerald went to the screening but afterward agreed only to give Lillian Hellman a ride to Dorothy Parker's, where Hemingway and others were to appear. Despite Fitzgerald's driving ten or twelve miles an hour down Sunset Boulevard, they eventually reached Dottie's home. Miss Hellman tried to persuade Scott to go in. "No," said Scott, "I'm riding low now. I'm scared of Ernest, I guess, scared of being sober when—" and his voice trailed off.[10]

Then Parker invited Scott to a dinner dance, a benefit for the Screenwriters Guild, on July 22 at the Ambassador Hotel. Dottie had taken an entire table where Scott, adorned in his tuxedo, black coat, and white tie, sat as her guest. Despite their two-night stand in New York three years earlier, Scott disliked Dottie's cynicism, her laziness, and her shrill conversion to communism that he considered a mere facade to veil her own lack of care for anyone except herself. Yet it was Scott's own brand of socialism that brought him to this event. Oddly, Fitzgerald had attained an undeserved reputation during the 1930s as a bourgeois reactionary, a perception that not only baffled him but hurt his literary reputation. Apparently, being a Socialist since the age of twenty was inadequate for these revolutionary times in Hollywood.

But Scott *was* there. While he was sympathetic to workers' struggles in the steel mills of the East, he found it difficult to be passionate about the "labor struggles" of workers who resided in mansions in Beverly Hills. Fitzgerald was simply amused when he saw Dorothy Parker dressed in a ruffled peasant blouse, flat-heeled shoes, a baggy skirt, and a babushka tied about her head as if she were a Soviet farmworker (a "peasant" earning five thousand dollars a week). Though he seldom laughed, Scott smiled deeply when amused. It was a mischievous, all-knowing smile that set his cold green eyes twinkling. When he played little jokes on people or when he was listening to Dottie, he would look downright impish and young.

Suddenly the table was empty except for him. As he looked about the room, he saw—at the table next to him—the English girl he had met at Benchley's bungalow. She also was alone. Across the smoky divide, "the white table," he wrote, "lengthened and became an altar where the priestess sat alone. Vitality welled up in him...."[11]

"I like you," he said.

Sheilah smiled. "I like *you*," she replied.[12] She then asked him to dance. Lovely as she was, Scott thought that she was *too* bold, her curves too dangerous—too forward for a woman. Scott begged off, saying that he had promised the next dance to, of all people, Dottie Parker. Still, two days later, Scott asked Eddie Mayer, a fellow screenwriter, if he knew a girl that he might like—"Nothing serious, of course." Eddie immediately thought of Sheilah, who was "engaged to an earl, he's in London," and presumed that she didn't want anything serious, either.

"Blond hair, green eyes, a complexion like smooth notepaper, a marvelous mouth, a great smile, and a great flirt."[13] Scott was describing Sheilah. Eddie agreed—it *was* Sheilah Graham. A phone call from Eddie to Sheilah delivered her and a friend to Eddie's bungalow and Scott and she were formally introduced. Then, they drove to the Clover Club nearby on Sunset Boulevard for dinner and dancing. At the bar they ran into Humphrey Bogart and his wife at the time, Mayo Methot.[14] Sheilah noted that Bogart seemed to have great respect for Scott. When Bogart asked Scott to have a drink with them, Scott smiled and shook his head, saying that he was not drinking these days. Bogart, a quite heavy drinker himself *and* a great actor, nonetheless could not hide his surprise. Scott, Sheilah, Eddie, and Sheilah's other friend continued upstairs to be near the band.

Soon Scott and Sheilah were dancing cheek to cheek. Three little words of exchange reveal all.

"I *love* dancing!" she cried.

"*I* do, too."[15]

On the dance floor Scott was at his most playful. He began to experiment with amazing tango steps, the "silliest tango" Sheilah had ever seen. Laughing, Sheilah tried to follow his steps. To her, Scott seemed young and wild. But when Scott asked *her* age, Sheilah subtracted five years.

"Twenty-seven," she lied.[16]

Still, with women—alongside his handsome, elegant appearance—Fitzgerald's greatest asset was his skillful use of words to charm. To Sheilah, as to other women, Scott spoke the language of love and romance. Still, she continued to be sufficiently aggressive that the relatively prudish Midwesterner considered her to be a "tart," despite his attraction. Moreover, love and romance were threatened by Scottie's decision to come west to visit her father under the watchful eyes of actress Helen Hayes and her husband, Charles MacArthur, the playwright. Among many old connections, Hayes and MacArthur were part of the Algonquin Round Table and Fitzgerald knew them well. Around that table and time (1922), Charles had a brief affair with Dorothy Parker, a pregnancy and an abortion

Sheilah about the time of meeting Scott. This was one of three publicity stills taken on the same day to promote her syndicated column, "Hollywood Today."

being the sequel. Dottie said it served her right for having "put all her eggs in one bastard."[17] At a dinner with Sheilah, Scottie, and two of Scottie's male friends, Scott was so nervous about Scottie's doing *the right things* that Sheilah thought him to be an irritable, prissy, middle-aged man—not the young, amusing tango dancer of an earlier night. Scott lit one cigarette after another and drummed his large fingers on the table. Sheilah sided with Scottie.

Once Scott and Sheilah had arrived at Sheilah's doorstep, alone again, that old blue magic returned.

"You look like a blue rose," he said softly, as their faces came closer.

"Please don't go, come in," she said.

Pulling Scott close to her, they kissed. Sheilah took his hand

and led him through her front door and upstairs to her bedroom. Their hot sexual relationship began.[18]

But it was more than that, much more. Not only did Scott make Sheilah laugh, she liked the way he listened to her every word. She felt *important*. Scott played Ping-Pong with the same imagination that he danced. He would cross his eyes, look one way and hit the ball the other way, then perform an absurd pirouette between shots. Other times he would shadowbox about the living room, imitating tough guy James Cagney—voice and all—challenging Sheilah to a "fight." To Sheilah, Scott was not only charming but had an astonishing breadth of knowledge. Even in conversation, he spoke in a theatrical manner, lowering and raising his voice in a dramatic way, throwing his arms about.

The stories Scott told were as imaginative and passionate as his written words. To those who knew him well, including Sheilah, he had the gift of intimacy. Most everyone, Hemingway possibly excepted, loved him because Scott would not have it any other way. More important perhaps, women and the prospect of romance seemed always to revitalize Fitzgerald.

Early in their relationship Scott and Sheilah went to dinner with friends such as Dorothy Parker, the Ira Gershwins, the Ogden Nashes, or the Nathanael Wests. More often than not, they went to Romanoff's on Rodeo Drive, a place in which Robert Benchley, John O'Hara, Dorothy Parker, and Jock Whitney were partners with Prince Mike Romanoff. Romanoff—really Harry Geguzunoff from little Lithuania—was inspired to pretend to be a member of the Russian imperial family while working as a tailor in New York. The screenwriters and actors knew that "Prince Romanoff" was a fraud, but they made his restaurant *the* place to go, perhaps because they considered *him* to be one of them. They did not know that Sheilah Graham too had invented herself. When Scott and Sheilah wanted to dine alone, they often went to the Brown Derby in Beverly Hills (which actually did have a very large brown derby atop its roof). In *The Last Tycoon,* Scott called the Derby "a languid restaurant patronized for its food by clients who always look as if they'd like to lie down."[19]

✧ ✧ ✧

Scott had always been very inquisitive; it was the instinct of a novelist to gather material wherever he could find it. Besides, he was truly interested in people. Economists examine the insides of data banks; novelists look at the innards of persons to find out how they tick. Scott did it so often and with such relentlessness that his targets often got "ticked off," a reaction often leading to lengthy apologies from Fitzgerald. It is easy, therefore, to imagine how threatened Sheilah was becoming from similar interrogations. Worse, she feared that Scott would unmask her as a fraud.

Even into the fall, Sheilah continued to accept occasional dates from other men such as the writer (and heavy drinker) John O'Hara, Eddie Mayer, and Arthur Kober, a writer once married to Lillian Hellman and now working on Marx Brothers movies. Though she was determined to make light of her love affair with Fitzgerald, she found other men dull and joyless in comparison. And, although Scott was not pleased with Sheilah's seeing other men, he, as with Ginevra and Zelda, found her more attractive when other men did as well. It reassured him about his judgment. Still, Scott had his doubts about *this* romance. He told Sheilah that he could never abandon his "poor lost Zelda," though Scott, as noted, had contemplated divorce several times.

At first blush it seems that Fitzgerald was using the same kind of falsehood that he had written for Tom Buchanan, who could not divorce Daisy in *The Great Gatsby*. Scott was not above using such theatrics, especially during times of uncertainty. More likely, Fitzgerald was not sure whether he could handle what he saw as his responsibilities to Zelda and Scottie, write screenplays, and maintain a new relationship. Although Zelda was still in Highland Hospital in Asheville, Scott felt a responsibility to her (as well as to Scottie) to visit her and take his small family on short vacations. Still, Sheilah currently was the "top girl," but neither she nor Scott was certain whether their summer romance would survive the cold truth of winter. Storm clouds already were forming in the distance.

The first clouds moved in near the end of the summer of 1937 in Malibu, of all unlikely places. Scott had driven Sheilah to lunch at a favorite small restaurant there. He began his usual round of questions about the woman's past—men, sex, relatives, and so on. He knew that she had been one of Cochran's Young Ladies and could guess that they had quite active love lives. Sheilah became increasingly defensive because of her fears that Scott would learn about her past. Scott, "a man of dignity and integrity," then would reject little Lily Shiel. Finally, on the way back along Sunset Boulevard, almost to Beverly Hills, she could not contain her sense of guilt and began to sob hysterically.

Sheilah began to tell Scott everything—well, almost everything—even as an astonished Scott protested that she need not tell him anything she didn't want to. She was a fraud and virtually everything Scott "knew" about her was false. Even her family photographs were fakes. "I'm sorry," he said repeatedly, "I'm always so curious about everything. Don't cry."[20]

A part of Sheilah's story included many lovers. Scott, the great romantic, was tormented by the images of those other men, images made clearer than Sheilah could remember by Fitzgerald's jealousy. Soon thereafter, at the end of summer 1937, he attempted to exorcise those images with a "love poem," entitled "For Sheilah: A Beloved Infidel." Among the lines are

I found the oldest, richest wine
On lips made soft by other men.

Touched, flattered—from that moment on, Sheilah thought of herself as Scott's beloved infidel, a term that transformed her past pagan amorality into glamorous virtue. She broke her engagement with Donegal. Shortly thereafter, Sheilah was soaking in a tub at Scott's bungalow when Scott came into the room and put a small pillow under her head for comfort, kindly smiling as his eyes met hers, yet strayed from the lovely, large breasts that had always been an embarrassment to her but gravitated to by men—an optical diversion no other man had ever achieved. This sensitive act won her heart as long as Scott lived.

Endnotes

1. Sheilah Graham (and Gerold Frank), *Beloved Infidel* (New York: Quality Paperback Book Club, 1958), p. 143.

2. Quoted in Robert Westbrook, *Intimate Lies: F. Scott Fitzgerald and Sheilah Graham* (New York: HarperCollins, 1995), p. 89. The book is written by Sheilah's son and corrects some mistakes, ambiguities, and exclusions of his mother's *Beloved Infidel*.

3. Ibid., p. 174.

4. Letter from Orrick Johns, Secretary, Organization Committee, American Writers Congress, to F. Scott Fitzgerald, March 21, 1935, Fitzgerald Papers, Princeton University Library.

5. Call for an American writers' congress, Fitzgerald Papers, Princeton University Library.

6. F. Scott Fitzgerald, "Pasting It Together" (March 1936), in Edmund Wilson, ed., *The Crack-Up* (New York: New Directions, 1956 [1945]), p. 79.

7. John Dos Passos, *The Best Times: An Informal Memoir* (New York: New American Library, 1966), p. 172.

8. Anthony Buttitta, *After the Good Gay Times* (New York: Viking Press, 1974), p. 31.

9. Fitzgerald Papers, Princeton University Library. The quote is from a Screen Writers Guild, Inc. memo dated August 26, 1939, and mailed to all its members. A copy was found in Fitzgerald's papers at the time of his death. He probably kept it as part of his research for *The Last Tycoon*.

10. Quoted by Lillian Hellman in her *An Unfinished Woman* (Boston: Little, Brown, 1969), p. 68.

11. F. Scott Fitzgerald, *The Love of The Last Tycoon* (New York: Simon & Schuster, 1993 [1941]), p. 73. Kathleen, Monroe Stahr's love interest, is based on Sheilah Graham. Some words and phrases exchanged between Scott and Sheilah are used verbatim in draft of the novel.

12. Sheilah Graham, *Garden of Allah* (New York: Crown Publishers, 1970), p. 98.

13. The quotes are from Sheilah Graham, *A State of Heat* (New York: Grosset & Dunlap, 1972), p. 140.

14. At least, in Sheilah's *Beloved Infidel* account (p. 177), Bogart is with Methot. Sheilah's son has Bogart with Mary Phillips in his *Intimate Lies* (p. 106). We took Sheilah's word as the correct account.

15. Graham, *Beloved Infidel,* p. 178.

16. Ibid.

17. Marion Meade, *Dorothy Parker: What Fresh Hell Is This?* (New York: Penguin Books, 1989), p. 105.

18. The reference to the "blue rose" appears only in a draft of *Beloved Infidel,* Princeton University Library. Sheilah's reply appears intact in *Beloved Infidel,* p. 182. In Scott's fictional version of the event, Kathleen and Stahr nearly enter Kathleen's home, but she impulsively decides that they should go to his house, where their affair begins (*The Last Tycoon,* pp. 86–87). This provides a good example of how Fitzgerald often put real-world happenings into not only different words but also different contexts to serve motivations within his fiction.

19. Fitzgerald, *The Last Tycoon*, p. 102.

20. Graham, *Beloved Infidel*, p. 193.

Sixteen

Writing Screenplays for the MGM Stars

THOUGH HE KNEW THAT HE AND ZELDA HAD LOST WHATEVER THEY HAD, Scott did not go to Hollywood to fall in love, but to work, to pay the bills, and to restore his reputation. His first project at MGM was to polish the dialogue on *A Yank at Oxford,* a film starring handsome Robert Taylor as an American Rhodes scholar and the beautiful Maureen O'Sullivan as his British lover. Different writers lined up, worked on the script, sometimes at the same time and often unknown to the others. It was Irving Thalberg's adaptation of Henry Ford's assembly line system. Scott, of course, found this to be very awkward and did not last long on this script—two or three weeks. A few of his lines survived the screening, but he did not receive the coveted screen credit. Later, in *The Last Tycoon,* Scott would detail Thalberg's screenplay writing system as Monroe Stahr's.

The highlight of working on *A Yank at Oxford* for Scott was lunch with Maureen O'Sullivan. Fitzgerald seldom failed to fall in love with actresses, Joan Crawford being a notable, even celebrated, exception. Ms. O'Sullivan had her own agenda: She wanted Scott to expand her role—"to liven it up, to make it more interesting, to come up with an angle." Scott, as ever, greatly enjoyed being in the same room, alone, with one of the most beautiful women in the world. He was further warmed by the mint juleps that O'Sullivan had prepared in advance. He was a changed man. "He seemed flamboyant," recalls O'Sullivan. "He seemed vital. He was great fun. He strode about the room with his arms waving in the air. It was a wonderful afternoon."[1] Hardly the afternoon of a vanquished author.

Doubtless inspired by Ms. O'Sullivan, if not the mint juleps, Scott began to rewrite the script as a cultural battle between an American (Robert Taylor) and an Englishwoman (Maureen O'Sullivan). He totally rewrote the first scene to a send-off of Taylor at the train depot, as if he were going off to war—a cultural war—as it would turn out in the comedy. Since Ms. O'Sullivan was bored just thinking about her first-scripted role, Fitzgerald decided to broaden the plot from just another boy-girl romance to an America-England affair, so he continued to rewrite.

The most original of his rewrites has Molly (O'Sullivan) and Lee (Taylor) motoring through the English countryside in a rattletrap Ford (similar to Scott's). At some point Lee stops and uses a bar of soap to decorate the car in what he says is American college fashion, scrawling slogans, such as "LEAP-IN—LIMP OUT; HELLO, CHICKEN, HERE'S YOUR COOP; FAIR CONDITIONED—110° HERE."

Molly decides that she too wants to play this game. "Oh, I've got a good one. Why is our car like a baby? Because it has a rattle." Scott (via Molly) was describing his own car. Scott understood that in the movies the camera does the "seeing," not a reader. Yet, he was ingeniously using *words,* in this instance to be *viewed by the camera.*

Well, as to the Yank and the Englishwoman, they really do not speak the same language. But what separates them even more is culture. Neither understands the other. As the old Ford rattles back into Oxford with its graffiti, Lee tells Molly, "It's good to see yourself as others see you." But he doesn't see the citizens of Oxford laughing as the Ford rolls past. As Aaron Latham correctly notes, Fitzgerald had learned that the camera could do more than simply frame a story; it could shape it. The camera became a perfect tool for picturing irony. Whereas Fitzgerald seemingly put the audience over the shoulders of the actors in his written stories, in his screenplay the audience could see what Molly and Lee could not—that they were the town's joke.[2] When Molly finally does see the fun, she jumps out of the car, embarrassed, but Lee, the American, never catches on. Anyway, someone, perhaps Mayer himself, did not like Fitzgerald's treatment, and it was cut from the script.

At first, Scott was philosophical. "Suffice to summarize," Fitzgerald wrote Mrs. Harold Ober, "I have seen Hollywood—talked with [Robert] Taylor, dined with [Fredric] March, danced with Ginger Rogers (this will burn Scottie up but it's true), been in Rosalind Russell's dressing room, wisecracked with [Robert] Montgomery, drunk (ginger ale) with Zukor and Lasky, lunched alone with Maureen O'Sullivan, watched [Joan] Crawford act, and lost my heart to a beautiful half-caste Chinese girl whose name I've forgotten."[3] Fitzgerald remained a talented ballroom dancer to the end.

✧   ✧   ✧

The critics did not like *A Yank in Oxford*. Judging from their catty comments, we could conclude that the film would have fared better if the studio had kept Scott's rewritten scenes.

Scott's prospects soon improved. He was assigned to write the movie adaptation of Erich Maria Remarque's novel of post–World War I Germany, *Three Comrades*. The novel was very left-wing for Hollywood because of its antifascist sentiments. This time Scott began working alone on the film, but under the supervision of Joseph Mankiewicz, a producer-writer. The "comrades" were three friends, all former members of the German air force, who start an auto repair shop after the Great War—attempting to survive a deepening economic depression in the shadows of rising Nazism. Robert Taylor again was to star along with Franchot Tone and Robert Young as the other comrades, and Margaret Sullavan as Taylor's love interest. Sullavan portrayed a woman slowly dying of tuberculosis, an immensely popular cause of death at the time—so popular that Fitzgerald thought for sure that he too would die from it.

For Scott this was a great opportunity. For inexplicable reasons he was viewed as the protector of the rich even though he was an avowed Socialist; not only would he be writing a love story, his forte, but he also could reestablish his persona as "far left." Moreover, he fully understood how the economic conditions in Germany were contributing to the rise of fascism. Scott could kill two birds with *Three Comrades*. Among his innovations was the division of the story into three "acts," a device still used today by Hollywood screenwriters.

Two-thirds through the script by September 4, however, Zelda once again intervened. Scott was scheduled to take one week off to visit her in Asheville, North Carolina. She was not any better. Zelda's latest obsession was religion and her claim to be in direct communion with Christ. God knows, Scott was careful not to mention Sheilah. Zelda's jealousy—almost always barely under the surface—could easily unbalance her delicate mental state. By the time Scott had returned to Hollywood, Mankiewicz had a cowriter for Scott, Ted E. Paramore, whom even Mankiewicz considered a hack. Ironically, Scott had known but not admired Paramore years before in New York, depicting him as "Fred E. Paramore" in *The Beautiful and Damned:* The satirical take had sufficient bite to end their fragile friendship. Scott was doomed to collaborate on *Three Comrades* with the enemy.

In the midst of this professional frustration, Scott had other mishaps. In an attempt to cheer him up, Sheilah told Scott that she wanted to read *all* of his books. After a search among the bookstores along Hollywood Boulevard, they could find *none* in stock. One bookseller was shocked that he was talking with Mr. Fitzgerald himself because he, like so many, had presumed the author dead. Sheilah's attempt to lift Scott's spirits had backfired.

Still, Scott found time and energy to help Sheilah with her career. She was preparing to do a five-minute radio spot and broadcast the latest Hollywood gossip. The show was to originate live from Chicago, with her spot spliced in from a studio in Los Angeles. She was terrified at the prospect, however, and wrote and rewrote her five-minute script. Scott looked at it and began to rewrite it, using his usual stubby pencil and his stubby right hand. When he finished, the script was transformed into beautifully flowing words. On the air, however, Sheilah was so nervous that she struggled for air and was swallowing every few words. Worse, her British accent returned with a vengeance so that she sounded like a "parody of some absurd colonel's daughter in an India regiment."[4] Scott was kind about her performance, but her sponsors in Chicago were honest and insisted on hiring a professional actress to read the script in her place. Scott, taking on his imperialist persona, said "Absolutely not!"[5] *Scott* decided that he and Sheilah would fly to Chicago to make her case. In the interim a classic Fitzgerald event was about to unfold.

✧   ✧   ✧

Just before Scott and Sheilah's trip, Scott would see Ginevra, his first Golden Girl, one last time. Buddy, Ginevra's mentally retarded son, had been placed in a special school in Santa Barbara, not far from Hollywood. Josephine Ordway, a mutual friend in St. Paul, had told Scott of Ginevra's plan to visit her son. It is *Scott,* contrary to earlier biographical accounts, who first contacts Ginevra and suggests getting together. Ginevra's first marriage is nearing an end; whether either Scott or Ginevra knew of the marital situation of the other is not known for sure, but we suspect that Josephine Ordway would have been a reliable source for both parties. Ginevra agrees to meet Scott; both are very nervous about the reunion. On October 6 Ginevra wires Scott an invitation to a dinner party at a friend's house on Saturday, October 9. Scott demurs; he has been avoiding parties. Instead, she travels down the coast to Hollywood to see him on the eleventh. They have lunch at the Beverly Wilshire Hotel, where she is staying.[6]

This reunion reminds us of the great importance of Ginevra to Scott. Not only was she Scott's first Golden Girl, she had been the good or better *parts* of Isabelle in *This Side of Paradise,* Judy Jones of "Winter Dreams," and Daisy Buchanan of *The Great Gatsby,* as well as most of the best—Josephine in the Basil and Josephine short stories. Two days after Ginevra's invitation, Scott writes to Scottie: "She was the first girl I ever loved and I have faithfully avoided seeing her up to this moment to keep that illusion perfect, because she ended up by throwing me over with the most supreme boredom and indifference." He concluded, "I don't know whether I should go or not…. These great beauties are often something else at thirty-eight, but Ginevra had a great deal besides beauty."[7] Indeed, she did.

Scott was in an emotional turmoil. Anyone, however, who understands Fitzgerald, knows precisely what he would do. He, of course, "rushed" as fast as he would allow his rickety, old Ford coupe to trundle to the side of Ginevra. Like Jay Gatsby's longing for Daisy, this was a woman whom Scott still yearned for but never could fully possess. Again, life was imitating art, imitating life. In the frenzy of the moment Sheilah was no competition for the grand romantic imagination of Scott's youth. Though he was in his own afternoon, or perhaps evening, as a man, Scott decided to be young for at least one more afternoon. So, on October 11, Scott arrived at the Beverly Wilshire for lunch.

Ginevra, as the wife of the singularly rich William H. Mitchell III, and wealthy in her own right had done what rich girls did in her day—among other things, dividing her leisure time between such exotic places as Palm Beach and Santa Barbara. She also had the leisure time and resources to be intelligent and transcendently attractive at thirty-eight. Some years later Ginevra remembers her reunion with Scott as being a much better time than she had anticipated. At first, things went well; Scott had no alcohol at lunch, telling her that he had been on the wagon for several months. Afterward, however, after following Ginevra into the hotel bar to wait for a friend who was to meet her, Scott began ordering double shots of gin with Tom Collins. More than likely, too, Scott had braced himself with gin *before* lunch. Ginevra, who had chaired the Illinois division of the Women's Organization for National Prohibition Reform, settled for lemonade. Then, in a discussion of Scott's fiction, she asked him which characters he had based on her. "Which bitch do you think you are?" he asked.[8] Thus ended the reunion.

"I was heartsick," she later writes, "as he had been behaving himself for some months before that. For the next few days I was besieged with calls, but as he was in love with someone in Hollywood, I believe, he soon gave up the pursuit."[9] Ginevra never revealed her motivation for agreeing to meet Scott for lunch; perhaps, with her marriage ending, she wanted a second chance to renew a romance that had been so intense. But, she chose to reject him, as before, the reason again left untold; perhaps it was the same, the difficulties of leaving behind Chicago's society. Scott, who never let any good story go untold, wrote the last of his many stories about himself and Ginevra—this one based on their reunion. "Three Hours between Planes" appeared in *Esquire* after Scott's death. In the story a man calls his old flame while waiting for his next flight; for him, it turns out to be a mistake.

Those Tom Collins's meant that Scott was drinking again. It was a drinking binge that he had been long resisting: It continued as Scott and Sheilah prepared for their flight to Chicago. Once again, Fitzgerald had been undone by Ginevra. Though Sheilah at first thought he was drinking tumblers of water, Scott downed at least six double gins at the airport. He continued to drink on the plane and created quite a scene, emphatically telling the man across the aisle that *he,* F. Scott Fitzgerald, was the famous author of *The Great Gatsby.* Worse, Sheilah also heard Scott tell the man that *she* was "a great lay."[10] Sheilah had great respect for the distinguished version of Scott, but was mortified for her and for Scott disgracing himself in this manner.

Perhaps the worst moments came when they visited Sheilah's radio producer. At some point the producer was unclear as to whether he would allow Sheilah her own performance on the radio show. Scott took serious exception to this and proceeded to take an awkward swing at the producer, obliquely hitting him in the mouth with sufficient force to cause bleeding. Still, the blow struck on behalf of Sheilah may have worked its wonders. The producer agreed to let Sheilah perform on her own show. Then, after a misadventuresome trip with a drunken Scott back to Hollywood, he assured Sheilah that he had decided to go back on the wagon. With his instincts trumping his inclinations, Scott decided that he loved Sheilah very much. On December 7, MGM renewed Scott's six-month contract for an additional year, giving him a raise in the process from $1,000 to $1,250 a week.

✧   ✧   ✧

For the moment Scott was back on top of the world, *his* world. Scott began to talk about the serious novel he planned to write; it would be about Hollywood and its main characters would be based on Irving Thalberg and Louis B. Mayer. Scott knew that *the* novel of Hollywood had yet to be written. The novel would, of course, have Fitzgerald-like moral themes and contrasts—the good forces of art versus the dark forces of money, the good forces of quality against the dark forces of commercialism. Scott had been greatly impressed with Thalberg when he had first met him in 1927 during his oxymoric, semi-virginal trip to Hollywood. He imagined Thalberg exercising his great power over the industry with style and grace. Thalberg represented the *best* of Hollywood—integrity, intelligence, and great dreams. Louis B. Mayer represented the *worst*—sentimental money-grubbing, all that was sordid. Thalberg's character trumped his use of an assembly line of writers.

Thalberg's death September 14, 1936, marks remotely the inception of *The Last Tycoon*. As noted, Fitzgerald wrote Maxwell Perkins of his planned novel a month later. Although Scott considered Thalberg an enemy, he liked and respected him enormously. Fitzgerald had done enough to be a source of friction with the producer. As also noted, Thalberg may have wrongly suspected that his actress wife, Norma, had an affair with Fitzgerald. Then, there was that late-night alcoholic phone call plus a drunken Fitzgerald reciting "Dog" at the Thalbergs' party.

During Christmastime 1937, Sheilah was left alone as Scott flew back to Asheville to visit Zelda. Scott's absence was painful for Sheilah, whose love had deepened. But Scott could not totally abandon Zelda, or betray—as he put it—that "old bond of justice that existed between us." Frances Kroll Ring, Scott's young secretary for the final twenty months of his life, who saw him almost daily, later confirmed Fitzgerald's sincerity.

> And Zelda: despite their separate lives, her well-being and treatment were his trust. She might never be well again, but he would never abandon her. For himself, he lived modestly, needing only books and records—a far cry from the extravagance of his youth.[11]

Scott nonetheless was tormented by Zelda's irresponsible spending early in the marriage and his "necessary" spending now, on Zelda's medical bills. The wounds were deep and Scott had no further sexual interest in Zelda, an interest that had waned early in the marriage. This time, as so many times before, the tension of seeing Zelda ended with a three-day drunk. For once, Sheilah, Scottie, and Zelda were never to learn of *this* binge. And, inexplicably, the drunken disaster in Chicago had led to a deeper commitment between Scott and Sheilah. Her 1938 New Year's resolution was to no longer have dates with other men. The hopelessly romantic Scott had prevailed.

Sheilah and Scott began a secret world together. Fitzgerald often telephoned five or six times a day, not only to say hello but also to ask his insistent questions. He sent flowers with little notes such as "Missing you is a luxury like everything about knowing you, lovely, lovely, Sheilah." Not only was the attention hard to resist, Scott was always entertaining her with wild parodies of Fred Astaire dancing, or reciting T. S. Eliot's "The Boston Evening Transcript" while doing the "Shuffle Off To Buffalo." And, of course, Scott enjoyed Sheilah's laughter when he went into his shadowboxing routine. Sheilah was unaware that he had done all this before and entertained other women in the same way in other rooms in the past. Still, he certainly did not seem to be an old man whose time had come and gone. He left the same impression on Frances Kroll Ring. "He was," she writes, "to me a kind, gentle, and extraordinarily considerate man, as he was to his many friends."[12] The announcements of the death of F. Scott Fitzgerald—literary and otherwise—were premature.

Scott had continued to work on *Three Comrades* throughout the autumn of 1937 and the first months of 1938. Despite the awkward collaboration with the "disgusting" Ted Paramore, they somehow completed six drafts of the screenplay and submitted their final draft on February 1, 1938. After declaring it one of the best screenplays he had ever read, Joe Mankiewicz rewrote it himself so that it was barely recognizable to Fitzgerald and Paramore. Other writers expected to be rewritten by Mankiewicz, but not, of course, *F. Scott Fitzgerald*. He wrote an angry letter to Joe that Scott considered diplomatic.[13] Mankiewicz ignored Scott's lectures. Sheilah talked Scott out of sending another letter filled with outrageous insults.

Years later, in 1969 to be exact, Joe Mankiewicz told his side of the story in an interview. As he explained, he could not count on Scott *or* Hemingway, Steinbeck, *or* Sinclair Lewis for dialogue. "In a novel, the dialogue enters through the mind. The reader endows it with a certain quality. Dialogue spoken from the stage enters through the ear rather than the mind. It has an immediate emotional impact. Scott's dialogue lacked bite, color, rhythm."[14] Mankiewicz was not the only producer to make a sharp distinction between novels and movies, but he may have been one of the first to fully appreciate it and do the rewrite. After Ogden Nash had labored on a script for months, Mankiewicz rewrote it in twenty-four hours and denied Nash credit for the picture. Joe still used more of Scott's ideas than Scott, blinded by anger, could see. In Scott's view, the script now was so awful that Joan Crawford might as well play the Maggie part. Ironically, according to Aaron Latham, Mankiewicz "used more of what the author wrote than any other Hollywood producer before or since."[15]

Mankiewicz was the boss and he had his way, a way in some respects more imperial—as difficult as that is to believe—than Fitzgerald's. Joe's great stubborn streak earned Scott's respect in one important regard. MGM worried that *Three Comrades* might be perceived as too critical of Nazi Germany. The threat was not an idle one; Adolf Hitler had his own journalistic organ in Los Angeles, the *Weckruf und Beobachter*. Thus, in winter 1938, Louis B. Mayer invited a representative of the Nazi regime plus an official censor from the dreaded Hays Office, Joseph Breen, to watch the screening of the movie with Joe. The Nazi was quite upset, claiming that the movie was the vilest Communist propaganda because it painted his government as being "anti-Semitic," of all improbable claims.

Earlier, Scott had told Sheilah Graham how Hitler and his speeches infuriated him. He would jump up and walk restlessly around the room of their little beach house. "They're going to do it again," Scott would say. "They're going to have another war—and we'll be in it, too." Then, he would sit down, light a cigarette, and listen again to the ranting, hysterical voice, the thunderous "Sieg

Heil! Sieg Heil! Sieg Heil!" Then Scott would turn to Sheilah. "I'd like to fly over there and assassinate Hitler before he starts another war. I'd do it, too, by God!"[16] Scott again reminded Sheilah that he had wanted to fight in the last war, but the armistice came too soon.

Breen suggested that several scenes be refilmed so that it would appear that Germany's problems were due to the communists, *not* the Nazis. Louis B. Mayer, a Jew and an archenemy of the "communistic" Screenwriters Guild, happily agreed. Joe Mankiewicz (also Jewish), however, stubbornly refused. He instead threatened to resign from the studio if any Nazi were allowed to touch his film; furthermore, his resignation would be loudly public. This action took courage; even non-Jewish actors feared the wrath of the 10,000-strong band of pro-German Americans. Rather than lose a prize producer and be exposed to Joe's public denunciation, the thick, tank-shaped Mayer backed down. The day after Scott heard of Mankiewicz's courageous stand, he threw his arms around Joe in the MGM commissary and kissed him. It was Fitzgerald's excessive exuberance at one of its few apt moments.

Scott's reconciliation with Joe lasted only until he saw the movie premier in June 1938. He was especially anguished that even the ending to the movie had been changed. At Sheilah's home later in the evening, Scott punched the wall hard with his fist. "That s.o.b.," he cried. "My God, doesn't he know what he's done?" The next day, he went on another of his three-day binges. He required round-the-clock nurses while drying out. The pattern was now clear to Sheilah.

As to the disputed ending to the movie, Scott's intuition once again was exactly on target. In Fitzgerald's version, the movie's closing moments are in a cemetery where the surviving comrades (Bobby and Koster) have come to visit Pat (Margaret Sullavan). Koster (Franchot Tone) says, "There's fighting in the city." These are the only words spoken. There is the sound of a gun and they walk down the hill like the descent from Calvary. Scott thought it the perfect ending. They, including the dead Sullavan character, heroic and unconquerable, side by side go back into the fight. Scott wrote a last-ditch plea to Mr. Mannix and Mr. Katz, Mankiewicz's assistants: "To every reviewer or teacher in America, the idea of the comrades going back into the fight in the spirit of 'My Head is Bloody but unbowed' is infinitely stronger and more cheerful than that they should be quitting—all the fine talk, the death of their friends and countrymen in vain." And, at the end of the letter: *"The march of four people, living and dead, heroic and unconquerable, side by side back into the fight."*[17]

"Monkeybitch" thought that the ending could be improved. He had the surviving comrades running away *to South America*. Fitzgerald thought that this changed the story from tragedy to escapism. After World War II thousands of Nazis *would* flee Germany for South America, perhaps retracing the steps of the comrades. As it turns out, Scott correctly saw the story as a tragedy, and history would make it so, even as history vindicated his intuition that "escape" for the comrades would coarsen their fate in South America. Early on, Scott had seen through the facade of fascism as well as communism.

Still, *Three Comrades* was a Hollywood victory for Fitzgerald, even if his professionalism made it a personal defeat. By most accounts Fitzgerald's script was heavily rewritten because both the actress (Sullavan) and producer Mankiewicz found Scott's approach too literary with unspeakable dialogue.[18] Despite the unlikely collaboration of Scott, Paramore, and Monkeybitch, somehow *Three Comrades* made it to the screen and the credits read "Writers: F. Scott Fitzgerald, Edward (Ted) Paramore," Scott's first and only screen credit.

Fitzgerald summed his feelings about the experience in a letter to Beatrice Dance, March 4, 1938:

"Three Comrades," the picture I have just finished, is in production and though it bears my name, my producer could not resist the fascination of a pencil and managed to obviate most signs of my personality. Nonetheless, I am now considered a success in Hollywood because something which I did not write is going on under my name, and something which I did write has been quietly buried without any fuss or row—not even a squeak from me. The change from regarding this as a potential art to looking at it as a cynical business has begun. But I still think that some time during my stay out here I will be able to get something of my own on the screen that I can ask my friends to see. But if you go to see "Three Comrades," only credit me with the parts you like.[19]

Still, Scott had labored successfully to strengthen Margaret Sullavan's role. She won the New York Film Critics Award as "Best Actress" (1938), the British National Award, and was nominated "Best Actress" by the Academy Awards (1938). The film was among the top ten of the year, a year of great competition.[20] Scott's name appeared in the 1939 edition of FAME. Once again, however, those who counted accepted Scott's own judgment that he had failed, but that judgment, as ever, was against his own unattainable standards.

Fitzgerald's next project was a film that he really cared about even though it was to star Joan Crawford. It was to be called *Infidelity* and it read a lot like *The Great Gatsby* revisited. Scott began work on the script in February 1938. Seven years earlier Fitzgerald's script for *The Redheaded Woman* had not been used; rather, a very funny script by Anita Loos had replaced his. The Hays Office was not happy about that film. That the Redhead (Jean Harlow) slept around through most of the movie did not bother the censors. What bothered them was that she ended up as the *happy* mistress of a French nobleman (Charles Boyer, before stardom). She was not punished for her awful transgressions. As a direct result of this terrible offense, the Hays Office issued an explicit edict: "Adultery, sometimes necessary plot material, must not be explicitly treated, or justified, or presented attractively."[21] Moreover, Louis B. Mayer, who respected motherhood and the family on screen though spending a great deal of time admiring (at *his* eye level) Hedy Lamarr's breasts off-screen, was opposed to the project.[22] What could Scott do with a movie titled *Infidelity* to begin with? Scott was once again up against Joe Breen of the Hays Office.

Fitzgerald had studied Joan Crawford's movies and concluded that she must be serious from the first and must have direct, consuming purpose in mind at all points of the story—nothing ever ambiguous. It was an amazingly accurate description of Crawford's performances; it reminds us that Fitzgerald had done quite a few performances himself both on and off stage, though he was an amateur compared with Ms. Crawford. Scott wrote to Gerald Murphy, "Also, you can never give her such a stage direction as 'telling a lie,' because if you did, she would practically give a representation of Benedict Arnold selling West Point to the British."[23]

When Scott first met Ms. Crawford, he told her, "I'm going to write your next picture."

"Good," she said, doing her best imitation of Joan Crawford by drawing her face into the serious, driven expression Fitzgerald had admired in her films. "Write hard, Mr. Fitzgerald, write hard!"[24]

Gary Cooper, it was thought, would be man enough to costar in the movie.

Hunt Stromberg, the film's director, agreed to the rare privilege of allowing Fitzgerald to work at home some of the time. Scott began to write a screenplay with very little dialogue, creating an air of mystery. For example, in one scene Fitzgerald has two characters at a nightclub on the roof of the Waldorf observing couples at faraway tables through opera glasses. The scenes were to be photographed through a frame of opera glasses; then, the audience would see movement and the couples' lips moving, but not hear any dialogue. This was how the audience would "see" the story.

Scott used what he had felt during Zelda and Edouard Jozan's love affair as the emotion behind the infidelity. He reverses the roles, however, and it is the man, Nicolas, who strays and ends up cutting himself off from even those to whom he once belonged. Throughout, Fitzgerald emphasizes sight over sound, pictures over words. We will never know whether these techniques would have worked. With only about fifteen or twenty pages to be written, Joe Breen decided that the film would not be made. By now the only kind of movie that was acceptable was some version of Andy Hardy (Mickey Rooney) living next door to a little girl that could sing (Judy Garland). *Infidelity* was not long for this world. Joe Breen, not Mayer, was the most powerful person in Hollywood. Fitzgerald's script, a labor of love, was the censor's latest victim.

Scott had made a gallant but little-noted effort to save the film from the Breen Office. In his new treatment he has Myrna Loy in love with Clark Gable and Robert Taylor. But one has to lose her. (Fitzgerald always liked to pick the actors for his movies.) At the beginning Clark and Myrna are married but unhappy, living behind closed doors. Myrna, while in Europe visiting her mother, comes across Robert Taylor, the man she loved and almost married five years ago. He will always love her. Meanwhile, in America, Clark has run across his former secretary and drifts into an affair with her. Returning unexpectedly from Europe, Myrna finds them together. She is unable to forgive. Robert Taylor returns from Europe, and Myrna's encouragement of his attentions provokes a divorce. Myrna immediately marries Taylor. After five years of Myrna and Robert living happily, Gable comes back into Myrna's life. She now finds Clark more exciting than Robert and is physically attracted to Gable. Something interrupts this new situation and they are thrown back into their old worlds again. In a roundabout way Robert finds how close she has been to Clark for that week or two. Now, she is guilty of the same behavior for which she condemned Clark, five years before. She is trapped by an old love, bringing her to the point of *Infidelity*—so close that Robert thinks that she has been unfaithful.

Can she now forgive Clark? If so, it seems likely that Robert, being a sensitive man, would gracefully retire from the situation. Whichever way Myrna goes, staying with Robert or remarrying Clark, the script shows how, when faced with a situation parallel to the one that her husband faced, Myrna might have yielded, too. Years of tragedy are unnecessarily visited on all three.[25] Earlier, Scott had summed up the theme of the movie in Gable's "last statement." "There were other women in my life but you were the only one. That's what you couldn't understand…. Too late she understands that there may have been many women in a man's life."[26] This, and a deep bow to the censor. It was a brilliant if convoluted effort to save the film, but Joe Breen still would not buy it.

In late March 1938, Scott had arranged a reunion with his small family—Zelda and Scottie. They stayed at the Cavalier Hotel in Virginia Beach, a languid resort hotel greatly resembling a country club. Zelda looked awful: Her face was craggy and immobile, resembling a wooden Indian. She became increasingly irritated with her golf and tennis pros at the hotel. Zelda began correcting Scottie over minor matters until Scottie retorted sharply, filling Zelda with rage. Zelda stormed to Scott's side to accuse him of training her daughter to attack her. Scott, who was using all his remaining energy and resources to earn the money needed for Zelda's doctors and Scottie's school, reached for the nearest bottle of gin. Seeing Scott reeling from the effects of many glasses of gin, Zelda decided *he* was the crazy one, but *she* had been declared unfairly insane and put into an asylum. It was the typical trick of the sociopathic personality.

It was not a pleasant reunion, and Scott went on one of his epic drinking sprees, which continued after returning to California.

✧ ✧ ✧

Sheilah Graham decided that she was going to *save* F. Scott Fitzgerald. As noted, the Garden of Allah, despite its suggestion of a religion impatient with hard liquor, was hardly a dry apartment dwelling. Scott was surrounded with heavy-drinking friends, not a good environment for his goal of sobriety. Sheilah believed that he needed sunlight, sand, and crisp ocean breezes—exactly what were tonics for her. Sheilah found a white clapboard cottage for two hundred dollars a month with a six-month lease among the sand dunes at 114 Malibu Beach. It cost less than what Scott was paying for his bungalow at the Garden of Allah. The cottage had four bedrooms and Sheilah could keep an office here and visit evenings and weekends. If Scott needed to be in town, he could stay at her house on Kings Road. Scott, now perched precariously between drinks and a hangover, did not protest. She did not realize that Scott considered the sun to be a friend of his tuberculosis.

Scott's next on and then off-again assignment was to write the screenplay for Irving Thalberg's original picture *Marie Antoinette*. The movie was to be Thalberg's masterpiece and Fitzgerald correctly sensed it. Thalberg's premature death, however, postponed the project. Scott worked for a brief time for producer Hunt Stromberg on the re-born film in May, but was quickly reassigned to Hunt Stromberg's *The Women*. As Fitzgerald began to write the history of the Clare Booth character (Mary), he decided that she would not be of the beautiful and damned. Rather, Mary was much more like Sheilah Graham. Zelda had required so much care, but Sheilah had taken care of Scott. Stromberg did not like Scott's idea.

In the end, *The Women* was not much of a challenge for Fitzgerald. Mostly, he used the conversations in Clare Booth's well-written play—almost word-for-word. The play was about women gossiping. Scott could not sharpen Clare's already razorlike tongue, but he did often have to take the edge off it for Joe Breen. For example, the character Sylvia philosophizes about men, swearing, "I wouldn't be sure of the Apostle Paul." Of course, Fitzgerald, a non-practicing but spiritual Catholic, knew that Breen, a *devout* Catholic, *would* be sure. The Apostle Paul was cut from the script. Scott, not exactly a hack, had learned how to hack.

Miss Booth had written a tough little play. Scott nevertheless introduces sentimentality about hearth and home throughout. With Sheilah, Scott seemed to have a new sense of home and its importance. He, of course, had lost his own. In one scene he has Mary telling her friends that home means "everything in the world" to her.[27] In his screenplay Scott has the good rich using their money to strengthen the home and the bad rich neglecting their families. It was a new and different Scott Fitzgerald.

After one forgettable collaborator on the screenplay, Stromberg decided to team Fitzgerald with his old friend from St. Paul, Great Neck, and Paris—Donald Ogden Stewart. Stewart had written a number of successful film scripts, and Stromberg may have felt that Fitzgerald needed something like Stewart's experience in the summer of 1938. Stewart had greatly disliked "The Crack-Up" essays and, having not seen Scott for about a decade, did not know whether he had become a deplorable drunk or not. Stewart was pleasantly surprised and recalls, "He wasn't drinking, and he was, in fact, much more understanding than before, and infinitely more human. In our month together our old friendship came back, and it was like those starry-eyed days in St. Paul when he was reading Masefield to me in front of the fire in his living room." Scott was reading: "Be with me, beauty, for the fire is dying." But, as Stewart suggests, "The fire still wasn't dying—in either of us."[28]

Despite the great promise of this writing team, *The Women* met a fate similar to that of *Infidelity*. The play's satire was quite daring for 1938 and even Stewart's professionalism combined with Fitzgerald could not please Stromberg. Joe Breen would be harder to please. Besides, *The Women*'s script needed a woman's touch. Perhaps. After four months of frustration, Scott was reassigned to *Madame Curie,* probably only to keep him occupied until his contract with MGM expired. Although some of Fitzgerald's lines remained in *The Women* (released in 1939), Anita Loos and Jane Murfin were given the credits. Fitzgerald was told to make *Madame Curie* more of an MGM "love story" rather than a story of science, more like the successful *Barretts of Wimpole Street* (1934), a theme that Scott and the producer "were bucking." (Eventually the film did appear in 1943, as a "love story" starring actress Greer Garson.) Halfway through the script at Christmas, Scott was fired and his contract was not renewed. Some eighteen months of working at MGM had ended and Fitzgerald was on his own again. As Scott wrote to Ober, he never knew why he was fired, but he added, "Baby am I glad to get out! I've hated the place since Monkeybitch rewrote 3 Comrades!"[29] It may have come down to economics: Fitzgerald was being paid fifteen hundred dollars a week, a princely sum for an MGM writer.

More exactly, the decision to fire Scott probably was slightly more complicated. He did very little drinking while working at MGM, but when he did, he did it in the usual flamboyant Fitzgerald style and it led to lost time from work. With only one official screen credit, the studio might have judged Scott too great a risk at such a high price. Anyway, he was loaned to David O. Selznick for some final work on *Gone with the Wind* during his final two weeks. Selznick had gone through at least a dozen screenwriters who were forbidden to use any words except those of Margaret Mitchell. Fitzgerald would have loved to have the same imperial conditions for screen versions of *his* novels. He worked on all of the big scenes including the famous staircase scene in which an exasperated Clark Gable

Ann Sheridan and Budd Schulberg at work on Winter Carnival

said to Scarlet, "Frankly, my dear, I don't give a damn!" Those words, sounding much as Scott might have felt, however, were in the original novel and sailed past Joe Breen.

What happened next not only added to the Fitzgerald legend but did him great professional harm. In February 1939, Scott became a freelance screenwriter with H. N. Swanson and, later, the legendary Leland Hayward as his agents. Almost immediately Swanson secured a writing assignment on Walter Wanger's production of *Winter Carnival,* a forgettable college romance picture at Dartmouth starring Ann Sheridan. Wanger had hired the twenty-four-year-old Budd Schulberg to write the screenplay. Scott and Budd were to collaborate. The reason for hiring Scott was the same as that for hiring him for *A Yank at Oxford*: It was a college film. The story of Budd and Scott's snowy week in Hanover, New Hampshire, has been told many times.

Kindness compels us to quickly sum it up. Against Fitzgerald's wishes, he flew east with Wanger and Schulberg to "experience" the Dartmouth Winter Carnival that year. Thanks to an innocent gift of champagne from Budd's father (at the time, in charge of Paramount Studio), Scott got very drunk on the plane and stayed that way, more or less, for the entire event. There were many embarrassing incidents, with Fitzgerald often in a state of near collapse. However, even when Scott looked as if he were falling-down drunk, his brilliant mind went on and on. At one party a group of Dartmouth English professors gave unsolicited criticism of the movie in the making. Scott sank deeply into a chair to listen; when he had heard enough, he rose and said, "You know, I'd love to be a professor in a university like this with all the security and smug niceties, instead of having to put up with the things we have to put up with out there in the world. I bid you good night, gentlemen."[30]

Budd Schulberg later said: "One of the things that impressed me most in the course of that arctic weekend hell was the quality of Scott's creative intelligence and the courage of his humor. He was constantly noticing little things that amazed me—details of academic life as exact as the lexicon of O'Hara.... At the very moment when the faculty and student onlookers were laughing at him as a drunk and a clown, his accuracy toward them was muffled but deadly."[31] Still, Budd and Scott did not prevail.

Wanger fired both, putting them on a train bound for New York City. By now Fitzgerald appeared to have pneumonia. Because of Budd and Scott's shoddy physical appearance, the result of a week of drinking, hotels denied them a room. Sheilah Graham was summoned to care for the nearly comatose Fitzgerald and he was admitted to Doctors Hospital. Schulberg eventually was rehired to complete the screenplay.

All of this would have been quickly forgotten save for Budd Schulberg's *own* account of it in his novel *The Disenchanted*. Schulberg depicts Manley Halliday, the Fitzgerald character, as anything but a writer and a man lacking in personal dignity. Even in the worst of circumstances, Scott rarely fit that description. The novel was written a decade after the events with the help of Arthur Mizener, who was writing about Fitzgerald in what became *The Far Side of Paradise*. Borrowing from fiction, Mizener relies on Schulberg's novel as well as from his several magazine pieces, for his damning Fitzgerald biography. The two books combined depict Fitzgerald as a drunken sot and shattered wreck in his Hollywood years. This legend has been difficult to dispel; ironically, someone who otherwise had such great respect for Scott's talents ignited it.[32] Fitzgerald, ever the professional, was able to use the Winter Carnival experience in the development of one his characters in *The Last Tycoon*.

Still, Dartmouth was costly spiritually and financially. After roughly a year of sobriety, Scott began to drink more frequently. It began to look like a replay of the worst days of 1935 and 1936, requiring the care of expensive doctors and nurses, sometimes around-the-clock. During these months of the spring and summer of 1939, Sheilah Graham believed that Scott was trying to kill himself with drink. Her love, care, and sympathy probably kept him alive.

He nonetheless tried Sheilah's patience. After a short stint on a film in March 1939, he took a trip to Asheville to pick up Zelda and take her to Cuba for a brief holiday from the Highlands Sanitarium. Scott had left Hollywood in a rage after a bitter and drunken quarrel with Sheilah. He continued to drink heavily on a trip that turned out to be one of those legendary Fitzgerald disasters. The trip ended with Scott in a state of total exhaustion at the Algonquin Hotel in New York—site of many meetings around its Round Table. Zelda put him once again in Doctors Hospital while she returned with her sister, Rosalind, to Asheville. It was the last time that Scott and Zelda ever would see each other.

✧ ✧ ✧

Fitzgerald's financial prospects, bad as they once had been, again deepened. Although all his nine books were still in print, their combined sales for 1939 produced royalties of only $33. Sales for 1938 had been even worse. There were a few, scattered, brief freelance screen assignments—*Air Raid* for Paramount in March 1939, *Open that Door* for Universal in August, *Everything Happens at Night* for 20th Century Fox and *Raffles* with David Niven for Goldwyn in September. Then, there were no screenwriting jobs as far as Scott could see, and he was left with no choice except to write short stories. For him, now, he had no other source of income. Ironically, in what seems like a Hollywood ending squared, Scott soon would write his best screenplay and, perhaps, what would have been his greatest novel.

Endnotes

1. The quotes from O'Sullivan are based on interviews with Aaron Latham. See Aaron Latham, *Crazy Sundays: F. Scott Fitzgerald in Hollywood* (New York: The Viking Press, 1970), p 111.

2. Ibid., p. 115.

3. Andrew Turnbull, ed., *The Letters of F. Scott Fitzgerald* (New York: Charles Scribners Sons, 1963), pp. 574–75.

4. Robert Westbrook, *Intimate Lies: F. Scott Fitzgerald and Sheilah Graham, Her Son's Story* (New York: HarperCollins), p. 171.

5. Ibid.

6. The correct details of this meeting are presented for the first time in James L. W. West III, *The Perfect Hour: The Romance of F. Scott Fitzgerald and Ginevra King, His First Love* (New York: Random House, 2005), pp. 85–87. Earlier biographies have Ginevra initiating a meeting taking place in Santa Barbara and having Scott being well behaved (despite having quite a few drinks).

7. Scott to Scottie, October 8, 1937 in Turnbull, *Letters, op. cit.,* p. 19.

8. Quoted by James L. W. West III, *op. cit.,* p. 87.

9. Quotes are from a letter by Ginevra to the author, *The Far Side of Paradise,* p. 275.

10. Sheilah Graham, *The Real F. Scott Fitzgerald: Thirty-Five Years Later* (New York: Grosset & Dunlap, 1976), p. 103.

11. Frances Kroll Ring, "Memories of Scott," in Jackson R. Bryer, Alan Margolies, and Ruth Prigozy, eds., *F. Scott Fitzgerald: New Perspectives* (Athens and London: University of Georgia Press, 2000), p. 19. This bond that united Scott and Zelda forever also is demonstrated in their final correspondence in Jackson R. Bryer and Cathy W. Barks, *Dear Scott, Dearest Zelda* (New York: St. Martins Press, 2002), especially in pages 270–383.

12. Ibid.

13. Edmund Wilson wanted to include the letter in *The Crack-Up,* but Mankiewicz dissuaded him with a very thoughtful letter. In it, he writes, "Aside from the extremely unpleasant characterization of me that emanates from the letter, I do not want it published for reasons that have to do also with Scott, his good taste and his sense of criticism." See letter from Joseph L. Mankiewicz to John Biggs, May 1, 1944, Fitzgerald Collection, Princeton University Library.

14. Latham, *Crazy Sundays*, pp. 563–64.

15. Ibid., p. 148.

16. Sheilah Graham (and Gerald Frank), *Beloved Infidel*, (New York: Quality Paperback Book Club, 1989 [1958]) p. 175.

17. Letter from F. Scott Fitzgerald to Mr. Mannix, Mr. Katz, undated, Fitzgerald Collection, Princeton University Library.

18. See, for example, Tom Dardis, *Some Time in the Sun: The Hollywood Years of F. Scott Fitzgerald, William Faulkner, Nathanael West, Aldous Huxley, and James Agee* (New York: Charles Scribner's Sons, 1976), p. 39.

19. Letter from F. Scott Fitzgerald to Mrs. Beatrice Dance, March 4, 1938, Fitzgerald Collection, Princeton University Library.

20. Martin Connors and Jim Craddock, eds., *VideoHound's Golden Movie Retriever* (Detroit/New York/Toronto/London: Visible Ink, 1998)

21. Bob Thomas, *Thalberg: Life and Legend* (New York: Doubleday, 1969), p. 210.

22. See Hedy Lamarr, *Ecstasy and Me: My Life as a Woman* (New York: Fawcett Crest World Library, 1968), pp. 29–31.

23. Turnbull, *Letters*, p. 446.

24. Graham, *Beloved Infidel*, p. 161.

25. See *Infidelity,* from F. Scott Fitzgerald to Hunt Stromberg, June 27, 1938, Fitzgerald Collection, Princeton University Library. The full treatment runs five pages.

26. *Infidelity,* from F. Scott Fitzgerald (apparently to Stromberg), May 25, 1938, Fitzgerald Collection, Princeton University Library.

27. F. Scott Fitzgerald, "The Women," MS, dated July 9, 1938, in MGM archives, p. 25. Quoted by Latham, *Crazy Sundays*, p. 187.

28. Matthew J. Bruccoli, C. E. Clark, C. E. Frazer, Jr., eds. *The Fitzgerald-Hemingway Annual* (Washington, D.C.: NCR Microcard Books, 1971). p. 188.

29. Turnbull, *Letters,* p. 39.

30. Andrew Turnbull, *Scott Fitzgerald* (New York: Charles Scribners Sons, 1962), pp. 295–96.

31. Quoted by Latham, *Crazy Sundays*, p. 227.

32. See, for example, Schulberg's tribute, "Remembering Scott," in Jackson R. Bryer, Alan Margolies, and Ruth Prigozy, *F. Scott Fitzgerald: New Perspectives* (Athens and London: University of Georgia Press, 2000), pp. 3–17.

Seventeen

Hollywood Endings

FITZGERALD WAS BACK TO WRITING SHORT STORIES—NOW, ABOUT A screenwriting hack named Pat Hobby. Scott resourcefully used his plight as Hollywood "factory" worker to advantage in these stories, satirizing the industry that treated its writers so condescendingly. It is easy to dismiss the Pat Hobby stories as trite Hollywood trash, and although they are surely beneath Scott's manifest artistic capabilities, they are nevertheless delightfully humorous and carefully crafted. More important, Arnold Gingrich of *Esquire* paid Scott $250 per story in a series of seventeen. They ran at the beginning of 1940 to May of 1941. They advanced Fitzgerald's main goal—financial survival so that he could continue writing a book about Hollywood.

Scott spoke for himself as well as many Depression-era Americans in his "Pat Hobby Does His Bit" with the comic economic truth that "it is exceedingly difficult to borrow money when one needs it" and situates Pat Hobby in the position of an unemployed worker in the process of being divorced from his only remaining capital. We learn that the borrowing is to "save his car," hardly worth saving "but, because of Hollywood's great distances, it was an indispensable tool of the writer's trade."[1] Fitzgerald had Hobby driving a car very much like his own—a very used, rattletrap Ford coupe. As Hobby attempts to borrow money from an actor during a filming, he inadvertently gets caught on film in a scene with the leading lady, and, because the actress has left the country before the mistake is found, several scenes with Pat must be shot to complete the film. Fitzgerald had not lost his sense of irony or humor.

As in Charlie Chaplin's film satirizing assembly line work, *Modern Times*—with which Scott was familiar as an acquaintance of Chaplin—a single error by a single person can halt an entire production. Moreover, errors on an assembly line inevitably compound themselves. Rather than being a mere nuisance to be cut from the film, Pat's mistake threatens to be a film-stopping boner. The rigid schedule deciding the movements of the leading lady imply that she has already been whisked off to England. The saving grace is that actors—like scriptwriters—are mostly interchangeable parts in the Hollywood machine, so Pat is fully capable of doing an acting "bit."

The parallel with the Chaplin film's satire does not end there. In one of the more famous scenes from *Modern Times,* the assembly

Scene from Chaplin's Modern Times

line worker, Charley, is the subject of an experiment in Taylorism when a feeding machine that goes haywire treats him inhumanely. Similarly, coerced into being a stunt man, Pat Hobby is strapped into a metal jacket and is to be literally run over in a scene which itself goes awry. Like the harassed Chaplin, Pat is forgotten in the excitement when the car turns over and ruins the shooting.

✧　✧　✧

Fitzgerald had returned to a Marxist theme from his early stories—worker alienation. This and other Pat Hobby stories show Scott retaining his artistic conscience in a climate that repeatedly, perhaps inevitably, extracts dignity from the worker. Writer and actors alike, like the art itself, are assumed to be mechanically reproducible and, as a result, people as well as the work of art lose their aura. Little concern is given to the danger of wrecking the man, "just don't wreck the picture." As in Marx (Karl, not Groucho), product is more important than the person as humanity and creativity are sacrificed in the name of mechanistic production and profit. Pat Hobby is left alone, abandoned in his metal casing of a jacket—a feeling shared by Scott himself, whose aura had long faded and whose search for authenticity was confined to working sporadically on what was to be his last novel.

Although Scott assigned himself a "D" in Marxian Economics while designing Sheilah Graham's *College of One* course, this grade greatly understates the lifelong influence of Marx. In a January 1939 letter to Scottie, Scott writes, "Most questions in life have an economic basis (at least according to us Marxians)."[2] Later, in a 1940 letter to Max Perkins, Scott expresses his intellectual debt to Marx and Spengler: They "are the only modern philosophers that still manage to make sense in this horrible mess."[3] Although the focal point of Scott's fiction clearly was not the working class, his treatment of and identification with Jim Powell, Dick Diver, and Pat Hobby's estrangement displays his class consciousness. True, the proletariat is submerged. But, as noted earlier, way back in 1920 in the short story. "The Camel's Back," Scott was depicting the working-class experience under capitalism in Marxian tones. In the beginning as well as near the end, Marxism provided an intellectual as well as sentimental subtext for Scott's fiction.

As adequately noted, Fitzgerald's understanding of Wells, Shaw, and Spengler had greatly softened Scott's Marxism. Although Marxism functioned as more than sentimental attachment in Scott's life and writings, it was never an intellectual or political panacea. What is markedly missing in Marx's deterministic vision but present in Spengler's philosophy is Scott's belief in the role of personality and the extraordinary leader in shaping the modern world. It was the kind of hero-leader that would dominate what would be Scott's final novel, *The Last Tycoon*. In Spengler's depiction of the decline of Western culture, powerful money interests increasingly dictate control of the economic and political world and from this emerges the formation of class interests along economic lines (through both representative democracy and socialism), but, in a departure from Marx, Spengler foresaw that this is followed by "the age of great individuals in a formless world."[4] The preeminent of these Caesar-men are able to command through personality as well as through the power of money, either benignly like Monroe Stahr in *The Last Tycoon* or malignantly like Adolf Hitler, whose emergence Spengler anticipated and whose Nazi-socialism Scott detested and recognized as fascist.

To Spengler, what is true about personality in the political realm is also true in the business realm. In opposition to Marx, Spengler celebrates the entrepreneur whose "personality...vouches for a corresponding heightening of the economic energy of his field" and without whose "creations" workers would become "soulless, will-less, empty shells."[5] This view instructs Fitzgerald's *The Last Tycoon* in which Monroe Stahr is portrayed in these life-infusing expressions. But Stahr's unique position of authority is precarious and faltering. In the final scene of the unfinished novel, Stahr is unwilling to relinquish authorial or artistic control to the Writers Guild in his meeting with Brimmer, a communist organizer. But it is the "broad-shouldered" Brimmer who easily deflects a drunken Stahr's pathetic personal assault, and one is led to believe that the combined forces of socialism and capitalism were destined to snuff out the fading light of a star.[6] Monroe Stahr would indeed be "the last tycoon." Having witnessed the efforts of writers and actors to unionize—to gain power and recognition from the "benevolent" studio producers—Scott wanted to dramatize these actions in his novel.

✧   ✧   ✧

These were Scott's thoughts as he wrote his final fiction. As it turns out, however, Hollywood was not finished with Scott. In March 1940, Lester Cowan, an independent movie producer, approached Scott about writing a script based on "Babylon Revisited" (1931), one of the best of Fitzgerald's short fiction, set in Europe in the aftermath of the 1929 stock market crash. Cowan bought the film rights from Scott for $800 plus $300 a week while Scott worked on the screenplay, for a total payment of $5,000. The offer came at a time when Fitzgerald thought his days as a screenwriter were over.

Scott's short story, "Babylon Revisited," concerns a father's attempt to redeem himself and reclaim guardianship over his daughter following a life of excess, including a fateful winter night in which his drinking and negligence is thought by his wife's sister to have contributed to the death of his wife of pneumonia after he mistakenly locks her out of the house. Like so many of Fitzgerald's great short stories, the story has powerful yet subtle social, political, and economic undercurrents: The father's (Charles Wales') futile attempt to regain custody of his daughter (Honoria) is a microcosm of America's problem of legitimizing its authority against the backdrop of twenties excess and corruption, which by most accounts, including Fitzgerald's in "Echoes of the Jazz Age" (1931), contributed to the economic collapse and general disorder of the thirties. The original story also has biographical overtones: As noted earlier, Zelda's sister Rosalind (Marion in the story) not only repeatedly accused Scott of being a reckless, irresponsible husband and parent, but the direct cause of Zelda's mental illness. Rosalind, as also noted, attempted to adopt Scottie to "save her" from Scott.

Despite reservations about writing movie scripts based on his own fiction and his increasing disillusion with Hollywood following *Three Comrades* and *Infidelity,* Scott was interested. The initial attraction, aside from his desperate need for money, stemmed from Scott's belief that he could avoid the usual Hollywood bureaucracy and maintain artistic control over the script. Scott was paid "on spec" with a bonus if the film was ever produced. Scott also was intrigued with the film's thoughtful possibilities: He would at once deepen the main character and the historical reach of the film by making Wales a stock market leader during its boom-to-bust era. At the same time, he would revisit the profound universal yet highly personal themes contained in the original short story—the nature of innocence, corruption, redemption, authority, and leadership. Unlike the movie script for *Tender Is the Night,* which deteriorated into a comic condensation of a sophisticated novel, this project promised to expand into a significant new work of art portraying a historical era as well as complex developments within Scott's own life.

Although the final screenplay was titled *Cosmopolitan,* it began as *Honoria.* To highlight Fitzgerald's basis for deepening and broadening the story, we pay close attention to this first script. The final script differs greatly from the short story; in particular, it is much darker. Along the way Honoria becomes Victoria.

We discovered the source material for *Cosmopolitan* at Princeton University Library. Scott uses Earl Sparling's *Mystery Men of Wall Street* to further develop the character of Charles Wales and research the history of the boom-to-bust economy of the late twenties.[7] The refurbished Wales is based on Sparling's portrayal of a new breed of business tycoon emerging on Wall Street in the postwar era—successors to the railroad (James Hill of St. Paul) and banking (J. P. Morgan) moguls of the Gilded Age. In Sparling's telling, these men operate in the stock market on a scale never dreamed of before, speak casually of billions as the men of the old Wall Street spoke of millions, destroying precedent and tradition.

> They have ushered in an era of major manipulation, of
> tidal movements in speculation, of pools and syndicates
> so enormous that the operating combinations of other

days are dwarfed to toy proportions. They move so vastly that the outmoded machinery of the New York Stock Exchange has collapsed under the strain of keeping pace and must be rebuilded in high-speed steel.[8]

These new tycoons of Wall Street resembled their Gilded Age predecessors with their audacity and secret dealings, yet their daring and bullish outlook stood in contrast to the more bearish and conservative Eastern Wall Street establishment. As Sparling puts it, "The difference has been that the Eastern market players, including most of the Stock Exchange members, have been playing the market by note, following customs, precedents, rules of order and established theories." In contrast, he continues, "The Westerners have been playing by ear and they have gotten away with it."[9]

Although in some respects a composite of the dozen "Mystery Men" portrayed by Sparling, Wales is most closely modeled after William Durant, who, like Scott's depiction of Wales in the original script, is a former "automobile man," Durant having founded General Motors in 1908.[10] Durant subsequently lost ownership of GM in the recession of 1920–21 along with his $90 million personal fortune, which he threw "into the financial whirlpool trying to save, not himself, but his friends…[who] had invested in General Motors on his recommendation…"[11]

After his financial ruin in 1920, Durant turned from producer of automobiles to stock speculator, where he made millions as leader of the bull market and as head of a "prosperity consortium" whose purpose was to protect the bull market from the bears of the East.[12] However, unlike the unsuspecting public and other followers of the bull market that he had helped create, Durant began withdrawing his investments in the spring of 1929 after a clandestine meeting with President Herbert Hoover convinced Durant of the Federal Reserve's resolve to adhere to a tight credit policy, which Durant predicted (correctly) would cause the collapse of the bull market.

Scott not only selected aspects of Durant's life to further develop the character of Charles Wales, but he also freely borrowed snatch phrases, sounds, and descriptions from Sparling's book to help recreate the atmosphere of Wall Street before and during the 1929 crash. The rhythmic "clack, clack, clack"[13] of the stock ticker stuttering "the finale of an era,"[14] is used in the script as an audio device to communicate both the uncontrollable and unsustainable pace of the late twenties as well as the insanity of Charles's wife (Mrs. Wales is never visually present nor named in the script, but she is more akin to Zelda than Charles's wife Helen is in the short story).

When Charles leaves with his family for Europe in the spring of 1929 (having retired from the stock market in an attempt to

Wall Street on the day of the Crash. A man came to work on a high building; the crowd waited impatiently for him to jump.

restore his wife's sanity), he liquidates his holdings (as Durant did in spring 1929) and remarks to his former business partner that "the market is leaderless," a statement made by Durant taken verbatim, though out of context, from Sparling's book. Sparling also portrays Durant as possessing a natural feel for the market, speculating by ear rather than by studious attention to the ticker tape, an intuitive ability Scott possessed and incorporated into the characterization of Wales, who is blessed with "That gift of the—divine guess."[15] For example, when the stock tickers lag hopelessly behind during the crash, Wales speculates on instinct and successfully conducts his stock manipulations independent of mechanical failure as "America fell literally into a financial chaos, an example in miniature of the anarchy civilization as a whole might revert to if all means of communication failed."[16]

Beyond those intuitive abilities, Scott was undoubtedly intrigued by Durant because he was an industry leader who managed to resurrect himself from seeming ruin in one industry to effectively lead in another, an imperialistic urge Scott secretly harbored when he went to Hollywood for a third time in 1937. In a letter to his daughter written in July 1937, as he traveled literally and figuratively through the Rocky Mountains aboard that train bound for Hollywood, Scott reflected upon his two previous Hollywood failures: "I want to profit by these two experiences—I must be very tactful but keep my hand on the wheel from the start—find out the key man among the bosses + the most malleable among the collaborators—then fight the rest tooth + nail until, in fact or in effect, I'm alone on the picture."[17] Although considerably chastened by his nearly three years in Hollywood (conceding to Scottie in a letter written in the winter of 1939 that he was now willing to settle for "Assistant Czar")[18] Scott was unable to suppress this imperialistic urge. The screenplay for "Babylon Revisited" was a golden, ultimately final, opportunity to fly to the top solo.

A resurrection story of an individual, however, had to be more than Horatio Alger writ large for the Hollywood screen: Scott had come a long way from the boy from St. Paul who had first looked up Summit Avenue and saw James Hill's lit-up mansion and wondered about the American Dream. Instead, Scott's alienating Hollywood experience would be transformed to reveal an utterly modern truth he first discovered during the arduous process of writing *Tender Is the Night*: True creativity—originality in its purest, most mysterious and incalculable form—arose in the presence, indeed out of the experience, of nothingness. *Cosmopolitan* would revolve around the glamour, waste, and refuse of wealth—that was Scott's conjuncture—but it would reflect the profundity that true leadership consists of the courage to create in the face of disorder, relative poverty, and absolute despair.

Spiritually and financially impoverished, but bravely beating against the current with a glimpse of that distant green light, Scott set to work on April 12 and on May 29 completed a draft of *Cosmopolitan,* titling it "Honoria" after Charles Wales' daughter (named originally in honor of Sara and Gerald Murphy's daughter). Although the original script was not flawless, Scott was unusually pleased with it, informing his agent Bill Dozier on May 15: "I think I have a pretty fine continuity here if I can have another week's peace of mind about it. Though I've sweated over it, it's been pleasant sweat, so to speak, and rather more fun than I've ever had in pictures."[19]

One of Scott's accomplishments is establishing the perspective of a child in an adult world. The effect is ironic: A complex, disorderly, and hostile adult world characterized by hypocrisy, greed, concealment, and manipulation envelops Honoria—a symbol of simplicity, purity, and innocence. The most obvious corruption and source of conflict is Wales' former business partner—Lloyd Garside in the original script and a slightly more disguised but no less sinister Dwight Schuyler in the final script. Garside threatens Honoria's future by robbing her trust fund during Wales' debilitating guilt-ridden depression following his wife's suicide, and then attempts to murder Wales to cover his theft and losses from the stock market crash. In contrast to Wales' creative genius—his gift for prophecy and ability to create even amidst the disorder—Garside is parasitic, a false leader riding the wave of prosperity created by Wales.

After realizing that Garside has lost Honoria's trust fund in the crash, Wales is forced to sell his remaining holdings short in the market to save himself and his family. Ironically, Garside views this as traitorous: "You selling short? You've never been a bear before. You selling America short? Why you—"[20] although it is clear that Garside's treachery and excess have *forced* Wales to turn bearish in the market. Similarly, Scott was accused by Hemingway and others of selling out in the late twenties and early thirties when, in truth, charitable motives (familial duties to Zelda and Scottie) were mostly directing that decision.

Like Durant in finance, Scott had created and led a bull market, a writer's bubble with his flapper stories. Again, like Durant, Scott's prescience would have had him out of the market, the *Saturday Evening Post* market, well prior to the 1929 crash. However, financial exigencies arising from the need to support Zelda and Scottie coupled with the public's incessant demands for "feel good" stories about youth and glamour in the *Post* forced him to "sell short." At the same time *Tender Is the Night* (and his less upbeat short stories rejected by the popular magazines) were disappointing his mass market audience and invited accusations of abandoning ship from *Post* and other editors. Under the circumstances, Scott too must have felt like an innocent child in a hostile world.

The cinematic technique devised by Scott to accentuate the juxtaposition between innocence and corruption was to periodically place the camera at the child's level. The adult world thereby frequently filters through to the audience audibly but not visibly. The insanity, greed, and other dangers of the twenties are always lurking yet are strangely removed and never fully grasped by Honoria and, it is implied, by a naively hopeful age of celebration. In this sense, the script resembles *The Great Gatsby* wherein a pure and promising transcendent American Dream is imperiled by a false, malevolent, and corrupting version of that dream. In fact, the contrast is sharper in this movie script than in the novel since Honoria's innocence remains purer than the tainted naïveté of Gatsby, who is afflicted by corrupt means and false dreams.

It is doubly ironic that Scott's original script, evidently so nicely situated for Hollywood's good-versus-evil formula, was subjected to adulteration by Lester Cowan's insistence that the script be modified to cast Shirley Temple in the lead child's role. Scott was impressed with Temple but feared that she appeared too worldly for the part and would detract from the aura of innocence otherwise framed by Honoria's character.

Cowan also wanted clarification as to the cause of Mrs. Wales' suicide, which occurs after Charles returns to his speculative vocation aboard the ship; Scott had subtly and deliberately left it ambiguous (as it was in his own mind regarding Zelda's "death") whether husband, wife, both, or neither were responsible for the suicide. This ambiguity is in notable contrast to the short story where Mrs. Wales' death is attributed by her sister to the husband. Another obscurity of the original script is Wales' initial motivation for reentering the stock market on the transatlantic journey to Europe in July 1929, an important nuance since Wales' reentry temporarily separates him from his wife and seemingly precipitates her suicide. An innocent query by Honoria leads Wales to the brokerage office located aboard the ship and, despite knowingly opening a Pandora's box, Wales cannot resist entering. Once inside, an innate draw to his vocation coupled with public pressure keeps him there.

In the original (May 1929) version, Wales picks up the ticker tape and exclaims "Good Lord! They're pounding McDonough Radio!"[21] which was revised for the August 1940 version to read "Good Lord! They're pounding Radio! Poor old Bill Bonniman!"[22] Bill Bonniman, a new character Scott introduced into the August 1940 script, is a small-town banker friend from Wales' hometown whose investments are threatened by the end of the bull market. Radio stock was symbolic of the bull market as its price "rose from $25 in 1924 to $570 on a split share basis in May, 1929, without any dividends having been paid at all."[23] Wales' concern about the drop in Radio's share price is not due to any personal financial loss, because he had already liquidated his stock holdings. Nevertheless, Wales does feel a personal affront and (in the August rewrite) an added sense of guilt about the end of the bull market he helped create but had abandoned.

Scott's decision to introduce a new character, Bill Bonniman, underscores rather than removes the complexity surrounding Wales' motivations for reentering the market, suggesting charitable motives as well as personal pride in his work. By depicting an industry leader who neglects his wife partly because of an innate talent and absorption with his work, partly because of personal pride and guilt in abandoning a profession he helped construct, and partly because of public pressure and charitable concern for others to continue working, Scott was developing a highly complex and autobiographical script. Whatever the shortcomings of Scott's script from a Hollywood perspective, it was not from lack of grandiose plans.

Although the script's plot and action revolve around the stock market crash and Charles Wales' guilt-ridden depression, Scott was not primarily interested in the forces of deterioration. The process of dissipation (or what, in the short story, is the ability "to make nothing out of something")[24] was a subject Scott had already masterfully depicted in *Tender Is the Night* and personally experienced in the late twenties and early thirties in full recognition of the humiliating fact that he, like Dick Diver, was increasingly perceived as an ex-emperor without clothes. Instead, Scott returned to the main theme underlying his short story, the problem of redemption. Restoring and legitimizing personal and professional authority and, more broadly, restoring leadership to the modern world had haunted Scott in 1930 when he first wrote the short story, and it was equally acute in 1940, three years after packing his dream of professional recovery with his luggage when he boarded that train bound for Hollywood. Moreover, redemption (making something out of nothing) was a theme suitable for Scott's hoped-for Hollywood ending.

The "ironic paperweight" that stood on Fitzgerald's desk in various places and, finally, in Hollywood.

The issue of leadership and authority is played out in the

Cosmopolitan script mainly in the guardianship rights to Honoria. Marion, the bitter and jealous sister of Mrs. Wales, is convinced that Wales' absorption with his work and wealth has caused her sister's suicide. Initially out of a sense of guilt and self-disgust, and later out of a tacit conspiracy between Garside and Marion, Wales loses custody of his child. With the help of a nurse, however, Wales recovers from his depression and learns of Garside's treachery. In the original script, Garside responds by hatching another sinister plot: He uses Marion's husband's unwitting role in the loss of Honoria's trust fund to make a phone call that dupes Wales into traveling to Switzerland on the pretense that Honoria is there. Garside's intention is to murder Wales by faking his suicide, a plot foiled by the unexpected appearance of Honoria, who has resourcefully traveled to Switzerland on her own upon knowledge that her father is there.

Honoria's arrival creates a tension. Wales now knows he is the target of a murder plot and wishes to protect Honoria. However, it is Honoria's innocence that actually protects her father by delaying his murder. The next morning, as Garside's contracted killer leads Wales down a mountain path, a desperate but nevertheless resourceful maneuver saves Wales. He deliberately throws himself off a cliff and survives the fall, a metaphor for how a bear can survive a market crash by going short and how creativity can turn adversity and disorder to advantage. In the obligatory (yet sophisticated) happy Hollywood ending Scott initially envisioned, Wales is saved by a combination of his own agility, his daughter's life-infusing innocence and creativity, and the restorative force of his nurse, who fortuitously arrives in a sleigh just as Wales reaches the bottom of the cliff.

✧   ✧   ✧

In Hollywood happy endings were possible, or so Scott believed, in contrast to *The Last Tycoon* wherein Monroe Stahr's creativity was doomed by overpowering commercial and bureaucratic forces. In a Hollywood screenplay, Scott could explore a more upbeat alternative to Monroe Stahr's fate—how an industry leader escapes from the excesses of the boom, avoids ruin during an enveloping crash, and reemerges an industry leader. It would be a script foreshadowing Scott's hoped-for return to prominence. Instead, his almost single-handedly fashioned original script had to be revised to suit Hollywood and was interminably delayed.

In the beginning Cowan and Fitzgerald both considered Cary Grant (or possibly Clark Gable) as well as Shirley Temple for the leading roles. At some point, however, Scott changed his mind and thought the story good enough to make stars of some unknown actors. Cowan nonetheless still wanted Ms. Temple for the part of Honoria. Then, Honoria's pure innocence (which Scott hoped to portray through the anonymity of an unknown child actress) had to be diluted to suit a sophisticated but better box office draw—Shirley Temple at age twelve going on twenty. Fitzgerald himself spent almost an entire day in July trying to persuade the child actress's mother to permit her rapidly aging young star's appearance in the film. Scott wrote Scottie describing the meeting and called Shirley "a sweet little girl." He had earlier written Lester Cowan about how Honoria could be played as an eleven-year-old: "If she's been well brought up she is beginning to realize her social responsibilities (in that regard I was very impressed with the Temple kid—no trace of coyness or cuteness yet a real dignity and gentleness).... If the personality that she has in private life could be carried *almost without heightening* over into the picture, I believe she would be perfect."[25]

To complete "our picture," we should note that Honoria became Victoria (in honor of Budd Schulberg's daughter) in the second draft of *Cosmopolitan* (August 1940).

As reported in a letter written September 14, however, Temple was unavailable at that time because her current film work was being held up to find a suitable costar. After telling Cowan on September 28 that he thought Temple was inappropriate for the part, an October 19 letter to Zelda indicates that Scott was resigned to it being a Temple film. On November 5, Scott wrote his agent, Bill Dozier, "If anything more comes in from Lester I think I can finish it *[The Last Tycoon]*," but ended the letter on a less hopeful note regarding his Hollywood career. "When I see you we can discuss what future, if any, I seem to have in this business."[26] Fitzgerald continued to work on the screenplay for several months after his weekly payments had ended.

Despite Scott's great effort, including his tendency to act out scenes, speaking the dialogue, Fitzgerald's screenplay was never produced. In one especially emotional scene played to Cowan over the phone, the producer wept. Fitzgerald told Frances, his devoted secretary, "At last I've made a son-of-a-bitch producer cry."[27] Poetically, it was a full decade before Lester Cowan recovered his investment in *Cosmopolitan*. Cowan hired the Epstein twins *(Casablanca)* to do a rewrite, which he sold to MGM for $100,000, under the title of Elliot Paul's novel *The Last Time I Saw Paris,* which starred Elizabeth Taylor when it was released in 1954.[28] Film histories still have the movie "based on a short story by F. Scott Fitzgerald."

Shopping around Hollywood with the *Cosmopolitan* script did restore some of Scott's lost luster in the film colony. 20th Century Fox hired him for a brief stint. Shortly thereafter, Zanuck and Nunnally Johnson gave him a ten-week job revising their script for Emlyn William's *The Light of Heart*. They paid him $700 a week and a total of $7,000, much better than the roughly $250-a-month for the Pat Hobby stories. Still, Fitzgerald's script about a broken-down alcoholic actor was "too glum" for Hollywood and was rewritten by Johnson a couple years later as *Life Begins at Eight-Thirty*, starring Monty Wooley. It was Scott's final film assignment. Though the income was desperately needed, it was earned at a cost of time foregone on his new novel. He had served as a Pat Hobby workaday laborer beholden to those in possession of the wealth.

✧　✧　✧

No longer the owner of the *Cosmopolitan* script, Scott returned to his novel. Ironically, Scott was right about commercial and bureaucratic forces overwhelming leadership and originality—also one of the themes of *The Last Tycoon*. He had started blocking out the novel in May 1939, five years after the publication of his last novel, *Tender Is the Night*. Since it would be the first serious novel about Hollywood and filmmaking, Scott was careful to conceal its subject from everyone except Sheilah, and convey its subject only obliquely to Max Perkins. To Max he wrote: "It is distinctly not about Hollywood (and if it were it is the last impression that I would want to get about.)"[29] Fitzgerald did not tell Scottie about the novel until October: Then he is very upbeat about it and writes that it may even be great.

In September Scott submitted the outline of the novel to Kenneth Littauer of *Collier's*. They were prepared to pay $15,000 for the serial rights to the book, only half as much as Fitzgerald expected. He nonetheless submitted the first six thousand words (now the first chapter of *The Last Tycoon*) to Littauer in November. Littauer wanted more: In a rage, Scott suspended all dealings with *Collier's*. It was sent to the *Saturday Evening Post*, which expressed absolutely no interest. Despite these disappointments compounded by bad business decisions and interruptions to do his screenplay work, Scott continued to work on the manuscript during 1940.

We should perhaps be reminded that *The Last Tycoon* is an unfinished novel, despite its editing by Scott's "friend" Edmund Wilson and its publication by Scribners. At this point of development of the novel, it was quite different from Fitzgerald's earlier fiction. He created Monroe Stahr in the tradition of the Horatio Alger unflawed hero—rising from office boy to boss. Fitzgerald returns for the final time to the American Dream. Not only that, Stahr is actually successful. He is the perfect professional, unbroken by loss but with a capacity to love again. Stahr is very much what Fitzgerald had been and had become. Stahr is not only committed to his work, he is *responsible*. He makes only one great mistake, he delays the decision to go away with Kathleen, his true love, by one day, and during that day he loses her. Moreover, Fitzgerald's women had always been stronger than his men: Now, Fitzgerald had created his first strong male hero. Perhaps it was Fitzgerald in his final self-realization. His guilt about his own irresponsibility may have come to an end. If so, it was a happy—Hollywood—ending.

F. Scott Fitzgerald had come full circle with *The Last Tycoon*. He was the author of *This Side of Paradise* at twenty-three, of *The*

Great Gatsby at twenty-eight, and was a mental basket case at thirty-eight. At age forty, Scott had started over in a new industry. He had grown up aware of his father's failure in business and understood his conditions as a poor boy at rich-boy schools. Stahr, like Scott, always remains ambitious throughout. His envy, like Fitzgerald's, is qualified by his understanding of the negative aspects of success. What defeats Stahr in the end is not himself but the character of the modern corporation. Part of Scott Fitzgerald's great dream was to create and manage some important enterprise. His last version of this dream was to take command of Hollywood, as Stahr does, temporarily. Stahr (Irving Thalberg) is told by his doctors that if he doesn't stop working, he will die. Fitzgerald was told the same by his doctor. Stahr, like Fitzgerald, refuses to stop.

✧　✧　✧

His major biographers' cavalier treatment of Scott Fitzgerald's contributions to films and to writing while in Hollywood is difficult to understand. Not only was he fascinated by films, he fully understood their making. He had a gift for dialogue, and he understood the difference between written words and the visual medium.

To gain some perspective, we can compare Scott's record with that of a "successful" novelist and screenwriter during the same era. As noted, Fitzgerald was not the only writer who went to Hollywood. Among the notables was William Faulkner, who spent more than four years there, divided into uneven durations, starting in 1932 and ending in 1955. Despite the similarities between the two, Faulkner's life is treated with much greater tenderness than is Fitzgerald's. The reasons for the disparate treatments are difficult to pin down.

Like Hemingway, drinking was part of the Faulkner legend. Hemingway and Faulkner were not simply heavy drinkers; they were alcoholics. While Fitzgerald made ill-fated efforts to conceal his drinking habit, Faulkner was quite public about his. Unlike Scott, but like Hemingway, Faulkner could "hold his liquor." When Faulkner worked with Darryl F. Zanuck and 20th Century Fox in November 1935 until the late summer of 1937, he became a legend in his own cups. Faulkner's principal French translator, Maurice Coindreau, visited Faulkner in the early summer of 1937 and said, "While I was staying at his home, he drank constantly, but without seeming to be affected by it...."[30]

Just before finishing the movie script for *The Road To Glory,* Faulkner went on a week's drinking binge. He was either bored with the picture or may possibly have been celebrating his completion of *Absalom, Absalom!*—one of his best novels.[31] The binge put him in a hospital. During 1943 and 1954, Faulkner was frequently hospitalized for detoxification, both in Mississippi and in New York. After his last binge in 1962, he died at Wright's Sanitarium in the backwoods of Byhalia, Mississippi.

Although Faulkner's Hollywood history covers a longer period than Fitzgerald's, he too received few film credits. Faulkner's first two series of visits yielded only three screen credits—*Today We Live, The Road To Glory,* and *Slave Ship.* According to Tom Dardis, had it not been for Faulkner's contributions to two classics, *To Have and Have Not* and *The Big Sleep,* "Faulkner's time in Hollywood would been largely wasted."[32] Both movies starred Humphrey Bogart and both were writing collaborations with the formidable Howard Hawks. *To Have and Have Not,* to its credit, was closer to Bogart's *Casablanca* than to Hemingway's "socially conscious" novel of Cuba and Florida in the mid-1930s. Unlike Fitzgerald, Faulkner was quite willing to take a backseat and collaborate with other writers, especially Hawks, who also was a noted director. Importantly, Faulkner also was willing to work for only three hundred dollars a month. Faulkner never had any ambitions to contribute artistically to this newly dominant medium; unlike Fitzgerald, he never aspired to be a "professional" screenwriter or movie director.

The absence of invidious comparison does not end with the drinking or differences in professional ambitions. Standing next to Faulkner, who was only five feet, Fitzgerald looked quite tall. Yet little has been made of Faulkner's height, perhaps because his pretensions were to be a pilot, not an athlete. Although Fitzgerald and his "friends" fretted about the paucity of sales of his books during his lifetime, most of Faulkner's books sold no more than a thousand copies during his time. Such sales would be comparable today to that of an abstract economist's monograph on the mathematics of foreign exchange. It is little wonder then that William Faulkner, who also put in time at MGM but disliked the work, wrote screenplays for the same reason as Parker—for the money.

Francis Goodrich and Albert Hackett, a screenwriter wife-husband team of classics such as *The Thin Man* (1934) and *It's a Wonderful Life* (1946), also were in Hollywood during its Golden Age and knew Scott Fitzgerald while staying at the Garden of Allah. Knowing that Goodrich had graduated from Vassar, Scott sometimes stopped by the Hacketts' MGM office to read his letters to Scottie aloud, letters that Francis called "beautiful." Goodrich also referred to Graham as Fitzgerald's "salvation," helping him drink less and urging him to complete *The Last Tycoon*.[33] Goodrich and Hackett were once given an office that Faulkner had recently vacated. Looking for anything left behind by the famous and respected author, Hackett said, "There was nothing except a large yellow pad on the desk. Faulkner had drawn a calendar and had circled every payday. But the only words he'd written on the whole pad were 'Boy Meets Girl.'"[34]

Sometime in 1939, Scott autographed the Hacketts' copy of *The Great Gatsby* with the poem:

When anyone dances
It's liable to be Frances
While a quiet and malicious racket
Is liable to proceed from Albert Hackett
(Writing this way is rash
In the presence of Ogden Nash)[35]

As to Fitzgerald's screenplays, Scott got fewer credits than he deserved. His biggest assignments, including that for *Cosmopolitan,* were essentially impossible projects. For reasons outside of Fitzgerald's control, they could not be brought to the screen. The faith of directors and producers in Scott's abilities in the face of his alcoholic reputation must have been exceptional; otherwise, he would not have been given such tough assignments or been paid so much. Although *Cosmopolitan* eventually appeared in the greatly rewritten *The Last Time I Saw Paris,* in which "a successful writer [Fitzgersald] reminisces about his love affair with a wealthy American girl in post-WWII Paris," the shift of the time frame from the 1920s to post-WWII Paris was a huge mistake. The credited screenplay writers were Richard Brooks, Julius J. Epstein, and Philip C. Epstein.

The censors undid both *Lipstick* and *Infidelity.* The same can be said for *The Women,* even though much from Scott's screenplay eventually made it

Sheilah Graham and Marilyn Monroe at Ciro's, 1955 or '56

into the theaters. *Lipstick* was delayed much longer, not making it to the big screen until 1976 in the post-Breen age. The credited writer is David Rayfiel: Scott is not mentioned, for which he would be grateful. Ironically, Ernest Hemingway's two granddaughters are among the cast—Margaux Hemingway as the star and her kid sister Mariel, in her debut. It is based loosely on Scott's story. In the film, fashion model Margaux seeks revenge on the man who brutally attacked and raped her, after he preys on her kid sister (real-life Mariel). It is an exquisitely exploitative excuse for entertainment.

Much, little though it was, of Fitzgerald's two weeks of work on *Gone With the Wind* made it to the screen. Today the screenplay credit goes to Sidney Howard, but with the assistance of "producer Selznick and novelist F. Scott Fitzgerald."[36] That certainly has been a successful film. Among its Academy Awards in 1939 were Best Screenplay, Best Picture, Best Actress (Vivien Leigh) and nominations for Best Actor (Clark Gable) and Best Supporting Actress (Olivia de Havilland).

Even if Fitzgerald would have had no important influence as a screenwriter, his short stories and novels led to one motion picture after another. *The Great Gatsby* was filmed twice, the first time with a very short Alan Ladd, the second with the slightly more believable Robert Redford. Even the second film, however, was not an unqualified success. Then, too, the title of the poem that Scott wrote for Sheilah Graham became a book title and a movie. Sheilah's autobiographical *Beloved Infidel* was briefly a best-seller in 1958. In 1959 it became a film with Deborah Kerr as Sheilah and, even more improbably, Gregory Peck as Scott. Graham thought the film hideously miscast. Gregory Peck was much too tall and too wooden for his part. Her preference was for Richard Basehart. Deborah Kerr also was all wrong—too thin, too controlled, and too ladylike. According to Wendy Fairey, Sheilah's daughter, Sheilah thought Marilyn Monroe right for the part.[37]

Sheilah thought that her and Marilyn Monroe's lives were similar in some respects. They both had bleak childhoods, neither raised by their mothers. Both were raised in orphanages. Both learned early of the power of their sexual bodies; both had used men and sex, and vice versa. Both were Pygmalions at the hands of famous authors: Monroe's Henry Higgins being the dramatist Arthur Miller. Each married and divorced three husbands. More to the immediate point, Marilyn Monroe's earthy sexuality was a good match for Sheilah's.[38] We can sense the latter in a picture from an industry dinner at Ciro's in Hollywood taken in 1955 or '56. Sheilah is around fifty years of age, Marilyn around thirty-one. Sheilah holds her own with the younger, famous star: Graham is still glamorous in an open V-neckline black satin dress that highlights her attractive bosom. Marilyn is, well…Marilyn Monroe.

✧ ✧ ✧

For the final time we return to F. Scott Fitzgerald in Hollywood. Scott had been stone sober for more than nine months. By October he was again reading *The Last Tycoon* to Sheilah. She had discovered fascinating parallels between Scott's and her story and that of Stahr and Kathleen. In the novel, Kathleen is a young Englishwoman from a lowly background cavorting with British royalty. By now Scott and Sheilah were living in a world bounded by their apartments and by Schwab's Drugstore, their routine well established and calm. By now, too, Sheilah loved Scott deeply and believed that she possessed "something precious and irreplaceable in this man..."[39]

Unlike his opinions of Zelda, Edmund Wilson had only good things to say about Sheilah and her relationship with Scott. Wilson had visited them in Hollywood and had seen Sheilah after Scott's death, and later on. She stayed with the Wilsons when Edmund was editing *The Last Tycoon*. "In Scott's case," he writes, "she took over somebody who was unreliable in certain ways, and needed support." Despite all that Sheilah had done for Scott, "after Scott's death, she made no attempt to exploit her relationship with him." Wilson praised her helpfulness with his editing of *The Last Tycoon* and "her quietly responsible relationship with Scottie." He greatly admired Sheilah's "British good sense and her intelligent grasp of what Scott was doing." He also found her "amusing and very realistic about Hollywood."[40] Wilson understood that Scott finally had established a mature relationship with a Golden Girl.

On a Thursday afternoon in November, a dull, gray day, Scott said, "I'm going to Schwab's for cigarettes." Twenty minutes later, when Scott returned, Sheilah did not hear him. She looked up and saw a gray and trembling Scott, letting himself slowly into his easy chair. Alarmed, she asked, "Is anything the matter, Scott?"

He lit a cigarette carefully and then spoke, " I almost fainted at Schwab's," he said. "Everything started to fade. I think I'd better see Dr. Wilson in the morning." After a morning drive downtown to Dr. Wilson's office, Scott returns—he said, "I had a cardiac spasm."

"Is that a heart attack?"

Scott was vague, but Sheilah knew the truth—especially when he told her that he had to be put to bed and could not walk stairs.[41]

Scott began to struggle with *The Last Tycoon*. It was December 20, 1940. Although Dr. Wilson was due in an hour to take a cardiogram, Scott asked Sheilah to call, tell him to come tomorrow, because his progress on the novel was going too well to be interrupted. He announced that he had just solved a difficult problem.

He kissed her. "Let's celebrate." He was in high spirits. Sheilah had tickets to a press preview of *This Thing Called Love,* a comedy starring Rosalind Russell and Melvyn Douglas. When the film had ended, Scott stood up, then staggered. Sheilah hurried to him and took his arm. In a low, strained voice, he said, "I feel awful—everything started to go as it did in Schwab's." Sheilah held him tightly. Scott said, "I suppose people will think I'm drunk."

Sheilah thought that Scott should call Dr. Wilson. He said no. Wilson was coming tomorrow after lunch, anyway—no reason to make a fuss.[42]

In contrast to the day before, the next day, as Sheilah recalls it, was a bright sunny day. Scott was pacing up and down, dictating. He was wearing slacks, slippers, and a sweater over his shirt. Sheilah was typing a letter to Scottie and asked Scott what she should write. Scott, of course, began to dictate as she typed. Sheilah added "P.S. Your father has not been well, but he's getting better now. He hasn't had a drink for over a year."

Frances Kroll, Scott's secretary, dropped by, bringing Scott's mail (still going to his apartment). *She* remembered the day as damp and gloomy. Scott's mail included a few bills, some advertisements, and the current issue of the *Princeton Alumni Weekly*. Sheilah prepared sandwiches and coffee for lunch; Scott glanced though the newspapers and the news about the mutual-aid pact among Germany, Italy, and Japan. He said that this would take the United States into the war. Then, if his book is a success, he would like to go to Europe and write about the war. Hemingway was sending special dispatches from Europe. "Ernest won't have that field all to himself, then," Scott said with a rueful smile.

After lunch, Sheilah put Beethoven's Third Symphony, *Eroica*, on the phonograph. Beethoven's thunder filled the room. Scott lounged in a green armchair and began to munch on a Hershey bar and read the *Princeton Alumni Weekly*, making notes on the margin of an article about the Princeton football team. Their eyes met: he grinned. Scott seemed calm, content, and happy. Scott's attention turned in a final moment to the game that he loved, no doubt recalling the cheering crowds and the players running down the green field.

Beethoven's symphony was rising to a climax. Suddenly, Scott stood straight up out of his chair as if jerked by a wire connected to the ceiling, clutched the white mantelpiece above the fireplace, and fell silently to the floor. Fitzgerald's pencil shot off the page of the Princeton publication in a squiggly line, the final mark he ever made on paper. He was flat on his back, eyes closed, and breathing heavily. Sheilah summoned medical help, but it was too late.[43]

F. Scott Fitzgerald was gone—at forty-four; as he had said, the heart does not stop until it has run its race. Scott's heart, compromised by his father's genes, damaged by alcoholism and cigarettes, had crossed the finish line. Some firemen arrived; they covered his body with a white sheet.[44] Scott's friend Nathanael West, age thirty-six, and his wife Eileen, were killed in an automobile crash the next day in El Centro, California.

Fitzgerald's body was taken to the Wordsworth Room of Pierce Brothers Mortuary at 720 West Washington Boulevard; it was in a seedy part of downtown Los Angeles and poetically unjust. A cosmetic mortician had highly rouged Scott's cheeks so that he looked like a cross between a floorwalker and a wax dummy, but in Technicolor. It took a cosmetic mortician to take away Scott's last chance to retain his dignity. When Dorothy Parker, one of the few visitors in the funeral home, saw Scott, she quoted Owl-eyes's comment on Jay Gatsby's body: "The poor son-of-a-bitch." Fitzgerald's own words conveyed the sadness of the scene.

Frances conducted her final business as Fitzgerald's secretary. At the request of Judge Biggs, she had Scott's body shipped to Baltimore. Scott remained with his friend as Nathanael West's body went back east on the same train. Both would be home for Christmas. Frances stored Fitzgerald's few possessions and personally delivered a copy of *The Last Tycoon* manuscript along with Scott's old briefcase (absent any Coca-Colas) to Biggs in Delaware. She then went on to New York, as Fitzgerald had done so many times before.

Nineteen-year-old Scottie was distraught, Zelda gave strange orders for the disposition of the body, then collapsed, and Sheilah was tactfully excluded from Scott's funeral. Zelda was not well enough to attend. Scott had wanted a Catholic service in St. Mary's Church in Rockville; instead he had an Episcopal service on December 27 in the Pumphrey Funeral Home in Bethesda. At dusk Scott was buried at the Union Cemetery in Rockville, Maryland, having been denied a Catholic burial because he was not a practicing Catholic at the time of death and had not received last rites. He would have expected that decision, made by an official with the Baltimore Diocese. Among the twenty or twenty-five people there were Scottie, Scott's brother-in-law Newman Smith (representing Zelda), Gerald and Sara Murphy, Max and Louise Perkins, Harold Ober, John and Anna Biggs, Ludlow Fowler (the best man at Scott's wedding), and the Turnbulls. The two greatest loves of Scott's life were the notable absentees. Scott, once a celebrated member of the leisure class, had no assets, and his estate mainly derived from his life insurance policy, all of which came to $44,000 gross and about $32,000 after his few remaining debts had been paid.

Late in December 1940, Zelda recovered sufficient equilibrium to pay tribute to Scott's generous nature in two moving letters to Harold Ober and the Murphys.

> He was as spiritually generous a soul as ever was…. In retrospect it seems as if he was always planning happinesses for Scottie, and for me. Books to read—places to go. Life seemed so promisory always when he was around: and I always believed that he could take care of anything.

> I grieve for his brilliant talent, his faithful effort to keep me under the best of very expensive care and Scottie in school; his devotion to those that he felt were contributing to the aesthetic and spiritual purposes of life—and for his generous and vibrant soul that never spared itself, and never found anything too much trouble save the fundamentals of life itself.[45]

Zelda, Scottie, and Sheilah were the loving survivors.
With Scott's estate, the ever-loyal Biggs purchased an annuity

that brought Zelda fifty dollars a month; he also obtained a monthly veteran widow's pension for an additional $35. He put whatever cash was left into El Paso Natural Gas and Panhandle Eastern Pipeline stock. The greatest financial benefit, however, flowed from royalties that Biggs had collected from Fitzgerald's writing by having unpublished material printed, and by licensing the literary rights to *The Great Gatsby* and *Tender Is the Night* for film projects and television. In this way F. Scott Fitzgerald continued to pay for most everything. With loans from Ober, Perkins, and Murphy, Biggs paid Scottie's Vassar bills, and she was able to remain in the expensive school.

The unfinished draft of *The Last Tycoon*, edited by Edmund Wilson, appeared in October 1941. Even in its unfinished form, it received great praise from critics at the *Chicago Tribune* and *The New Yorker*. Despite some privately insulting comments about Scott, in his preface Edmund Wilson called *The Last Tycoon* "Fitzgerald's most mature piece of work" and "the best novel we have had about Hollywood." The 1976 movie adaptation was, by most accounts, the best of the films based on Fitzgerald's novels. In part, this relative success probably was because Scott had mastered the style of the screenplay even as he used that style to parody Hollywood.

As Fitzgerald had expected, Zelda was in and out of Highland during the next eight years. Her symptoms became more pronounced, the interventions more dramatic. By now insulin and electroshock therapies were standard practice. They could only relieve symptoms temporarily, not cure mental illness. The treatments did enable Zelda to live several of the eight years following Scott's death in Montgomery with her mother in her little white bungalow at 322 Sayre Street. She continued to practice ballet and to paint. She also continued to work on "Caesar's Things," which increasingly became a collage of fantasy, autobiography, and religious delusions. During some periods her speech would become unintelligible and she would refuse to bathe or get dressed. Late in fall 1947 her mental state had deteriorated to the point where even the smallest incidents brought her to tears.

On November 2, 1947, Zelda again boarded a train for Asheville to voluntarily reenter Highland. She told her mother not to worry, she was "not afraid to die." Her skin reflected the long-term effects of her illness and treatment. Her personality now had a hard, cynical edge. She had long periods of solitude, mostly avoiding others. For the remainder of her insulin treatments, she was moved to the top floor of Highland's main building; there the insulin patients were carefully monitored for delayed shocks.

Around midnight on March 10, 1948, an electrical fire broke out, starting in the first-floor kitchen of the main building, and quickly spread up a small dumbwaiter shaft leading to the roof, spewing flames onto each landing. The stairways were cut off as the blaze engulfed the interior of the building. Now that the fire was real, Zelda did not turn in an alarm to the fire department. In fact, an alarm was not turned in until thirty minutes after the fire began, and when the firemen arrived the building had been burning for forty-five minutes. By 4:00 A.M. the blaze was out of control and the central building's three-story structure was rubble. Although patients on the lower floors were saved, Zelda's third-floor room was unreachable. Had she not been asleep, she might have escaped before being trapped. Zelda, along with eight others, perished in the fire. Dental records and a single burned slipper found beneath her charred body identified her remains. Unlike the salamander, the flames had consumed her.

On St. Patrick's Day, Zelda was buried beside Scott in Union Cemetery in Rockville, Maryland. Scott and Zelda were together again.

Fitzgerald had once prophesied, "Zelda and I will snuggle up together under a stone in some old graveyard there [in Maryland, the ancestral home]." Scottie, determined to have her parents re-buried in consecrated ground, finally convinced Catholic authorities in 1975 to place her father and mother in the Fitzgerald family plot at St. Mary's Church in downtown Rockville, Maryland. In death, as in life, the Fitzgeralds always seemed to be restless. At the reinterment on November 7, Matthew Bruccoli read from Fitzgerald's work, and a new stone was inscribed with the last lines of *The Great Gatsby*— "So we beat on, boats against the current, borne back ceaselessly into the past."

The death scenes for Scott and for Zelda had been as dramatic as the lives of the Fitzgeralds. Scott's remains, however, experienced a different Hollywood ending: dead of a heart attack, forgotten and virtually alone, grotesquely smeared with makeup at his embalming, he was given a make-believe ending fit for a second-rate actor. Nothing could have been less or more suitable. The sources of creativity, like genius, are mysterious and unfathomable. The fact that Scott had discovered late in life the fortitude to remain artistically inventive is perhaps no more surprising than the fact that people were no longer reading him. Dubbed in his youth as the spokesman for America's dreamy gay and glamorous times, Scott in life was more often well ahead of his readers, as he was in death. He left the remains of a wonderful screenplay and an unfinished novel exploring the incompleteness of modern life conjoined to his own. *The Last Tycoon*, even in its unfinished condition, was at the time and perhaps since, the best novel ever written about Hollywood. Ironically, it did *not* have a Hollywood ending. In fact, as it stands, no ending has been written.

Endnotes

1. F. Scott Fitzgerald, "Pat Hobby Does His Bit" (September 1940), contained in *The Pat Hobby Stories* (New York: Simon & Schuster, 1995), p. 81.

2. Andrew Turnbull, ed., *The Letters of F. Scott Fitzgerald* (New York: Scribners, 1963), p. 47.

3. *Ibid.* p. 290.

4. Oswald Spengler, *The Decline of the West, vol. 2* (New York: Alfred A. Knopf, 1928), p. 416.

5. *Ibid.* p. 492.

6. F. Scott Fitzgerald, *The Love of the Last Tycoon* (New York: Simon & Schuster, 1993 [1941]), p. 124. Bruccoli, the "editor" of this edition, insists that Fitzgerald had intended to use this title for *The Last Tycoon*. The subtitle chosen by Bruccoli is "A Western." Scott often was involved in selecting titles for his works; if indeed this is what he intended, surely he would have been persuaded to use the shorter and more exact title, *The Last Tycoon*. The idea that it was a "Western" was probably Scott's usual play on words, whereby he meant it to be satirical about Hollywood on the new American frontier of California.

7. Earl Sparling, *Mystery Men of Wall Street* (New York: Greenberg, 1930). Extensive underlinings and marginalia in Scott's distinct handwriting appear throughout Fitzgerald's well-used copy of Sparling's book in the Princeton University Library.

8. Ibid., pp. ix–x.

9. Ibid., p. 196.

10. From F. Scott Fitzgerald's "Honoria" script, May 29, 1940, Princeton University Library, p. 25.

11. Sparling, *Mystery Men*, p. 35.

12. Ibid., p. 10.

13. Ibid., p. 92.

14. Ibid., p. 119.

15. F. Scott Fitzgerald, *Babylon Revisited: The Screenplay* (New York: Carroll & Graf, 1993), p. 43.

16. Sparling, *Mystery Men*, p. 189.

17. Matthew J. Bruccoli, ed., *F. Scott Fitzgerald: A Life in Letters* (New York: Charles Scribner's Sons, 1994), p. 331.

18. Ibid., p. 384.

19. Matthew J. Bruccoli and Margaret M. Duggan, eds. *Correspondence of F. Scott Fitzgerald* (New York: Random House, 1980), p. 596.

20. Fitzgerald, "Honoria," May 29, 1940, Princeton University Library, p. 107.

21. Ibid., p. 34.

22. Fitzgerald, *Babylon Revisited: The Screenplay*, p. 58.

23. Sparling, *Mystery Men*, p. xvii.

24. F. Scott Fitzgerald, "Babylon Revisited," in *The Stories of F. Scott Fitzgerald* (New York: Macmillan, 1951), p. 389.

25. Letter from F. Scott Fitzgerald to Lester Cowan, June 26, 1940, Fitzgerald Collection, Princeton University Library.

26. Bruccoli and Duggan, eds. *Correspondence of F. Scott Fitzgerald*, p. 612.

27. Frances Kroll Ring, "Memories of Scott," in Jackson R. Bryer, Alan Margolies, and Ruth Prigozy, eds., *F. Scott Fitzgerald: New Perspectives* (Athens and London: University of Georgia Press, 2000), p. 20.

28. Fitzgerald, *Babylon Revisited: The Screenplay*, pp. 11–12.

29. Letter of May 22, 1939, in John Kuehl and Jackson R. Bryer, eds., *Dear Scott/Dear Max: The Fitzgerald-Perkins Correspondence* (New York: Scribners, 1971), p. 285.

30. Maurice Edgar Coindreau, "The Faulkner I Knew" *Shenandoah* 16, no. 2 (Winter 1965): p. 30.

31. These and other Faulkner stories are related in Tom Dardis, *Some Time in the Sun* (New York: Charles Scribner's Sons, 1976), pp. 100–107.

32. Ibid., p. 128.

33. David L. Goodrich, *The Real Nick and Nora: Frances Goodrich and Albert Hackett, Writers of Stage and Screen Classics* (Carbondale and Edwardsville: Southern Illinois University Press, 2001), pp. 119, 120.

34. An observation quoted in the *St. Louis Post-Dispatch*, April 19, 1987, p. 36.

35. Aaron Latham, *Crazy Sundays: F. Scott Fitzgerald in Hollywood* (New York: Viking, 1971), p. 14.

36. Martin Connors and Jim Craddock, eds., *VideoHound's Golden Movie Retriever* (New York: Visible Ink Press, 1998), p. 849.

37. Sheilah's preference for Marilyn Monroe is revealed by Sheilah's daughter in Wendy W. Fairey, "My Mother and Marilyn Monroe," *The F. Scott Fitzgerald Review:* 1 (2002) p. 88.

38. These similarities are recounted by Sheilah's daughter in ibid., pp. 93–96.

39. Sheilah Graham (with Gerold Frank), *Beloved Infidel* (New York: Holt, Rinehart & Winston, 1958), p. 321.

40. David Castronovo and Janet Groth, eds., *Edmund Wilson: The Man in Letters* (Athens, Ohio: Ohio University Press, 2001), p. 79. The quotes are from a letter from Wilson to Dawn Powell, January 26, 1959.

41. Graham, *Beloved Infidel*, pp. 322–23.

42. Ibid., pp. 325–27.

43. Ibid., pp. 328–32. The account of the final days is similar to that of Robert Westbrook, *Intimate Lies*, pp. 435–41, but he adds the detail about Frances Kroll's account and of Beethoven's symphony.

44. Ibid., pp. 321–29.

45. Matthew J. Bruccoli and Jennifer M. Atkinson *As Ever, Scott Fitz—*, (Philadelphia and New York: J. B. Lippincott, 1972), p. 424; *Letters from the Lost Generation*, p. 261.

Eighteen

Ever Afterward

ONCE, SCOTT FITZGERALD SUMMED UP HIS THEORY OF WRITING IN ONE sentence. "An author ought to write for the youth of his own generation, the critics of the next, and the schoolmasters of ever afterward." In life he had achieved only that first goal as an author with *Paradise* and his many *Post* stories. At the end he was working hard on a Hollywood novel that, he hoped, would make him immortal. At death, his books were still in print, still listed in Scribners' catalog, still not selling. According to Charles Scribner III, the *fourth* Charles Scribner to be involved in publishing Fitzgerald's works, today more copies of Fitzgerald's books are sold *yearly* than the entire cumulative sale during his lifetime.[1] His novels *and* short fiction are required reading in virtually every college, university, and high school in America. Fitzgerald marvelously met his second and third goals, if posthumously.

From a young age, Fitzgerald's writing talents were perceptible. In his review of Fitzgerald's early fiction, biographer Henry Dan Piper, in a rare tribute to Scott by him, notes the solid literary reputation Fitzgerald built at Princeton and concludes that "as early as 1917" there "is evidence already of Fitzgerald's special gift for voicing the feelings and attitudes of his own generation then just coming of age."[2] Remarkably, as he matured as a writer, Fitzgerald did not always speak in the present tense. There is a powerful historic and sometimes prophetic voice underlying Fitzgerald's later short stories and novels that virtually assures his reputation among "the schoolmasters of ever afterward," as he had passionately hoped.

The schoolmasters still find Fitzgerald relevant. Substitute cocaine or oxycodin for alcohol, false corporate accounting for bootlegging, CEO stock options instead of stock, insider trading for watered down stock, Rush Limbaugh for Tom Buchanan, Britney Spears for Zelda at twenty-two, Donald Trump for Gatsby, Bill Gates for James J. Hill, George W. Bush for Warren G. Harding, Tonya Harding for Jordan Baker, John Kenneth Galbraith for Thorstein Veblen, pecuniary emulation for pecuniary emulation, Tiger Woods for Bobby Jones, a lopsided wealth distribution for a lopsided wealth distribution, and—to paraphrase Bing Crosby in *High Society*—you've got today's version of the Jazz Age. *The Great Gatsby* is a classic because it speaks of an age, conditions, and behaviors that keep reappearing. Even Social Darwinism has made a comeback, just in time to excuse obscene wealth accumulations. But, then too, a Galbraithian revival has begun. And, so on.

During Fitzgerald's lifetime, however, that deeper blend of talent of his (when noticed) was more often attributed to facileness or intuition than to intelligence. As we have again and again verified with his words and actions, he possessed both. True to his gift for prophecy, Fitzgerald correctly sensed that a positive critical assessment of his literary career would be subject to a lag. It was the kind of institutional lag of which Thorstein Veblen wrote. A reassessment of Fitzgerald's literary stature began in the 1950s and an academic periodical bearing his name soon followed, but it is only recently that a scholarly journal has devoted itself exclusively to Fitzgerald and his work.

Fitzgerald's gift for prophecy, however, failed him in two crucial and related respects. First, he misjudged his friendship with Hemingway, or, more accurately, Hemingway's friendship with him. Second, he failed to fully comprehend the complex realities of becoming the spokesperson for that "youthful generation" to which he aspired and succeeded in attaining with *Paradise* and with Zelda.

Although pivotal to his literary career and in some respects liberating, the publication of *Paradise* followed by his short stories about the young and rich created an authorial image that Fitzgerald could not escape. However entertaining, writing about youth and wealth is all too easily put down as immature and shallow, a reproach Hemingway never resisted.

The depth and historical reach of Fitzgerald's satire of the rich was overlooked in *The Beautiful and Damned* as well as in his sophisticated short stories such as "The Rich Boy," and they went underappreciated. As a celebrity author, Fitzgerald underestimated the cost of having a captivating public image. To his credit, Fitzgerald responded by displaying a deep understanding of the power of image in the modern world in *The Great Gatsby*. Still, the multifaceted brilliance of that novel—which he hoped would propel him to literary greatness while retaining his mass popularity—would have to wait. By the time *Tender Is the Night* was published, Fitzgerald was well prepared for it and for him to be labeled a "noble failure" (with the help of Hemingway, Wilson, and Bishop, of course).

Stephen Vincent Benét, in his review for the *Saturday Review of Literature,* thought Fitzgerald to be working at the height of his powers with *The Last Tycoon*. "You can take off your hats now, gentlemen," he writes, "and I think perhaps you had better. This is not a legend, this is a reputation—and, seen in perspective, it may well be one of the most secure reputations of our time." In the *New York Times*, J. Donald Adams writes: "It is the best piece of creative writing that we have about one phase of American life—Hollywood and the movies." Hemingway disagrees, concluding, "The old magic was gone," comparing the novel with "moldy bacon." Fitzgerald, had he lived, would never have finished the novel. Disparaging Wilson's choice of Fitzgerald's stories to reprint, he predictably calls "The Rich Boy" "profoundly silly" and "The Diamond as Big as the Ritz" "simply trash." Literary history has not been kind to Hemingway's assessment even as it has elevated the value of Fitzgerald's fiction.

Fitzgerald's work in Hollywood also remains greatly underrated, perhaps because of his first movie ventures. In his book *The*

Cinematic Vision of F. Scott Fitzgerald (1986), Wheeler Dixon reports of Scott's early failures as a scriptwriter because of a literary heavy-handedness, his relative lack of knowledge regarding cinematic perspective, and his difficulties adjusting to collaborative writing. However, by his third trip to Hollywood in 1937, Dixon argues that Fitzgerald's scripts for *Three Comrades* and *Infidelity* demonstrate that he had developed a more sophisticated understanding of the importance of camera angle and other cinematic techniques and, in fact, was employing many of them in his new novel, *The Last Tycoon*. At one point, Scott considered titling his novel *The Love of the Last Tycoon: A Western,* which Dixon argues might have been a tip of the hat to Hollywood director John Ford, whose Western films are often suffused with the same sense of the "tragiheroic past," of a time now irrecoverably lost, and often centered around one predominant figure of authority who attempts to impose his ideas and values upon those around him. Ford's heroes, like Monroe Stahr, shape events rather than react to them.[3]

Astonishingly, in his time even the academic world was not kind to Fitzgerald. It was not until the summer of 1948 that the Princeton English Department offered a course in British and American literature published since 1900. A young assistant professor named John Hite taught the course. For the first time, F. Scott Fitzgerald was *officially* taught at his own school. The students were assigned *The Portable F. Scott Fitzgerald,* wherein *Gatsby* was assigned as well as some parts of *The Crack-Up*. George Garrett, now retired Henry Hoyns Professor of Creative Writing at the University of Virginia, a member of the class, recalls that as late as that summer, first editions of Fitzgerald's books rested openly on the stacks of the library. Not for long, perhaps. The class was also assigned *The Waste Land, The Sun Also Rises*, and *The Sound and the Fury*. Fitzgerald would have loyally welcomed at least the first two selections.[4]

✧   ✧   ✧

As Fitzgerald wrote famously in the conclusion to *The Great Gatsby,* we are "borne back ceaselessly into the past," and so we take one final backward glance to that first short story published in the *Nassau Literary Magazine* when Scott was just eighteen years old, aptly and prophetically titled "Shadow Laurels." Set in a dark tavern in Paris (soon to be a familiar environ for Scott), the story concerns a son's (Jacques Chandelle's) search for the identity of his dead father (Jean), whose life and fate he learns about from his father's former drinking comrades (Pitou, Destage, Lamarque, and François). Told with melodramatic humor, the story is nevertheless haunting because it simultaneously speaks of Scott's past—the aspirations and failures of his father and Scott's deep but ambivalent love for him—while prophesizing much of Scott's future.

Pitou remembers Jacques' father as "a terrible drunkard," unfairly reputed to be a cheater, who died in a tavern brawl. Pitou protests, "No—no—I never believed he cheated. They were laying for him—," a conclusion we share regarding trumped-up accusations of plagiarism and other conspiratorial attacks on Scott's character traced to his alcoholism. Another comrade, Destage, remembers him as "attractive" and "a wonderful talker—when he wished, he could amuse the whole wine room," but more ambivalently recollects that "he worked feverishly hard, but he was always drunk, night and day," a tragically accurate depiction of episodes in Scott Fitzgerald's life. When Lamarque recalls, "He was educated. God knows how," we also recall a view shared by many of Scott's Princeton classmates and biographers. Finally, an inebriated François exuberantly proclaims: "He knew everything, he could tell anything—he used to tell me poetry. Oh, what poetry! And I would listen and dream—."[5]

Although completely under the influence, François speaks accurately of Scott's poetic aspirations and prophetically of the lasting effect of his writings on his audience. Fitzgerald hardly "knew everything," but he read widely and with profound understanding, and no poet has so successfully tapped into the American capacity to wonder and dream. Moreover, Fitzgerald's life and writings span America—from the rolling hills of the North, the "green breast" of the Midwest, to small Southern towns with their proud but waning aristocratic heritage; from the bright white lights of New York City to the dream-dotted world of Hollywood.

With his comprehensive but exacting survey of the social, economic, moral, and spiritual landscape of early-twentieth-century America, Fitzgerald staked a considerable claim to being the first *modern* American writer uniquely positioned to live and experience many of its ambiguities and contradictory forces. Endowed with a youthful belief in autonomy and self-determination, Fitzgerald gained an early glimpse into the constraining influences of mass media. As a living representative of the élan vital of the Jazz Age, Fitzgerald later experienced his personal version of the waste and dissipation of the Great Depression. A self-proclaimed authority of failure, he successfully authored the many failures of Western culture.

A multimillionaire (in today's dollars) during his lifetime who partied with the wealthy in New York City, the Riviera, and Hollywood, he also lived in almost constant debt and empathized with the downtrodden and oppressed. Imperialist by nature, he had a strong communal ethic, political as well as familial. Belligerent and childish when drunk, he was fundamentally a kind and generous soul who possessed wisdom beyond his years. Frequently vilified, he more often deserved praise. In appreciation of all these ambiguities and contradictory elements, we join Jacques Chandelle in his final toast to his fictional father: He was one "who drank of gall and wore a wreath of shadow laurels—" and only a tumbler of straight gin could properly toast Destage and François' final assessment that "he was more than a genius to be admired…Don't you see, he stood for us as well as himself."

Endnotes

1. Charles Scribner III, "F. Scott Fitzgerald, A Publisher's Perspective," in Jackson R. Bryer, Alan Margolies, and Ruth Prigozy, eds., *F. Scott Fitzgerald: New Perspectives* (Athens and London: University of Georgia Press, 2000), p. 22.

2. Henry Dan Piper, "Scott Fitzgerald's Prep-School Writings," *Princeton University Library Chronicle*, autumn 1955, as quoted in John Kuehle, ed., *The Apprentice Fiction of F. Scott Fitzgerald, 1909–1917* (New Brunswick, N.J.: Rutgers University Press, 1965), p. 66.

3. Wheeler Winston Dixon, *The Cinematic Vision of F. Scott Fitzgerald* (Ann Arbor, Mich.: UMI Research Press, 1986), p. 83.

4. This story is told by George Garrett, "The Good Ghost of Scott Fitzgerald," in Bryer, Margolies, and Prigozy, *F. Scott Fitzgerald: New Perspectives,* pp. 28–35.

5. In Kuehl, ed., *Apprentice Fiction*, pp. 71, 72, 73, 74, 73 and 74, respectively.

Acknowledgements

THE AUTHORS HAVE ENJOYED CONSIDERABLE AND NECESSARY ASSISTANCE
and cooperation from many. In the spirit of collaboration, we thank
them all. Princeton University Library gave Thomas Birch pain-
less access to materials in its Department of Rare Books & Special
Collections. Craig Tenney at Harold Ober Associates and Don Skemer
at Princeton University Library skillfully guided us through what
otherwise would have been a minefield of permissions. In addition
to permissions for the use of numerous illustrations (see Illustrations
and Credits), Harold Ober and Associates Incorporated provided permission to use the following materials: Scott Fitzgerald's Newman
transcript; Scott's note to Sheila Graham on the flyleaf of his copy
of Frank Norris's *Octopus*; Scott and Zelda's golf score card at the
Yacht Club, White Bear Lake; Scott's list of his investments; medical
evaluation of Zelda's illness, Malmaison Clinic Report; letter from
Scott Fitzgerald to Dr. Adolf Meyer, April 10, 1933; extracts from
Dr. Rennie's transcript of May 28, 1933; medical history of Zelda's
condition, Craig House files; quotes from Zelda's draft of her novel,
Caesar's Things; the Scott Fitzgerald (and Robert Spafford) movie
script, *Gracie at Sea*; Scott's notes in his copy of Froude's *Caesar*;
letter from Scott Fitzgerald to Beatrice Dance, March 4, 1938; letter
from Scott to Beatrice Dance, October 11, 1938; a memo from Scott
Fitzgerald to Mr. Mannix and Mr. Katz in Hollywood; letter from

Zelda to Ludlow Fowler, December 22, 1921; letter from Zelda to Scott, fall 1930; letter from Zelda to Scott, undated; letter from Zelda to Scott, April 1934; quotations from Zelda's spiral notebook; letter from Scottie Fitzgerald to Arthur Mizener, March 10, 1950.

Ray Canterbery specifically thanks the Association for Evolutionary Economics (AFFE) for the invitation to present a paper first revealing the connections between Fitzgerald and Veblen. The occasion was the geneses for this biography as well as an opportunity to meet Thomas Birch. Canterbery is also grateful to all those who have contributed to the Fitzgerald literature, especially those academics bravely traveling where no writers have gone before, explorations greatly shortening an otherwise long road. And, of roads *not* traveled, Ray is grateful for his wife Carolyn, not only for her strong support and attentiveness, but also for her graciously and generously postponing our trip to Istanbul so that proofs could be returned, more or less on time. He thanks Rosemary Yokoi at Paragon House, for her more or less equal patience. Finally, Ray thanks Maggie, his dog who often shares his office, for not eating any pages

Thomas Birch particularly thanks AFFE for the opportunity to meet Ray Canterbery, and holds an open mind regarding Maggie, a dog un-met. Birch also thanks the student participants in "American Culture and Communication Through the Life and Work of F. Scott Fitzgerald," a seminar at the University of New Hampshire at Manchester, and especially his colleague, Jeff Klenotic, whose many talents make this team-taught experience stimulating and memorable. Many other colleagues, library staff and friends, also have been enormously helpful, including another team-teaching colleague, Fred Metting, as well as Annie Donahue, Paula Galvin, Karla Vogel, Jack Resch, Cindy Tremblay, Jennifer Lee, Chris Payne, Donna McIntire, Ellen Ruggles, Ray Boozer, Justin Moore, Patty Kenny, Carolyn White, Heather White, Don Skemer and the library staffs at Princeton University and the University of New Hampshire at Manchester. Finally, Tom is grateful for his wife and children— Anne, Rosalind and Emerson—and for their steadfast support.

Illustrations (and Credits)

Note: Permissions from Harold Ober Associates are on behalf of The Estate of F. Scott and Zelda Fitzgerald.

Index

Page numbers in italics indicate photographs.